Hell's
Broke Loose
in Georgia

Hell's Broke Loose in Georgia

Survival in a Civil War Regiment

SCOTT WALKER

The University of Georgia Press
Athens & London

© 2005 by The University of Georgia Press
Athens, Georgia 30602
All rights reserved
Designed by Emily Cavett Taff
Set in 10/13 New Caledonia by BookComp, Inc.
Printed and bound by Maple-Vail

The paper in this book meets the guidelines for permanence
and durability of the Committee on Production Guidelines
for Book Longevity of the Council on Library Resources.

Printed in the United States of America
10 09 08 07 06 C 6 5 4 3 2

Library of Congress Cataloging-in-Publication Data
Walker, Scott, 1950–
Hell's broke loose in Georgia : survival in a Civil War
regiment / Scott Walker.
          p.   cm.
Includes bibliographical references and index.
ISBN 0-8203-2605-4 (hardcover : alk. paper)
1. Confederate States of America. Army. Georgia Infantry
Regiment, 57th. 2. Georgia—History—Civil War, 1861–1865—
Regimental histories. 3. United States—History—Civil War,
1861–1865—Regimental histories. 4. Confederate States of
America. Army. Georgia Infantry Regiment, 57th—Biography.
5. Soldiers—Georgia—Biography. 6. Georgia—History—Civil
War, 1861–1865—Biography. 7. United States—History—Civil
War, 1861–1865—Biography. 8. Confederate States of America.
Army—Military life. 9. United States—History—Civil War,
1861–1865—Social aspects. I. Title.
E559.5 57th .W35 2005
973.7'458—dc22   2005008517

ISBN-13 978-0-8203-2605-4 (hardcover : alk. paper)

British Library Cataloging-in-Publication Data available

In grateful memory of my friend Abdah Johnson (Chip) Conyers.
Our forefathers served together and so did we.

Contents

Illustrations

Maps

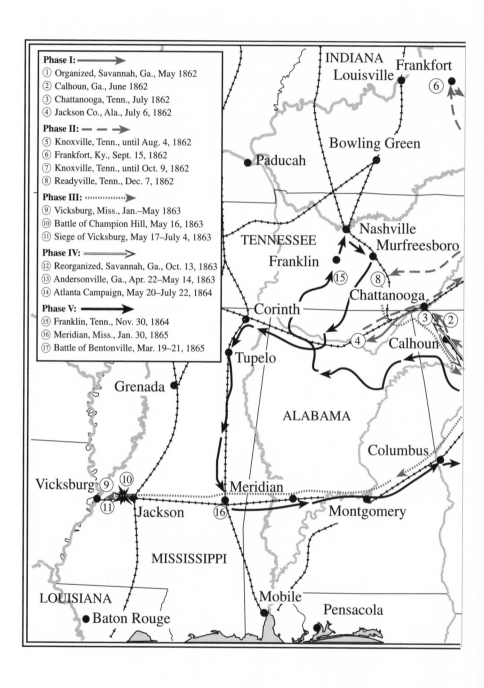

Phase I: ——————→
① Organized, Savannah, Ga., May 1862
② Calhoun, Ga., June 1862
③ Chattanooga, Tenn., July 1862
④ Jackson Co., Ala., July 6, 1862

Phase II: — — — →
⑤ Knoxville, Tenn., until Aug. 4, 1862
⑥ Frankfort, Ky., Sept. 15, 1862
⑦ Knoxville, Tenn., until Oct. 9, 1862
⑧ Readyville, Tenn., Dec. 7, 1862

Phase III: ·················→
⑨ Vicksburg, Miss., Jan.–May 1863
⑩ Battle of Champion Hill, May 16, 1863
⑪ Siege of Vicksburg, May 17–July 4, 1863

Phase IV: ————→
⑫ Reorganized, Savannah, Ga., Oct. 13, 1863
⑬ Andersonville, Ga., Apr. 22–May 14, 1863
⑭ Atlanta Campaign, May 20–July 22, 1864

Phase V: ——————→
⑮ Franklin, Tenn., Nov. 30, 1864
⑯ Meridian, Miss., Jan. 30, 1865
⑰ Battle of Bentonville, Mar. 19–21, 1865

INDIANA

Frankfort

Louisville

⑥

Bowling Green

Paducah

Nashville

TENNESSEE

Murfreesboro

Franklin

⑮

⑧

Chattanooga

Corinth

③ ②

④

Calhoun

Tupelo

Grenada

ALABAMA

Columbus

Vicksburg ⑨ ⑩

Meridian

⑪

Jackson ⑯

Montgomery

MISSISSIPPI

LOUISIANA

Mobile

Pensacola

Baton Rouge

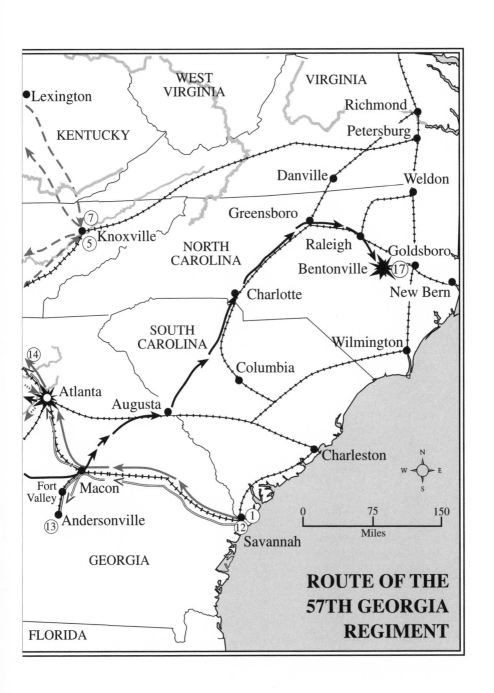

**ROUTE OF THE
57TH GEORGIA
REGIMENT**

I was in midsabbatical at the University of Georgia, hard at work writing a novel in a corner of the university library late at night. As midnight approached, I yawned, stretched, and pushed back from my desk. With bleary eyes I looked at my surroundings as if for the first time.

A student was fast asleep, her head cradled on her folded arms on the table next to me. I grinned, remembering my own frenetic college days. My eyes drifted slowly to the stacks immediately before me. Squinting, I scanned the titles, discovering that I was in the American history section of the library.

Most of these books were about the Civil War, a subject I did not know well. Though I am a Southerner by birth and heritage, the Civil War never meant much to me. It was an American epic lost in the distant past. I knew that this brothers' war had been a horrendous, tragic, and formative chapter in American history. My great-grandmother had even told me a few stories about my great-great-grandfather who had fought in the war. But the pain and the bloodshed were reason enough to put the past behind and get on with living. I saw little purpose in reenacting battles, rehashing old arguments, and keeping the suffering alive.

As my eyes roved the dusty spines, I spied a six-volume work entitled *Roster of the Confederate Soldiers of Georgia, 1861–1865*. Suddenly, I was curious: I knew my Civil War ancestor's name and that he was from Georgia. I wondered whether I would find him. I thumbed through the index, an innocent act that would change my life and the course of the next fourteen years.

My great-great-grandfather's name was there. All the roster said was that he fought with the Fifty-seventh Georgia Infantry Regiment. But it was enough to intrigue me. I spent the next hour flipping through Civil War books in a futile effort to find information about the Fifty-seventh Georgia. After the library closed and I walked out into the cool night, I sensed that curiosity had seized my reason.

During the next few years I pursued intensive research on the Fifty-seventh Georgia. Captivated, I temporarily shelved my unfinished novel. How had I become so caught up in this project?

My research was turning up clues to an incredible story. Because little had been written about the Fifty-seventh Georgia, I was forced to do primary research at the Georgia Division of Archives and History in Atlanta. There I unearthed letters, diaries, and journals of men who lived more than a century ago and are now forgotten. Some collections of letters had been stashed in files for years and never transcribed. The pages were yellow, faint, barely legible. One packet of letters between a husband and wife still contained a locket of hair. And the stories that flowed from these forgotten witnesses were amazing.

Spurred on, I slowly made the rounds of the Georgia counties where these men had lived. I researched courthouse records, perused books and manuscripts in county libraries, interviewed descendants, and encountered colorful local historians. It was a rich experience.

Over time, the dead came alive. Men like Wright Vinson, Edwin Davis, Jim Kuglar, Cincinnatus Guyton, William Barkuloo, Charles Olmstead, Robert Braswell, and Seaborn Mims walked forth from the grave. And the story they told was powerful, more powerful than any fiction I could write. Their story was real, one that I became convinced must be told. Hence my decision to shelve my novel.

This is a story that is *bigger* than the Civil War, for it really is a story about you and me, about what it is to be a human being in the midst of the greatest conflicts and passions of life.

The reader should understand several points. First, this book is not historical fiction. Rather, it is *narrative history,* a genre of history that is factual, carefully researched, extensively footnoted, and based on primary resources yet reads as a well-told story. In telling that story, I sometimes found that, because detailed description is minimal or lacking in the primary resource, I had to construct a scene to describe a known event. Or, as is sometimes the case with a character in this book such as Robert Braswell, I describe thoughts or emotions that he probably had but are not made explicit by a primary source. Such description is informed by either the event or inference. Thus you are reading well-researched and -documented history, expressed through the rich craft of narrative.

Second, although I chronicle the Fifty-seventh Georgia Regiment as well as Mercer's brigade, my primary intention is not to develop a regimental history but to relate how one small group of Confederate soldiers struggled to survive and remain sane through the ravages and rigors of the Civil War. Granted, I tell the regimental and brigade histories in detail. But the heart of the book illustrates how simple soldiers find themselves at the vortex of powers and struggles that they seldom comprehend, yet they hold fast to their personal values to the end.

Third, I believe that it is important, whenever possible, to allow the historical characters to describe their own circumstances and experiences. For this reason I include extensive quotations from letters, memoirs, and journals. For the novelist this is problematic. Such quotes can break and distract from the story line. And verbatim quotations often are not as gripping or cogent as finely crafted dialogue. But for the historian I think that direct quotation puts the reader into the character's frame of mind and provides nuances of a bygone day.

Fourth, I write simultaneously for both the first-time reader of Civil War history and the Civil War scholar. Although this is difficult, I do not believe that it is an impossible task. I ask the historian to be patient when I am painting a broad picture that might seem obvious. I also ask the novice reader to understand the need for historical detail and annotation.

Finally, this book is not meant primarily to recount military history. Rather, it is meant to depict the human drama and the incalculable struggle endured by a generation of Americans who wore both the blue and the gray. This book is a testament to their competing devotion, to the best and the worst within the human race. It is a mirror in which we can glimpse not only our past but also our present and future. I hope that this is a story in which you will see your own face.

Acknowledgments

I am profoundly grateful to many people for their contributions and encouragement during the process of completing this project. A book is always a collaborative effort by friends and colleagues, an expression of shared labor, commitment, and love.

My agent, Claudia Cross, guided the writing of this book over the course of many years. Her patience, encouragement, direction, and friendship, shaped the character of this story and honed my skills as an author.

Michael Parrish, professor of history at Baylor University, is the epitome of the finest qualities to be found in a professor and scholar. His guidance, advice, insight, and editorial skills were indispensable in crafting this book. Above all, his belief that this story must be told gave me the courage to persevere. He has taught me much about the meaning of scholarship and friendship.

Many people helped me discover the primary sources that are woven together in the fabric of this human epic. Sandy Boling, a research specialist at the Georgia Division of Archives and History, played a most significant role in my fact-finding process. I am deeply grateful for her assistance and expertise.

Don Frazier, professor of history at McMurry University, served as the cartographer for this book. I am grateful to him for his skill, expertise, and patient spirit.

The folks at the University of Georgia Press, as well as my fine copy editor, played significant roles in the final formation of this book. I am thankful for their craft and professionalism.

Finally, I am profoundly grateful to my wife, Beth, and my children, Drew, Luke, and Jodi, for their love, support, and encouragement during the fourteen years we have shared together in the writing of this book. This process has been a "family affair" that has enriched all of our lives.

Birth of a Regiment

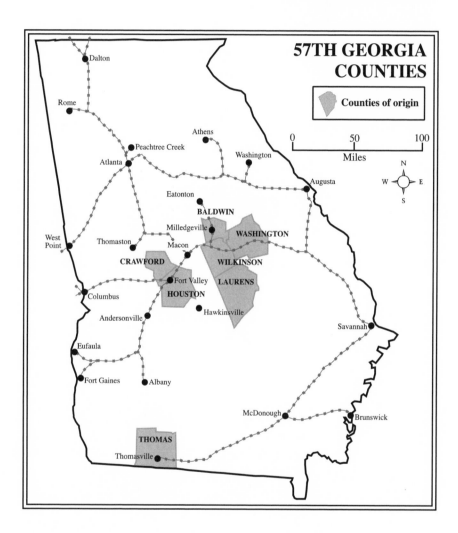

57TH GEORGIA COUNTIES

Counties of origin

0   50   100
Miles

N
W ⊕ E
S

Dalton

Rome

Athens

Peachtree Creek

Washington

Atlanta

Augusta

Eatonton

BALDWIN

Milledgeville

WASHINGTON

West Point

Thomaston

Macon

CRAWFORD

WILKINSON

Fort Valley

LAURENS

Columbus

HOUSTON

Andersonville

Hawkinsville

Savannah

Eufaula

Fort Gaines

Albany

McDonough

Brunswick

THOMAS

Thomasville

1

War Fever

The threat of war could not have loomed at a worse time for Sarah Anne Braswell. Widowed in her late twenties, she had struggled alone for twelve years to raise and protect three willful, strapping boys. Her parents had helped, but her task had been overwhelming and lonely. Now, anxious and frayed beyond her forty years, she feared her world was teetering on the brink of tragedy once more.

Sarah Anne's sons were fast becoming sturdy and independent young men. William, the eldest at twenty-one, had been named for his father. Because Billy had shouldered the family mantel from an early age, he was serious, at times to the point of grimness. He had recently apprenticed to become a doctor, and already his friends teased him by calling him "Dr. Billy."[1]

Samuel, seventeen, was a typical middle child. He felt keenly the presence of his older brother's precocious shadow, and Samuel now struggled to grasp his own identity. He was slightly built, had the delicate face of an artist, and was a follower who dreamed of being a leader, of breaking away into the larger world beyond the rural realms of his home, Fort Valley, Georgia.

The so-called baby, Robert, was a lanky fourteen-year-old. He was bucking his way into manhood with a handsome face not yet nicked by a razor. And he was so delighted that he was already taller than his brothers that he always stood ramrod straight. On the surface Robert was jovial. But he had also inherited the family trait of stubbornness. He could be mulish and opinionated, pushing his mother to tears of frustration.

Though they would deny it, Samuel and Robert worshiped their older brother. Billy had recently come down with a bad case of war fever, and Sarah Anne was aware that it was proving contagious to his brothers.

Indeed, in this explosive year of 1861 war fever had consumed the South, including almost every inch of Georgia. The small rural town of Fort Valley in middle Georgia had not been spared. Hardly a family in Fort Valley had escaped its effect.[2]

Nationally, the disease had been festering for years. Even before the Revolutionary War the Northern and Southern colonies were economic rivals and great competitors. As the young nation grew and gained identity, these sibling regions heightened their quest for power and political sway. Now a strong and adolescent tension was rending this tenuous family union. Civil war threatened.

Master Sergeant William (Billy) Braswell
(Courtesy of Phil Van Duivendyk)

Some of the ill will was spawned by things as petty yet human as regional variance in custom, diet, pronunciation, and manners. Southerners and Northerners were different, and each would quickly say so. But more basic and definable issues had also arisen and solidified. As a more industrial and vigorous economy took root in the North, the rural and agrarian South feared that its ability to govern and shape its own destiny was eroding. People vehemently argued the issues of states' rights and slavery. But the deeper issue for white Southerners was not so much whether they should or should not own slaves—most did not—but whether they should have the choice of doing so. Southerners regarded this as a simple matter, one that they colloquially referred to as "freedom," with nary a hint of irony.

Billy Braswell accepted this point of view. He did not own a slave. But his maternal grandfather, Williamson Mims, owned and ruled eighty-five African slaves and was one of the wealthiest planters in Fort Valley, a town in Houston County that had about a thousand white residents and double that number of slaves.[3] Billy would not deny his grandfather the freedom to own slaves, right or wrong. After all, freedom was all about self-governance. And, if the North would not let the South govern itself, then Southerners must do as their patriot forefathers and fight. Or so went the argument that was preached and repeated in thousands of Southern homes and hamlets. Many Southerners did not approve of slavery. Few hated the United States of America. But almost everyone rallied around the white-hot issue of "freedom."

Private Samuel Braswell
(Courtesy of Phil Van Duivendyk)

As firebrands in the North and South gained visibility and credence, more Americans anticipated war and bloodshed. After Abraham Lincoln was elected president in November 1860, Georgia became the scene of a series of dramatic and swift events. The contentious governor, Joseph Emerson Brown, was an avid secessionist and slaveholder. Anticipating conflict with the federal government, he took bold and preemptive action. Brown commanded the First Volunteer Regiment of Georgia to seize the unoccupied Fort Pulaski, which guarded the entrance to the port of Savannah, from the U.S. government. The regiment occupied the fort without resistance on January 2, 1861. Then, in response to South Carolina's adoption of the Ordinance of Secession from the United States on December 20, 1860, the Georgia legislature called a special convention in the state capital of Milledgeville. On January 19, 1861, Georgia seceded from the Union too.[4]

Writing of these days many years later, Mariah Austin Kersh, a resident of Fort Valley and a cousin of the Braswell brothers', reflected:

> In 1860 much uneasiness and fear were in the land, for there was much wrangling in Congress, especially among the senators from the South, who saw the war clouds and heard the thundering of evil times just ahead. Talk in every gathering was of secession, and everyone knew that meant war.
>
> Military companies were organized in every city and town to be ready to go to war. Fort Valley then had two full companies, one hundred men each. The

Private Robert Braswell
(Courtesy of Phil Van Duivendyk)

"Governor's Guards" was the pride of the town; the "Fort Valley Riflemen" was the other company. . . .

When secession was decreed, many towns and cities celebrated. Macon was ablaze with light. Many went from here to see the bright illumination, something new. I wanted to go with the crowd, but my father, a Whig opposed to secession and war, said, "No, you cannot go. Soon they will be hanging crepe on their doors instead of lights in their windows." How true his words were and how soon we realized it. Everything was in confusion and chaos.[5]

Everything might have been "in confusion and chaos," but one thing was clear in the mind of Billy Braswell: he was ready to go to war. He and his friend Tom Massee caught the train to Macon and enlisted on March 18, 1861, in Governor Brown's Riflemen.[6] They had a hunch that this company would be one of the first to see combat.

It is now difficult to imagine the chivalry, gaiety, and excitement that seized small Southern towns. Southerners regarded the looming war as a grand competition that would be short lived and glorious. They would show those uppity Yankees their place and preserve the Southern way of life. The war also offered young men an exceptional means to seek adventure and a shortcut to local heroism; to middle-aged men it beckoned with a final fling at youthful exuberance. It even gave tedious old men something to discuss that guaranteed an attentive ear. War seemed a grand and glorious affair and life was full of promise.

Indeed, Mariah Kersh offers a fine description of those days:

> Every Friday evening, one or the other [of our local military companies]
> would drill through the town, headed by a splendid band of music. . . . The
> governor's Guards uniform was a blue coat and trousers trimmed with white
> braid and army brass buttons and beautiful hats with white plumes. The
> Riflemen had dark blue uniforms trimmed with yellow braid and brass buttons,
> and a large hat with yellow plumes. . . . We were proud of our soldier boys, so
> handsome and manly, so brave and true; little did we dream what was in the
> future for them and for us.
>
> In the Spring, the Fort Valley Companies invited the Companies of Macon,
> The Macon Guards and Riflemen, to Fort Valley to camp a week together. . . .
> Tents were put up, light stands built. The white tents and handsome boys in
> beautiful uniforms made a picture never to be forgotten. It was a gala week for
> Fort Valley. Ladies came from Macon, Perry, and Marshallville to enjoy the
> occasion with the boys. An encampment was something new.[7]

Such unusual events were heady wine for small and isolated communities.

Billy Braswell and Tom Massee were among the first Fort Valley boys to leave for
the war, but within weeks the little town said farewell to most of its military-age
men.[8] Soon the Governor's Guards became part of the Third Regiment Georgia
Volunteers, and the Fort Valley Riflemen were incorporated into the Sixth Regiment Georgia Volunteers. Both regiments were sent north to fight in Virginia.[9]

Even so, the Confederacy had an urgent need for more troops. Already Fort
Valley had strained to furnish and supply the two full companies for the war. The
town was depleted of manpower and drained of its economic resources. Raising
and outfitting another company of men must have seemed an insurmountable
task.

In the meantime some older boys and middle-aged men began to drill infor-
mally. Most were not of prime military age, yet they wanted to be part of the war
effort, prepared to defend their homeland if Georgia were invaded. Robert and
Samuel Braswell became a part of this ragtag organization and for weeks spent
long hours learning to march and bark military commands.

The war gradually intensified as 1861 wore on. The North exerted its enormous
power and probed for points of Southern weakness. In the West it soon became
obvious that the Union army and navy would try to capture the entire length of
the Mississippi River, splitting the South and clamping a major artery of commerce and transportation. At the same time the Union navy and army combined
forces to blockade the Atlantic and Gulf coasts and seize primary port cities. On
August 28, 1861, Fort Hatteras, North Carolina, surrendered to Union forces.

Confederate Army Organization

UNIT	COMPOSITION	MEN	COMMANDER	EXAMPLE
Company		100	Captain	Company E
Regiment	10 companies	1,000	Colonel	57th Georgia Infantry
Brigade	3–6 regiments	4,000	Brig. general	Mercer's brigade
Division	3–6 brigades	12,000	Maj. general	Cleburne's division
Corps	2–4 divisions	36,000	Lt. general	Hardee's corps
Army	2–4 corps	75,000	General	Army of Tennessee

Note: The troop strength for each unit is both approximate and theoretical. In reality, by 1863 effective troop strength (troops present and able to fight) was usually only 30 to 60 percent of the numbers given. For instance, Mercer's brigade began the Atlanta campaign with 2,800 troops in May 1864 and was the largest brigade in the Army of Tennessee. However, following the Battle of Atlanta, Mercer's brigade was reduced to 1,871 troops.

More ominously, Port Royal, South Carolina, fell on November 7, 1861, leaving Savannah, Georgia, vulnerable.

As pressure mounted, the small militia of men and boys drilling in Fort Valley formalized into an official company that was fully equipped by one of the town's wealthy citizens, J. Abb Everett. Its members elected A. H. Long captain and dubbed itself the Everett Guards.[10]

As the Everett Guards prepared to join the state militia, Sarah Anne Braswell knew that Samuel would be going. He was seventeen and she could not hold him back. But Robert was another matter. At fourteen he was much too young. Yet Robert insisted on enlisting. The anguished Sarah Anne realized that she could do nothing to stop this bullheaded youngster from going to war. And the Confederate army would gladly accept him.

On the other end of the spectrum stood the stout and stooped fifty-six-year-old William "Will" Holly Sr. The average life expectancy in 1861 was less than fifty, which made Holly a grizzled old man. His family had made its contribution: his son had already enlisted. But Holly insisted on joining up, signing the company roster along with Robert Braswell.[11]

The Everett Guards were officially mustered into state service on October 18, 1861, as part of the First Independent Battalion, First Brigade, Georgia State Troops. The men enlisted for a six-month commitment and were immediately sent to defend Savannah.[12] As Mariah Austin Kersh's father predicted in late 1861, families in Fort Valley and thousands of other American towns would "soon be hanging crepe on their doors instead of lights in their windows."

2

Savannah

As Robert and Samuel Braswell rode the rails to Savannah with the Everett Guards, other young men were making life-changing decisions. Nestled in the hamlet of Penfield, Georgia, was a small Baptist school, Mercer University. Early in 1861 an energetic mathematics professor, S. P. Sanford, formed a student military company called the Mercer University Cadets. Soon more than one hundred young men were drilling every Saturday. Dressed in white pants, black coats, military belts, and colorful sashes, these Mercer students were imbued with the cause of Southern patriotism.[1] Indeed, the senior class of 1861 enlisted in the Confederate army virtually en masse. Of the thirty-one members, nine would soon die in battle.[2]

As the Christmas holidays of 1861 approached and final examinations drew near, one of the youngest cadets, nineteen-year-old Edwin Tralona Davis, struggled with his conscience and contemplated his future. He was filled with military ardor, restless, and considering enlistment. On December 12, 1861, Edwin placed an empty notebook on his desk and began a diary with a one-sentence entry: "Having determined to become one of the defenders of an invaded country, on this day I take my departure from Mercer University Ga., en route to the army, via Riddleville, my home in Washington Co. Ga."[3]

Fifteen miles north of Fort Valley in neighboring Crawford County, a young farmer, Wright Vinson, gazed at his pregnant wife, Christiana, and felt painfully torn. He longed to experience the birth of his first child, and his parents needed him; he was the oldest of nine children and carried much responsibility within the family and its farming enterprise.[4]

Yet on October 14, 1861, Wright and his younger brother William followed many of their childhood friends into the ranks of Company F, Second Regiment, First Brigade of the Georgia State Troops. Marching to the train depot in nearby Fort Valley, they departed for Savannah to fulfill a six-month obligation.

Many Georgia boys looked around Savannah with astonishment. They came primarily from farming communities and had never seen a city, much less one so stately. Reflecting an English grandeur, the city's streets were bisected by lovely parks and were flanked by grand, elegant houses. Savannah was a queen city.

However, some soldiers found Savannah to be quite odd. A seventeen-year-old from Athens, Thomas Barrow, wrote home that Savannah was "an old-

Private Edwin Tralona Davis (Courtesy of the Thomasville Genealogical, History, and Fine Arts Library, Thomasville, Ga.)

looking place with ill-shapen houses and narrow streets on which the sand was about a foot deep. . . . [Its citizens are] a set of stuck up know nothing fools."[5]

Savannah was quickly being transformed from a socially conscious port city focused on commerce to a major military staging center. Thousands of Georgians received their primary recruitment and training in Savannah and from there were deployed to the battlefront.[6] "Probably there is no city in the Confederacy where you would be so struck by the military air that pervades everything here," wrote the war correspondent Felix Gregory de Fontaine. "In the Park, if a lady has an escort, it wears a uniform, while in the surroundings of the City where are encamped the various brigades you will see the fine essence of soldierly esprit de corps. These regiments, are just such as one might expect to find in Georgia— strong in numbers, and made up of all degrees of humanity from the wealthiest to the poorest and from the white haired veteran to the boy of thirteen."[7]

Yet soldiers assigned to defend Savannah were not likely to spend much time escorting women around city parks. Rather, most were deployed to isolated forts and stations on the barrier islands surrounding the city, islands with strange names such as Whitemarsh, Tybee, Wassaw, Cockspur, Bird, Hog, Turtle, Ski-daway, and Isle of Hope. On these lonely sandy citadels the new recruits spent many hours drilling and serving picket duty, for the Yankees would first have to capture these islands if they were to seize Savannah by sea.

For soldiers from the north Georgia mountains or the fertile fields and river valleys of middle Georgia, being on the coast was a mixed blessing. Most had never seen the ocean. Many fell in love with its beauty and exuberance. However, the bone-chilling sea breeze in winter and the steamy dank humidity of summer were unpleasant. The pungent smell of pluff mud (the thick, gooey, sulphurous mud of tidal marshes) and the nuisance of sand (it penetrated everything) made many Georgia boys long for the red clay and mountain freshness of home.

Perhaps more than anything, they were tormented by swarms of tropical insects. Mosquitoes, fleas, and sand flies were everywhere. Malaria was rampant, and the troops suffered serious outbreaks of measles and dysentery. Farm boys who had never lived bunched together were discovering the harsh truth of the Civil War: disease eventually killed twice as many soldiers as did combat.[8]

As young men such as Robert Braswell, Wright Vinson, and Edwin Davis adjusted to the demands and rigors of soldier life in Savannah, military events swirled rapidly around them. In October 1861 a powerful Union fleet of seventy-four vessels secretly slipped out of Hampton Roads, Virginia, and headed south, landing troops on Hilton Head Island, South Carolina, twenty-five miles north of Savannah.[9] Port Royal fell to the Union on November 7, 1861, as did nearby Forts Walker and Beauregard.

"On Thursday the great Yankee fleet attacked the batteries at Port Royal, and after a fierce bombardment of five hours dismounted nearly all the guns and rendered the batteries untenable. Our forces retreated safely, with the loss of some ten killed and twenty wounded," George A. Mercer of Savannah noted in his diary. "The Yankees have possession of Hilton Head Island, and have secured a fine harbor in Broad river; Savannah is thus placed in a perilous position and many of our people are removing their families and valuables. . . . Vigorous measures are being adopted to defend Savannah. . . . We hope the Yankees will give us time to prepare a vigorous and effective defense."[10]

As the Georgia State Troops dug in and waited, they were hampered by lack of armament. Many recruits had only the hunting rifles and muskets that they had brought from home. Little, if anything, was standardized, and the problems of ordnance and supply were persistent. Into the midst of this nightmare sailed a miracle of deliverance. The blockade runner *Fingal* slipped into Savannah from England, bringing much-needed weapons. A young Confederate officer, Clement Evans, wrote to his wife on November 13, "Sure enough the 'Steel Clad Steamer' has come in and a glorious looking vessel she is. Completely mailed with steel so as to be cannon proof—She brought over 12,000 Enfield rifles—several rifled cannon—ammunition in abundance—millions of percussion caps—4000 kegs of powder—cartridge boxes—leather etc. . . . Her arrival is a victory in itself."[11]

Yet despite this good fortune, Savannah trembled. On November 24, 1861, Union troops landed on nearby Tybee and Wassaw islands and entrenched. From Goat Point on Tybee Island, Yankee soldiers could gaze seventeen hundred yards across a narrow channel toward the walls of Fort Pulaski, which was supposed to save Savannah from Union attack.

In 1829 a second lieutenant fresh from West Point had been assigned to help construct Fort Pulaski. Thirty-two years later that same officer was a full general in the Confederate army and in command of the District of South Carolina and Georgia. Now he was called to defend the fort that he had seen constructed. His name was Robert E. Lee.[12]

Farther west, in Tennessee, the Union army advanced as 1862 began. In February a little-known Union general, Ulysses S. Grant, moved his forces up the Tennessee and Cumberland rivers, capturing Forts Henry and Donelson. The vital city of Nashville capitulated to the Union on February 23. In a few short days the Confederacy had lost Kentucky and western Tennessee.

Alarmed by these defeats, the Georgia State Troops in Savannah determined to defend their city and state. Expecting a naval assault and amphibious invasion, they reinforced Fort Pulaski and toiled frantically to build fortifications near Fort Jackson. However, as winter progressed, Union efforts near Savannah appeared to slow. This was a deception. Union soldiers worked quietly but steadily on Tybee Island to install the powerful new Parrot and James rifled cannons that could propel a spinning shell against traditional fortifications with devastating effect. Working only at night, they hid these artillery pieces behind sand dunes, thus leaving no noticeable alteration of the island's features. When they were finished, they armed the siege guns and aimed them at the walls of Fort Pulaski, which were less than a mile away.

The crisis came at dawn on April 10, 1862, when Union commanders demanded that Fort Pulaski surrender or be obliterated by artillery fire. The fort's commander, Colonel Charles Olmstead, who was twenty-five and inexperienced at combat, faced a difficult decision. Neither he nor General Lee understood the power of the Union's new weaponry. With masonry walls seven and a half feet thick and twenty-five feet high, Fort Pulaski was a formidable target. Only days before, Olmstead and Lee had stood on the ramparts of the fort and gazed at the Union activity on Tybee Island. Lee had remarked to Olmstead, "They will make it pretty hot for you with shells, but they cannot breach your walls at that distance."[13]

Banking on Lee's assessment and the formidable architecture of the fort, Olmstead responded to the Union demand for surrender: "In reply, I can only say that I am here to defend the Fort not to surrender it."

At 7:40 A.M. Union forces fired the first rifled cannons and mortars. By eve-

Colonel Charles H. Olmstead
(Courtesy of the Georgia
Historical Society)

ning the powerful new Parrott and James rifles had breached the brick walls of Fort Pulaski. Early the next morning, April 11, the Union bombardment continued, soon striking the fort's magazine: detonation would obliterate Fort Pulaski. Olmstead had no option but to surrender. Savannah's mainstay of defense fell in less than two days.

As Union troops occupied Fort Pulaski and the fate of Savannah grew precarious, the six-month term of enlistment concluded for most Georgia State Troops defending the city. The majority had signed up in November and could not be legally held in Savannah beyond the time of their contractual agreement.

However, they had heard rumors for several months that the Confederate government might declare a military draft. This was a controversial action that had never been taken by the national government or that of any state. Nevertheless, on April 16, 1862, the Confederate government declared the first of three conscription acts and required all men aged eighteen to thirty-five to join the army. [14]

The Conscription Act angered many Georgia State Troops. Most men felt committed to the Southern cause. But they perceived that the Conscription Act deprived them of personal freedom and undercut their sense of patriotic voluntarism. To ease the tension the Confederacy furloughed many Georgia State

Troops so they could go home for a few days to get their affairs in order and prepare for a long war. Now state military organizations would become Confederate units. Young men such as Robert Braswell, Wright Vinson, and Edwin Davis suddenly realized that the war would not be short and that it would require great sacrifices.

3

Birth of a Confederate Regiment

The Fort Valley train station teemed with men from the middle Georgia area who were rushing home for a thirty-day furlough before they reported for duty with a Confederate regiment. Wright Vinson's feet hit the station platform running, so eager was he to cover the fifteen miles to his home in Crawford County. While he was away in Savannah, Christiana had given birth to their first child, a robust little boy named Charley, but Wright had not yet laid eyes on him.

As Wright neared his home, he undoubtedly felt both joy and anxiety. Now he was a father, but with the passage of the Conscription Act, he had no choice about being a soldier for the duration of the war. His quiet and simple youth was over. His world was speeding up, expanding, changing, becoming perilous.

Wright Vinson had much to do in a short time. Before leaving for his six-month enlistment in Savannah, he had started construction on a small house. Now he had to finish the house and move his family before reporting for duty once more. He was also worried about the farm. He needed far more time at home than his furlough would allow. But the thought of seeing Christiana briefly eased his fears.

Robert and Samuel Braswell were also elated to be home. They did not see their brother, Billy, however. Billy's unit, Brown's Rifles, had been shipped off to Florida a year earlier, in April 1861, to guard Pensacola Harbor. Incorporated into the First Confederate Regiment Georgia Volunteers, his unit had spent ten months exchanging fire with Union troops at Fort Pickens on Santa Rosa Island. When the Confederates abandoned Pensacola in the winter of 1862, the First Confederate Regiment was sent to reinforce the harbor defenses of Mobile, Alabama. Billy was now stationed at Fort Gaines, overlooking Mobile Bay.[1] He would not be home for months.

As Robert and Samuel enjoyed their mother's cooking and reveled in a new appreciation of home, they faced pressing decisions. Samuel, now eighteen, had no option but to return to the army. But he could choose the regiment in which he would serve. Having seen enough of Savannah, he decided to go to Mobile and join Billy in the First Confederate Regiment.

This left Robert in a quandary. At fifteen he was legally underage to enlist. He might not be accepted into his brother's regiment. Yet he was assured a place if he stayed with his Fort Valley friends. His decision to opt for the bird in hand was more fateful than he could know. While his brothers would quietly guard a harbor fort in Mobile for the next two years, he would march hundreds of miles and be baptized in brutal combat.

As her boys made their decisions, Sarah Anne Braswell took comfort in the return home on furlough of her youngest brother, Seaborn Mims, who had been fighting in Virginia with the Sixth Georgia Regiment. Married and the father of two small children, the twenty-nine-year-old Mims decided to transfer to the Everett Guards. Now he could keep an eye on his young nephew Robert. This reassured Sarah Ann and helped her support Samuel's decision to join Billy in Mobile.[2]

As the Everett Guards drilled in Fort Valley, reorganization became necessary. The company's name was changed to the Fort Valley Infantry. Charles Richardson was elected captain, and Seaborn Mims was appointed first sergeant. Robert Braswell probably was elated. It never hurt to have your company's first sergeant on your side.

Edwin Davis left Savannah on April 6 and returned home to Riddleville on furlough. Quickly bored with small-town life, he perhaps thought of going to see his buddies at Mercer University. But most were already gone, serving in the army. Instead, he traveled to south Georgia to visit a friend in Thomasville. While there he made a sudden decision that he noted in his journal: "Today my friend, B. F. Oswald and myself went to Thomasville and joined the 'Dixie Boys', Capt. Lucius C. Bryan of Thomas Co."[3] This impulsive act would shape the direction and character of Davis's life for the next three years.

While soldiers squeezed all they could out of their furloughs, many Confederate officers in Savannah were jockeying for position, trying to be named to the command of new Confederate regiments. Colonel William Barkuloo was bolder than most. He saw an opportunity for career advancement and moved aggressively.

Barkuloo, forty, was a most unusual candidate for colonel of a Confederate regiment. To hear his accent was to know immediately that he was a Yankee. Born in New York in 1822, he had moved south and married a Georgia girl, Mary Margaret Anderson. He never moved back to New York.[4]

During the Mexican War, Barkuloo served in the U.S. Army with the Palmetto Regiment from South Carolina and was seriously wounded.[5] By 1850, while still recovering, he had moved to Columbia, South Carolina, where he was a clerk.[6] Later Barkuloo moved his family to Fernandina, Florida, and then to Brunswick, Georgia, which became the Barkuloos' permanent home.

As war fever spread through Brunswick in 1860, William Barkuloo became the coorganizer of the Brunswick Riflemen. In January 1861 he was commissioned a major, in command of the Eighth Battalion, Georgia Militia. On October 14, 1861, he was promoted to colonel, commanding the Second Regiment, First Brigade, Georgia State Troops.[7]

William Barkuloo was a feisty character. As colonel of the Second Regiment, he was infuriated when his men did not receive adequate camp equipment and tents and angrily marched his troops to a railroad siding where a supply train was stopped. He armed some of his men with axes and ordered the rest to fix bayonets and commandeer the train. They chopped through the boxcar doors and secured tents and supplies. This endeared him to his men, but he was initially placed under military arrest. However, Barkuloo was eventually released and retained his command.[8]

With the same bullishness with which he attacked the supply train, Barkuloo decided to form his own regiment when it became evident that all Georgia State Troops must become incorporated into Confederate military units. On March 3, 1862, he wrote a demanding letter to the adjutant general of the Confederate States of America stating, "I have the honor to request you to send me General Orders No. 1 and No. 6. Also *all the blanks* necessary for mustering six months state troops in the confederate service for *the war.* . . . I want blanks for *three* Regiments. I want authority to give my men (and those of cooperating Regiments) *furloughs* for forty or sixty days, to *pay them* the bounty, and *muster them,* elect all officers etc., *before they go home*" (emphasis Barkuloo's).[9]

Barkuloo clearly wanted to get the state troops under his present command corralled into his new Confederate regiment "before they go home." His quick work paid off. Seven of his ten state troop companies signed on, and Barkuloo needed only three more unattached companies to complete the regiment.

As the furlough for the state troops ended and soldiers drifted back to Savannah, Wright Vinson was in a mess. He had not been able to finish his house and get his family settled. After returning to Camp Barkuloo in Savannah, he expressed his frustration in a letter to Christiana on May 11, 1862:

> Darling I reach Savannah safe and sound and came up to camps and found all the boys well and harty and well satisfied. Sow they say. But I don't believe a word of it because I now [know] I don't like to stay away from you and the baby. . . .
>
> Darling I want you to write back to me, how they is getting along with your house. And I want you to write when you move sow I will now where to gow to when I come home. . . .
>
> Darling the regiment is not made up yet but I think it will bee in a day or too. They have got 7 companeys here now and the Colnel [Barkuloo] says that they is some more that we can get. Sow, I record [reckoned] it will be first next week.
>
> Darling, wee have got about 100 and so men in our company now. They is a right smart proud of us.[10]

As the Fort Valley Infantry detrained in Savannah, it had not committed to a Confederate regiment and was fair game for the marauding William Barkuloo. Before the men could unpack, they were persuaded to join. By the end of May, Barkuloo's regiment was fully formed with ten companies. On May 28, 1862, Barkuloo telegraphed General George W. Randolph, Confederate secretary of war, and reported: "The Second Rgt., Georgia State Troops, having been tendered by the governor of Georgia is now in camp and the muster rolls of ten full companies have been forwarded by express. Are they accepted? Wm. Barkuloo, Col., commdg."[11]

The regiment was accepted into Confederate military service and became the Fifty-seventh Regiment Georgia Volunteer Infantry. Three long years of warfare lay before its soldiers.

The approximately one thousand troops composing the Fifty-seventh Georgia were a homogeneous lot. Nine of the ten companies were from the rich agrarian region of middle Georgia. With the exception of Company A, "the Dixie Boys," who were from Thomas County in south Georgia, all the men lived within eighty miles of each other. Five companies were comprised of men from Laurens and Wilkinson counties. The remaining companies were from Houston, Crawford, Washington, Baldwin, and Thomas counties.

When the regiment was completed, the troops elected their officers. Colonel Barkuloo was affirmed as the founding officer of the regiment. Reflecting the voting majority of the men from Laurens and Wilkinson counties, the troops elected Cincinnatus Guyton as lieutenant colonel. A recent graduate of Mercer University, Thomas Jefferson Dyson of Monroe County, was elected adjutant.

Guyton was twenty-eight and popular with his men. More than a century earlier the Protestant Huguenot Guyton family had fled France for South Carolina to escape religious persecution. In the early 1800s the Guytons moved to Laurens County, Georgia. With the purchase of extensive landholdings in the Buckeye region of the county, they soon became prosperous planters, with hundreds of slaves.

Cincinnatus Guyton's father was a member of the Georgia House of Representatives. When his father died, Cincinnatus followed in his footsteps and was elected a state senator. Throughout the war Guyton would take temporary leave when possible to attend the senate sessions.[12]

Describing Guyton after the war, one of his brigade commanders, Colonel Charles H. Olmstead, said, "Lieut. Col. C. S. Guyton I like exceedingly. He was a man of middle size with a face of much refinement, gentle in speech yet possessing a resolution of character that never failed him in any emergency."[13]

Lieutenant Colonel Guyton would give excellent leadership to the Fifty-seventh Georgia. His courage and levelheadedness were a balance to the more impetuous and temperamental William Barkuloo.

Colonel Cincinnatus Guyton
(Courtesy of Laurens County
Historical Society)

The adjutant, Thomas Dyson, was young but capable. He was elected because of his obvious administrative skills and literary ability. After the war one of his Mercer professors, J. B. Willet, described Dyson as a "quiet, unassuming, kind, generous lad and brave to a fault." Dyson would be challenged to coordinate the administrative affairs of the new regiment.[14]

Once gathered and organized in Savannah, the Fifty-seventh Georgia did not have to wait long for its orders. On May 31, 1862, it was directed to report to Camp Randolph, in Gordon County, northwest Georgia.[15] Rumor was that the men were on their way to Tennessee. Now Savannah and the seacoast would be behind them. They would confront the strong Yankee force advancing toward north Georgia.

The Kentucky Campaign

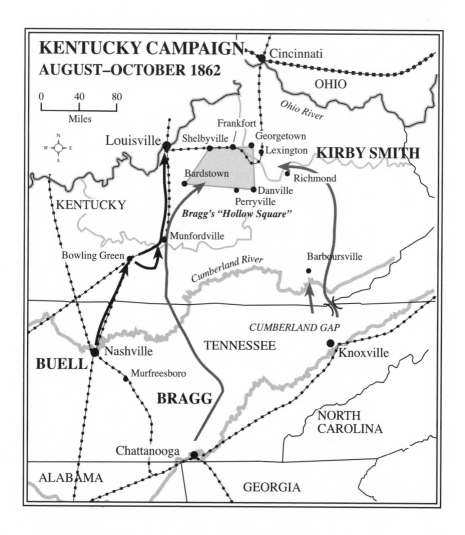

KENTUCKY CAMPAIGN
AUGUST–OCTOBER 1862

Cincinnati

OHIO

0   40   80
Miles

Ohio River

N
W   E
S

Louisville

Frankfort
Shelbyville /
Georgetown
Lexington

KIRBY SMITH

Bardstown

Richmond

KENTUCKY

Danville
Perryville

Bragg's "Hollow Square"

Munfordville

Bowling Green

Barboursville

Cumberland River

CUMBERLAND GAP

Nashville

TENNESSEE

Knoxville

BUELL

Murfreesboro

BRAGG

NORTH
CAROLINA

Chattanooga

ALABAMA

GEORGIA

4

In Sight of the Yankees

Although it seemed that Savannah faced imminent attack in the spring of 1862, the assault did not come. Indeed, Savannah would not fall until 1864, when General William T. Sherman concluded his notorious March to the Sea.

As 1862 progressed, conditions grew worse for the Confederacy. On the northern front Union armies were camped outside Richmond. Along the Atlantic coast Norfolk had fallen, Charleston was besieged, Savannah was sealed up, and only the port of Wilmington, North Carolina, remained open. The Gulf coast fared no better. New Orleans and Pensacola had surrendered, and Mobile was tightly blockaded. The Union navy was effectively squeezing the South.

In the West, Confederate armies were reeling. When Major General Ulysses S. Grant had captured Fort Donelson in Tennessee on February 23, 1862, he opened Kentucky and much of Tennessee to Union control. Later, in April, following the disastrous retreat of Confederate troops after the Battle of Shiloh, northern Mississippi and Alabama also became vulnerable to Union occupation. Now there was clear indication that the Union army intended to attack Chattanooga, Tennessee.

If Chattanooga fell, it would mean catastrophe for Georgia, as it would open the front door to Georgia and the crucial railroad and industrial hub of Atlanta. Though Savannah remained in danger, it became imperative that all available troops in Georgia be sent to defend Chattanooga.

As the ten companies of the Fifty-seventh Georgia returned to Savannah from their furlough, they received orders to move by train to north Georgia and report to a camp of instruction. On June 14, 1862, they arrived at Camp Randolph, three miles from Calhoun, Georgia.

For many men in the Fifty-seventh Georgia, this was their first experience of living in a mountainous region far from home. Wright Vinson had spent his life on a small secluded farm in Crawford County. He had received a meager education; his perspective was narrow and his experience limited. Now looking wide eyed at his new surroundings from a troop train, he wrote to Christiana with a childlike simplicity:

> Darling, I have eat up my old hen all but one whing. I have got some bread yet but not much. Darling I am now setting in the engine riting [writing].

Darling I have seen some poor lands since I left and some verry good and some of the worst hills that I ever saw in my life.

Wee went through a cut about two hundred feet deep. . . . [Then] we run under the ground about 700 yards long [a tunnel]. We pass through it about twelve o'clock in the day and it was as dark as the dead hours of midnight. Darling, I wish that you cold just see it. It looks bad to start in that plase. It looks like that you had started in to bee kill but it runs through in five minutes. . . .

Darling, they is a mountain in four miles of our camps. You can gow on the top of it and look as far as [your] eyes will let you. A man looks like a pea from the top of it.[1]

The men of the Fifty-seventh Georgia had much to learn, not only about mountains and railroads but about how to fight a war. From June 15 until July 3 they drilled under the eye of the camp commander, Major John Dunwoody. Though they spent long hours learning commands and attack formations, they had not been issued arms. They were like children marching with broomsticks. They could not master the use of their weapons or improve their marksmanship.[2]

On July 2 the Fifty-seventh Georgia received orders to advance to Chattanooga. The men now came under the authority of Major General Edmund Kirby Smith, commanding the Department of East Tennessee. The Fifty-seventh Georgia was assigned to the brigade of Brigadier General Danville Leadbetter, commander of the Chattanooga post.

Though still unarmed, the Fifty-seventh Georgia struck camp on July 3 and spent the next day in crowded troop trains careening around narrow mountain curves and chugging up steep slopes. After arriving in Chattanooga, they received arms on July 5: Harpers Ferry rifles and Springfield rifle muskets.[3] With weapons in hand the gravity of their situation seeped in. No longer were they a home guard close to their families. Now they were part of a raging war that embroiled the whole nation. Their fate was not in their grasp.

Writing to Christiana, Wright Vinson related his uncertainty, loneliness, and a desire to escape from his emerging nightmare:

I take my seat in Tennessee for the first time to let you now [know] where I have got to. Darling I am in tolerable health at this time and I hope when this comes to hand it may find you all the same. . . .

Darling I have sent my trunk to Fort Valley and I want you to keep a lookin for it and get it home. I cant care [carry] it no further with me. . . . Write wether you get the trunk and key . . . for the Lord nose when I well get to come home. I may never get ther any more or not. I want to get to see your face one more time and the baby. . . .

I want you to tell Gap to get mee a subtute [substitute—someone paid to serve in his stead] if can find one and send him on to mee. Tell him to give 400 dollars. . . . Darling if they cant get nare one [substitute], I want you to take the train and gow up to Macon and get yours and the baby type [daguerreotype] taken and send it to mee if it costs 50 dollars. My life ant now satisfaction to mee now how and I dont recond [reckon] yourn is ether. Sow I want your type if I cant get to come home.[4]

The Georgians did not have long to wait around and grow depressed. On July 6 they received orders to go to Camp Davis in Jackson County, Alabama, thirty-five miles southwest of Chattanooga.[5]

It was now clear that the Union army intended to occupy eastern Tennessee, where the population was largely loyal to the Union. If Union forces could capture Chattanooga, they would control the hub of the railroad system for the entire central South. After the Confederate general P. G. T. Beauregard retreated from northern Mississippi, Major General Henry W. Halleck, commander of the Union Department of the Mississippi, ordered Major General Don Carlos Buell to advance his Army of the Ohio toward Chattanooga. Following the Memphis and Charleston Railroad due east across northern Mississippi and Alabama, Buell's Yankee troops made slow progress, halting to repair the railroad as they advanced.

By June 29 the Army of the Ohio had arrived at Huntsville, Alabama. An advanced detachment was at Battle Creek below Chattanooga, guarding engineers who were building pontoon bridges at Stevenson and Bridgeport, Alabama.[6] When the Fifty-seventh Georgia arrived at Camp Davis in Alabama, it was nose to nose with Buell's advanced troops. Wright Vinson described the situation in a letter to his father-in-law:

Wee are in sight of the yankees. They say that they ant [ain't] more than ten thousand here. They are station on tenessee river about 35 miles from Chattanooga. Wee taken three of them this weake prison. One of them said that they had just as well quit for they never wold whip us.

I was out on picket the other day about 3 hundred yards from them and I saw about one hundred in the river a washing. I never heard sow much fuss in my life as they did keep. Wee have got about 40 thousand between here and Chattanooga. Wee have got men enough to whip all the yankees they is here.[7]

As the Fifty-seventh Georgia settled into a combat zone, life became more rugged and dangerous. Wright Vinson did not like his soldier's life and told his wife so:

I got in last night about midnight after picket. I have been gone 7 days. Darling that is the worst trip that I ever taken in my life. Wee was gone six nights and in the six nights I was up 4. You may now that it went hard. Wee didnt have now tents with us. Wee had to be on the ground ever night. Just like a hastle of hogs and it rained too days. I was wet about three days. It have give mee a coal but not bad yet. . . .

We are lying here in sight of the yankees. Wee can heare their drums any time we want to. Our picket taken three of them prison last weake. They was in the river washing and when the picket taken them they was start naked as they came in the world. Wee give them some close to put on. Sow that is a nugh [enough] on that subject. . . .

Darling I havent slep in my tent in 8 nights. Dear wee thought that wee seed harde times when we was at Savannah but that ant nothing. You may take my word for that. . . .

Darling wee are looking for a fight ever day. I ant able to say wen it will take place.

Darling I am going out in the country this evening to see if I cant get mee a subtute [substitute]. I heard that they was some up here. Sow I must close for this time.[8]

Before Wright Vinson could succumb to his homesickness and find a substitute, the Fifty-seventh Georgia received orders to return to Chattanooga. Everyone sensed a major battle was looming.

5

Dreams of Kentucky

Major General Edmund Kirby Smith was a handsome, sensitive, and dashing young man. A Floridian, he was raised in a home where success and recognition were stressed. His overbearing father, Joseph Lee Smith, a federal judge, decided when his son was a child that the boy would pursue a military career. Packed off to a Virginia preparatory school at twelve, Edmund seemed destined to go to West Point, and he fulfilled this parental decree when he entered the military academy in 1841.

After graduating twenty-fifth in the West Point class of 1845, the green lieutenant was soon embroiled in the Mexican War and rose quickly through the ranks because of his bravery and aptitude in battle. Later Smith, who was known as "Kirby," was assigned to commands in the West that thrust him into the brutal Indian campaigns. Although Kirby Smith held strong allegiance to the Union, his allegiance to his home state apparently was stronger. After Florida seceded, Smith resigned his commission and entered Confederate service as a lieutenant colonel.

Smith served initially in the Shenandoah Valley under Joseph E. Johnston, became an overnight hero at First Manassas, and soon was named a division commander in northern Virginia. However, when Jefferson Davis began to look for promising and vigorous leadership for the sputtering Western theater, his eye fell on Kirby Smith. Smith reluctantly accepted a transfer and became the commander of the newly formed Department of East Tennessee.

When Smith arrived in Chattanooga in the frigid February of 1862, about the time that Ulysses S. Grant was taking Fort Donelson, Smith faced a desperate situation. The population of eastern Tennessee was strongly Unionist, and he felt like an invader, holding the lid down tight on an occupied and resentful people. Danger was always in the air.

The mountainous Department of East Tennessee included eastern Tennessee, the portion of North Carolina west of the Blue Ridge Mountains, and a segment of Georgia north of the railroad from Augusta to Atlanta to West Point. Unlike many regional commanders, who reported to General Braxton Bragg, the commander of the Western Department,[1] Smith held an independent command and reported directly to Jefferson Davis.

Smith soon discovered that he was being squeezed in an escalating Union pincer movement and had inadequate forces with which to respond. To the north was the mountainous bastion of Cumberland Gap that towered over the Tennessee-Kentucky border. From its impregnable heights General George W. Morgan commanded a Union division that threatened to mount a strong offensive into Tennessee.

To the south Major General Don Carlos Buell's forces increasingly threatened Chattanooga as the Northerners advanced slowly from the west across Alabama. Between the converging forces of Morgan and Buell was a Unionist population bent on guerilla warfare. Kirby Smith had only nine thousand troops with which to police and defend his embattled district.

Of his two crisis points, Chattanooga was the more critical. Should Chattanooga fall, the soft underbelly of the entire South would be exposed and its rail system paralyzed. Chattanooga must be held at all costs. Yet how could Smith's small army keep Morgan's troops at bay at Cumberland Gap while repulsing Buell's thirty thousand troops, which were closing in on Chattanooga? It was impossible without massive reinforcements, and few were available.

As Smith scrambled for a solution, he considered unconventional and drastic measures. It occurred to him during the summer of 1862 that sometimes the best defense is a strong and daring offense. He began to dream of leading a Confederate invasion into neighboring Kentucky.

Why Kentucky? Kentucky was a border state. More Southern than Northern by nature, Kentucky nevertheless had maintained official neutrality in the present civil strife. Yet Jefferson Davis and other Confederate leaders had long maintained that if Kentucky had to choose, it would go with the South. However, the strong presence of Union forces in such cities as Louisville and Cincinnati had coerced Kentuckians into a forced neutrality. Smith reasoned that if he could show a strong military presence in Kentucky, the support of Kentuckians would swing quickly to the South.

But how could Smith abandon the defense of Chattanooga to venture into Kentucky? And how could he invade Kentucky with so few troops? Clearly, he would need the full help and military support of Braxton Bragg.

Bragg was also facing a grim and deteriorating situation in northern Mississippi. As a result of the early Confederate fiasco at Shiloh in April 1862 and the subsequent retreat to Tupelo, Mississippi, Union forces had bled the Army of Mississippi to thirty-one thousand effective troops (that is, enlisted men who were present for duty, healthy, combat ready, and equipped). The country north of Tupelo was barren and dry, with no prospects for forage. Bragg's chances of moving north toward Corinth, Mississippi, to regain the offensive against Halleck and his Department of the Mississippi were slim to suicidal. Yet Bragg yearned to strike the Yankees, avenge the defeat at Shiloh, and retake control of central Tennessee. Bragg was as perplexed as Kirby Smith as to how he might crush such superior forces.

During July 1862 a wily Kirby Smith began to court a vulnerable and frustrated Braxton Bragg and to unveil his bold offensive strategy. Rather than fight superior Union forces in separate and isolated actions with little chance of success, Smith argued, Bragg should quickly transport the bulk of his troops to Chattanooga from whence he and Smith would jointly conduct a lightning raid into central Tennessee and the heartland of Kentucky. Certainly, such bold Confederate action would force Halleck and Buell to suspend offensive operations in the South and withdraw their armies north to defend their home bases and supply centers.[2] Thus Chattanooga, southern Mississippi, and northern Alabama would be saved from further Union attack. And Smith and Bragg would realize the delightful additional benefit of forcing England and France to notice such bold Confederate success, which might induce them to officially recognize the Confederate States of America.

Although the plan was risky, it nevertheless had a chance of succeeding with spectacular results. It certainly was better than waiting to be overpowered by superior Union forces. The new elements of surprise, rapid mobility, and coordination of forces just might work. Bragg decided that it was worth a try.

On July 23, 1862, Bragg's first troop train left Tupelo en route to Chattanooga. By July 29 his entire army was riding the rails across the Southland. It was a risky operation, and Bragg handled the massive transfer of troops masterfully.

Kirby Smith arrived at Bragg's headquarters in Chattanooga for a council of war on July 31. The situation was awkward and uncomfortable. Bragg was known to be irascible and sour. He was seven years Smith's senior and a fellow West Point graduate. He had distinguished himself in the Mexican War and had a reputation for being an excellent administrator. His ability as a battlefield commander, however, was yet to be proved. Bragg had been promoted and placed in command of the Army of Mississippi largely because of his personal friendship with Jefferson Davis, which they had forged in the heat of the Mexican War.

As Kirby Smith entered Bragg's headquarters, he faced an officer who outranked him and commanded a much larger army. But Bragg was technically in Kirby Smith's territory because the Department of East Tennessee was an independent command, separate from the Army of Mississippi. The touchy subject of authority and command hung heavily in the air as the two men greeted each other.

Bragg and Smith waltzed around the issue of command. They finally decided that they would operate independently and under their own command while their armies were physically separated from each other. Only when the two commands were merged together for joint operation would Bragg command both armies.[3] This decision was at best a compromise. And a compromised command always spells trouble. As an old military maxim states, "*One* bad general is better than *two* good ones."

Studying maps of Tennessee and Kentucky, Bragg and Smith sought to clarify their objectives. Bragg established, and Smith agreed, that Smith would first march against Cumberland Gap, Kentucky. By attack or by siege, Smith would force the Yankees to surrender or retreat, thus removing an enemy presence from his unguarded back. At the same time Bragg would move into middle Tennessee to assault a surprised and destabilized Buell. If Smith could make quick work of the Cumberland Gap, he would then advance rapidly west to join forces with Bragg and crush Buell. With this mission accomplished, Bragg and Smith could then merge forces and invade Kentucky. On the surface the plan seemed simple enough.

6

Crossing Big Creek Gap

As the rank-and-file of the Fifty-seventh Georgia milled around their camp near Chattanooga, few cared about such issues as command structure, battle objectives, supply, and communication. Simple soldiers, like fifteen-year-old Private Robert Braswell, knew only that tension was mounting, quartermasters were working furiously, and something big was fixing to happen. Finally, the Fifty-seventh Georgia received orders to proceed by rail to Knoxville. Rumor had it that they'd be attacking the Yankees at Cumberland Gap.

As they were herded into rickety boxcars to move northeast in early August 1862, the men of the Fifty-seventh Georgia were troubled. A homesick Wright Vinson worried about losing touch with his wife. Only a month before he had mailed his letter begging her to have a daguerreotype made of herself and sent to him. Now he fretted that the photograph would be lost. He also worried about how to send his bounty [salary] safely home to support his family. As Vinson waited for the troop train to depart, he hastily scratched out a letter:

> Dear, I just got a letter from you that was wrote on the 28 and was glad
> to heare that you was well and harty. Dear you needent to send your type
> [daguerreotype] till I write to you. We are move up to Chattanooga and have
> got orders to go up to Knoxville Tennessee. . . . Dear, I want you to send your
> type by male when I write to you again and if you get any chance to send it by
> hand you can do sow.
>
> Dear, you said something about my bounty. You said Will [Wright's younger
> brother] had sent his home. I have got mine but I hant sent home yet but
> I will. I will send it by Mr. Booker. I will send 55 dollars. I wold send more
> but Allen [Allen R. Davis] wants 10 dollars and I have got to keep some with
> mee for wee hant got nothing to eat nor hant had in two days. I had to by my
> breakfast this morning.
>
> Dear I will have to quit for I hant got the chance to write . . . The train is
> moveing sow I cant set still. Yours truly loving husband,
>
> Wright Vinson[1]

Not all the men boarding the troop trains with the Fifty-seventh Georgia were white and of European heritage. Many black slaves also boarded the train, rode in wagons, or walked toward Knoxville. It is an often neglected fact that men and women of color have served in all of America's wars. During the American Civil War black Americans played a vital role in both the Union and Confederate armies.

A conservative estimate is that fifty to sixty thousand black Americans—men and women—worked as servants, bodyguards, musicians, nurses, cooks, scouts, barbers, teamsters, and construction laborers within the operations of the Confederate army. Six hundred thousand to one million white men served in the Confederate army, which means that approximately 5 to 10 percent of the people involved in Confederate military operations were of African descent. Indeed, according to one estimate, 25 percent of the Confederate Ordnance Department consisted of black men.[2]

While most blacks did not serve officially as soldiers in the Confederate war effort, they sometimes did perform combat duties. Records show, for example, that early in the war black Confederate sharpshooters saw combat in Virginia and that a black slave served as chaplain in a Tennessee regiment. In the final months of the war the Confederate Congress reluctantly approved a bill allowing black Americans to serve as soldiers.[3]

One black American boarding the troop train with the Fifty-seventh Georgia was a thirty-seven-year-old slave named Scott. Scott was the "camp servant" of Lieutenant Archibald C. McKinley of Milledgeville, a twenty-year-old graduate of the Georgia Military Institute and an officer in Company H of the Fifty-seventh Georgia. Scott was seventeen when McKinley was born and had looked after McKinley ever since. Now he followed McKinley into the war, cooking his food, washing his clothes, building his campfires, and serving him in myriad other ways. No doubt, this was a relationship of forced servitude. But Scott and McKinley also had a deep mutual commitment to one another. Throughout the next three years of intense combat and privation, the bond between Scott and McKinley would be tested and found strong.[4]

The Fifty-seventh Georgia was now enmeshed in a large and complex military operation. Kirby Smith's Army of East Tennessee had four divisions. The Fifty-seventh Georgia was assigned to the Second Division under the command of Brigadier General Henry Heth. Within Heth's division were four brigades. The Fifty-seventh Georgia was detailed to the First Brigade under the command of Brigadier General Daniel Leadbetter.

Upon its incorporation into the Army of East Tennessee, the Fifty-seventh Georgia was temporarily reclassified as the Fifty-fourth Georgia.[5] In Leadbetter's First Brigade the Fifty-seventh joined the Fifty-sixth Georgia (led by Colonel Elisha Watkins), the Fifty-ninth Georgia (under Colonel James A. W. Johnson), and Waddell's Alabama Artillery (led by Captain J. F. Waddell).[6] These four regiments would serve together throughout the Kentucky campaign.

After a day and night in Knoxville, Smith's army began three months of grueling marching. Heth's division left Knoxville on August 4 and marched eighteen miles to the village of Clinton on the Clinch River and encamped.

Years later Private Jim Kuglar of the Fifty-sixth Georgia, a twenty-one-year-old farmer from Carroll County, Georgia, recounted their first day of march:

> Our regiment turned over its tents, and most of its cooking utensils, to the quartermaster at Knoxville, Tennessee, and began to march in the direction of Kentucky. The day was bright and clear, and the rays of heat from the midday sun came down upon us with almost melting power. The dust rose around us like smoke from the burning prairie; this, together with the cartridge box buckled around the waist, gun on the shoulder, and a heavy knapsack of clothing and a blanket on the back, proved to be very tiresome and disagreeable to the soldier, and especially to the members of our 56th regiment, many of whom were strangers to the hardships of the soldier's life. As we marched along numbers from every company fell out of ranks, and little did we think that we had that day begun a campaign of three months almost incessant marching, day and night, part of the time with nothing to eat and no water to drink.[7]

Wright Vinson also wrote to Christiana about his introduction to hard marching, "Dear, wee march 18 miles a foot and when wee got heare wee all was worn out. Wee had to toat all of our things. Dear wee have had to throw all of our things a way. Only what wee can toat. We have left our tent and have to ly in the woods rain or shine and wee have had to leave our camps chest two and ever thing else that wee have got."[8]

Weary from the march, Kirby Smith's green troops tended to their blistered feet and rested for ten days. During this time Smith played his cards skillfully to convince Bragg that it was time to invade Kentucky. During his initial meeting with Bragg in Chattanooga on July 31, Smith had agreed that he would knock out Union general George Morgan's forces at Cumberland Gap, either by direct attack or by siege. Only after the defeat or retreat of Morgan would Smith then march to join Bragg in a move against Buell in middle Tennessee or perhaps Kentucky. However, in recent days Smith had become aware that Morgan had ample provisions to withstand at least a thirty-day siege. Kirby Smith did not want to wait that long before entering Kentucky.

On August 9 the impatient Smith sent a message to Bragg asking permission to bypass Morgan and move immediately into Kentucky. Bragg was uneasy about this request but granted permission.[9] Smith immediately put his troops into motion on August 14, leaving to Carter Stevenson's First Division the job of hemming Morgan in at Cumberland Gap.

Smith assigned the Fifty-seventh Georgia and the other three thousand men of Heth's Second Division the arduous duty of convoying the ponderous supply wagons across the steep Cumberland Mountains through Big Creek Gap, descending into Barboursville, Kentucky. Smith himself would take a second route with the crack troops of Thomas Churchill's Third Division and Patrick Cleburne's Fourth Division, both of which were on loan from Bragg. These six thousand troops would veer northeast and cross the Cumberlands at Roger's Gap, flanking Morgan's position a scant eighteen miles southwest—in other words, Smith planned to maneuver around Morgan's extreme right side (flank), thereby gaining access to the vulnerable rear of his army, in effect surrounding him. Kirby Smith's dream of invading Kentucky was about to become a reality.

As the Fifty-seventh Georgia and the rest of Heth's division prepared to leave Clinton for Kentucky, doctors were examining the growing number of sick—some had dysentery or other illnesses, others were faking it—and either declaring them fit to march or sending them back to Knoxville. Such decisions often put the brigade surgeon, Dr. George W. Peddy, in a difficult and unpopular position. He alone could determine whether a man was truly ill or shirking duty. Many soldiers grew angry when he returned them to active duty. As he wrote to his wife, Kittie, in Franklin, Georgia, the doctor tried to ease her fears that he would suffer reprisal:

> No doubt their are many in the Regt. that dislike me because I will not give them furloughs & discharges, & also frequently mark them for duty when they are trying to play off. . . . Honey, you must not listen to the tails you hear of my miss treating the men. It's all falts, & so far as being killed in battle by them is concerned, I do not fear them in the least. If the Yankees were to attack us I would be more uneasy for fear they would run over me in retreating if I were behind them than to think they would shoot me, & so far as my partiality extends if any difference I have shown it from the company from our county. The whole staff think the world of me. Col. Watkins & Slaughter tell evry body that they have got the best Surgeon in the world.[10]

Wright Vinson wondered whether the doctor would send him back to Knoxville. Weak from physical illness and contemplating the march through Big Creek Gap, he wrote Christiana:

> Dear I was verry sick yesterday all day. But I feel better this morning. Wee have got orders to send all the sick two the horsepitle today. Wee have got to march 150 miles. The sick will be left at Clinton or at Knoxville one. Sow if they leave mee I will write where I am at and if I get wors I shall write for you to come and wait on me for the soldiers dont wait on us heare. The women had rather kill us than to wait on us. . . .
>
> I saw Henry Cheaves and he cald mee and I went to him and he gave mee your type [daguerreotype] and a letter. I open your type and it is sow much like

*Dr. George Washington Peddy
(From Cuttino, ed.,* Saddle Bag, *ii;
courtesy of Mercer University Press)*

you it look like it ought to speke. And our baby is as sweet as it cold bee. Dear
you type is a little to dark. Dear I look at it two and three times ever day. I have
got it lying on my paper now. Dear I sleep with you ever night. Sow I must
close. [11]

Though weakened by exertion, exposure, and camp food, Vinson was declared
fit for duty and began the trek into Kentucky. Many more men fell ill as they
approached the Bluegrass State.

As Leadbetter's brigade pulled out of Clinton with Heth's Second Division,
Edwin Davis was temporarily detached from the Fifty-seventh Georgia and
placed in command of a pioneer corps. [12] The pioneers moved in advance of the
army and were in charge of clearing the roads and pathways for the oncoming
troops and wagon trains. Repairing the narrow trail through the rugged Cumberland Mountains with picks, shovels, and teams of mules was difficult. For a
young man only recently removed from Mercer University, such hard work was
a jolt. Davis's hands were soon covered with blisters, and every muscle in his
lean body ached.

The Cumberlands are part of the Appalachian Mountains, a range that de-
scends from Maine to northern Georgia and Alabama. As the mountains merge
into Tennessee from southwestern Virginia and southeastern Kentucky, they
evolve into a wide elevated plateau with jagged slopes twenty-five hundred to
forty-five hundred feet high. The Cumberland Gap serves as a doorway through

the mountains. Although it was a natural invasion route for both armies, the passage is extremely steep, rugged, and difficult for transporting wagons and artillery.

Private Jim Kuglar of the Fifty-sixth Georgia described the passage of the supply train:

> On August 14 we again took up the line of march, passed through Jacksboro, Tennessee, crossed the Cumberland Mountain at Big Creek gap. In a few days or so we started over this steep mountain about midnight; it was so steep that we hitched about twelve horses to each piece of artillery, fastened a long rope to the end of the tongue, which the men took hold of, and by that means the men and horses pulled them up the mountain. Near the top we halted to rest. Although it was then about the middle of August, we were so cold that we kindled a fire to keep from suffering. At dawn of day we reached the top. In viewing the beautiful scenery, its wildness and sublimity filled me with emotions of pleasure to which I had been a stranger.[13]

As Heth's troops descended into Kentucky, the pioneer corps ran into the first sign of organized opposition. Backwoodsmen with Union loyalties, better known as "bushwhackers," attempted to blockade the narrow road. They felled countless numbers of large trees across the path and rolled large boulders into the passageway. The Confederate pioneer corps worked furiously to clear the path for the advancing supply train.

Despite the obstructions, the long convoy made slow but steady progress that August of 1862. Within five days it had crossed the Cumberlands into Kentucky. With their backs to the mountains, Kirby Smith's troops had passed the point of easy retreat. Now they had committed themselves to invasion and war.

7

First Blood

Robert Braswell and David Fuller crossed through Big Creek Gap with the Fort Valley Infantry. For the first time both fifteen-year-olds felt that their lives were endangered. Now they saw bushwhackers in every shadow. They had heard gruesome tales of what these fierce mountain men would do to captured Confederates. Seeking each other's protection, all the men drew closer together as they trudged deeper into the dense green mountains.

Laboring up and down the steep rocky paths, Heth's Division snaked through the mountains and emerged into Kentucky on August 18, 1862. The first village that the Georgians approached was Boston. Soldier Paul Hammond described Boston as "a dirty little village, of some twenty houses, hemmed in on all sides by the mountains."[1]

A mile from Boston, the advance regiment of Leadbetter's brigade, Colonel J. S. W. Johnson's Fifty-ninth Georgia, began crossing the Elkhorn River near a running gristmill. As the point men waded the stream, thirty to forty bushwhackers fired on their flank from the mill and a field. Panic erupted as the surprised Georgians struggled to return the fire. Hammond recorded their inexperience in battle:

> A curious, but at the time, not amusing illustration was given in this little affair of the ignorance of some of our volunteer officers, when first engaged in actual warfare.
>
> This Georgia regiment [the Fifty-ninth] . . . was a magnificent body of men, but had been mustered into service within a few weeks only, and were now on their first campaign. Their colonel [Johnson], a brave man, who afterwards made an excellent officer, was a county lawyer and politician, and had been elected far more on account of his personal popularity than for any acquaintance with the art of war. When his men came running down the lane, as thick and disorderly as a drove of cattle, confined within the fences, but keen for the fray, Brent [Colonel William G. Brent of Virginia], a veteran who had seen much service, said to him, "Colonel, form your men into line of battle, throw out skirmishers and skirmish that piece of woods, we do not know what is concealed there, this may be a serious movement on the part of the enemy."
>
> "No, no, sir, I will not risk my men in that way," the Colonel answered.

"Why," said Brent, "That is the way to save your men, if the enemy have a field piece they will rake you fore and aft down this lane."

But the Colonel would not "risk" his men, while a discharge of grape or canister [encased artillery shot], or a round shot ploughing through the living mass, would have sent us, sensibly, skirmishing to the rear at a pace which would have done more credit to the hew in our legs than the Colonel's prudence did to his knowledge of tactics. [2]

Despite the Georgians' confusion, they returned fire, killed six bushwhackers, and captured twenty-five, whom the Georgians released when the Northerners agreed to take the oath of allegiance to the Confederate government. [3] The Confederates suffered no casualties.

As they filed past the ambush site, the Georgians gawked and flinched as they looked upon their first combat fatalities. David Fuller would forever remember the sight of the miller lying dead, sprawled in front of his spinning mill wheel. [4] And Wright Vinson, writing to his wife three days later, still stared at the fresh scene in his memory:

> Darling, I have seen sights since wee got here in this country. Wee got right a munks the yankees. Wee made them scatered. Wee taken the plase wee are at now. Boston is the name of the plase.
>
> Darling, wee taken some priseners and kill some. I saw one man lying in the jam of the fence killed. He was shot right through the heart. I walk up to him and look at him good. I saw the hole that he was shot. [5]

Within weeks, these same young soldiers would think nothing of seeing human bodies bloated and ripped apart.

Heth's Second Division remained in Boston for three days, resting and waiting for the last supply wagon to lumber down out of the mountains. Then the troops set out on August 21 to link up with the rest of Kirby Smith's Army of East Tennessee, which had crossed at Rogers Gap and was now at Barbourville. As they marched, they encountered their primary challenges, thirst and hunger. Jim Kuglar remembered that "our diet was green corn and roasted apples. It was just two days march to Barbourville, and we traveled both days without having any water to drink, except a little we took from the run of dried-up branches, which was warm, muddy and very scarce. This was the beginning of our suffering with thirst, for suffer we did, as the weather was extremely hot." [6]

When Heth's Second Division finally reached Barbourville with the supply train and artillery, it found Kirby Smith eager to move farther into Kentucky. Smith had learned that Colonel John Scott's Rebel cavalry had swooped down on London, Kentucky, and captured 150 Union supply wagons en route to fortify General Morgan at Cumberland Gap. Scott had also ripped up the tracks of the

Louisville and Nashville Railroad at Gallatin. Morgan was now completely cut off and without supplies.

Yet Kirby Smith was facing his own supply problems and decided to use this predicament to his advantage. Smith's desperately hungry army was in a desolate section of southern Kentucky aptly called "the barrens": forage was scarce and the people hostile. Smith knew that Braxton Bragg did not want him to immediately proceed farther into Kentucky to try to free the state to join the Confederacy. So Smith informed Bragg that his lack of food and water mandated that he proceed toward Lexington. Incredibly, Bragg granted permission, jettisoning any hope that Bragg and Smith could combine forces to attack Buell in Tennessee.

In a letter to Bragg dated August 24, Smith further clarified his intentions. He stated that he wished to push on to Lexington and gamble that the locals would not only supply his army but flock to the Confederate cause. Then, dropping all pretense, he invited Bragg to ignore Buell in Tennessee, cross the Cumberland River into Kentucky, and mount a united offensive to the Ohio River.[7]

By the next day, August 25, Smith was moving his forces north toward Lexington without waiting for the slow mail service to bring a response from Bragg. Thomas Churchill's Third Division and Patrick Cleburne's Fourth Division led the advance toward Lexington through Big Hill and Richmond. Heth's Second Division was again assigned to convoy the ponderous supply wagons. However, the Fifty-seventh Georgia and the rest of Leadbetter's brigade were detached and sent back to temporarily reinforce Carter Stevenson's First Division, which was hemming Morgan in at Cumberland Gap.

As the Georgians grumbled and retraced their steps through the mountains, they again came under sniper fire from the Unionist bushwhackers. The regimental surgeon, George W. Peddy, penned his thoughts to his wife, Kittie:

> Once more, after passing through the land of Bushwhackers over the Cumberland mountains to the rear of Cumberland gap, I am permitted through the intervention of kind providence to perform the delightful task of writing to you again. . . . If I am not killed by one of those Bushwhackers, I think I will see you between this & Christmas.
>
> We have the Yankees between our force in front & rear. We captured their supply train consisting of about three hundred wagons & teams, the best you ever saw, loaded with Sugar, Coffee, Flour, Bacon, & evry thing that is eaten by the Yankee army. We will starve the enemy out at the gap in a few days. I think they will be compelled to surrender, if a very heavy force does not come to their rescue in a few days.
>
> Our Regt. is quite healthy at this time. I suppose when we leave here we will go on towards Lexington, Ky., if we do not meet with to strong a force.[8]

When Leadbetter's brigade arrived at Cumberland Gap, General Carter Stevenson, commander of the First Division, directed the brigade to block nearby Cumberland Ford. Jim Kuglar of the Fifty-sixth Georgia described their position: "There were sixteen yankee regiments at the gap . . . and their only route of escape was by the way of Cumberland Ford, which is twelve miles in the rear. It is closed in by mountains and has a defile just wide enough for a wagon road. Our brigade, numbering about twenty-five hundred, guarded this narrow passage."[9]

While Leadbetter's brigade dug in at Cumberland Ford, Kirby Smith marched toward Lexington. Soon he encountered his advance cavalry, which was bringing the news that seven Union regiments were positioned nine miles ahead near Richmond, blocking the Confederates' progress toward Lexington.

Because he would rather engage the Federals in open country than have them fall back to the high bluffs overlooking the Kentucky River near Lexington, Smith decided to attack immediately. With Pat Cleburne spearheading his offensive, Smith plowed into the Union forces under General William "Bull" Nelson on August 30.

Cleburne's and Churchill's veterans rolled back the raw Union recruits and, in a desperate win-or-lose fight, achieved one of the most complete Confederate victories of the Civil War. The 6,350 Confederate infantry and cavalry killed, wounded, or captured 5,300 of the 6,500 Union soldiers and took their supply train, suffering but 459 casualties in the process. Union survivors fled to Louisville and the safety of the Ohio River. Now Kirby Smith could walk into Lexington uncontested.

On September 1 the mayor of Lexington quietly surrendered his city to Kirby Smith's advance troops. It appeared that Smith had succeeded in his quixotic quest: Kentucky was in the hands of the Confederacy—for now.

8

By Marching, Not Fighting

Far to the south at Cumberland Ford, Brigadier General Daniel Leadbetter's detached brigade had received orders from Kirby Smith to move north once again to rejoin Heth's division. General Humphry Marshall, who commanded three thousand Confederate infantry in the Western Virginia Department, moved in to replace the Georgians at Cumberland Ford. On August 30—for the third time in two weeks—Leadbetter marched his footsore Georgians over the rugged mountains toward Richmond and Lexington.

Following the Union route at Richmond, Kentucky, Smith had ordered Heth's slowly advancing supply train to halt momentarily at the Richmond battlefield. He directed Heth to parole Union prisoners, secure field hospitals, and transport the wounded. Within twenty-four hours Heth's Second Division was on its way to link up with Smith in Lexington.[1]

Leadbetter's detached brigade finally arrived at the Richmond battlefield on September 2 after Heth had left. The grotesque scenes were etched in Jim Kuglar's memory:

> The distance from Big Hill to Richmond is eighteen miles. Our company was vanguard that day. . . . We soon arrived at the place where the battle commenced. A scene then presented itself which was new to most of the regiment. Fences were taken down by the retreating Yankees to form breastworks on both sides of the long and beautiful [lanes]; rails were torn and split to pieces with shot and shell; the earth was ploughed up in many places with lead from the rebel's guns; the residences were crowded with the wounded of both armies. New graves could be seen on the road side.
>
> One grave we noticed in particular was a Yankee's, as I discovered from his blue uniform; he was buried in this style: the fence was laid down and at the corner where the rails lapped, a hole was dug the length of the man, and about one foot deep. He was laid in this hole and a little dirt thrown over him, and the fence was put up again. When we passed I supposed he had been buried about three days. A portion of the dirt by some means had been removed from the top of his body, and there he lay about half exposed, and the green flies swarming around him like bees around a hive.[2]

Wright Vinson also encountered the gruesome results of war. In the last letter that he would be able to post to Christiana for two months, he scribbled:

Dear, I have walk over the battle field. It was fought between Richmond and Lexington. Our men whip them bad. What they dident kill they taken prisoner.

Darling that was a sight to look at the wounded. Dear I went in the horsepittle where they was. It was the worst sight I ever saw in my life. Some with there arms off and some with their legs off and other plases. Our Regtment hant had nare fight yet.[3]

Disappointed at missing the battle yet relieved not to be among the shredded casualties in the "horsepittle," Leadbetter's Georgians pushed on toward Lexington. Jim Kuglar wrote:

Late in the afternoon we left Richmond and traveled half the night, or later. The boys felt pretty lively, as rations of whiskey had been issued that afternoon. "It was a calm night," and we marched by the light of the "silver shining moon." Crowds of ladies and countrymen flocked to the road, and while we were passing they shouted at the top of their voices: "Hurrah for the Georgia boys;" while we would reply, "Hurrah for the ladies of Kentucky!" The ladies requested us to sing "Dixie". We sang "Dixie" and a few other Southern songs as we marched along.[4]

Filled with a surge of patriotism, Leadbetter's unscathed troops, the tail end of Kirby Smith's invasion force, crossed the Kentucky River and finally arrived on the outskirts of Lexington on September 3. According to Kuglar, they entered Lexington with great flourish:

We arose early in the morning, ate a hearty camp breakfast, loaded our baggage, and formed our regiment to march in the following order: Colonel Barkaloo [Fifty-seventh Georgia], with a brass band at the head of his regiment, in front, Colonel Watkins [Fifty-sixth Georgia] in the rear. Thus formed, we advanced with the route step slowly up the road, until we reached the suburbs in the city. . . .

General Leadbetter on his fine bay horse rode in advance of his brigade. All the windows and porches of the tall city buildings were crowded with ladies and children, who were waving handkerchiefs and shouting hurrahs to us. Confederate banners were floating in the breeze, from the tops of the highest houses. Numbers of ladies and gentlemen came in from the country in buggies, carriages, and on horseback. . . . It was said to be the grandest day that had ever been in Lexington except the day that Henry Clay was buried. It reminded one of the picture of the entrance of the American army into the Grand Plaza of the City of Mexico.[5]

These Georgia boys were experiencing the romantic highlight of their war years. Never again would they bask in a victory parade.

As grateful partisan crowds flocked around his army, Kirby Smith appeared correct in his assumption that the men of Kentucky would rally to the Confederate banner. Caught up in the moment, an ebullient Dr. Peddy exclaimed to Kittie:

> I never saw people so enthusiastic in my life. Our presence fills them with so much joy they are nearly crazy. The road sides are thronged with Ladies waiving their handkerchiefs & Confederate flaggs. We can hardly get about our camps for them. They bring loads of provisions to our camp evry day. They have been oppressed by the Federals so long that in a great many instances they burst into tears at our approach. Nothing they have is to good for us. . . .
>
> Honey, I cannot portray the intensity of the excitement in this country. The k[entuck]yans have made up for the Confederacy in this country today two Regts. of infantry & one company of Cavalry. We will get at least fifty or sixty thousand troops for the Confederacy out of this state.[6]

The truth was that those troops never showed. Kentuckians understood and valued their neutrality. Even if they championed the Southern cause, they still lived in a border state subject to changing winds. Should a man place his bet on Confederate fortunes and lose, he might forfeit his house, property, business, and future to invading Federals. If Kirby Smith needed Kentucky reinforcements to win his campaign, he was in deep peril.

Now that Smith had seized Lexington and Frankfort, he could advance on weakly defended Louisville or Cincinnati and send shock waves through the Union. Or he could join the slowly advancing Bragg and together crush Buell with one unified thrust. However, as Smith stood on the edge of victory, he hesitated, became confused, and lost his offensive momentum.

Four days before Smith's triumphal entry into Lexington on September 2, Braxton Bragg had finally left Chattanooga, headed north. Bragg's plans and destination were unknown to Smith. However, Bragg had a force of only 27,816 men, compared to Buell's horde of 45,000 to 59,000, which would indicate that Bragg was trying to join Smith before engaging Buell.[7] But from August 27 until September 13, Bragg's intentions were a mystery to Smith. Smith did not know where Bragg was or what to do next.[8] This lack of communication and clear strategic objectives was what ultimately lost the Kentucky campaign for the Confederacy.

While Bragg advanced in silence, General Buell initially feared that Bragg's destination was Nashville. Buell therefore concentrated his Union troops and supplies around Nashville and waited for the onslaught. Kirby Smith, on the other hand, consolidated his gains while waiting for Bragg. Smith ordered his 12,500 troops to spread out over a two-hundred-mile line from Cumberland

Gap to within thirty miles of the Ohio River, a defensive rather than an offensive maneuver.

On September 6 Kirby Smith ordered General Leadbetter's Georgia brigade to leave Lexington and advance southwest to Lebanon to drive off a small Union force and capture its supplies. The brigade marched for two hard days, only to find that the Yankees had withdrawn northwest to Louisville. Smith then ordered Leadbetter to proceed southeast to Frankfort to secure the center of Kirby Smith's occupation line. After another hard march the Georgians reached Frankfort on September 15.[9]

As Leadbetter's Georgia boys were getting a dusty tour of the Bluegrass State, General Bragg steadily made his way from Chattanooga toward Kentucky. By September 14 Bragg had reached Glasgow in north-central Tennessee, abandoning any intention of penetrating middle Tennessee. By now General Buell realized that Bragg would not attack Nashville and hurriedly sent half his command to intersect with Bragg and reinforce Louisville.

Back in Glasgow, Bragg was paralyzed by his lack of information and indecision. He was uncertain how many Union troops were driving to overtake him. He also knew that his supplies were low and forage sparse. He assumed that Buell's forces outnumbered his, and he was separated from Kirby Smith's reinforcements, which were two hundred miles to the northeast. If Bragg were to stand a chance against Buell, he must quickly link up with Smith's army.

Bragg decided that he and Smith should combine forces in Bardstown, forty miles southeast of Louisville, and then attack the weakly defended Louisville. This strategic river city was the Union's supply center for Tennessee and Kentucky, and its capture would disable Buell's army. On September 15, the day that the Fifty-seventh Georgia trudged into Frankfort, Bragg finally contacted Kirby Smith and directed him to hold his force in readiness for a combined assault on Louisville by September 23, 1862.

Inexplicably, Bragg, still in Glasgow, now lost his zeal for the offense. For three days he vacillated over his options while awaiting information from cavalry scouts under Joseph Wheeler, Bragg's chief of cavalry, regarding Buell's advance from Nashville. Meanwhile, Buell was charging aggressively ahead. Bragg ran out of time. Buell slipped past the Confederate forces and entered Louisville, reinforcing the Union garrison and dashing Bragg's opportunity to capture the vital city.

As Bragg pondered his lost opportunity and moved to meet up with Smith, Bragg was heard to murmur, "This campaign must be won by marching, not fighting."[10] As the Fifty-seventh Georgia was discovering, the Kentucky campaign would indeed be characterized mostly by marching.

9

Winning the Battle and Losing the War

As General Buell made his rapid march from Nashville to defend Louisville, dramatic actions were taking place on the opposite side of Kentucky. On September 18 General Morgan abandoned Cumberland Gap, broke through the Confederate encirclement, and raced north toward the Ohio River. Kirby Smith attempted to intercept and capture Morgan but failed. Jim Kuglar of the Fifty-sixth Georgia jotted in his diary, "General Morgan gave [us] the dodge . . . and went out through the mountains by the way of Trouton, and crossed over into Ohio."[1]

Smith rushed his Army of East Tennessee back from his futile expedition to corral Morgan and linked up with Bragg's Army of Mississippi on October 2. The Confederate command was at last unified. However, rather than placing his consolidated force in a strong, unified defensive line facing Buell in Louisville, Bragg unwisely dispersed his troops in a broad square east of Louisville. The average distance between the four cities at the corners of the square was forty-four miles. General Leonidas Polk and the majority of the Army of Mississippi guarded Bragg's headquarters at Bardstown—forty-one miles southeast of Louisville—and formed the southwest corner of the square. Patrick Cleburne and Preston Smith held the northwest corner at Shelbyville. Harry Heth's troops—including the Fifty-seventh Georgia—held the northeast corner at Georgetown, and Carter Stevenson's troops held the southeast corner at Danville. Although this was a politic move—it gave maximum exposure to a Confederate presence in Kentucky—it spread Bragg's troops dangerously thin patrolling the 176-mile periphery of the square and did not focus on the primary objective, which was defeating Buell.[2]

As Bragg watched the Union forces strengthen and fortify Louisville, he concluded that an exhausted Buell would stay there for a while to regroup and resupply. However, Buell was under intense criticism from Washington for allowing Bragg to unite his forces with Kirby Smith's. Buell was aware that he might soon be relieved of command, and he was eager to attack Bragg.

Rather than preparing for battle, Bragg allowed himself to be distracted by an attempt to inaugurate a new Kentucky governor sympathetic to the Confederacy. Such a governor could immediately gain passage of a state conscription act, which would force Kentucky men to join the Confederate army. In the middle of an elaborate ceremony on October 4 in the state House of Representatives in Frankfort, Bragg stepped to the podium and presented Richard C. Hawes as governor. As Hawes began to speak, cannons roared from the opposite side of the Kentucky River. Buell had begun a massive offensive. The inaugural ceremony was hastily concluded, and the Confederate administration ended before it began.[3]

Several days before the inauguration, Buell had quietly marched sixty thousand Union troops out of Louisville in four columns. Three of the columns fanned out to the southeast—traveling on separate roads a day's march apart—to converge on Bragg's Army of Mississippi, temporarily commanded by General Leonidas Polk in the vicinity of Bardstown. Buell sent the fourth Union column, comprised of only two divisions, due east to confront a portion of Kirby Smith's Army of East Tennessee at Frankfort and prevent those troops from reinforcing Bragg's Army of Mississippi. This fourth column was the one that rudely interrupted Bragg's inaugural celebration.

Because he was receiving poor intelligence, Bragg initially thought that Buell's main attack was aimed at Kirby Smith's forces in Frankfort, where Bragg remained. Bragg immediately ordered Polk to send reinforcements to Smith. Only later did Bragg realize that the bulk of Buell's force was bearing down on Bragg's own Army of Mississippi in Bardstown. Belatedly rushing to relieve Polk and take command personally, Bragg found his officer corps confused and his forces scattered. Before Bragg could pull his far-flung divisions and brigades together and develop coherent battle plans, part of Buell's advancing Union force—twenty-five thousand troops—collided with sixteen thousand Confederate troops near the small village of Perryville, near Danville.

Unaware that he was significantly outnumbered, Bragg decided to take the offensive and strike first on October 8. Hurling his troops against Buell's arriving force, Bragg encountered initial success. In one of the fiercest battles of the Civil War, the smaller Confederate force miraculously gouged out a tactical victory over the larger Union army under Buell, who had access to massive reinforcements. As night fell, the Union had incurred 4,211 casualties, whereas the Confederates had lost 3,396.[4]

By now, however, Bragg was aware that he was not confronting an inferior force but rather the bulk of Buell's army. Relieved that he had not been annihilated, he ordered a retreat during the night, and Confederate forces melted away in the darkness toward Harrodsburg, a few miles to the northeast. At Harrodsburg Bragg intended to consolidate his far-flung forces and counter any attempt by Buell to cut the Confederate line of retreat to Tennessee.

Yet Bragg was clearly losing his desire to fight. The word *retreat* was becoming dominant in his mind. Bragg was disillusioned, his troops were exhausted from incessant marching, their supplies were low, water was scarce and—most disheartening—Kentucky had not joined the Confederate ranks. Even if Bragg could win a staged battle against Buell at Harrodsburg, would he only be delaying an inevitable defeat? Would Bragg win the battle and lose the war? Bragg privately decided to withdraw from Kentucky and save his army for another day.

When Bragg arrived at Harrodsburg on October 9, he had already set into motion orders to retreat east across Dick's River to his supply base at Bryantsville.[5] The next day Polk's army limped in from Perryville and joined Smith's Army of East Tennessee. Bragg was at last able to present a unified defensive front.

Buell left Perryville on October 11 and pursued Bragg to Harrodsburg. That night the two armies faced each other, confident that the dawn would bring the long-anticipated and decisive battle. In a council of war Bragg surprised his generals with his decision to again retreat. Kirby Smith objected and expressed a strong desire to fight. However, Bragg pointed out that only four days of rations remained, Union troops were already threatening the Confederate retreat routes, and fall rains would soon make passage over the mountains impossible.

Scholars have long debated whether Bragg's decision was wise or yet more evidence of a general who was reluctant to fight. Perhaps both factors were at work. But certainly Bragg's decision to retreat took Southern troops by surprise and dumbfounded Buell. But right or wrong, Bragg and his wing commanders— Leonidas Polk and William Hardee—as well as Kirby Smith, had made the decision.

Jim Kuglar recorded how Leadbetter's Georgia brigade learned of the new orders:

> The night was dark, drizzly and cool. All rails on the surrounding fences were burned that night, as we kept large fires until morning. We were then in sight of General Bragg's army which lay in line of battle, while the enemy, under General Buell, was in line of battle one mile beyond.
>
> The next day the drum "beat" early, which warned us to "fall in". The men soon formed in two ranks behind the stack of guns. Almost every one thought that in a short time he would be out on the line of battle, ready to "pitch into" his enemy, just a short distance beyond.
>
> Colonel Watkins mounted his nice little roan animal, which he called "Sallie McGrundy," appeared in front of his regiment [the Fifty-sixth Georgia], and after giving the commands preparatory to starting, gave the command, "Forward, march." Instead of marching toward the line of battle, we marched back through Harrodsburg, and camped that night a few miles from "Camp Dick Robinson." Here we began to prepare to leave the state.
>
> It is said that the enemy, whose force at that time was very large, had us almost surrounded, having us hemmed in the shape of a horseshoe. All the captains tore up their tents to make haversacks for the men to carry rations in.[6]

Bragg ordered the retreating Confederates to move in two separate columns toward Cumberland Gap. Bragg's Army of Mississippi would march through Lancaster and Crab Orchard, while Smith's Army of East Tennessee would move over Big Hill and through Barbourville. Smith's troops would have the dangerous task of accompanying the slow supply wagons. Joe Wheeler's cavalry would serve as rear guard.

The Confederates had four days of rations to make a twelve-day forced march. Leadbetter's Georgia brigade stumbled on good fortune when it struck camp. Jim Kuglar wrote: "Late in the evening [of October 13] our whole army was put in motion, and soon found itself at Camp Dick Robinson. Here were hundreds of pounds of pickled pork, which our regiment anticipated destroying to prevent its falling into the hands of the enemy. Consequently every soldier was ordered to take as much of it as he was willing to carry. Most every one took a piece, which he carried on his bayonet."[7]

Ham hocks on bayonets only contributed to the ludicrous appearance of Bragg's entourage. Many Kentuckians were fleeing with the Southern army, driving dozens of civilian carriages, buggies, and farm wagons laden with household furnishings. Texas cowboys had been detached from their units to herd the cattle, sheep, and hogs that formed Bragg's mobile commissary. An absurd circus atmosphere enveloped the Confederates. Most symbolically, packed into the wagon trains were the unopened crates of thousands of rifles that Bragg had imported for use by the hordes of Kentuckians who never flocked to the Southern cause.

As Robert Braswell marched alongside his uncle, Seaborn Mims, the boy was a weary, wide-eyed, footsore soldier. He was also worried about his buddy from Fort Valley, David Fuller. The teenager had become ill and had been hospitalized. Now he was trapped behind Union lines. What Braswell could not know was that Fuller was already making his escape. Fuller later told this tale:

> A few nights [after being hospitalized], I heard the clatter of horses' feet on
> the streets, and was told our command was retiring from Kentucky. I quit that
> hospital bunk, climbed on top a freight car and went to Danville. Having taken
> command of myself, I went on foot to Camp Dick Robertson. A regiment of
> cavalry, the rear guard, overtook me, and a trooper allowed me to ride a horse
> he was leading. . . . The next day at 5 P.M. I came upon my command, went to
> Gen. Ledbetter's headquarters for something to eat, and was pointed to a pile
> of corn and told to help myself.[8]

As Braswell worried and wore his shoes out, his buddy rode with the cavalry.

Separating from Bragg's column, Smith's Army of East Tennessee approached Big Hill and quickly ran into trouble. The column ground to a halt as the supply train faltered on the steep terrain. A seven-mile line of stalled wagons blocked all movement. Bragg's column was now miles away and could be of no help as Buell's Union cavalry nipped at Smith's heels. Calling his staff together, Smith said, "It is necessary for me, gentlemen, to call upon you for the exercise of all your energies. I consider my army in great danger. I am determined to save it, though I may be forced to destroy the trains. Park the wagons out of the road ready for burning, then move forward those which contain commissary and quartermaster's stores, but keep the road open for my troops."[9]

As the wagons crept over Big Hill, Heth's division, including Leadbetter's Georgians, was ordered to manhandle the wagons and push them along. Paul Hammond described the scene:

> The soldiers lined the road on either side from the foot to the summit of this immense and rugged hill, and as the starved and tired mules faltered and fell, seized the wagons and lifted them by sheer force over the worst places. All day, and throughout the night and until noon the next day, the trains, in one unbroken stream, continued to pour over Big Hill, and then the troops followed.
>
> We were now again in the region of bushwhackers, who were even more active than upon our entrance into the State. Their savage ferocity spared none who fell into their hand, and they audaciously fired upon the soldiers in their very camps. But, altogether, their hostility was rather serviceable than otherwise, as, in a great measure, it prevented straggling.[10]

Even as Smith's soldiers were encumbered by wagons and annoyed by bushwhackers, hunger, thirst, and disease were escalating. As the exhausted men hobbled along, many without shoes, they found no forage or water. Soldiers often sifted through dirt to find leftover kernels of corn after a horse had eaten its grain. A diet of only one or two biscuits a day was typical for many regiments. Some units reported going for three days with no rations.[11] "Water was extremely scarce," Jim Kuglar recalled. "Some dipped a few cupfuls of water from the horses tracks. Our men began to suffer with hunger, having subsisted since the thirteenth principally on parched corn, while cabbage patches, orchards and Chinese sugar cane were shown no quarter by our army."[12]

Malnutrition made the men all the more susceptible to disease. During the two-hundred-mile retreat, at least fifteen thousand troops contracted typhoid, scurvy, dysentery, and pneumonia.[13] Hundreds died. Horses and mules were worked until they dropped. It seemed like a death march.

To add to the Confederates' misery and fear, Buell's cavalry continually harassed their flanks and rear. Wheeler's rear guard fought twenty-six separate engagements in five days and nights.[14] If Buell had pursued aggressively, he likely would have captured Smith's supply train and a significant portion of his army.

Buell, however, felt an urgent need to return to Tennessee and reinforce

Nashville. He feared that once Bragg crossed the mountains, the Confederates would make a dash toward Nashville by railroad. If so, Buell might be caught in the interior of Kentucky, and Nashville would fall to Bragg. Thus Buell's pursuit of Smith and Bragg became halfhearted and ground to a halt once Smith passed through London, Kentucky. Buell decided to let the Rebels go and moved rapidly back to Nashville. He had saved Kentucky. Now he must do the same for Tennessee.

Smith's troops slowly made their way to Cumberland Gap. Jim Kuglar recalled a trip marked by hunger, tedium, cold, and death:

> On October 20th we stacked arms at 2 o'clock in the evening along the Cumberland river two miles from Flat Lick and five miles from Cumberland Ford in Knox County, Ky. A mill stood in front of our gun stacks, and in a field on the opposite side of the river was a quantity of threshed wheat which was not well fanned. Our Colonel sent after the wheat, pressed the mill and started it to grinding. The mill ran all night, and by morning enough was ground to give the regiment a scanty meal. We took a small quantity of the flour in our tin cups, kneaded it and baked it on an iron for our supper. A portion of the flour was brand and chaff. Beef was issued that night without any salt.
>
> The next day we moved one mile south of Cumberland Ford and halted to camp. About ten o'clock at night a small portion of bread was given to each man. No wood being handy, we lay down, each man having one blanket, but we could not keep warm as the night was very cool.
>
> On the following day we traveled sixteen miles. We passed Cumberland Gap and camped five miles south of it on the bank of Powell's river. During our march we saw between the "ford" and the "gap" the distance of which is about twelve miles, twenty-seven dead horses and mules. [15]

The thinly clad and starving Johnny Rebs were desperate. Buell would have found them easy prey. As it was, disease and fatigue nearly did the job for the Union.

Finally, Smith's gray column crossed into Tennessee. Jim Kuglar captured well the memorable moment of standing on the mountain ridges and looking back into Kentucky:

> From the top of the mountain, the country is visible for many miles around. There one can get a glance at what we termed "beautiful mountain scenery." A few paces from the very summit, on the south side, stands the corner stone of three states, Kentucky, Virginia, and Tennessee. As we stepped over the line into Tennessee, and felt the cool soft and pleasant breeze of "Dixie", Oscar Alexander Cantrell declared that it called to his mind the reading of that chapter in the Holy Bible, which tells about the children of Israel crossing

the Red Sea after which they sat down and sang and played on their musical instruments; and I do believe at that time music would have been the sweetest sound in the world to me. Thus ended our campaign in Kentucky.[16]

According to the historian Robert Selph Henry, the collapse of the Kentucky campaign heralded decline for the Confederacy: "Those days in September of 1862, not the July days of Gettysburg and Vicksburg in 1863, marked the definite point when the tide of fortune for the Confederacy turned and began its ebb."[17] Though ferocious battles remained to be fought, and the Confederates would score significant victories, never again would the Union lose the offensive initiative in the western theater. From this point forward, the Confederacy's chances of obtaining recognition or substantial aid from European powers were greatly diminished. A grueling war of attrition had begun.

Leadbetter's Georgia boys had marched more than one thousand miles in eleven weeks. The Kentucky campaign covered more territory than any other campaign of the entire war. Yet the brigade had not fired a single shot at the Yankees. What had the Georgians accomplished? That was the question they now had time—too much time—to mull and curse. The romance of war had disappeared for young men like Robert Braswell. Good men had died for no apparent reason.

The Vicksburg Campaign

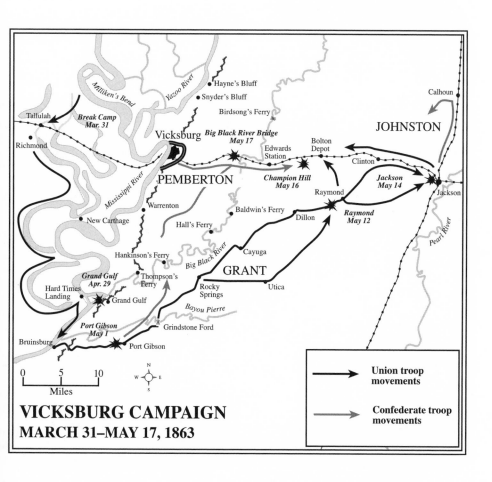

VICKSBURG CAMPAIGN
MARCH 31–MAY 17, 1863

10

Hard Decisions

As Southern troops neared Knoxville, the first snow fell. No one could remember when it had snowed in October in Tennessee. Many felt that it was an omen. The troops built huge bonfires and huddled under thin blankets. They did not have tents. It would be a winter of despair.

George Peddy, the surgeon for Leadbetter's brigade, wrote to his wife, Kittie: "Our troops are well nigh worne down. We lost a great many men that had to be left in consequence of sickness. We have been into no fight since we left, but come very near several times. . . . Honey, I am as near naked as I have been in my life. I want you to send my close on just as soon as you can. I wish a roundabout, coat, vest, and pants, and some wolen shirts of some kind. I will need some socks also. . . . The Confederacy owes me now over eight hundred dollars, and I will send it to you as soon as I get it."[1]

When the commanders of the Fifth-sixth and Fifty-seventh Georgia called the rolls of their thin and ragged troops and compiled casualty reports, they found that the Fifty-sixth had lost 46 men to disease, and the Fifty-seventh had buried 87, more than a tenth of the regiment.[2] Nearly 15,000 soldiers were crowded into hospitals from eastern Tennessee to northern Georgia.[3] Of greatest concern, Bragg had left 900 patients at Perryville, 1,700 at Harrodsburg, and 400 at Danville. Now these 3,000 soldiers were prisoners of war.[4]

Straggling and desertion were also increasing. Although Smith had retreated from Bryantsville with sixteen thousand able-bodied troops, by the time he passed through Cumberland Gap only six thousand were healthy and ready for battle. One-third of his Army of East Tennessee was gone—to combat death and capture, desertion, and especially disease—and his effective strength was only half what it had been in his summer reports.[5] These Confederate soldiers were sick in heart and body, and many were ready to go home.

Within the officer corps displeasure at the conduct of the Kentucky campaign was intense. Officers, enlisted men, and the press publicly criticized Braxton Bragg. General Harry Heth had received orders transferring him back to the Army of Northern Virginia, and he minced no words:

> As far as I can judge, Bragg's management of this campaign was as faulty and badly-managed as any military operation of the war. . . . In discussing

Bragg's course in Kentucky, General [Kirby] Smith and I came to the conclusion that Bragg had lost his mind, and Smith said he would so state in his report to Mr. [Jefferson] Davis. After preparing his report he gave it to me to read. I said, "You have not stated that you thought Bragg has lost his mind."

"No," Smith replied, "I have not. I think it would be better of you to state that to the President when you go to Richmond."

I told Mr. Davis what conclusion General Smith and I had formed in Kentucky after witnessing Bragg's incompetence in this campaign. There was no man in either of the contending armies who was General Bragg's superior as an organizer and a disciplinarian, but when he was in the presence of an enemy he lost his head.[6]

Heth and Smith did not stand alone. Generals Polk and Hardee were also outspoken in their disapproval. A Confederate senator from Tennessee, Gustavus Adolphus Henry, summed up the situation: "Never have I heard so much dissatisfaction as the army expresses at the result of General Bragg's campaign. The army is clamoring for Joe Johnston to lead them, or for [General P. G. T.] Beauregard. The safety of the army depends upon a change of commanders."[7]

Jefferson Davis could not turn a deaf ear to such pervasive criticism. Nor was he happy with the outcome of the Kentucky campaign. When Bragg reached Knoxville, he received orders on October 23, 1862, to depart for Richmond to report to the president.

Fortunately for Bragg, if Jefferson Davis liked you, you were a friend for life. He could also be an inveterate enemy. Davis shared with Bragg a foxhole friendship welded in the heat of the Mexican War. Though Bragg would give Davis problems throughout the Civil War, Davis would remain loyal to Bragg, and Bragg to Davis.

Davis decided to reorganize the western command structure. He divided it into three separate armies or departments: the soon-to-be-formed Army of Tennessee under Braxton Bragg; the Department of Mississippi and East Louisiana under John Pemberton; and the Department of the Trans-Mississippi under Kirby Smith. Davis then selected General Joseph E. Johnston to have overall command of the western theater.

Believing that he had resolved his command dilemma, Davis then turned to the problem of military operations and strategy. When Bragg visited Davis in Richmond, he brought with him a plan of operations. Smarting from the Kentucky campaign, Bragg felt strongly that the western Confederate forces must reestablish the offensive initiative before the Union could regroup and coordinate its vastly larger army. He reasoned that the Confederacy's only hope for success lay in keeping the Yankees off balance.

Bragg recommended that he be allowed to rapidly transfer his army west to Murfreesboro, Tennessee, and make a lightning strike against Nashville from there. This must be done immediately, before Union forces could be deployed south from Kentucky into northern Alabama and Mississippi. Such a bold strike would also relieve John Pemberton in Vicksburg of the pressure that was mounting as Union general Ulysses S. Grant tried to extend his possession of the Mississippi River. Davis agreed to the offensive plan. Bragg renamed his army the Army of Tennessee—a title that it would keep throughout the war—and had his troops riding the rails toward Murfreesboro by the first week in November.

This reorganization brought change to the Fifty-seventh Georgia. Its division commander, Harry Heth, had been transferred to Virginia. The Fifty-seventh's brigade commander, Daniel Leadbetter, was temporarily transferred to Mobile, Alabama. Even Kirby Smith's Army of East Tennessee was dissolved and integrated into the new Army of Tennessee.

The Fifty-seventh Georgia was reassigned to the Army of Tennessee as part of the division led by Major General Carter L. Stevenson and the brigade under Brigadier General Thomas H. Taylor. This was an all-Georgian brigade made up of five regiments: the Thirty-fourth Georgia, Thirty-sixth Georgia, Thirty-ninth Georgia, Fifty-sixth Georgia, and Fifty-seventh Georgia. The Cherokee (Georgia) Artillery was assigned to support Taylor's brigade.[8]

As the men of Taylor's brigade made their way toward Murfreesboro, Tennessee, about twenty-five miles southeast of Nashville, they stopped for eighteen days at Lenoir's Station on the East Tennessee and Georgia Railroad. Here they received tents and cooking utensils. On November 17, 1862, they went by rail to Tullahoma and then on to Manchester, where they camped on the Duck River. On December 7 they moved to Readyville, twelve miles east of Murfreesboro.[9]

During the seven weeks between the return of the Fifty-seventh Georgia to Tennessee on October 17 and its arrival at Readyville on December 7, the soldiers knew little of what was occurring beyond their camp or why. This is clearly reflected in Private Wright Vinson's correspondence with his wife, Christiana, back in Crawford County, Georgia.

On November 6 Vinson wrote his first letter to Christiana in more than two months because constant marching in Kentucky had made correspondence impossible. Vinson scrawled:

> I seat myself this morning to pen you a few lines. These lines leave me enjoying very good health at presant. Hoping these few lines may come to hand and find you all enjoying all the sweets of life.
>
> But it is far to the contrary with me. When I left you I left all my joy behind. I have nothing to write you that will interest you in any way whatever though I will do the best I can.
>
> I can't tell how long we will stay here. . . . It is unknown to us where we will go when we leave here. Reports say we will [move] to Chattanooga the first place we go to.

We have had one of the sweetest trips up in Kentucky you ever hear of. We marched all most day and night ever since we left Long Island [Alabama] and a portion of the time with nothing scarcely to eat. I have seen hard times since I saw you. I am fearful we are going to see some more hard times.

I now think we can get furlows as soon as we get stationed for the winter and if there is any chance for a furlow, Wright is going to have one.

I never wanted to hear from home as bad in my life. I have not heard a word from you since we crossed the mountain going into Kentucky. I would like to see my boy [his infant son, Charley] running about. I know if he has kept hearty he can walk in this time and I would like rite well to see the little fellow.

About this time they come up and report here in camps that they are abought to make peace. But when they do it then I will believe and not before. But I wish to God they could make peace on some terms or other for I am getting tired of the war. You may depend if every body was of the same notion I am it would soon come to a close. But if we have to fight it out it will take a long time. . . . If I live to be a hundred years old I never want to see Kentucky again. . . . If peace was made now I would be one of the happyest boys you ever saw in your life. I long to see the day when I can go home and stay.[10]

Wright Vinson

Furlough was little more than a pipe dream. Only one officer from each company was allowed to go home, to bring supplies back for his men. Most soldiers realized that they were in service for the duration of the war.

As winter lengthened, married men became severely concerned about their wives and children, worrying that they might not have food on the table. Five days after his last letter home, Wright Vinson expressed this uneasiness to Christiana:

My loveing Wife,

I take my pen in hand to ancer your kind letter. It come safe to hand on the 10th and was gladly receive.

Darling I was glad to heare that you and Charley was well and getting harty. I was sorry to hear that you had two spells of the childs [chills]. Dear, you said that it went hard with you. I now it did. Dear, I wish that I cold been there to waited on you. . . .

Darling wee have a grate deal of sickness in camps now. When wee left home wee cold drill 60 and some times a hundred men [Co. F] and now it takes our best to drill 30. Wee have had severl to die and severl to perrole by the yanks and has got severl sick now. Our trip up in Kentucky has killed severl men. The brigade that wee are in does have a man to berry every day and sometime two.

Darling I want you to write to mee in your next letter wether pa has killed that cow or not and if he hant I want you to tell him to doo it, that is if she is fat a nough to kill. And tell him to keep the hide for I shall want it when I get home. . . . You had better keep the taller [tallow] for you will stand in need of it. . . .

Darling I must say something about the hogs. I recond you had better kill all of them but the sow. I recond you have got corn a nough to faten them. And I want to know how maney pigs the sow has got . . . ,

Dear their is a nother thing I want to now and that is I want to now how your pervisions is helt out. Whether you have had plenty to doo you without bying any more or not. Dear write what flour is selling at. Dear when you get out of any thing you must by it. Dont wait to write to mee a bout it. Get it.

Darling they is one thing that I hant told you yet. While wee was in Kentucky I lost all the money that I had and my pocket book to. They was 14 dollars in it. Somebody may stole it for all I now. I lost it in the city of Lexington. . . .

Dear, I have got your type. You both looks nice. Good by, honey.

Wright Vinson

p.s. Dear I dream of hugging you and wake up and bee hugging the boys and then I wold bee mad. Darling I wish I was their to sleep with you tonight. I now I wold sleep warm and more than that I cold hug up with you, though I cant doo it. But I hope the time ant far off [when I] can sleep with you all the time. Sow nothing more. [11]

While the generals and politicians worried about offensive strategy and command structure and indulged in political intrigue, the men worried about cows, hogs, "pervisions," a child's first step, and a wife sleeping in an empty bed back home. Even through the gloom Wright Vinson's humor held out as he "hugged the boys." Humor and friendship were all that most had to cling to.

Increasingly, like Dr. Peddy's wife, families and friends had to provide soldiers of the Southern army with staple articles such as clothing. During the winter of 1862 threadbare soldiers suffered, and many relatives traveled through the lines to resupply their menfolk. Wright Vinson's father visited him:

Darling, I was supprised on [Nov.] 12th. I went down to the station to carry a letter and when I got back to camps I heard that pa was their. And then I went back and you better believed it I was shore that I wold see you their. But I was fooled. He said that you and Charley was well and harty. He said that Charley was growing as fast as He cold and running ever where. . . .

Honey, I must tell you how my clothes fits. My coat fits just as nice as you ever saw in your life. My pants fits just wright. Dear you needent to send any more till I write for them. My socks I hant had them on yet. They will fit, I well know.

Dear, they is one thing that you can make mee and it is a pair of gloves. I lost the ones that I had. Knit them with fingers.

Dear, send mee another pair of suspenders. I hant got none but what you sent by pa. And they is another thing that I like to forgot and that is I wont you to make mee a over coat if you can get the cloth and send it when the captain comes.

Darling I will send your type [daguerreotype] back by pa. The reason I am going to send it is [it's] going to get broke. You keep it till I write to you for it. The case is a bout to get ruined and I woldent have it done for 10 dollars.[12]

For weeks Wright Vinson had cherished and coddled Christiana's "type," but now he was sending it home, a potent symbol of his sinking spirits. Sentimental soldiers were growing numb to the sharp edge of war.

As winter stretched on, disease ran rampant as camp life became squalid. Wright Vinson was not spared the discomfort:

Dear, it looks like that all of our men will soon get sick. . . . Wee left home with a bout 100 men and now wee hant got but 50. It won't take long to loose the rest if they drop off like they have for the last two months. . . .

I have just got done eating breakfast. I had bisquit and meat and corn coffee and gravy. . . . Wee get plenty to eat, such as flower and meat. That is all that wee get. Wee dont have now salt at all. Wee hant had none in 12 days. It is the worst eating that I ever done in my life. Certain it looks to mee like I cold eat up a hole sack [of salt] at one time. It will kill all of us in our bowels if wee dont get some soon. . . .

Wee hant got now soap either. Wee hant had a bit since pa left theirs. I hant wash my close [clothes] in a month and shant till I get soap. Ever thing that I have got is black as the black sow. . . .

Darling I'm a shame to tell you that I am lousey. It is the body louse. I have done my best to keep them off but god in heaven nowes [knows] they ant now chance to doo it. Sow, if I was to get the chance to come home you would hate to tech [touch] mee for you wold get them on you and I woldent have that done for 50 dollars. Dear, I can't keep them off unless I cold get soap to wash my close. Nothing more on the louse scrip.[13]

Early in the Fifty-seventh Georgia's stay outside Murfreesboro at Readyville, Wright Vinson's captain returned from furlough, bringing mail and supplies from Crawford County. One of Vinson's most poignant and telling letters to Christiana followed:

Darling, I received your kind letter when the Capt. [John F.] Vinson come. . . . I got the things that you sent mee. I got the overcoat and a pair of gloves and a pair suspenders. Honey, you ought to see how my coat fits. It is as good a fit as you ever saw in your life. I recond my gloves fits as well as they cold. My suspenders, I hant had them on yet.

Darling, I am much oblige to you for them things. When I get home I will kiss you and hug you and doo any thing you want mee to doo.

Darling, the Capt. treated mee mean a bout the provision you sent mee. He eat it all up before he got there. He eat up the cake and the pies and the butter and had ruin the light bread. I dident get a bit of it. When he got there and I found it was eat up I was mad a nough to give him a whipping. . . . I thought he was a gentleman but I find it not sow. I want say anything more a bout it for it makes [me] mad ever time I think of it and when I get mad I cant right at all. . . .

Darling, I never wanted to gow home as bad in my life as I doo now and if they don't give mee a furlow I am going any how. I will have to desert. The men is deserting more or less ever night. They leave in droves ever night and when I right to you that I am comeing and cant get a furlow, you may now that I have runaway. And I dont [want] you to say a word a bought it for when I come I expect to die right there.

Darling, the army will soon brake up if they keep leaveing like they have been for the last week.

Darling, I want to now what you think of it [desertion]. If you dont want mee to doo it, right back. My life ant now satisfaction to mee and I had just as soon die as to live.

Darling, I understand that 2000 of Bragg's men had left and they say that they expect to doo their fighting at home. They hant none of our company left yet but I am looking for it ever night. . . . Write what you think about mee leaving. Yours as ever,

Wright Vinson[14]

Desertion was a major problem in both the Confederate and Union armies. Many men deserted for a short period of time, checked on their families, harvested a crop, and then reenlisted or returned to their regiment. Others would slip quietly away, never to be heard from again. By the war's end one in eight Confederates and one in ten Federals had deserted.[15] Yet deserting one's comrades was no easy choice. The men in a regimental company usually were from the same locale. A deserter knew he might meet these same men face to face again and be held accountable.

Then, too, soldiers felt a deep, though gradually diminishing, commitment to patriotism and the "Southern cause." Confederate armies were fighting all across the South. But even the simplest of rural minds was recognizing the superior manpower and resources of the Union army. Was the Southern way of life worth dying for? And if defeat was inevitable, why risk death on the battlefield?

But more than anything, the men were concerned about their families. With few men at home wives and children were truly suffering. Anxious letters from home told the tale. Planting and harvesting crops was enormously difficult. The Southern economy was falling apart and prices were skyrocketing. Where did a soldier's allegiance lie? with the South? or a state? or pride and patriotism? or with loyalty to family?

But desertion was as dangerous as staying in the army. If Wright Vinson deserted, he could not simply return home to Christiana and Charley. Desertion was illegal and punishable by death. Desertion for Wright Vinson meant hiding in the swamps and woods of Crawford County and being a fugitive until the end of the war.

Of course, there were legal alternatives to desertion—if a soldier was fortunate. Private James N. Mathews, also from Crawford County, was fighting with Jeb Stuart's cavalry in the Army of Northern Virginia. When he joined the army in 1861, he was thirty-four, older than most soldiers, and left a wife and four children at home. Two years later, after he had participated in several bloody battles, including the carnage of Gettysburg, Mathews was sent back to Georgia to requisition horses for the Confederate cavalry. While visiting Crawford County, he allowed his name to be placed on the ballot for county sheriff and won the election. Robert E. Lee signed Mathews's honorable discharge from the army due to "civil service."[16]

So there were ways to leave the army without deserting—paying a substitute, working in civil service, transferring to a less dangerous theater of operations. But these options were not open to most men. Still, what was remarkable was not how many men chose to desert but how many chose to stay and face another battle and the grinding discomfort of soldier life.[17] As it happened, Wright Vinson and the other men of the Fifty-seventh Georgia would have few nights to sit and grow despondent in Tennessee. Soon they would be ordered west, farther from home than ever.

Dust to Dust

While the Army of Tennessee was encamped around Murfreesboro, the Union army massed to meet the Southern forces. A furious U.S. War Department had relieved Don Carlos Buell of command on October 24, 1862, for his failure to aggressively pursue and destroy Bragg's retreating army before it escaped from Kentucky. Major General William Rosecrans assumed Buell's command, and his three corps were designated the Army of the Cumberland.

Bragg worked frantically to pull together 40,000 Rebels to face the 60,000 Yankees entrenched around Nashville. Rosecrans had another 35,000 reserve troops poised to advance from Kentucky. Bragg assumed that both armies would settle into winter camp and clash in early spring.

As Rosecrans and Bragg faced each other, Joseph Johnston assumed command of Confederate forces in the western theater and hurried to forge a strategy. He soon came into conflict with Jefferson Davis. Johnston felt strongly that the highest priority in the west should be to secure Tennessee. Should Bragg be defeated in Tennessee, Johnston reasoned, Georgia and Alabama would be open to a Union advance and the South would collapse.

Jefferson Davis disagreed. Although he recognized the importance of Tennessee, he believed that the Union's strategy had two basic objectives: the capture of the Confederate capital in Richmond, Virginia, and control of the Mississippi River. Thus Davis was convinced that Johnston's highest priority in the western theater must be the strengthening of John Pemberton's Department of Mississippi and East Louisiana.[1]

Both Pemberton and Bragg desperately needed immediate reinforcements in order to defend their spheres of operation. The only Confederate troops available were thirty thousand soldiers in Arkansas under the command of General H. T. Holmes. In a face-to-face conference with Davis, Johnston and Bragg argued vehemently that Holmes's troops should be sent to reinforce Pemberton in Mississippi. Davis refused to remove them from the defense of Arkansas.[2] Instead, Davis ordered Bragg to prepare Carter Stevenson's division of nine thousand men—one-fourth of Bragg's army—to leave Tennessee to reinforce Pemberton at Vicksburg. This critically weakened Bragg's Army of Tennessee and delighted Rosecrans.

By December 18 Stevenson's troops—including the Fifty-seventh Georgia and Taylor's Georgia brigade—had left Tennessee and begun a three-week trip by rail to Mississippi. Most of these men had never dreamed that they would end up in Mississippi. Their circuitous route seemed ludicrous. To travel west, they first had to go east to Chattanooga and Atlanta before traveling west through Mobile to Jackson, Mississippi.

The troop train carrying the soldiers of the Fifty-seventh Georgia entered their home state and stopped in Atlanta a few days before Christmas. In this sentimental season and so close to home, many men grew increasingly lonely and were tempted to desert. Many did. In a pensive moment Wright Vinson wrote to Christiana, who was less than a hundred miles away:

> Dear, wee are on our way two Mississippi and wee have got as far as Atlanta on the way. Wee will leave here to day, I recond.
> Darling, I want [wasn't] with you last Christmas and won't bee this [Christmas]. I have done my best to get off but the General Taylor ant here and the Colnel wont sign a pass. Sow I cant get off unless I was to dessert. I am afraid to doo it. They were a few men running last night.
> Dear, I want you to send me a cover for I want one. I nearly freeze. . . .
> I received a letter that you sent by Tom Booker and a little bag of salt. Your letter said that you sent some soap, but I dident get it. Sow I must close for this time. Yours as ever.[3]
>
> Wright Vinson

At the Atlanta railway station Wright Vinson saw his younger brother, William, who begged Wright to desert and go home to his wife and son. As the train whistled and began to pull away, Wright Vinson faced the biggest decision of his life. Slowly, he stepped back on the train. For reasons he could not fully explain, he could not leave his regiment.[4] Talking about deserting and actually doing it were two different things.

Relieved to be temporarily at a distance from the squalor of winter camp and the threat of imminent battle, Carter Stevenson's troops relaxed and became jovial. Some soon relieved their tensions by preying on vulnerable citizens. Jim Kuglar of the Fifty-sixth Georgia wrote:

> Orders were very strick then against any one selling whiskey to a soldier. A citizen informed one of the boys that he had a canteen of whiskey, and that he would let him have it for eight dollars. His reply was, "A trade, as soon as I step and get my canteen." While the citizen was getting the canteen, the soldier whispered to some of his comrades, "Watch me, and when you see him emptying the whiskey in my canteen, rush up with your guns and take him prisoner."

At last when the man returned with the whiskey one of the soldiers addressed him in a severe manner, "What have you in that canteen?" The man replied, "Water." "Let me see," said the soldier, at the same time pulling out the stopper and placing his nose to the mouth of the canteen. "Water, oh! Bring him down to headquarters, boys!"

The citizen fearing they would arrest him for selling the whiskey, ran off without his eight gallons, and probably thought he had escaped without being arrested. The boys proceeded to the camp, stacked arms, and had a fine time drinking and laughing over their cleverness.

A soldier who witnessed these tricks, seeing that they were well managed, concluded to try his luck. An old lady came up with a bucket of pies, and while she was telling the prices, the soldier slipped a pie out of the basket. The old lady having watched somewhat closer than he anticipated, lifted his hat from his head, remarking at the same time: "A fair exchange is no open robbery." The boys who were crowded around began to laugh at the soldier, who saw he was caught, laid the pie in the basket, and the old lady returned his hat.[5]

The soldiers also picked on black slaves, who were always defenseless:

It was Christmas times and during the day some of the boys had taken a little more than the average supply of whiskey, which caused them to be a little bit thirsty. [After leaving Atlanta] the train halted for a few minutes, and they called to a negro who was standing near the car, to bring them water, quick! The negro ran and in the shortest time imaginable handed a bucket into the car. One of the boys began to drink out of the bucket. The whistle blew and the train began moving off slowly. The negro ran along keeping up with the train until it began running at full speed, exclaiming, "Master, please gim me de bucket! Master, please gim me de bucket!"

The last the negro saw of the bucket, the thirsty soldier was standing with it almost bottom side up, in the door of the car drinking as though he didn't intend to cease until he had swallowed its contents. . . .

Before we reached West Point the train again stopped and two negroes came up to the car offering potatoes for sale. One of the boys lifted the sack into the car and began to distribute them among his comrades, who were crowded very thickly around him. One of the negroes said "Master, ain't you gwine to pay me for the taters?". The soldier pointed his gun toward the negro and told him if he didn't "skedaddle" he would shoot him.

The negro ran off about ten paces and said, "Master, if you won't pay me for de taters, gim me de sack." About that time the gun fired and the negroes leaped behind a tree. Another soldier held up his gun and fired at the top of the tree. The negroes then began running. Here they went at full speed through the woods, leaping over logs, rocks, sticks and bushes. The boys only intended to have some fun out of them and then pay them for the potatoes, but the negroes understood the joke to be strictly sincere.[6]

The fear of the hapless slaves was valid. Homesick, youthful soldiers, racism, and stout whiskey were a volatile combination.

From West Point, Georgia, Stevenson's troops proceeded to Montgomery, Alabama. From the trains they boarded steamers and cruised down the Alabama River to Selma, where they reconnected with the railway and rode to Demopolis, Alabama. A feast was waiting for them. Jim Kuglar recalled:

> Down the street we could see it crowded with beautiful women, and a short distance beyond them we saw a long table under a row of beautiful trees which stood along the sidewalk. Provisions cooked in the best style were soon placed on the tables and the whole car load of soldiers, consisting of two regiments, were invited to dinner. We marched up to one side of the table, while the ladies stood on the other side and waited upon us with the greatest pleasure and politeness. We were informed that they had been feeding soldiers seven days and had provisions enough prepared to feed them seven more days, and if the soldiers continued passing through, they intended to feed them as long as Demopolis could furnish a pound of meat or a loaf of bread.[7]

The officer corps may have tolerated "boyish hijinks" as long as the soldiers were plaguing mere citizens and slaves, but as the troops journeyed toward Mississippi and a soldier in the Fifty-sixth Georgia helped himself to others' possessions, he learned how harsh disciplinary measures could be:

> Captain Rowland placed his boots near his head when he retired. When he arose the boots were missing. By searching around in his bare feet, he found them, together with other articles which were missing from the regiment, in the possession of a young lad named Rataree, who already bore the reputation of being a considerable rogue. For punishment his shirt was taken off and one hundred and one stripes placed upon his bare back, the hair shaved off one side of his head, marched through the encampment in advance of a large crowd of soldiers who followed close behind under sound of the tune called the "Rogue's March", with his hat in his hand. When this was done he was considered fully discharged.[8]

When Stevenson's division reached Jackson, Mississippi, in early January 1863, the men set up temporary camp before advancing to Vicksburg. While in Jackson, Wright Vinson became seriously ill. To scrawl a letter to Christiana, he had to make his own ink and find a rare scrap of paper:

Dear, it looks like that all of our men will die. I heard the other day that James Hammock had died and James Hartley died and James Morris he died too. That makes ten men that wee have had to die. . . .

I have been quite sick with pains in my head and back. The Doctor says that it is the Rheumatism. Though I am a good deal better. I have been in hopes that I will be able to do my camp duty in a few days.

I don't want you to be uneasy about me for if I git any wors off I will let you now it. I am yet in camps with the balance of the boys. I don't think I will have to go to the horsepitle if I keep mending which I think I will for I have a good tent to stay in. The balance of the company is in good health that are here. We hant got but fifty here.[9]

Within six months Company F of the Fifty-seventh Georgia had been reduced from more than one hundred men to fewer than fifty. Fatigue, malnutrition, poor hygiene, and finally disease had become far more deadly than the Union army.

But Vinson's regimental doctor was wrong, and what appeared to be rheumatism was smallpox. On January 18 one of Wright Vinson's friends, Nathan Carswell, wrote Christiana:

Dear Maddam,

I this afternoon seat my self for the purpus of droping you a few lines to inform you that your husband is not well at this time but hopes these few lines may reach and find you all enjoying good health.

He was taken about one weak ago with Small pox. I was sent to the Hospital at Jackson and his brother William was not allowed to go with him. Consequently he was sent off by his Self. And Will and the fellows of his mess was sent off to a camp by them selves for fear they would take the Small pox. But none of the rest of them have taken it yet. And William got me to write to you for him because he said he was afraid to write to you his self for fear he might have the Small pox him Self and send it to you in a letter.

I heard from Wright this eaivining. He is very low but I hope he will get over it after all. God grant that he may at any rate.[10]

Three days later Christiana received another letter, from Lieutenant John B. Fowler, acting company commander:

Dear Madam,

It becomes my painful duty (at the instance of William D. Vinson) to inform you that your husband, Wright Vinson, died at the Institute hospital the 18th [of January] from Small pox. His brother W. D. Vinson was not allowed to stay at the hospital to wait on him. I used every means in my power and William went the second time, but was not allowed to ever see him. All of the mess are now quartered remote from the Regiment and quarantined in order if possible to arrest the disease. And they are all afraid to write in fear the disease might be sent by the letter.

William wishes you to write to him immediately after you receive this. He, William, has Wrights money and his clothes will be burned at the Hospital.[11]

It would be more than a month before William Vinson could write to his sister-in-law. His initial letter was lost in the mail. Finally, after receiving an inquiring letter from Christiana, he replied:

Christiana, I am verry sarrow to hear that you have not recieved my letter yet. I had ritten to you about 2 weaks ago. And I would have ritten to you before I did but I did not have any paper nor any money to get any with.

You wanted to now if I recieved the things that you sent to Wright. I recieved every thing that you sent to him. I recieved them the same eavening that he was sente to the horsepittle. The letter that you sente to him I sente that to him and the money that you sente I taken that out of the letter before I sente it off. And the cake and butter I kept it till after he died and then I and Allen eat it. And the head quilt that you sente we have it yet and the money to.

Chris, you wanted me to rite to you how longe he was sick and how he was treated during his sickness. Chris, I cant tell how he was treated after he was into the horsepittle, only what they told me. They told me that he was treated very kind by both the doctor and his nurse. He only stayed with us five days after he was taken [sick]. He only lived about seven dayes after he went there.

Chris, while he stayed where I could wait own him he did not suffer for any thing that I could do for him. I done all that I could to get to go to wait own him but they would not let me. Chris, it hurt me very bad to think that he had to lie there and die without any of us with him.

I do not know what they done with his things. I know that he was burid in one suit of his close and the rest of them was burnt I recon.

Chris, you wanted me to fetch him home when I come if I could. I will sea if I can and if I can I will be shore to do it for I don't want any of my folks to be left in this old state. I do hate it worse than any place I have ever bin at yet.

I am sorrow to my hart that he dident go home when we was at Atlanta. I done my best to get him to go home then but he would not go. Maybe if he had a went he would a bin a living yet. But I am in hope that he is in a better world than this where there is now more war nor trubles.

I want you to kiss Charley for me. Tell him to be a good boy till I come home and I will bring him a present. Nothing more only this remains your loveing brother untill death,

W. D. Vinson[12]

It had been a long struggle for Wright Vinson—a struggle to be faithful to causes, events, and passions far beyond his understanding and control. As a soldier he never fired a shot in battle. He died for the sake of loyalty—loyalty that became a cause in and of itself, a loyalty that sounded a hollow answer to widows who cried in the night and children who never saw their father's face.

A Georgia boy returned to dust in Mississippi, and to this day no one knows where his grave lies.

12

The Battle of Champion Hill

During the three weeks that Carter Stevenson's division and the Fifty-seventh Georgia were traveling to Mississippi, the situation in the western theater changed greatly, and the Fifty-seventh Georgia narrowly missed a bloodletting in Tennessee.

When Rosecrans heard that one-fourth of Bragg's troops had left for Vicksburg, he disrupted Christmas holidays and immediately marched 47,000 Union soldiers to Murfreesboro on December 26, 1862. He engaged Bragg's 38,000 Rebs along Stones River, and a vicious seesaw battle ensued for four days. On January 3, 1863, Bragg retreated, fearing that overwhelming Union reinforcements from Nashville were approaching. The Battle of Stones River was costly: 12,906 casualties for the North and 11,739 for the South.

Although tactically the Battle of Stones River was a draw, Rosecrans had driven Bragg out of central Tennessee and left his soldiers demoralized. Bragg lost his offensive zeal, and Joe Johnston's fears were proved true: Tennessee was falling to the Union, opening Georgia and Alabama, and then all of the South, to the Yankees. Bragg was now on the defensive in eastern Tennessee with little hope of reinforcements, and Grant was poised to administer a severe blow to Pemberton in Mississippi.

Toward the end of January 1863, the Fifty-seventh Georgia proceeded with Stevenson's division from Jackson to Vicksburg, Mississippi. For the next three months the Fifty-seventh Georgia was involved in garrison duty and brief forays into the countryside surrounding Vicksburg. However, with the budding of spring Grant moved south down the Mississippi River toward Vicksburg. On the night of April 16 Grant loaded a large infantry assault force onto Admiral David Porter's transports, floated quietly down the darkened Mississippi, and slipped under the massive defensive guns at Vicksburg. Grant caught Confederate officers attending a gala ball and lost only one transport and a few supply barges to Rebel fire. Proceeding sixty miles south of Vicksburg, Grant eventually landed unopposed at Bruinsburg, Mississippi. He was joined by an additional Union force, which had marched south along the western bank of the Mississippi. Moving rapidly, Grant overran Brigadier General John Bowen's fifty-five hundred Rebels at Port Gibson and secured a beachhead for reinforcements as Union forces prepared to strike inland.

Grant swiftly moved his troops toward the state capitol at Jackson, in north-central Mississippi, dumbfounding the Confederate command.[1] On May 9 Joseph Johnston, who was recovering from a severe illness, received orders from Richmond to immediately leave his headquarters at Tullahoma, Tennessee, and take personal command in Mississippi. When he arrived in Jackson on May 13, he found that he could assemble only 12,000 disjointed troops to defend against Grant's 20,000 disciplined veterans. Johnston knew that his only hope was to somehow combine his limited troops in Jackson with a portion of the 32,000 soldiers under Pemberton in Vicksburg, which was forty-five miles due west through flat, forested terrain.

As Johnston scrambled to get Pemberton to send major reinforcements from Vicksburg before Grant struck Jackson, communication and a clear chain of command quickly broke down. Previously, Jefferson Davis had telegraphed Pemberton from Richmond, strongly stating that he was to hold Vicksburg at all costs.[2] Now, on May 14, 1863, Davis's communiqué seemed to be contradicted by an urgent message from Pemberton's theater commander, Joe Johnston, ordering Pemberton to leave only a minimal crew to defend Vicksburg and to proceed immediately to join Johnston in Jackson.[3]

Faced with conflicting messages, Pemberton hesitated and sought clarification as Grant pounded toward Jackson. Time ran out, Grant's troops captured Jackson, and Johnston retreated north, mounting minimal opposition against Union forces. Johnston knew that his meager troops could not defeat Grant and should not be wasted. Grant's army quickly destroyed the rail hub that any Confederate reinforcements for Vicksburg would have had to use, and left Jackson in flames. Grant then wheeled and turned west toward Vicksburg.

As May 15 dawned, Pemberton—unaware that Jackson had fallen—concluded that he could not risk joining Johnston to confront Grant. Instead he temporarily moved his headquarters from Vicksburg to the small community of Edwards Station, which straddled the railroad line twelve miles east of Vicksburg. Pemberton left ten thousand troops to man the stout defenses of Vicksburg and brought twenty-two thousand with him. He reasoned that as Grant would move toward Vicksburg, he would follow the railroad line across the Big Black River and through Edwards Station. If Pemberton could array his army along the steep banks of the Big Black, he might be able to defeat Grant and avoid being trapped and besieged in Vicksburg.

Pemberton then moved to sever Grant's supply line at Dillon's Plantation, seven miles west of Raymond and due south of Edwards Station. Pemberton established a raiding party of three divisions. In the vanguard was a division from the Department of Mississippi and East Louisiana, commanded by William Wing Loring, followed by the division led by John Bowen. Carter Stevenson's division—including the Fifty-seventh Georgia—brought up the rear, guarding the supply wagons.

As the raiding party moved out at the dawn on May 15, nothing went right. After long delays the party finally reached the Jackson Road, only to learn from advance scouts that they had seen a large corps of Union troops advancing from Jackson on the Bolton Road. Pemberton was stunned. There were not supposed to be any Yankees in the vicinity. As darkness fell, Pemberton decided to sit tight until morning. He suspected that crisis was imminent.

When the sun rose on May 16, Robert Braswell of the Fifty-seventh Georgia was undoubtedly in a foul mood. He had marched through ankle-deep mud all night and had gotten only an hour of fitful sleep on soggy ground. His skinny sixteen-year-old body felt like an old man's arthritic frame, and he was hungry. Nobody was cooking breakfast, however. Everyone was listening to the rumble of artillery fire on the Raymond Road.

Through the dawn a lathered horse and rider galloped in from Jackson with new orders from Johnston. Aghast, Pemberton finally learned that the state capital had fallen and that Johnston had retreated. Johnston again was commanding Pemberton to march his troops northeast to join forces with him.[4] Pemberton decided to reverse direction and begin a forced march to unite with Johnston.[5]

As the Confederate column retreated, it soon became evident that a battle with Grant's advancing forces could not be avoided. For Pemberton to keep marching and not establish a line of battle would be suicide. He had no choice but to immediately turn and face the enemy.

As Pemberton frantically looked for good defensive ground upon which to deploy his three divisions, he had no idea of the size of the Union juggernaut bearing down upon him. Grant's seven divisions were coming from three directions on three roughly parallel highways: the Raymond Road to the south, the Middle Road in the center, and the Jackson Road to the north. All three highways converged near a 140-foot prominence called Champion Hill.

By 8:30 A.M. Pemberton aligned his troops on a three-mile battlefront stretching southwest to northeast, with Champion Hill anchoring the northeastern, or left, flank. Fortuitously, the land was excellent for waging a defensive battle. Loring held the right flank and faced the Raymond Road, where the initial contact with Union forces had been made. John Bowen's tough and tested troops held the center of the Confederate line and faced the Middle Road. Carter Stevenson anchored the left end of the Confederate line, with his left flank resting on the slope of Champion Hill.[6]

As the morning fog lifted and the sun rose higher on an already stifling day, Pemberton was able to momentarily slow the Union advance along the Raymond and Middle roads. However, at 9 A.M., Brigadier General Stephen D. Lee, commanding the second brigade of Stevenson's division on the far left flank of Pemberton's line, received word from a wide-eyed courier that a large body of Union

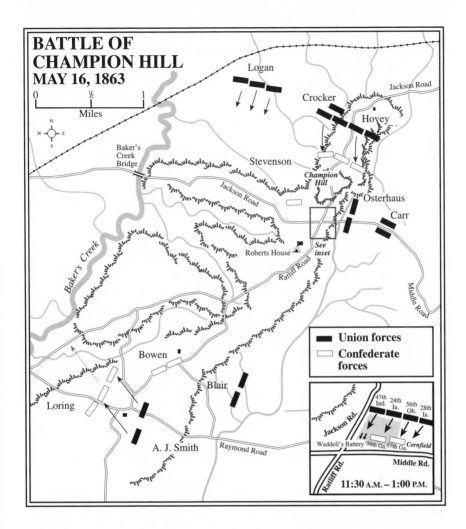

**BATTLE OF
CHAMPION HILL
MAY 16, 1863**

0   ½   1
Miles

Logan

Jackson Road

Crocker

Hovey

Baker's
Creek
Bridge

Stevenson

Champion
Hill

Osterhaus

Carr

Jackson Road

Roberts House   See
inset

Ratliff Road

Baker's Creek

Middle Road

■ **Union forces**
□ **Confederate
forces**

Bowen

Blair

47th   24th   56th   28th
Ind.   Ia.   Oh.   Ia.

Jackson Rd.

Loring

Waddell's Battery 56th Ga. 57th Ga.   Cornfield

A. J. Smith   Raymond Road

Middle Rd.

11:30 A.M. – **1:00** P.M.

Ratliff Rd.

troops was advancing from the northeast on the Jackson Road. Lee immediately
realized that he must move to his left to keep this new threat from turning the
Confederate left flank, capturing Edwards Station, and severing Pemberton's
line of retreat across the Baker's Creek bridge to Vicksburg.

As Lee shifted his alignment, his Alabama brigade ascended the slope of
Champion Hill, crossed its crest, and created a line of defense down the left, or
northwestern, slope. Lee's movement required that Stevenson's Third Brigade,
under Brigadier General Alfred Cumming, also shift his Georgians to the left in
order to stay connected to Lee's right flank.

Cumming, a Georgian and a West Point graduate, had replaced Thomas
Taylor as commander of the Georgia brigade only three days earlier.[7] Cumming

barely knew his regimental commanders by sight, and now he attempted to reposition them.[8] His brigade consisted of the Thirty-fourth, Thirty-sixth, Thirty-ninth, Fifty-sixth, and Fifty-seventh Regiments of Georgia. Although all these regiments had marched through the Kentucky campaign, none had seen actual combat.

After receiving permission from Carter Stevenson to shift with Lee to the left, Cumming personally led the Thirty-fourth, Thirty-sixth, and Thirty-ninth up the slope of Champion Hill. At the southeastern base of the hill was an important intersection of the Jackson and Middle roads called "the Crossroads." Waddell's Alabama Artillery had been posted at the Crossroads, facing east toward Osterhaus's and Carr's Union divisions, which were approaching down the Middle Road. Those divisions were a portion of the powerful Thirteenth Corps, commanded by Major General John A. McClernand. Waddell's Artillery could not be left unprotected. Cumming was confronted with a dilemma: the only way to hold the alignment with Lee on the left flank and also protect Waddell's artillery on the right was to split his brigade. Cumming had no choice. Reluctantly, he left the Fifty-sixth and Fifty-seventh Georgia at the Crossroads with the artillery, facing Osterhaus's and Carr's Union divisions on the Middle Road, while the other Confederate regiments clambered to the top of Champion Hill.[9]

As the men of the Fifty-seventh Georgia watched events unfold, they knew that they had been placed in imminent danger. Civil War–era textbooks on infantry tactics were emphatic: the flanks of a regiment should always be guarded by another regiment, a fortification, or a natural barricade such as a river. Left alone at the Crossroads, the Fifty-sixth and Fifty-seventh Georgia were separated by three hundred yards from the rest of Cumming's brigade to their left and rear and by nearly twelve hundred yards from Bowen's division to their right; Champion Hill was to the rear of the Georgians. Six hundred yards to their front were Osterhaus's and Carr's divisions, stalled only by a flimsy Rebel roadblock and temporary restraining orders from Grant. The troops at the Crossroads were vulnerable from all directions.

It was obvious to the men of the Fifty-sixth and Fifty-seventh Georgia that they would serve as little more than a warning to Stevenson if the Union troops advanced from the east. And if the Yankees poured over the crest of Champion Hill a few hundred yards to the north, the Georgia units would likewise be overwhelmed. *Cannon fodder* was the term heard most often in their ranks.

As Robert Braswell listened to Colonel Barkuloo shout orders in a New York accent, the boy could not help but think of the irony of the moment. Here was a Confederate regiment from Georgia, in Mississippi, under the command of two Yankees: Colonel Barkuloo of New York and General Pemberton of Philadelphia. Even their brigade commander in Kentucky, General Leadbetter, had been from Maine. Southern boys were placing their lives in the hands of a lot of Northern brass.

By 10 A.M., Generals Lee and Cumming could clearly see the endless line of blue troops marching down the Jackson Road and pooling at the northeast base of Champion Hill. The generals quickly sent couriers to Pemberton's headquarters, six hundred yards to their rear at the Roberts farm, to report that they would be overrun if not reinforced. Pemberton did not respond. He remained convinced that the main attack would come along the Raymond and Middle roads, due east of their position, and he refused to shift troops from Loring or Bowen.

Pemberton was mistaken. By now Grant had arrived from Jackson and was personally in command of the Union forces. He was headquartered with James McPherson's Seventeenth Corps and calmly directing the actions of Alvin Hovey's, John Logan's, and Marcellus Crocker's divisions. Grant decided to attack the Confederates from where he was, the Union right flank, and capture the strategic heights of Champion Hill.

At 10:30 A.M. Grant ordered Hovey and Logan to prepare to assault the heights with ten thousand men. Logan's division would attack Lee's Alabama brigade. Hovey's division, on the left, would engage Stevenson's Georgia brigade. Crocker's division, still en route, would serve as reinforcement. The four Union divisions on the Middle and Raymond roads would remain idle until the initial attack against Champion Hill was made and the results assessed.

As Hovey aligned his division for his attack against the Georgians, he placed Brigadier General George McGinnis's First Brigade on the right of his assault column and Colonel James R. Slack's Second Brigade on the left. They would be plowing straight up the wooded slopes of Champion Hill toward the lines of the Thirty-fourth, Thirty-sixth, and Thirty-ninth Georgia on the bald crest. Slack would later collide with the Fifty-sixth and Fifty-seventh Georgia as they defended Waddell's artillery at the Crossroads.

By 11:30, concealed by thick trees and foliage, the Union troops were quietly advancing up the hill, and Alfred Cumming was aligning his Georgia troops along the summit. He was alarmed by how thin his line was: the width of only one regiment with no reserves. These three regiments—the Thirty-fourth, Thirty-sixth, and Thirty-ninth Georgia—were missing eleven companies that had been detached earlier to fortify a roadblock and repair a bridge. Thus Cumming's line was nearly at half strength, with only six companies per regiment present.[10]

Further weakening his position was that Cumming's line was required to bend at a right angle in order to connect with the right flank of Stephen Lee's Alabama brigade. As Cumming surveyed his troops, he looked to his front and peered through the thick trees and brush, wondering where his pickets had vanished.[11] Suddenly, a "very heavy and destructive volley" of fire erupted out of the woods less than seventy-five yards away.[12] As Cumming later wrote, "The attack broke upon us with great impetuosity and vehemence, in overwhelming force, and in a manner wholly unexpected and unlooked for. [There were] no driven-in pickets, or scattering shots on either front, [which would] give intimation of the presence of the enemy."[13]

At such close range the surprised Georgians were able to fire only one volley before Hovey's nine regiments stormed into their ranks with fixed bayonets. For an eternity of five minutes, men from Georgia, Indiana, Wisconsin, Ohio, and Iowa gouged and swung at each other with musket butts, bayonets, cutlasses, daggers, and fists. At last the Thirty-ninth Georgia and four companies of the Thirty-fourth Georgia on Cumming's left crumpled and fled. As they were beaten down the slopes, they left the flank of the Thirty-sixth Georgia and two companies of the Thirty-fourth Georgia exposed. The Eleventh Indiana soon raked the remaining Georgians with deadly fire, and Colonel Jesse Glenn of the Thirty-sixth Georgia shouted for his men to retreat.

At the southeast corner of Champion Hill at the Crossroads, the Fifty-sixth and Fifty-seventh Georgia heard the savage fighting three hundred yards above them. As panicked Confederates began streaming down the hill, the Fifty-sixth and Fifty-seventh Georgia quickly ended their effort to block any Union advance down the Middle Road and swung around to their left and north to face Champion Hill. No sooner were they realigned than Stevenson's entire line collapsed. Gray-clad soldiers from the divisions of both Cumming and Lee poured down the slope, pursued by Hovey's and Logan's Yankees. Stevenson's division tried desperately to form a new line along the Jackson Road that skirted the southern base of the hill. The Crossroads now became the right flank of Stevenson's new line, with the Baker's Creek bridge on the left.[14]

After an hour and a half of desperate fighting, the Confederates struggled to stabilize on the Jackson Road. At 1:30 P.M. Slack's Union brigade finally broke through the dense undergrowth surrounding the base of Champion Hill and gazed across a clear expanse of cornfield. Two hundred yards away was the Crossroads. Behind a wooden fence was the battle line of the Fifty-sixth and Fifty-seventh Georgia, supported by Waddell's Artillery.[15]

Colonel Slack immediately formed the Forty-seventh Indiana, Twenty-fourth Iowa, Twenty-eighth Iowa, and the Fifty-sixth Ohio into a line of battle and led them in a rapid charge across the cornfield. The Twenty-fourth Iowa, a regiment composed of many clergymen and known as the "Preacher's Regiment," surged into the lead, firing on the run.[16]

On the Confederate side Colonel Barkuloo ordered the Fifty-seventh Georgia to commence firing. Thomas Dyson, the Fifty-seventh Georgia's young adjutant, was sitting on his horse but soon felt compelled to dismount. With sword in hand and waving his hat, he paced back and forth, encouraging his men to hold fast. A minié ball soon spun him around, mortally wounding him.[17]

To the immediate left of the Fifty-seventh Georgia, Colonel E. P. Watkins of the Fifty-sixth Georgia slowly mounted his horse and cantered to the front of his regiment. Seriously ill and out of the hospital for only a few days, Watkins was also struck down as minié balls rained through the trees.[18]

Recognizing that their lines would probably be overrun, Captain Waddell ordered his gunners to limber up, to harness the horses to their artillery pieces so that they could haul them away and avoid capture. The artillerymen brought the large horses forward to couple to the carriages, but the horses were shot down by the Union advance. Amid the kicking and flailing of dying animals, Waddell's gunners tried in vain to manhandle the guns to the rear.[19]

As the two Georgia regiments sought to hold off the charge of four Union regiments, Southerners began to fall. Robert Braswell of the Fifty-seventh Georgia and his uncle, Seaborn Mims, were crouched behind the rail fence, taking aim at moving human targets for the first time. Braswell heard Mims scream in pain and collapse, shot through the thigh.[20]

As Braswell whirled to check on Mims, Henry Harris dropped his rifle and grabbed his face. The tip of his nose had been shot cleanly away, cartilage and gore clearly showing.[21] The tough old man of the regiment, Will Holly, grunted and fell, dying instantly.[22] Only seconds of combat had transpired, and the Fort Valley Infantry already had paid a high price.

A few yards away Private Philo Harris of the Fifty-sixth Georgia stood behind an oak, drawing a bead on a Yankee officer. A minié ball shattered his rifle stock, passed through the six layers of blanket that he had rolled and draped diagonally across his shoulder to gain some limited protection, and buried in his chest muscle.[23] Harris thought he was dead. Knew he was dead. Knocked to the ground and struggling for breath, he was soon elated to discover that the ball had not penetrated his chest cavity.

Men in blue were falling as well. First Lieutenant T. J. Williams of the Fifty-sixth Ohio remembered those hellish moments:

> The enemy, as was their custom, presented a stubborn resistance, and we had to fight for every foot of ground. . . . Here, behind a strong rail fence they poured into us a deadly fire. After entering the field a short distance, the first of our company, Henry Richards, fell, shot through the brain. A little further along, as we halted to give them a volley, my brother, John Henry Williams, was shot through the heart. He had his gun at ready, about to take aim, and as he fell in death, he pitched his musket toward the enemy; it fell with the bayonet stuck in the ground, the stock standing up. Captain Williams instantly grasped the musket and gave the enemy its load. . . . The comrade on my left had his arm shot off. Other comrades in the company were being hit, but there was no halt. Closing up ranks we pressed on.[24]

Sgt. Charles L. Longley of the Twenty-fourth Iowa also recounted the Union charge:

[T]he Enfields of the twenty-fourth add their clamor to the hell of sound, and their missiles to the many that make the very air writhe. The more accustomed eye now detects here and there a gray-clad enemy marking their line at but a few rods distant. You note one, perhaps, striving to find shelter behind a slender tree—he is reloading, and hastily withdrawing his rammer, uncovers the upper part of his body—instantly you aim and fire, and when he falls backward, throwing the useless gun over his head, you forget that other bullets than your own have sped and scream aloud in the very frenzy of self congratulation. At this moment, while every human instinct is carried away by a torrent of passion, while kill, *kill,* **kill,** seems to fill your heart and be written over the face of all nature—at this instant you hear a command (it may have come from the clouds above, you know not), to "Fix bayonets, forward, charge!" and away you go with a wild yell in which all mouths join.

See! From the sunken road along the ridge, and now almost at your feet, there arises a line of gray. . . . As it runs parallel with the line, a full artillery team catches the eye just long enough to see a leader fall and the six horses almost stand on end as they go over and down in struggling confusion—now the battery itself is ours, and fairly won, and cheer follows cheer![25]

The Confederate soldiers barely had time to fire and reload their rifles two or three times before the Yankees overran their lines. The ranks quickly broke. The Fifty-sixth and Fifty-seventh Georgia retreated in confusion toward Pemberton's headquarters at the Roberts house. Israel Ritter of the Twenty-fourth Iowa recalled, "The Rebs ran like sheep!"[26]

As Slack's bloodied men captured the Crossroads, Slack called a halt to let his troops recover. Lieutenant T. J. Williams turned back during the lull to check on his brother's body. Later he wrote, "For a short time there was no firing in our immediate front, and by permission of our Captain I returned to my brother's body, thinking it would be my only chance. I spread his rubber blanket over him, which had been folded across his shoulder, and was perforated through the several folds by the ball that took his life."[27]

Slack's men had paid a heavy price for Waddell's four cannons, which they now turned and fired at the retreating Georgians. But the crucial Crossroads was theirs.

As the fury on Champion Hill increased and the signs of disintegration and retreat became unmistakable, Pemberton at last decided to reinforce Stevenson's mauled division. Around 1 P.M. Pemberton sent a staff officer to order Bowen and Loring to reinforce Stevenson's retreating forces. Bowen squinted at McClernand's massed divisions facing him on the Middle Road and refused to obey Pemberton's order unless peremptorily commanded to do so.[28]

When told of Bowen's refusal, Pemberton angrily dispatched orders requiring Bowen to send one of his brigades immediately to Stevenson's aid and to dispatch a second brigade as soon as possible. Bowen sent Colonel Francis M. Cockrell's crack Missouri brigade double-timing toward Stevenson's lines, followed by Brigadier General Martin E. Green's Missouri and Arkansas brigade. These two brigades were among the best fighting units in the Confederate army.[29]

Initially, Pemberton intended to send Bowen's reinforcements to aid the left side of Stevenson's line, where Lee's troops and those of Brigadier General Seth Barton had been smashed, exposing the vital Baker's Creek bridge. However, when Slack's Union surge captured the Crossroads, Pemberton redirected Bowen's two divisions there.[30]

As they approached the Crossroads, Cockrell's and Green's brigades found the men of the Fifty-sixth and Fifty-seventh Georgia still retreating with their wounded. Near the Roberts house General Pemberton personally reorganized these two broken Georgia regiments and gave them a spirited oration. Within minutes the soldiers of the Fifty-seventh Georgia pulled themselves together and hurried after Cockrell and Green, followed shortly by the Fifty-sixth Georgia.[31]

Around 2:30 P.M. Bowen directed Cockrell's and Green's troops to unleash a furious counterattack against Slack's four Union regiments at the Crossroads. Cockrell advanced on the left and Green on the right. Initially, the five thousand screaming Rebels paid a fearsome toll, but gradually Slack's forces began to crumple and retreat. As Bowen's troops gained momentum and overran the Crossroads, Cockrell's and Green's brigades began to separate, creating a dangerous gap in the middle of their advance. By this time the Fifty-sixth and Fifty-seventh Georgia had caught up with the Rebel assault and were able to plug themselves into the widening gap between Cockrell and Green. The Georgia boys were now literally in the middle of the fray.[32]

Proceeding beyond the Crossroads, Cockrell's Missourians crashed into McGinnis's brigade and pushed it back up Champion Hill. Soon the Confederates had recovered the crest of the hill, and Cockrell had the Bluecoats in full retreat down its far side.

Green had also managed to batter Slack's troops back across the cornfield. In less than an hour of incredibly ferocious combat, the Missouri, Arkansas, and Georgia troops had driven the Yankees back three-quarters of a mile. If the Fifty-sixth and Fifty-seventh Georgia had initially buckled under pressure, they were quickly redeeming themselves, emboldened by the presence of experienced troops and leadership.

Remembering years later the fierce Rebel counterattack at the Crossroads, First Lieutenant T. J. Williams of the Fifty-sixth Ohio recounted:

On our right the Twenty-fourth Iowa, being in open timber, was pushed back after the most desperate hand-to-hand fighting. . . . Our regiment was forced to leave the fence, for which the enemy made a rush. In a moment we were under the most scorching fire from two or three sides. Under this fire our men fell thick and fast. . . . Loading and firing, we fell slowly back, it being the first time for the Fifty-sixth Ohio to turn their backs to the enemy. Halting at every favorable opportunity, we would give them a few rounds.

At one point, while we were shooting from the same stump, Comrade Richard Davis fell dead across my feet, shot through the heart. He had just urged me to be more careful or they would hit me. . . .

As I turned to fire, my musket being at prime, a bullet from the enemy struck the barrel of my gun, the ball exploding. Four small pieces were buried in the back of my hand, and several larger ones in the stock of my musket. My Enfield was in the right place to save me from the fate of my fallen comrades. About the same time one of our boys had the top of his cap shot off his head; another had his canteen and haversack shot off, and another had the side of his pants below the knee cut off, all by pieces of shells bursting among us. It seems strange that any of us escaped.[33]

Sergeant Charles Longley also remembered the devastating effect of Bowen's counterattack upon the Twenty-fourth Iowa:

And look! There comes a new line of grey. Its head of column is already in our rear. See that orderly sergeant in advance making the ins and outs of the fence he is following. Shoot at him? Yes; and all the rest while you may, for now they halt, front and enfilade [rake] that road with a fire that patters in the dust like the big drops of a summer shower and makes the wounded wretches lying there writhe again in impotent agony and terror. But this is not all it does—it sweeps that hill, and while its occupants, late so full of conquering zeal, make all the resistance in their power, they are assailed upon the other side by the remnant of their earlier foes. They leave those guns [Waddell's] with desperate reluctance—alas! many never leave them; but leave they must who can, and in thirty minutes the battle of Champion Hill has ended, so far as one regiment, as a military organization, is concerned.[34]

Surging on, the men of the Fifty-seventh Georgia felt a sense of recklessness. Their momentum was carrying them farther and farther beyond Confederate lines. However, the Yanks were exacting a high cost from the Georgians. The Fifty-seventh Georgia had begun the battle with only 450 men, a greatly reduced regiment.[35] Now its ragged line showed gaping holes, and a trail of dreadfully wounded soldiers lay in its wake.

Years later John Keen of Company B, Laurens County, recalled that as the

Fifty-seventh Georgia pursued Slack's Yankees, the Fifty-seventh's color-bearer, J. J. Underwood, was immediately shot down. Another soldier snatched up the colors and was wounded. A third man grabbed the standard and was instantly killed. Finally, Underwood's brother carried the flag until the end of the battle.[36] Keen's recollection was characteristic of the ferocity of the combat.

As Bowen's men continued to press forward, Cumming and Lee were not able to engage their men in the Confederate counterattack. The result of their failure to advance placed Bowen in a precarious situation. As he drove the Union troops farther back, his left side was increasingly exposed to flanking or raking fire from Logan's Union troops. Without frontal pressure from Cumming and Lee, Logan's forces were able to turn their attention to Bowen, on their left.

Bowen's counterattack reached high tide within six hundred yards of the Union ordnance wagons and Grant's headquarters at the Champion house, about a half mile northeast of Champion Hill. Even steel-nerved Grant was shaken by the hell-bent Confederate charge. However, only minutes before, the advance units of Marcellus Crocker's Seventh Division had arrived. Three fresh Union brigades were immediately fed into the battle, while Hovey massed sixteen cannons to fire directly into the Confederates.[37]

Reeling and exhausted, General Bowen was forced to take stock of his predicament. He was facing what seemed to be an endless supply of fresh Union troops, and his ammunition was dangerously low. More ominously, Bowen had received word that to his rear McClernand's Union divisions were now beginning to advance along the Middle Road. Bowen wisely ordered an immediate retreat. As men from Missouri, Arkansas, and Georgia fell back, their organization and fortitude began to disintegrate. They ran for their lives, carrying their wounded as best they could.

As Edwin Davis of the Fifty-seventh Georgia limped back up Champion Hill, Mercer University and the sophomoric glories of war were another life away. Wounded in the leg, he had lost much blood and was weak. His mind must have been filled with worries of capture, amputation, bleeding to death. Many of his maimed comrades were screaming for help, pleading piteously not to be left behind. But now it was each man for himself. Davis would make it. Many others would not.[38]

While Bowen's men raced for the Jackson Road, Brigadier General Peter Osterhaus's Union division easily ran over the flimsy roadblock that the Confederates had established on the Middle Road early in the battle so that they would have some warning of when Osterhaus's troops were beginning to advance. As the Yanks advanced to the Crossroads, they could see Bowen's fleeing men as they plummeted down Champion Hill and reentered Confederate lines. Only stubborn artillery fire slowed Osterhaus's advance long enough for Bowen's men to escape. The Fifty-seventh Georgia had barely eluded capture.

As night mercifully enveloped the bloody hill, Pemberton ordered a retreat. Only one route to Vicksburg remained open. The bridge over Baker's Creek on the Jackson Road was in Union hands. His only salvation was to rush south toward the Baker's Creek bridge on the Raymond Road and hope that he beat the Union there. Pemberton ordered Brigadier General Lloyd Tilghman's First Brigade of Loring's division to stall the two Union divisions that were advancing down the Raymond Road. Loring instructed Tilghman to hold the road "at all hazards" until sundown. Tilghman did so courageously, dying in the process, and enabling most of Pemberton's troops to cross the Baker's Creek bridge.

The Fifty-sixth and Fifty-seventh Georgia were two of the last Confederate units to leave the battlefield and head toward Baker's Creek.[39] The Georgians mixed with Bowen's troops and crossed the bridge safely. Now they began to try to reunite with Stevenson's division.

Later, as the ten companies of the Fifty-seventh Georgia answered roll call, they were stunned at their losses. Particularly devastated was Company H, the Independent Volunteers of Baldwin County, Georgia. All their officers were wounded. Of the thirty-six men in the company who had fought in the battle, only five had escaped death, wounds, or capture.[40]

The regimental casualty count showed that of approximately 450 men in the Fifty-seventh Georgia who saw action, 27 were killed, 104 were wounded, 16 were prisoners of war, and 50 were missing and presumed dead. Casualties totaled 197, or 44 percent of the regiment.[41]

Casualties within Cumming's brigade were equally high. The brigade went into battle with approximately 2,500 troops. Of these, 121 were killed, 269 were wounded, and 605 were missing in action, for a total of 935 casualties, or nearly 40 percent of the brigade.[42]

As a whole, Cumming's brigade had not fought well and was duly criticized. But the men of the Fifty-sixth and Fifty-seventh Georgia could hold their heads up. They had counterattacked with Bowen and had been part of the Confederate force that had advanced farther than any other in the Southern counterattack under John Bowen. Now they were veterans who knew what it was to "see the elephant."[43]

Across the darkened ground of Champion Hill hundreds of torches flickered and bobbed as Union patrols searched for wounded soldiers. James N. Mathews of the Fifty-seventh Georgia, Company F, was found delirious with a shattered foot. Union surgeons soon amputated his lower leg. Considered dead by his family for many weeks, he later recovered, was paroled, and limped home to Crawford County.

The slave Scott, from Milledgeville, was frantic and crying as he searched the retreating Confederate wagons and ambulances piled high with dead and wounded. He had been told that his master, Lieutenant Archibald McKinley, had been shot through the shoulder and was dying. Scott finally found McKinley, gravely wounded but alive, and nursed him through the night and for days to come in the Vicksburg trenches. [44]

Many soldiers faced the surgeon's saw. Any bone that had been crushed by a minié ball or shell fragment required amputation of the limb. The Union army transformed the Champion house into a field hospital. The dining room table became an operating table. Blood flowed so freely that the surgeons ordered holes drilled in the wooden floors so that the pooled blood would drain. [45]

Thomas Dyson, the young adjutant of the Fifty-seventh Georgia, had been left seriously wounded where he fell at the Crossroads. He was brought to a Union field hospital and knew that his wound was mortal. During the three remaining days of his life, he wrote to his father in Monroe County, affirming, "I have done all I can, I die for my country." The Union soldiers attending Dyson did as promised and mailed the letter to his family. [46]

The Forty-seventh Indiana of Slack's brigade fared as badly as the Fifty-seventh Georgia. Squared off and firing into each other's faces, the soldiers of the Forty-seventh Indiana had overrun the Fifty-seventh Georgia, only to be mauled by Bowen's counterattack. The Indiana unit suffered 123 dead and wounded, and many Indianans still lay in the cornfield and in the ravines along the hillside. Among the wounded was William Aspinwall. His memoir poignantly captures the pathos of the Civil War:

> The last words I remember hearing before being shot were uttered by some of our officers who were begging our men to fall back as the rebels were flanking us. As I had my gun up to my shoulder three buck-shots, coming from the right flank, struck me in the right shoulder. My arm fell helpless by my side and not more than a second afterward a minie ball plowed across the top of my head cutting the scalp and chipping the skull, and cutting the hair across the head as neatly as it could have been done with a sharp pair of shears. I fell to the ground and our orderly sergeant, J. W. Whitmore, said I bounced around like a chicken with its head cut off. John E. Sturgis, one of our sergeants says he saw five of us boys, of our company, all wallowing around together in our own blood like stuck hogs.
>
> When I came to my senses I was inside the rebel line, the bullets falling around me like hail. It was some little time before I could make out my surroundings. A Confederate officer came and sat down on a little bank of earth beside me. He looked at the wound in my head and said, "My Boy, I am afraid you are done for." He gave me a drink of water out of his canteen, raising my head very gentle with one hand, so I could drink. He asked me what State I was from, I replied, "Indiana." I will never forget his kindness.
>
> After he left me I got up and started towards our lines, passing the retreating Johnnies, and almost rubbing clothes with them. . . . I succeeded in getting

into our lines and finding my captain, who got me in an ambulance and I was taken to the hospital which was in a corn field. . . .

In the evening some of my comrades brought me blankets, doing without themselves, and made me a bed in a fence corner outside of the hospital. In a little while a Confederate soldier came along. He had been shot somewhere in the bowels and was in great pain. I said—"Here partner, I will share my bed with you"—and he laid down beside me. He told me that he was from Savannah, Georgia, and that he could not get well. He wanted me to write to his wife and children and gave me a card with their address. I was to tell them that I had seen him and what had become of their beloved husband and father. Being weak and exhausted from the loss of blood, I dozed off to sleep and left him talking to me. In a little while I awoke and spoke to him two or three times, but he did not answer. I put my hand over on his face; he was cold in death. My foe and friend had crossed the river.

I laid there with him until daylight, then found a sergeant who dressed my wounds and a comrade who wrote two letters for me, one to my mother in Bluffton, Indiana, and one to this poor Confederate's family. I took the letters over to the Confederate hospital which was a short distance from ours in an adjoining cornfield. I found a Confederate officer and gave him the letter. He said I could rest assured that he would see to it that the dead soldier's family got the letter and he complimented me on my kindness.[47]

As the men of the Fifty-seventh Georgia crossed Baker's Creek late on the night of May 16 and raced through the dark for the Big Black River, they were no longer strangers to such tragedy and horror. Their memories were scarred forever by the early days of the Vicksburg campaign.

13

Siege and Surrender

Early in the predawn hours of Sunday, May 17, 1863, the exhausted men of the Fifty-sixth and Fifty-seventh Georgia caught up with Cumming's brigade, Stevenson's division, near Bovina Station, ten miles west of Champion Hill. Bovina, on the east side of the Big Black, was surrounded by earthworks that protected the Southern Mississippi Railroad bridge. Pemberton wanted Stevenson's troops to cross the river to safety, but they collapsed inside the Bovina earthworks and slept until dawn.[1] The next morning Stevenson's men passed over the Big Black, and Pemberton placed them in reserve while ordering Bowen's battered division to defend the bridgehead against Grant's advance.

Later in the day, when Union troops approached the bridge, a short but fierce battle ensued. Pemberton ordered the bridge burned. With Grant temporarily stalled at the unfordable Big Black, Pemberton continued a fast-paced retreat to Vicksburg, twelve miles to the west. It did not take long for Grant to erect pontoon bridges and nip at Pemberton's heels.

On this same day, May 17, Joe Johnston received a courier message from Pemberton reporting the disaster at Champion Hill. Stunned, he emphatically replied to Pemberton: "If . . . you are invested in Vicksburg, you must ultimately surrender. Under such circumstances, instead of losing both troops and place, we must, if possible, save the troops. If it is not too late, evacuate Vicksburg and its dependencies, and march to the northeast."[2]

Pemberton did not receive Johnston's order until noon of the next day, May 18, and by then his army was flooding into the Vicksburg perimeter. Calling a council of war, Pemberton and his generals unanimously voted to disregard Johnston's order as impossible to obey. Logical or not, Pemberton ignored another order from his theater commander and sealed his fate within the defenses of Vicksburg.

All during the day and night of May 17 and 18, wild-eyed gray hordes crowded into Vicksburg. Emma Balfour, a forty-five-year-old doctor's wife, scribbled in her diary:

> I hope never to witness again such a scene as the return of our routed army.
> From 12 o'clock until late in the night the streets and roads were jammed
> with wagons, cannons, horses, men, mules, stock, sheep, everything you can
> imagine that appertains to an army—being brought hurriedly within the

entrenchments. Nothing like order prevailed, of course, as divisions, brigades and regiments were broken and separated.

As the poor fellows passed, every house poured forth all it had to refresh them. I had every one on the lot and there were some visitors carrying buckets of water to the corner for the men. Then in the back gallery I had everything that was eatable put out—and fed as many as I could. Poor fellows, it made my heart ache to see them, for I knew from all I saw and heard that it was want of confidence in the General commanding that was the cause of our disaster. General Pemberton has not the confidence of Officers, people or men judging from all I am compelled to see and hear.[3]

Emma Balfour sounded a note that was being repeated all over Vicksburg: General Pemberton, the Yankee from Philadelphia, was a double agent and was intentionally folding before Grant's army. Private John Keen stated years after the war that the men of the Fifty-seventh Georgia firmly believed the rumor.[4] It was a time when the Confederate army doubted itself and its leadership.

As the troops poured into Vicksburg, Pemberton and his officers set to work, reuniting lost men with their regiments, establishing order, and positioning divisions and brigades into lines of battle around the seven-mile defensive perimeter. The perimeter was crescent shaped with the northern and southern tips arching back to touch the Mississippi River. Pemberton still had thirty thousand men to face Grant's forty-five thousand, more than enough to wage a successful defensive battle from behind stout earthworks and fortifications. Lack of food, not soldiers, was Pemberton's problem.

Because Carter Stevenson's division had been decimated at Champion Hill and as a whole did not fight well, Pemberton assigned those troops to defend a sector of the Confederate line that was not expected to receive a massive assault. The division extended along a four-mile southwestern front, stretching from the point at which the Southern Mississippi Railroad bisected the Confederate perimeter at the Railroad Redoubt all the way to South Fort on the Mississippi River.[5]

Stevenson placed the Fifty-seventh Georgia next to the Hall's Ferry Road, guarding its entrance to the Confederate defensive perimeter. The Fifty-sixth Georgia aligned with the Fifty-seventh Georgia's left flank, and Colonel Alexander Reynolds's Tennessee brigade protected the right flank of the Fifty-seventh Georgia. The terrain was hilly and covered with dense trees and undergrowth. The lush, green land seemed too pastoral for battle. Yet the topography was ideal for brutal defensive warfare.[6]

Within a day Grant had encircled the Vicksburg perimeter, drawing his noose tight around the city. Stevenson's division faced McClernand's Thirteenth Corps,

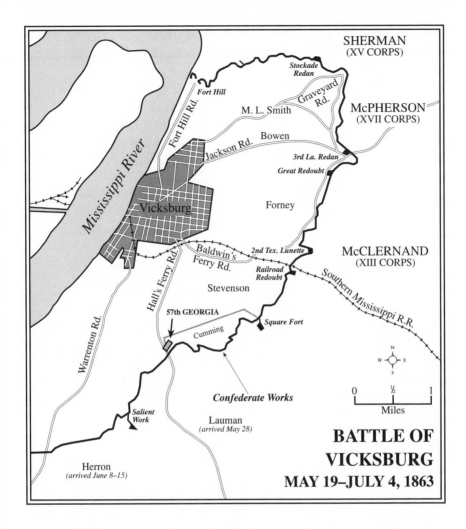

BATTLE OF VICKSBURG
MAY 19–JULY 4, 1863

a familiar foe from Champion Hill. Because Grant assumed that he faced a beaten and cowering foe, on May 19 he unleashed his Yanks against the northeast quadrant of the Vicksburg perimeter.

He learned that the Confederates had found their backbone. Firing straight into the Yankees' faces from behind stout earthworks studded with cannons, the Rebs shredded the advancing Fifteenth Corps of General William Tecumseh Sherman. By the end of the violent and bloody day, Grant had lost 942 men to Pemberton's 250.

Still, Grant was persistent. He wanted to seize Vicksburg quickly, before Johnston could move against his rear and sandwich him from the east and west. As Sherman would remark after the war, Johnston was the only Confederate general whom Grant admitted he feared.[7] This professional respect spurred

Grant on. If the Yanks could hit harder, Grant surmised, victory would be theirs. He stubbornly put his men to work preparing siege works for a second frontal assault.

On Friday, May 22, the dawn was heralded by an incredible artillery barrage from every Union battery. David Porter's gunboats joined the din, and one of the most intense shellings of the war lasted for four hours. Sure that such a pounding had smashed the Rebel ranks, the blue troops again charged the Confederate line. Once more they were savagely repulsed, and their attack turned into the bloodiest rout of the campaign. At day's end Union casualties totaled 3,199 men, but the Confederates had lost fewer than five hundred.[8] Anxiously peering to his rear for a glimpse of Johnston approaching from Jackson, Grant reluctantly settled in for a long siege.

The Fifty-seventh Georgia missed Grant's frontal assaults. General S. D. Lee's Alabama brigade held the left flank of Stevenson's Division. General Cumming's Georgia brigade connected to Lee's right flank at the Square Fort. Lee's Alabamans received the full brunt of the charge by McClernand's Thirteenth Corps and fiercely held down the far right end of the Confederate line. Cumming's Georgians, however, could only watch the onslaught from mere yards away and try to rake McClernand's troops with gunfire. The Georgians, including the Fifty-seventh, expected the battlefront to shift or another Yankee brigade to collide with their fieldworks at any minute, but it never happened. Except for heavy artillery barrages and countless stray minié balls, Cumming's Georgia brigade escaped Grant's attack.

The Georgians did not escape the horrors of the forty-seven-day siege, however. No sooner had the firing stopped than Grant sealed off Vicksburg. The Fifty-seventh Georgia, sitting astride the Hall's Ferry Road, soon was staring down the barrels of Colonel Isaac Pugh's brigade—the Forty-first Illinois, Fifty-third Illinois, Third Iowa, and Thirty-third Wisconsin infantry regiments. These men would make each other's lives miserable for the next forty-six days.

As soon as Grant resigned himself to a siege, he ordered his engineers to begin moving the Union lines closer to Vicksburg by using assault trenches, advanced artillery batteries, and underground tunnels to place mines under the city's defenses. Each night work details went out to dig approach tunnels, or "saps." The trenches were zigzagged to keep the Rebs from firing down their length. Grant's troops piled the excavated earth along the sides of the trenches for further protection.

Over the next six weeks the Union troops encroached upon the Confederate lines by advancing thirteen separate approaches via trenches around the Vicksburg perimeter. One of these approaches, carried out by General Jacob Lauman, would be directly opposite Cumming's brigade. Lauman's approach was the only one of the thirteen that Confederate raiding parties assaulted. The Fifty-seventh Georgia played a leading role in these counterattacks.

As Cumming's Georgians watched Lauman's men entrench on a wooded ridge four hundred yards in front of them, they were also watching the Union strategy unfold. The Yanks placed two artillery batteries on the ridge. By June 3 both batteries were firing continually, keeping the Georgians hemmed in their trenches.

Slowly, the Yankees zigzagged their trench work toward the Confederate lines. As they drew closer, they built additional artillery batteries. By June 21 they had advanced to within 275 yards of the Fifty-sixth Georgia's lines and had seven batteries firing relentlessly around the clock. Cumming's men were growing battle fatigued and shell shocked.

Lauman also deployed snipers. Exposed soldiers risked instant death. John Walden Jr., a young private in the Fort Valley Infantry, Fifty-seventh Georgia, was not aware that his anxious father had caught a train for Vicksburg to check on his son and bring supplies to the Fort Valley troops. Union sentinels stopped the senior Walden upon his arrival in the Vicksburg vicinity and denied him passage through the lines. He waited helplessly for days for word of his son.

After a particularly fierce shelling, young John Walden peered over the trench line for a brief moment. A Yankee sharpshooter placed a bullet cleanly through his forehead. Only after Vicksburg surrendered did his waiting father learn of his son's death and burial. Because of the war the grief-stricken father could not take the corpse home. Instead, the elder Walden returned home with the Fort Valley Infantry after the Vicksburg surrender and erected a simple monument in his son's memory that stands today in Fort Valley.[9]

As the Yankee trenches drew closer and the bombardment grew more intense, Alfred Cumming was the only Confederate brigade commander who decided to attack the Union lines. He selected Lieutenant Colonel Cincinnatus Guyton, second in command of the Fifty-seventh Georgia, to lead a series of night raids in an attempt to slow Lauman's trench campaign.[10]

On the night of June 21 the men of the Fifty-seventh Georgia heard members of the Thirty-third Wisconsin digging and extending their trenches toward the Salient Work, a prominent artillery battery near the Hall's Ferry Road that projected outward. After spraying the woods with artillery fire in the direction of the muffled voices, Guyton led a group of volunteers over the parapet and down into the dense-wooded ravine. The Georgians inched up on the Yanks and opened fire through the darkness. After a rapid exchange the Georgians melted back through the woods before the Union could mount a counterattack. Although the penned-up Rebs found the foray exhilarating, they killed only one Yank and wounded but two.

The next night Guyton tried his luck again. Leading a patrol of volunteers from the Fifty-seventh Georgia and Forty-third Tennessee, Guyton was surprised to find that a Union work detail of 350 men had carelessly failed to post sentinels and was taking a break. Opening up on the Yanks with a deafening volley, the Confederates sent the entire work detail running, killing four, wounding five, and capturing six.

Guyton, who had been ordered not to pursue, quickly commanded the men to pick up the work detail's abandoned shovels and fill the newly dug trenches. The men of the Fifty-seventh collected the dead and lowered them into the trenches. As the dirt showered down on the blue-clad bodies, one of the soldiers sprang up, declaring that he was willing to die for his country but not to be buried alive. Much to Guyton's surprise and delight, the Yankee Lazarus turned out to be Lieutenant Colonel William Camm of the Fourteenth Illinois, commander of the work detail. After crawling over the Salient Work parapet at dawn, the Rebs wasted no time presenting their chagrined prisoner to General Cumming.[11]

The next night the men of the Fifty-seventh Georgia ventured out on patrol, but the Federals had caught on to their game and were waiting. After a firefight in the woods, the Georgians retreated to their lines. Aware that future sorties would be futile without the element of surprise, Guyton and his men did not attack again. However, they held the proud record of being the only Confederate troops to take the offensive during Vicksburg siege.[12]

Life in the Vicksburg trenches was brutal and violent. The stench of diarrhea, urine, gangrene, and filthy bodies was ever present. Fresh air did not exist. A wound that healed or health that was restored constituted a miracle.

As the desperate days in the trenches continued, hunger and disease stalked the Confederates, thinning their ranks. The Union army, by contrast, had ample food and enough troops to rotate frontline duty. Because the Southerners could not know when Grant might unleash another assault, they were on guard at all times, never experiencing relief. The unremitting heat, disease, and tension debilitated more Southern men than did artillery shells and minié balls.

Thomas Lewis was one of the "boy soldiers" in the Fifty-seventh Georgia. Lewis had the proud distinction of being a company color-bearer until a minié ball ripped through his leg, shattering bone and tearing flesh. For several weeks he nursed the wound, resisting amputation. But the wound could not heal amid the squalor of trench life. Finally, the surgeon had no choice but to amputate. After the war Lewis described the moment to his children: "They rolled me over a barrel and sawed it off. You could have heard me holler all the way to Augusta."[13]

Hunger was severe and thirst constant. There was no clean water to drink. Wells were polluted, the river was rank, and dysentery soon became rampant. By the end of May Confederate soldiers were on half-rations. All beef and pork slowly disappeared. Rice, flour, and bread rations were reduced to four ounces per person per day. By the end of June most regiments allowed each soldier only one biscuit and a mouthful of bacon per day. Men were literally starving.

In the midst of this acute hunger Robert Braswell and several of his buddies from the Fifty-seventh Georgia slipped out of the trenches on a foraging detail. The pitiful-looking young men spied a woman on her porch and asked her for something to eat. She looked at sixteen-year-old Braswell's emaciated six-foot-four-inch frame, turned, and walked inside her house. She returned with the only food she had, a freshly baked pie.

The famished boys made quick work of the pie. With high praise for her cooking, they thanked the woman profusely. Braswell gushed, "That there's the best pie I ever ate, Ma'am," to which she replied, "Glad it is! That's the first rat pie I've ever baked." But Braswell and his buddies did not complain.[14]

Similar innovations in Southern cooking incorporated in their recipes the large numbers of dogs and cats that roamed the Vicksburg streets. Soon they were no longer to be seen. And when bread was depleted, army cooks made a greenish foul-tasting bread after someone found a large cache of dried peas.

For many starving Johnnies, however, the nadir of their experience came on June 28, when Confederate headquarters released this statement: "The Major General recommends to the troops, that when a mule is maimed by the fire of the enemy, it be made use of immediately for food: and is of the opinion that soup is, perhaps, the most palatable form in which the flesh can be used."

Some of the men in Brigadier General John Vaughn's Tennessee brigade tried the mule soup and published their opinion in the *(Vicksburg) Daily Citizen:* "It is sweet, savory and tender, and so long as we have a mule left, we are satisfied our soldiers will be content to subsist on it."[15]

By the first of July Pemberton knew that time was running out. Ammunition was ample, but only one week of half-rations remained. Johnston was nowhere in sight, and it was impossible to communicate with him because of the military situation. Pemberton was faced with the option of surrendering his army or trying to break out of Vicksburg.

As Pemberton struggled with his decision, Joseph Johnston was also facing a dilemma. For weeks he had been trying to raise enough troops to attack Grant's rear lines. Johnston knew that he would not have the strength to defeat Grant outright. But if he could hit hard enough, he might be able to destabilize the situation and allow Pemberton's troops to break out of the Vicksburg perimeter. Should this happen, Pemberton and Johnston could link up and together face Grant.

Fearing just this scenario, Grant had wisely detached one division from each of his three corps and sent them under the command of General Sherman to form a defensive line along the Big Black. If Johnston managed to advance, he would have to contend with Sherman first.

Grant need not have worried, however. Time and supply were on his side. Although Johnston was eventually able to pull together a force of thirty-two thousand men, Grant was adding troops every day. Cautious to a fault, Johnston delayed an attack for far too long. By the time he was prepared to move, Grant's total troop strength far exceeded Johnston's and Pemberton's armies combined.

Pemberton, unaware of either Grant's or Johnston's decisions, decided that the siege could not continue. On July 3 Pemberton sent a message to Grant under a flag of truce, proposing talks to arrange terms for surrender. Pemberton asked Major General John Bowen, a former neighbor of Grant's in St. Louis, to convey the message personally. Bowen, a man of unshakeable courage, was battling acute dysentery, which would kill him within two weeks.

Grant received Bowen's personal message but insisted that he would negotiate only with Pemberton. At 3 P.M. on July 3 Pemberton rode between the lines to meet Grant. No doubt, Pemberton's thoughts momentarily flashed back sixteen years to Mexico City, where he had officially commended a young lieutenant, Ulysses S. Grant, for bravery in battle. The irony was harsh.[16]

Accompanied by General Bowen and Colonel L. M. Montgomery, Pemberton met Grant under a wilted tree, two hundred feet from Confederate lines. Grant was accompanied by his staff and generals Ord, McPherson, Logan, and Smith. Grant's opening position was staunch: unconditional surrender. After negotiations, however, the terms that emerged were less than unconditional surrender. Rather than becoming prisoners of war, Pemberton's troops would be "paroled." As parolees, the Southern troops would take an oath not to fight against the North until Yankee prisoners were also released in a prisoner exchange. In addition, Pemberton's men would surrender their arms and their regimental colors. Officers would be allowed to retain their sidearms and one horse each. All prisoners would then be free to return home.

Pemberton and Bowen rode back into Confederate lines to seek counsel and mull over their decision. Late that night Pemberton notified Grant that he would accept the surrender terms. After forty-seven days of siege the Confederates surrendered Vicksburg on July 4, 1863, the eighty-seventh anniversary of Independence Day.

At 10 A.M. on July 4 white flags fluttered along Confederate lines. Upon orders from their regimental officers, each regiment marched out of its entrenchment, dressed ranks, stacked arms, and laid their regimental colors on the stacks of silent rifles.

Many regiments had cut their colors into small pieces and distributed them to the troops rather than face the disgrace of surrendering them. Most Rebs could remember the ceremony in which the colors had been bestowed upon their regiment. Made by women in small towns across the South, the regimental colors were a shield of honor, a symbol of virile pride. To surrender the colors was an act of shame.

Lieutenant Edwin T. Davis watched as the Fifty-seventh Georgia marched forward and surrendered its colors. Still hampered by a wound in the thigh from Champion Hill, he now winced again at the disgrace and humiliation of the moment. Worse still, each man was ordered to remove his knapsack, belt, cartridge box, and cap pouch and lay them on the ground. Stripped of pride and weaponry, the soldiers were then ordered back inside the entrenchments.

Davis noted carefully where the colors were laid. That night he slid over the Fifty-seventh's earthworks, crawled toward the stacked weapons, and crept within yards of the surrendered arms. To his surprise and delight the colors of the Fifty-seventh Georgia were still draped atop the rifles, and the Yankee sentinels were engaged in boisterous conversation yards away. Davis quietly cut the colors from the standard and slipped back into the darkness.

Davis and Lieutenant Robert H. Harris conferred about how to get the colors past Yankee inspection and back to Georgia. They remembered that Lieutenant Colonel Guyton had one of the few horses still alive, hidden in a cave. Sneaking into the cave, they found Guyton's saddle blanket and carefully slit it open. Folding the flag, they placed it inside the blanket and sewed up the border with a locust-thorn needle. Guyton never knew that he carried the regiment's colors all the way back to Georgia until he reached his home in Laurens County. The flag, riddled by more than two hundred bullet and shrapnel holes, was never returned to service and remains in the possession of Guyton's descendants.[17]

After the surrender Grant immediately ordered that the starving Southern troops receive food. General James McPherson was given the duty of paroling the Confederate troops. By the evening of July 10, 29,941 Rebs had signed their paroles. On July 11 all Confederates except Stevenson's division were mustered, inspected, and sent on the long march home. Stevenson's division was the last to be inspected and was released on July 12. More than thirty-six hundred wounded Confederates remained in field hospitals in Vicksburg.

The Union army almost did not release one member of the Fifty-seventh Georgia. Union troops harangued and taunted Scott, the slave, for wanting to stay with his master, Lieutenant Archibald McKinley. Five years after the war McKinley wrote, "[After surrender at Vicksburg, Scott] followed me in spite of Yankee threats & promises of freedom & good situation, back into Confederate lines . . . and remained with me true as steel." Scott accompanied the wounded McKinley to Milledgeville, Georgia, and throughout the rest of the war.[18]

Of course, Scott also wanted to go home and rejoin his wife and children. No one can ever know what he truly thought of the Fifty-seventh Georgia and the

Southern cause. But it is clear that he was loyal to McKinley and committed to his family in the South.

Already weakened by the disease and hunger of the siege, the paroled Confederates now had to walk long distances. Stevenson's division started with enough rations to reach Brandon, Mississippi, a distance of fifty miles, where the men expected to board railroad cars. However, because Joseph Johnston had used the railway in his army's recent retreat from Sherman's forces, and did not send the trains back, Stevenson's division had to march south of Jackson and on to Enterprise, Alabama, before Stevenson could obtain railroad transportation for his men. Many of the weakened men began to straggle as they marched. The troops found only green corn to eat. But the hope of reaching home kept most men struggling onward.[19]

When they reached Enterprise, the men were granted furloughs of fifteen to thirty days. The Georgians were to report to General Cumming in Atlanta at the end of thirty days.[20]

The gaunt and famished survivors of the Fifty-seventh Georgia had been in combat conditions for more than a year, hellacious months of continual marching, hunger, disease, slaughter, and now defeat. Their attitudes had changed greatly—youthful idealism had dwindled, martial fervor had dimmed, and the war had taken on a different hue.

At the same hour that Pemberton and Grant had wrangled over surrender terms on July 3, 1863, the Army of Northern Virginia under Robert E. Lee had suffered defeat at Gettysburg. Not only had Confederate troops in both the East and the West been defeated, but they had bled mercilessly.

For Robert Braswell, Edwin Davis, Cincinnatus Guyton, Scott, and other survivors of the Fifty-seventh Georgia, their only goal was to get safely home, eat home-cooked food, soak in a steaming tub, and wear clean clothes for thirty days before they had to face the dismal future.

Savannah and Andersonville

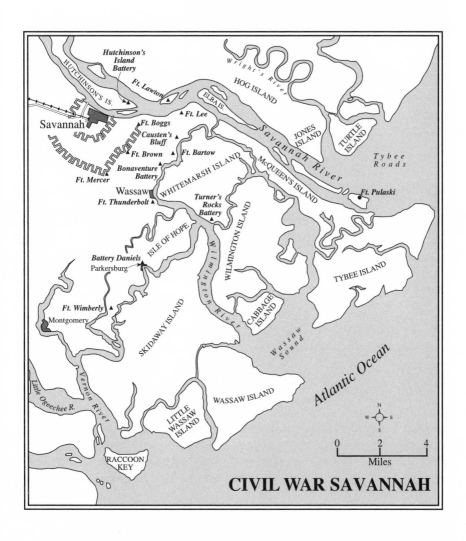

Hutchinson's
Island
Battery

Wright's River

HOG ISLAND

Ft. Lawton

ELBA IS.

HUTCHINSON'S IS.

Savannah

Ft. Boggs

Ft. Lee

JONES
ISLAND

TURTLE
ISLAND

Savannah River

Causten's
Bluff

Ft. Brown

Ft. Bartow

*Tybee
Roads*

Bonaventure
Battery

McQUEEN'S ISLAND

Ft. Mercer

WHITEMARSH ISLAND

Wassaw

Ft. Thunderbolt

Ft. Pulaski

Turner's
Rocks
Battery

WILMINGTON ISLAND

ISLE OF HOPE

Wilmington River

Battery Daniels

Parkersburg

TYBEE ISLAND

Ft. Wimberly

SKIDAWAY ISLAND

CABBAGE
ISLAND

Montgomery

*Wassaw
Sound*

Atlantic Ocean

Vernon River

Little Ogeechee R.

WASSAW ISLAND

N
W E
S

LITTLE
WASSAW
ISLAND

0   2   4
Miles

RACCOON
KEY

CIVIL WAR SAVANNAH

14

The Changing of the Guard

As the troops of Cumming's Georgia brigade neared Enterprise, Alabama, hundreds of feet and hoofs scuffed along dry dirt roads. Yellow dust swirled, nearly suffocating man and beast. Rasping coughs filled the searing air, and the smell of filthy bodies and oozing wounds was palpable. Most men trudged along, squinting their eyes, bowing their heads, and keeping a filthy handkerchief or rag tied over their mouth and nose.

Robert Braswell, now six feet, four inches tall, stood a head taller than most in his regiment. Even though malnourished, he had grown more than three inches in one year. Always broad boned but slender, he now looked skeletal. So did most other Southern soldiers. Dysentery and malnutrition had drained their strength and robbed their youth. Sunken eyes and hollow cheeks were their badge of honor.

Braswell kept an eye on his uncle, Seaborn Mims. A minié ball had passed through the thirty-one-year-old master sergeant's thigh at Champion Hill, nicking bone but sparing arteries. It was a miracle further blessed by lack of infection. Braswell probably nursed his uncle's wound by pouring his ration of whiskey into the puncture until the canteen ran dry. Mims took turns with the other walking wounded, riding in the back of the lone regimental wagon. The original mule team had died of exhaustion days earlier. So they had raided a hapless farmer's barn, and now Mississippi mules pulled the wagon toward the Alabama border.[1]

In Enterprise Cumming's men halted and waited for the next available troop train for Georgia. No one had a tent, and shade was at a premium. Every house found soldiers lying on the cool earth beneath it or draped across its broad porches. The men stripped bare the meager pantries of the townsfolk and kept their well pumps in constant use.

Finally, on July 22, Company E of the Fort Valley Infantry, and Company F, the Bragg Rifles of Crawford County, separated from the other companies in the Fifty-seventh Georgia, squeezed into boxcars, and rattled their way toward Columbus, Georgia.[2] From Columbus a spur of the Southwestern Railroad ran eighty miles east to Fort Valley. Braswell and Mims had never been so thankful that the patriarch of their clan, Williamson Mims, had invested in this rail line. His original stock had made him wealthy, and the railroad was now saving the lives of his son and grandson.

As the train drew close to Fort Valley, an incredible transformation came over the troops. Even the sick felt euphoric. Young Francis Fitzpatrick of Crawford County was dehydrated by dysentery, yet the anticipation of home brightened his hopeless eyes. Despite rest, love, and home cooking, however, he continued to waste away and died two weeks later. But he died at home. He did not lie in an unmarked grave.[3]

For men who months before could not wait to venture into the wide world, Fort Valley now seemed a notch above heaven. As the engine wheezed into the station, soldiers fought back tears, some openly weeping, others giddy with delight. From the boxcar doors the men gazed into the sea of gawking, smiling faces milling on the station platform. Wives were screaming as husbands jumped from the train cars to wildly embrace them. Embarrassed by their grime and smell, many other soldiers blushed and held loved ones at arm's length.

Among the crowd were also the tense, strained faces of parents and wives who refused to believe the casualty lists published in the newspapers and posted on courthouse walls. They prayed that there had been a mistake. Not until they talked to the person who had buried the body would they believe that their husbands or sons were dead.

The only account we have of the welcome that the men of the Fifty-seventh received upon their return to Fort Valley comes from a brief entry in the journal of Robert Braswell's cousin Mariah Kersh: "All that were left of Company E, Fifty-seventh Georgia Regiment, in Vicksburg were turned loose like a herd of cattle. They were starved; the poorest, thinnest, dirtiest set of men you ever saw, but how glad we were to have them get back to Fort Valley alive!"[4]

Robert Braswell returned to his mother's house several miles northeast of Fort Valley. His father, William Sr., a contractor, had died when Robert was a baby, forcing his mother to return to her father's plantation.[5] The Mims Place, as locals called it, contained fifteen hundred acres of corn and cotton fields, fruit orchards, pecan trees, pastureland, and dense woods bisected by meandering Mossy Creek. Williamson Mims had built an assortment of mills along the creek bank. It took all eighty-five of his slaves to plant and harvest crops, subdue nature, and master the skills and crafts needed to run a successful plantation.

Mims had built his daughter Sarah Ann a house nestled in a shallow valley, far enough away for privacy but close enough for him to keep an eye on his daughter and grandsons. He had given her several slaves for housework, farming, and chores: a married couple, Augustus and Harriet; three young men, Simon, Russel, and Allen; and a young mother, Julia, and her three children.[6] Mims kept Sarah Ann's pantry full and her children well clothed.

Robert was not home long before his mother broke the news that his grandfather was dying. While Robert and Seaborn Mims were pinned down in Vicksburg, Williamson Mims had summoned an attorney and written his last will and testament. He was eighty years old, and he was worried about a tightening in his chest, a growing pressure and pain.

After sleeping for hours, Robert saddled a horse and made his way to his grandfather's home. He dreaded seeing the shriveled body of a man who had once seemed larger than life, and Robert brooded about the future. His grandfather had held the Braswell world together for all the boy's life. And although Mims could be overbearing and manipulative, he stacked up next to God in Robert's mind. When his grandfather died, the foundations would shake.

The boy also thought about the war. Robert was young but no fool. He had seen the endless Yankee supplies and lines of blue troops that stretched forever. Robert sensed that the war was all but over. The only hope was for the South to endure long enough for Northern families to grow heartsick and broken by the endless slaughter and demand a negotiated peace at the polls. At best, the South could fight for time, waging a war of attrition that would be costly for the North. Robert prayed that he and his brothers could beat the odds and outlast the grim reaper.

But if the Yankees crushed the Southern armies, then the Mimses and Braswells would lose everything. They could not farm without slaves. And vast acreage was worthless without crops.

Robert joined Seaborn Mims for a hushed deathbed conversation with their patriarch. Struggling for clarity, the old man likely spoke of the future, what he had bequeathed to each of his eight children, his hopes and dreams for the plantation. But the young men noted that Williamson spoke as if the war did not exist, as if this quiet and ordered way of life in Fort Valley would never be touched by change of fortune or fate of battle. This moment—a prophetic moment—would lodge forever in Robert's memory.

While they were at home, many of the companies of the Fifty-seventh Georgia were feted with barbecues and picnics by their communities. The festivities, often held on nearby farms or courtyard squares, saw long lines of tables laden with food and surrounded by blankets and colorful quilts spread on the ground under shade trees. Pigs and chickens turned on skewers over pit fires. [7]

Mariah Kersh recorded the preparation for these events in Fort Valley, which occurred despite the blockades that made some goods impossible to obtain:

> Every farm raised everything to eat—corn, wheat, sugarcane, groundpeas, hogs, lambs, chickens and turkeys. . . . For coffee we used parched potatoes, rye and wheat, all of which when ground made a very good substitute. . . . When the soldiers got furloughs and came home, you may be sure that everyone tried to do his best for them. Parties, picnics and candy pullings were

arranged. Our refreshments were walnuts, parched groundpeas, popcorn, sugarcane, gingercakes and beer. No wedding feast was ever more enjoyed.[8]

Soldiers who told war stories were in great demand. Everyone wanted to hear about the battles, the struggles, the gore. Some men would spin mostly funny tales—the crazy things they did in camp, pranks they played on each other. But most were painfully silent. Recounting the war gave it life again. And there were no words to describe the horror, the violence, the profane slaughter.

Perhaps it was at such a gathering that Robert Braswell became infatuated with his doctor's daughter, fourteen-year-old Laura Love. In the dim past he probably had noticed her as a thin, gangly girl playing in the churchyard or walking the streets of Fort Valley on market day. But Laura Love was no longer a little girl. Now tall and shapely, she was moving into the full bloom of adolescence, with auburn hair, wide cheekbones, and dark brown eyes. She was beautiful.

For the rest of his furlough Robert could not see enough of Laura Love. Nor could several other aspiring suitors. But Robert was one step ahead. He knew her father, Dr. Henry Love, or at least Williamson Mims did. And, most important, Laura had taken a coy shine to Robert.

Five weeks after Robert returned home, Williamson Mims quietly died in his sleep on September 8, 1863. His adult children—four daughters and four sons— were summoned from across middle Georgia for the funeral. Robert and Seaborn were grateful to be home on furlough during this rare gathering of the clan. But Robert missed his brothers, who were guarding Fort Gaines on Mobile Bay, and knew that their grandfather would be long in the grave before they received word of his death. William, in particular, would be grieved.

Mims's last will and testament would be read after the funeral. The old man had lands scattered across Houston and Dooly counties and tried to treat each child fairly. Seaborn, the youngest of the children, received $3,000, five adult slaves, and "half of my Dooly [County] lands and mills." Robert's mother, Sarah Ann, received the three-hundred-acre tract on which her house had been built and ten slaves of varying ages. Mims's widow, Cynthia, though advanced in age, was bequeathed the fifteen-hundred-acre plantation in Houston County, all cash, stocks, and personal effects, and the majority of the slaves.[9]

Robert and his brothers were not immediate beneficiaries. However, Mims had specified that upon their mother's death, they would each receive one-third of her inheritance. Robert realized that one day he would own at least one hundred acres to farm and develop. A small corner of God's good earth would be his.

On September 30 the Fort Valley Infantry received orders to rejoin the Fifty-seventh Georgia in Savannah.[10] Surprised not to be going north to face a gathering storm on the Georgia-Tennessee border, the men experienced a strange feeling of returning to the past, of reliving the birth of the regiment in 1862. In one way this was fitting. The regiment had been so worn down and the ranks so decimated by disease and death that it would need to be reborn. Fresh bodies would fill the gaps and help provide a new sense of hope and determination among the veterans. Headquarters was correct in its assessment that the Fifty-seventh Georgia was not combat ready.

Robert's final days at home were frenetic. He now knew what to take to war. Above all, he wanted boots—the best boots he could find. Sarah Ann hastily sewed his clothes, not a uniform this time but rugged clothes that would stand the wear of camp and combat. Most critically, he needed a thick wool coat, knee length, to break the cold wind and serve as a blanket at night. Robert also gave his mother special instructions for making his pants: thick homespun cotton carded with wool, with double-layered knees and seat, the pockets deep enough for cartridges and caps. The most difficult task was finding a hat—not a dandy or-nament but a hat broad enough to block the sun and thick enough to shed rain or serve as a water bucket.

Finally, he needed tobacco to chew and tobacco to smoke. Although Robert had learned to carve pipes from roots to alleviate the boredom of trench life in Vicksburg, he did not crave smoking. But what he had learned in the Confed-erate economy was that a supply of tobacco was better than money. It was good for trade and barter. A man with tobacco did not go hungry.

Robert spent his remaining time courting Laura Love, being healed by her laughter and gentle touch. Robert had been thrust prematurely into manhood, and he was aware that Laura was not yet a woman. He was thankful for her naïvêté. In these uncertain times it was good that she was too young to marry, or make commitments, or realize that a woman should not lose her heart to a soldier.

Before he left for Savannah, Robert visited with Seaborn Mims, whose leg had not yet healed. He would not rejoin the regiment for several months. These two young men had found a new intensity to their relationship. With Williamson Mims's death they realized that it was their generation's turn to take the reins and guide the family, especially with the future so uncertain. This awareness drew Robert and Seaborn closer.

Finally, the day came to depart for Savannah. Sarah Ann watched as Robert walked out her front door and onto the porch to pick up his haversack stuffed with clothes and food. He looked like her boy again. Over the weeks at home he had gained weight and cleaned up well. Color was back in his face and he smiled more easily. But now he would be thrust again into that same kiln of battle that had hardened his youth and baked on him forever a glaze of sobriety.

As she fought back tears, Sarah Ann was comforted that Robert would be in Savannah, which was only a day's journey by train. And if safety could be found in the Confederate army, Savannah was a good bet. Sarah Ann breathed a prayer of thanksgiving that her three sons were not enmeshed in the battles in Virginia or Tennessee. Once again, she braced for the future and watched her youngest son go to war.

15

Dishonor

By October 13 two hundred members of the Fifty-seventh Georgia Infantry had reported for duty in Savannah.[1] Now under the regional command of Brigadier General Hugh Weedon Mercer, fifty-five, the regiment was placed in a brigade led by Brigadier General Raleigh E. Colston, recently transferred from Virginia. Included in Colston's brigade were the First Georgia Volunteers, under Colonel Charles Olmstead; the Fifty-seventh Regiment Georgia Volunteers, under Colonel William Barkuloo; the Sixty-third Regiment Georgia Volunteers, under Colonel George Gordon; the First Florida Battalion, under Lieutenant Colonel Charles Hopkins; and several smaller commands. The brigade was to defend the Savannah city lines and the batteries at Fort Bartow, Greenwich, Thunderbolt, Beaulieu, Rose Dew, and the Isle of Hope.[2]

The Fifty-seventh Georgia was ordered to camp near Fort Bartow.[3] Located on the Wilmington River directly across from Whitemarsh Island, Fort Bartow was three miles east of Savannah and a mile south of Fort Jackson on Causton's Bluff. Fort Bartow covered seventeen acres and was one of the largest and most complete fortified earthworks on the Atlantic coast. The fort provided both surveillance of the Wilmington River area and protection against a rear attack on Forts Jackson and Lee on the nearby Savannah River.[4]

Lacking the enthusiasm of raw recruits, the veterans of the Fifty-seventh Georgia dug in and quickly began to grumble about camp life. It was hard to return to both the discipline and the squalor of a military camp after an extended furlough at home. The weather was turning cold, and the dampness of the coastal plain penetrated the warmest clothing. Tents were thin and in short supply. Food was scarce and of poor quality. It was going to be a long and uncomfortable winter.

The Fifty-seventh Georgia soon found that it lacked the stability of strong leadership from its senior officers. Noticeably absent was Colonel William Barkuloo. He was confined to his home in Brunswick, Georgia, because of illness, and he would be absent from his command for virtually all the troubled six months that the Fifty-seventh Georgia was in Savannah.

The most effective leader of the Fifty-seventh Georgia, Lieutenant Colonel Cincinnatus Guyton, was also absent from October through December 1863, because he was attending the Georgia legislature as a state senator from Laurens County. He would rejoin the regiment in January.

Many other officers were missing or frequently absent. The adjutant, Thomas J. Dyson, had been killed at Champion Hill and not replaced. And the chaplain, Fitz Henry Ivey, had resigned from service. The Fifty-seventh Georgia faced a crisis in leadership.

The regiment was further weakened when companies B, D, and H were detached for temporary duty under Colonel R. C. Anderson's command. The only surviving muster report for this period shows 257 present for duty, 87 sick, 45 detached, 33 absent on extra duty, 15 on leave, 4 absent without leave, and 1 under arrest, 442 in all.[5] Thus the regiment was greatly reduced, fragmented, and lacking critical leadership and discipline.

Consequently, morale was poor. Many men voiced alarm at their perception of the terms of their Vicksburg parole agreement. Technically, the terms required prisoners to give a sworn oath that they would not take up arms against their captors until they were formally exchanged for an enemy captive of equal rank. Because the men of the Fifty-seventh Georgia had never been exchanged, they feared that if they were captured and identified, they would be executed for breach of terms. This anxiety further undermined the spirit of the regiment.[6]

As the Fifty-seventh Georgia attempted to strengthen its ranks, new recruits filtered in to join up. One was Private John Methvin, a seventeen-year-old from Jeffersonville, Georgia. Early in the war his two older brothers, Lieutenant William K. Methvin and Sergeant Thomas J. Methvin, had joined Company D of the Fifty-seventh Georgia and endured the Kentucky and Vicksburg campaigns. At the battle of Champion Hill William Methvin had been captured and was now interned in a Union prisoner-of-war camp at Johnson's Island, Ohio. John was enlisting to take his brother's place and keep his brother Tommy company.[7]

The Fifty-seventh Georgia was assigned to patrol duty, primarily on Whitemarsh Island. Union forces were nearby and the exchange of artillery fire was steady. Because of its decimated numbers the Fifty-seventh Georgia experienced strenuous and extended duty that kept the men exhausted. In a report to his superiors Brigadier General Colston wrote:

> Since the departure of two of my regiments for Florida I have been utterly unable to guard the [Whitemarsh] Island. . . . I had to strip the city lines of the necessary guards and impose such severe duties upon the rest of the troops that the surgeons are protesting against it, and with all my efforts I could not place on Whitemarsh more than 200 men, who have had to do the picket duty day after day without being relieved.
>
> . . . Whitemarsh Island is too large and too accessible, not only by numerous creeks, but over the marshes at high tide, to be guarded by a few men, and unless a considerable force is kept there what pickets we are able to establish must always be liable to be cut off.[8]

When Christmas came, most of the men were not granted furloughs because of the chronic shortage of Confederate troops to defend Savannah. Spirits plummeted and morale hit its lowest ebb in January and February 1864, a state that was revealed in two incidents that brought discredit and embarrassment to the Fifty-seventh Georgia.

In January 1864 an officer uncovered a conspiracy to mutiny by a segment of three companies of the Fifty-fourth Georgia Regiment that were garrisoned on Rose Dew Island. Though the number of troops actually involved in the scheme was small and their secret plans unexecuted, the plot stirred a tempest and implicated the Fifty-seventh Georgia. In his official report on the matter Brigadier General Colston wrote:

> On Tuesday, [January] 12th instant, a communication was received from Captain Hanleiter, commanding Beaulieu Battery, to the effect that a non-commissioned officer had informed him of the existence of a plot among the garrison at Rose Dew, the purpose of which was to abandon the post at Rose Dew with arms, ammunition, etc., to win over the troops at Beaulieu if possible, to advance toward Savannah, taking with them the Terrell Artillery at White Bluff, whose adhesion was considered certain, also some State troops camped on the Skidaway road, and to come to the camp of the Fifty-seventh Georgia, upon whom they seemed to rely as ready to join them, the whole to make their way to the interior of the country, their avowed purpose being to induce by their example as many of the troops as possible to imitate them and by refusing to bear arms any longer "to put an end to the war."[9]

George A. Mercer, serving on the staff of his father, Brigadier General Hugh Mercer, also scribbled his perceptions in his diary:

> [O]n a given night a portion of the troops (the number not ascertained, though several Regiments appear implicated) were to desert with their arms and ammunition, and to march immediately to the country, and then return to their homes: their idea seemed to be that this example would be followed by the army generally, which would disband, and the war, with its attendant hardships, cease. The chief grievances appeared to be deficient food and clothing, suffering families at home and the inability to obtain furloughs. It is probable that not a great many intended to participate in this scheme, though it seems that a written statement and pledge was circulated in several camps for signatures.[10]

Upon receiving information about the proposed mutiny, the senior Mercer acted quickly, dispatching troops to Rose Dew, arresting suspected ringleaders, and carefully monitoring the situation. Though involvement by the Fifty-seventh Georgia was never proved, the reputation of the regiment nevertheless took a beating. In his official recommendations following the quelled mutiny, Colston suggested to Mercer:

> [I recommend] that the Fifty-seventh Georgia Regiment be transferred either to the Army of Tennessee or of Virginia. The spirit of this regiment (the Fifty-seventh Georgia) is bad. The troops say that they have never been properly exchanged, and the impression prevails, probably with good reason, that they will not fight if brought before the enemy. They are demoralized by the influence of home, to which they are too near, their friends and relatives persuading them that they have not been properly exchanged and ought to be at home. Their presence here may have a bad effect upon the other troops and their spirit and tone may be improved by removal to more distant points.[11]

Right or wrong, the command staff in Savannah was convinced that the Fifty-seventh Georgia required stiff discipline. However, before the Fifty-seventh could be shunted off to another theater, a second event transpired that further sullied the regiment's reputation.

Early on Monday morning, February 22, a detachment of the Fifty-seventh Georgia was on picket duty on Whitemarsh Island at Gibson's house.[12] The men were bleary eyed and cooking breakfast, unaware that a Yankee amphibious assault was bearing down on them. As Brigadier General Colston later reported: "About 8 o'clock on Monday morning the enemy advanced toward Whitemarsh Island in two parties. One consisted of eleven surfboats, each carrying 20 men, and passed over the flats at high tide. The morning being hazy, and the high grass of the marsh covering them, they were enabled to effect a landing without being seen about 100 yards below the picket at Fleetwood's."[13]

The invasion force advanced to the Oatland Bridge, which connected the island to the mainland and Fort Bartow. If the Yankees captured the bridge, they would control the island, trapping the Confederate pickets and blocking their reinforcement. Fortunately, the Confederates recently had positioned a battery at the bridge and were able to hold it. Unable to achieve their primary objective, the Yankees wheeled and moved toward the Gibson house, where a detachment of the Fifty-seventh Georgia was supposed to be standing guard.

Although the Fifty-seventh probably knew that a Union force had landed on the island, the men were not aware that the Yankees had turned from the Oatland Bridge and were advancing. Meanwhile, the Fifty-seventh Georgia was focused on three Yankee ironclads that were steaming up to the docks at the Gibson house. Lieutenant Robert Harris of Company A described the scene in a letter to his wife:

> I started on a scout to Wilmington island this morning and had proceeded about a mile and a half when a courier overtook me and informed me that the Yankee gunboats were coming, whereupon I double-quicked my party back

to the Gibson Place and formed a line with rest of the detachment. Three iron-clad gunboats came right up to the landing and anchored. While we were watching the boats a large party landed from another direction and, cutting off our picket, came up in rear [the raiding party returning from being repulsed at Oatland Bridge]. We immediately attacked them and defeated them, but [with] two more parties flanking us in the meantime on our right and left, we had to fall back and, once started, the men became almost unmanageable and ran like sheep.[14]

Falling back in disarray and panicked by the prospect of being cut off and captured, the detachment of the Fifty-seventh Georgia retreated until it ran into the rest of the regiment, which had been ordered from Fort Bartow and drawn into line of battle. A reconnaissance squad was then sent to assess Union movement around the Gibson house. The scouts discovered that the Federals were boarding the gunboats and retreating. The Union command knew that further combat would be futile after its troops were foiled at the Oatland Bridge and unable to sever the island from Confederate reinforcement.

In the aftermath Colston severely criticized the Fifty-seventh Georgia for its battle performance. The brigadier general wrote in his official report, "The detachment of the Fifty-seventh at the Gibson house behaved very badly. Their officers deserve credit for their personal conduct, and are deeply mortified at the behavior of their men."[15]

The Fifty-seventh Georgia had hit bottom. Accused of complicity in mutiny and now charged with cowardice, its members awaited the reprimand or transfer that would certainly come. Most men were embarrassed by the escalating chain of events and wanted to do something to redeem the regiment's reputation. They decided to send a statement declaring their loyalty and allegiance to the Confederacy to the *Savannah Republican*. On March 7 it appeared under the headline "Reinlistment of the 57th Georgia Regiment":

The undersigned committee having been appointed to draft such resolutions as would give expression to the sentiments of the 57th Georgia Regiment, on the subject of their reballotment in the Confederate army—actuated by the same sentiments and guided by our knowledge of the patriotism and gallantry of the brave old 57th—we submit the following preamble and resolutions. . . .

Resolved, That the 57th Georgia Regiment, undismayed by the villainous threats of Beast Butler, and unconquered by their toils in Kentucky or the misfortunes of Middle Tennessee and Mississippi, do hereby reballot in the army of the Confederacy to serve during the war, determined never to lay down our arms until truth and justice be crowned with liberty in the glorious independence of our beloved country.

Resolved, That nothing has yet occurred to shake our confidence in the ability of the South finally to achieve her independence; and, in emulation of the deeds of our revolutionary fathers, we call upon all true Southern men to stand by our government in this hour of greatest peril, resolved on our own part, God being our support, to do our whole duty to the best of our ability.

Adopted by the regiment, and ordered to be published in the Savannah Republican, with the request that all other friendly papers in the State copy.[16]

Although the statement was earnest and passionate, it did not sway the opinion of the Confederate command that the Fifty-seventh Georgia must be removed from the environs of Savannah. The regiment—still under the command of Brigadier General Mercer—was detached to the backwaters of garrison duty at a newly constructed prisoner-of-war camp near Americus, in west-central Georgia. The camp was to become the most infamous prison camp of the Civil War: Andersonville. On April 22, 1864, the Fifty-seventh Georgia—now 625 strong—left for Anderson Station. Nine months earlier the men of the Fifty-seventh Georgia had been prisoners of the Union army in Vicksburg. Now they were to guard Union prisoners in the heartland of Georgia.[17]

16

Andersonville

As the men of the Fifty-seventh Georgia boarded a troop train and rattled toward middle Georgia, they were at least pleased to be moving temporarily closer to home. With each mile the controversy and humiliation of the last six months melted away. Although they knew they were a good regiment, having endured more combat and hardship than any other regiment in Savannah, the events of recent days had shaken their confidence and reputation.

When they arrived in Macon, they changed to the Georgia Southwestern Railroad and turned south toward Americus. As miles of dense forest and rich farmland flashed by, Robert Braswell grew sullen and angry. The Southwestern Railroad ran the length of Houston County, directly crossing the Mims plantation and bisecting Main Street in Fort Valley. Robert could clearly see his mother's house a mere half mile from the tracks. As the train slowed to a crawl through Fort Valley, Robert felt more like a prisoner headed to Andersonville than a soldier in his own state. Colston had been right when he had written, "They are demoralized by the influence of home, to which they are too near."[1]

Thirty miles south of Fort Valley stood a whistle-stop on the Southwestern Railroad named Anderson Station that had a prewar population of twenty people.[2] Located in the middle of Georgia's cotton and corn production region, this obscure hamlet became the unlikely site selected for a prisoner-of-war camp during the early days of 1864. Although its official name was Fort Sumter, prisoners remembered it as Andersonville.

Andersonville eventually became the largest and most notorious of all Confederate military prisons. The Richmond government built it under pressure to move large numbers of Yankee prisoners from Virginia to a remote place in the Deep South for greater security. During the fourteen months of its existence, more than forty-five thousand Union soldiers walked through its gates. Of these, nearly thirteen thousand died of malnutrition, neglect, disease, and exposure.

When the Fifty-seventh Georgia arrived on April 22, Andersonville was in its early stages. The first prisoners—five hundred from Bell Isle, Virginia—had arrived on February 18, 1864. They were interned in a treeless prison area of sixteen acres enclosed by a fifteen-foot-high stockade of hewed pine logs. Shaped like a parallelogram, the secured area was 1,620 feet long and 779 feet wide.

Inexcusably, no housing or shelter was provided for the prisoners. Men dug holes in the ground and tried to cover their dens with blankets, pine branches, or whatever material they could forage. The Yankee prisoners were constantly under the gaze of their Confederate captors. Sentry boxes, or "pigeon roosts," stood at thirty-yard intervals atop the stockade walls. Eight small earthworks around the perimeter of the prison were equipped with artillery to defend against Union cavalry attacks. These same cannons could be quickly wheeled to the prison gates and fired upon inmates should rebellion break out. Andersonville was not so much a military prison as a holding pen.

The Fifty-seventh Georgia, with 625 effective troops, joined the Twenty-sixth Alabama, Fifty-fifth Georgia, and the Florida Light Artillery, bringing the guard strength to 1,193. They pitched tents and formed camp outside the compound walls.[3] The putrid smell of the place immediately sickened them. The closest water supply was Sweetwater Creek, a ludicrous name, considering that it had become an open sewer. The stream trickled through the prison camp and was the only source of water for drinking, washing, and refuse. Its polluted waters spawned much disease and death.

Andersonville was designed to confine and support ten thousand prisoners. During the Fifty-seventh Georgia's first week of guard duty, the inmate population exceeded this maximum.[4] Yet the prison trains kept unloading their human cargo. By the end of August 1864 the inmate population peaked at thirty-three thousand, more than triple its intended capacity.

The result of such overcrowding was rampant disease, starvation, and the cruelty that inevitably erupts within such conditions. Even the Confederate guards were on reduced rations and subject to the same contagious diseases as the prisoners. Tempers were short and outbreaks of violence frequent. Prisoners preyed on each other for survival. Guards, usually humane, often became callous and cruel.

Perhaps the greatest symbol of violence at Andersonville was "the Dead Line." The guards created the Dead Line to keep prisoners at a safe distance. A crude one-rail fence ran parallel to the interior wall of the stockade, creating a fifteen-foot buffer zone between the prisoners and the wall. Guards in the "pigeon roosts" were ordered to shoot to kill any Yankee who crossed the Dead Line. Many died.

John McElroy was a prisoner who had enlisted in the Sixteenth Illinois Cavalry and was captured while guarding a supply route to Cumberland Gap during the Kentucky campaign in the winter of 1862–63. A journalist in civilian life, he recorded the following account of violence on the Dead Line on May 12, two days before the Fifty-seventh Georgia left Andersonville:

> The only man I ever knew to be killed by one of the 26th Alabama was named Hubbard from Chicago, a member of the 38th Illinois. He had lost one leg, and went hobbling about on crutches, chattering continually in a loud, discordant voice, saying all manner of hateful and annoying things, whenever

he saw an opportunity. This and his beak-like nose gained for him the name of "Poll Parrot." . . .

[Hubbard was accused of telling prison authorities of an escape attempt, and] a crowd caught the Parrot with the intention of lynching him. He succeeded in breaking away from them and ran under the Dead Line near where I was sitting in my tent. At first it looked as if he had done this to secure the protection of the guard. The latter, a 26th Alabamian, ordered him out. Poll Parrot rose up on his one leg, put his back against the Dead Line, faced the guard and said in his harsh cackling voice, "No! I won't go out." . . . The guard again ordered the Parrot out, but the latter, tearing open his blouse, cackled out, "No! I won't go; fire at me, guard. There's my heart; shoot me right there!"

There was no help for it. The rebel leveled his gun and fired. The charge struck the Parrot's lower jaw and carried it completely away, leaving his tongue and the roof of his mouth exposed. As he was carried back to die, he wagged his tongue vigorously in attempting to speak, but it was of no use. The guard set his gun down and buried his face in his hands. It was the only time that I saw a sentinel show anything but exultation at killing a yankee.[5]

Between April 1 and May 8, 728 prisoners died, most from disease, exposure, and malnutrition. Their bodies were stripped of shoes and any other useful clothing—often while they were still alive—and carried to the deadhouse. They were stacked like cordwood outside, and friends scribbled the deceased's name, rank, and regiment on a slip of paper and tied it to his big toe. Prisoners then transported the corpses to the prison cemetery in open wagons. No coffins were available, so they laid the bloated and putrid bodies side by side in long six-foot-wide trenches. Every day the cemetery grew larger until it had overgrown its bounds.

It was hard for Robert Braswell to comprehend that such inhumanity, cruelty, and depravity existed within thirty miles of his home. Always before, the horror of war had been in another state, on a battlefield hundreds of miles away. But now this human cesspool was near his mother, close to Laura Love and all that he held dear. It seemed that the whole world was corrupted, and Andersonville symbolized it all.

Fortunately for the Fifty-seventh Georgia, its banishment to Andersonville lasted only twenty-three days. Military events in northern Georgia were heating up and becoming critical. General William T. Sherman was leading a major Union advance out of Tennessee and driving south toward Atlanta. The Fifty-seventh Georgia was needed again on the battlefield.

To replace the troops on garrison duty in Andersonville, two regiments of the Georgia Reserves—young boys and older men not eligible for military duty—

had been sent from Atlanta. As the army regiments happily prepared to depart, the local belles gave them a grand send-off, complete with picnic and brass band. John Ransom, a twenty-year-old brigade quartermaster of the Ninth Michigan Cavalry, described the scene in his diary: "Making preparations for a grand picnic outside, given by the citizens of the vicinity to the troops about to leave. . . . A band of music from Macon yesterday to attend the picnic. A large crowd of women were present to grace the occasion. The grounds on which the festivities were held lay a mile off and in sight of all. In the evening a Bowery dance was one of the pleasures enjoyed. 'The Girl I Left Behind Me,' was about all they could play, and that very poorly."[6]

There was something repugnant about the scene as the smell of food and the sound of music drifted over the stockade wall to mix with the hunger and misery inside.

Hours after the Fifty-seventh Georgia left for north Georgia on May 14, 1864, a telegram arrived from Confederate Adjutant General Samuel Cooper, ordering the regiment to combat duty in Virginia. The order was immediately rescinded, and the Fifty-seventh Georgia narrowly avoided leaving its home state.[7]

As the Fifty-seventh Georgia steamed north, the men sensed that they were facing a new day filled with peril and urgency. For the last eight months they had marked time by guarding coastal islands around Savannah and prisoners of war in Andersonville. Life had become tedious and depressing. Now they were moving to the front lines to confront an attack on their homeland. Some of the cruel absurdity of Andersonville began to lift, and they sensed a vigor and idealism that they had not felt for months. They would now be fighting to protect their farms, towns, and families.

As they careened along the narrow tracks, Robert Braswell was pensive as the troop train neared Fort Valley once more. The inhumane suffering at Andersonville had affected him more deeply than any battle had. Now he knew not only the mask of death but also the leering face of evil. He no longer trusted a goodness in life that would somehow win out in the end.

As Robert passed by his family's fields, which were sprinkled with slaves who were plowing for spring planting, he silently pondered the future. Would he return to be a planter like his grandfather Mims, if he returned at all? Would the family still own land if the South lost this terrible war? Perhaps all that really mattered was the gift of life itself and a chance to marry Laura Love.

The thundering echo crossing Mossy Creek Bridge announced the last farewell for Robert. If and when he should return, the war would be over. But life as he had known it would never be the same. Kentucky, Tennessee, Champion Hill, Vicksburg, Savannah, Andersonville: what was it all for?

The Atlanta Campaign

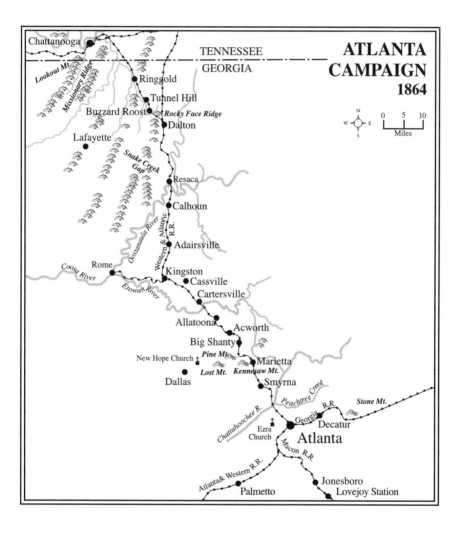

Chattanooga

TENNESSEE
GEORGIA

ATLANTA
CAMPAIGN
1864

Lookout Mt.

Missionary Ridge

Ringgold

Tunnel Hill

Buzzard Roost

Rocky Face Ridge

Dalton

0   5   10
Miles

Lafayette

Snake Creek Gap

Resaca

Calhoun

Oostanaula River

Western & Atlantic R.R.

Adairsville

Coosa River

Rome

Kingston

Cassville

Etowah River

Cartersville

Allatoona

Acworth

Big Shanty

New Hope Church

Pine Mt.

Marietta

Dallas

Lost Mt.

Kennesaw Mt.

Smyrna

Peachtree Creek

Georgia R.R.

Stone Mt.

Chattahoochee R.

Ezra
Church

Decatur

Atlanta

Macon R.R.

Atlanta & Western R.R.

Palmetto

Jonesboro

Lovejoy Station

17

We Expect to Show Them the Elephant

Much had happened to the Fifty-seventh Georgia's comrades in the Army of Tennessee in the ten months since the men had stacked their rifles and marched out of the trenches of Vicksburg.

On September 19–20, 1863, Braxton Bragg and the Army of Tennessee had paid William Rosencrans and his Yankee forces back for the Battle of Stones River the previous December. In a horrific battle a few miles southeast of Chattanooga, Tennessee, along the banks of Chickamauga Creek, Bragg had defeated Rosecrans, with combined casualties of 34,624. Rosecrans had retreated to Chattanooga, foundered under Confederate siege, and was relieved of his command.

A month later, on October 18, 1863, Ulysses S. Grant had taken command of the newly created Military Division of the Mississippi, giving him direct command of the Union's western theater. Grant quickly broke Bragg's siege of Chattanooga, defeated Confederate forces on the mountainous heights around the city, and sent Bragg reeling across the Georgia border. Bragg dug in at Dalton, Georgia, and Grant suspended his pursuit to settle into winter quarters.

Impressed by Grant's abilities, on March 12, 1864, Lincoln appointed him general in chief of the Armies of the United States; William T. Sherman assumed command of Union forces in the West. Grant directed that the Union's primary spring offensives would be in northern Virginia and northern Georgia. Grant would command the Army of the Potomac against Robert E. Lee's Army of Northern Virginia. Sherman would attack the Army of Tennessee.

Meanwhile, after Grant chased Bragg out of Chattanooga in late 1863, Jefferson Davis had decided to relieve Braxton Bragg of command of the Army of Tennessee by promoting him and transferring him to Richmond. The only available generals who were capable of replacing Bragg were Joseph Johnston and P. G. T. Beauregard. Davis disliked both choices and offered the command of the Army of Tennessee to Robert E. Lee, who firmly declined. Davis overlooked his strained personal relationship with Joseph Johnston and gave the command to him in December 1863.

Although Davis's relationship with Johnston long had been one of mutual animosity, the rank-and-file loved Johnston. The troops admired his experience, liked his immaculate military demeanor, and trusted him to take care of their basic needs. With Bragg kicked upstairs to assist Davis in Richmond, the morale of the Army of Tennessee rebounded.

When Johnston assumed command, he found a beaten army of forty-three thousand men. He immediately improved morale by providing better food, clothing, and shelter for his troops. Johnston then reorganized his seven infantry divisions into two corps. One corps was led by General William J. Hardee, a veteran and proven commander. The other corps was led by a recent youthful arrival from the Army of Northern Virginia, thirty-two-year-old General John Bell Hood. Later, General Leonidas Polk would supply a third corps with troops from the Department of Alabama, Mississippi, and East Louisiana.

Johnston's two corps commanders stood in sharp contrast to each other. Hardee, forty-eight, was sometimes slow but always stable, a recognized master of tactics and leadership. Hood was impetuous and mercurial. Despite his temperament, however, few officers in the Confederate Army were equal to John Bell Hood as an aggressive division commander. He had the wounds that proved his valor—his limp left arm had been shattered at Gettysburg, and his right leg had been amputated at the hip at Chickamauga. The severely crippled Hood had to be tied securely in his saddle. Constant pain and the effects of the narcotic laudanum further limited Hood's physical abilities as a corps commander.

Johnston's biggest problem was troop strength. His 45,000-man Army of Tennessee would be facing three Union armies—the armies of the Cumberland, the Tennessee, and the Ohio—with combined troop strength more than 100,000. The Confederate command began to frantically scavenge for troops from every available source. Soon General Hugh Mercer in Savannah received orders to move his brigade of four regiments—including the Fifty-seventh Georgia, which had been detailed to Andersonville—to north Georgia to join Johnston's army.

Hugh Weedon Mercer was the grandson and namesake of the Revolutionary War general Hugh Mercer, who had been killed at the Battle of Princeton. A native of Virginia, Hugh Weedon had graduated third in the West Point class of 1828. From 1832 through 1834 Mercer was honored to serve as aide-de-camp to Major General Winfield Scott and was commissioned first lieutenant of artillery in 1834. While stationed in Savannah, Hugh Weedon Mercer met and married Mary S. Anderson and resigned his commission in 1835.

From 1841 to 1861 Mercer was cashier of the Planter's Bank of Savannah. When Georgia seceded, Mercer entered Confederate service as colonel of the First Georgia Volunteers. He was promoted to brigadier general on October 29, 1861, and given command of a brigade to guard Savannah. From June 1862 through April 26, 1864, he served as commander of the Military District of Georgia. During those two years Mercer worked primarily to defend coastal Georgia despite an acute shortage of manpower.

Brigadier General Hugh W. Mercer

Mercer was fifty-six when he was ordered to join Johnston's army in north Georgia. Not in the best of health or physical conditioning, Mercer also lacked battlefield experience. Although a year younger than Johnston, Mercer was seen as a tottering elder statesman. Many feared that Mercer would be unable to endure the strain of a tough campaign.

Mercer's brigade was composed of four regiments—the First, Fifty-fourth, Fifty-seventh, and Sixty-third Georgia Volunteer Regiments—each with detached companies scattered between Charleston, Savannah, and Andersonville. The regiments were ordered to consolidate their troops and immediately join the Army of Tennessee. They would remain together as a fighting unit for the rest of the war and would be known as "Mercer's brigade," although others would lead it at various points.

The Sixty-third Georgia was the first to arrive in Dalton on April 30, followed on May 2 by the Fifty-fourth Georgia. The veterans of the Army of Tennessee stared and snickered as Mercer's troops detrained. Though various companies had seen sporadic combat in the defense of Charleston harbor during the autumn of 1863, the Fifty-fourth and Sixty-third Georgia had primarily spent their war years garrisoned around Savannah. Consequently, Mercer's brigade had a novice look about it.

As the Georgians marched to camp, dirty and grizzled veterans gawked at their fresh uniforms and regulation chevrons, something they had not seen for months. They taunted Mercer's troops as "band box soldiers," the "silver fork brigade," and "new issue." One incredulous Tennessee sergeant wrote home, "This morning I saw a regt, 1400 strong, just from Savannah. It has been in service nearly three years but has never been in a fight! We expect to show it the 'elephant' in a few days."[1]

The brigade was assigned to General William H. T. Walker's division of Hardee's corps and made camp three miles east of Dalton. Later these troops would be joined by the First Volunteers and the Fifty-seventh Georgia and would boast twenty-eight hundred men, the largest brigade in Johnston's army.[2]

Mercer was well acquainted with Walker, who was a West Point graduate of the class of 1837 and served as an officer in the U.S. Army until 1860. On December 20, 1860, Walker resigned his major's commission in the U.S. Army and entered the military service of Georgia, serving briefly under Hugh Mercer's command. Rising quickly through Confederate ranks, Walker was promoted major general by Joseph Johnston in May 1863.

Though Mercer had once been Walker's superior, he now accepted his subordinate role amiably. Walker would not, however, be the easiest general with whom to serve. His was a contentious and explosive personality, and he had a reputation as a Southern firebrand. Born in Augusta, Georgia, to a prominent family, Walker now was forty-seven and not in good health. The lead and shrapnel remaining in his body from the severe wounds he suffered in both the Seminole Wars and the Mexican War had given rise to his nickname, "Old Shotpouch." An asthmatic, he usually slept sitting up and was plagued by exhaustion, which intensified his fierce temper.

Despite his physical debility, Walker was an aggressive and fearless officer. Lieutenant General Richard Taylor wrote of Walker, "[His] character was one of the strangest I have met. No enterprise was too rash to awaken his ardor if it necessitated courage and selfless devotion."[3]

Over the years Walker had become embittered. He felt that his long military service and sacrifice had not been sufficiently recognized by promotion, rank, and command. Serving under this irascible son of Georgia would challenge General Mercer.

The first troops of Mercer's brigade arrived in Dalton on April 30, 1864, and on May 1 Sherman began his advance out of Tennessee. His primary objective was to capture Atlanta. To get there with his supply line intact, Sherman would have to remain close to the Western and Atlantic Railroad. Johnston knew this and wisely chose Dalton, which straddled the railroad thirty miles southeast of Chattanooga, as his first line of defense.

Dalton was naturally protected by a series of tall and easily defended ridges. The primary ridge, Rocky Face, was a wall of sheer stone that extended as high as fifteen hundred feet above the valley floor and for twenty miles on a north-south axis. The railroad bisected Rocky Face at Mill Creek Gap and descended

Major General William H. T. Walker
(Courtesy of the Virginia Historical Society,
Richmond, Va.)

to Dalton on the south side of the ridge. If Sherman was going to stay with the railroad, he would have to capture Dalton.

Johnston, a defensive specialist, studded the craggy heights of Rocky Ridge with artillery and rifle pits, crisscrossing the paths that Sherman's advance would have to follow. Sherman responded by adopting a plan proposed by Brigadier General George Thomas, "the Rock of Chickamauga," that used the tactic of "flanking," one that Sherman would rely on all the way to Atlanta. Rather than attack Johnston head on, Sherman positioned Thomas's Army of the Cumberland and John McAllister Schofield's Army of the Ohio squarely in front of Rocky Face Ridge to feint a major attack. While Johnston was preoccupied with this imminent danger, James Birdseye McPherson's Army of the Tennessee quietly moved southeast out of northern Alabama, passed through undefended Snake Creek Gap, and made a rapid advance to Resaca, sixteen miles south of Dalton on the Western and Atlantic Railroad. If McPherson seized Resaca, Johnston's Army of Tennessee would be sandwiched north and south and his supply line to Atlanta severed. When Sherman received word that McPherson was a mile and a half from Resaca, he pounded his fists on his dinner table and howled, "I've got Joe Johnston Dead!"[4]

As McPherson's advance elements reached the outskirts of Resaca at dusk on May 12, they came under fierce Confederate fire. McPherson peered through the darkness and assumed that he was facing superior forces. In fact, he was snookered by the bluff and bluster of Brigadier General James Cantey's lone

Confederate brigade. With night falling, McPherson made the mistake of his career and withdrew to await reinforcements. Had he advanced, he would have had a 5–1 troop superiority and would have slammed the back door shut on Johnston.

Johnston now realized that despite his excellent defensive position in Dalton, the real danger was to his rear in Resaca. During the night of May 12 Johnston abandoned Dalton and withdrew to Resaca, arriving on the morning of May 13. Intense skirmishing soon developed into major infantry assaults during that day and the next, north and west of Resaca. Casualties escalated and a major battle seemed imminent. However, Sherman again decided to flank Johnston, dispatching Brigadier General Thomas Sweeny southward with orders to cross the Oostenaula River near Calhoun and seize the railroad at Johnston's rear.

When Johnston learned that Sherman was again leapfrogging past him, he had no choice but to withdraw to a more defensible position. A major tactical truth was becoming clear. As long as Sherman had significant manpower superiority, he would be able to pin Johnston down with his left hand and flank him with his right, forcing Johnston to retreat. Johnston had to either find topography that did not lend itself to a flanking movement or devise a way to force Sherman to divide his forces, allowing Johnston to defeat segments of Sherman's army one at a time.

Johnston needed to do one more thing. He desperately needed to impede or sever Sherman's railroad supply line as it rolled out of Tennessee and into Georgia. If he could drastically reduce Sherman's supplies, the Union general would be unable to support his massive army and would have to retreat.

Johnston was adamant that he did not have adequate cavalry both to support his infantry and send detachments to raid and destroy Sherman's railway. Therefore Johnston asked Jefferson Davis to reassign the large cavalry units guarding Alabama and Mississippi—especially the vaunted horsemen of Major General Nathan Bedford Forrest—to sever Sherman's supply line.

Fearing just such a strategy, Sherman ordered Union raiding expeditions to descend out of occupied Tennessee into Mississippi and Alabama to keep Forrest's cavalry busy. And Jefferson Davis, loathe to further threaten his home state of Mississippi or destabilize Alabama, refused to release the Confederate cavalry units to reinforce Johnston in Georgia. The result was that Sherman's railroad supply line kept the Union forces in Georgia well reinforced and supplied.[5]

As Johnston's troops filed out of Resaca, crossing and burning bridges as they headed south, Walker's division—including Mercer's brigade—was attached to Hardee's rear guard. Walker's division had played primarily a supportive role to date, serving as a reserve unit. Although the division had experienced some casualties, it had not been fully committed to battle. Instead, the men were being shuttled from position to position, enduring long marches primarily under the cover of darkness. The result was that Mercer's brigade was being marched into shape. Captain George Mercer, General Mercer's son, scribbled in his journal, "the men completely broken down by loss of sleep, fatigue and insufficient food."[6] And they had not yet seen the elephant.

Johnston retreated south and chose the small college town of Cassville for his next confrontation with Sherman. Johnston's decision was predicated on geography: there were few roads in this rugged isolated region. If Sherman pursued Johnston closely, he would be forced to divide his large army on two highways to speed their advance, splitting his troops into two columns seven to eight miles apart. Johnston believed that he could consolidate his Confederate forces and smash one of the Union columns at Cassville before Sherman could unify his army. It was a brilliant plan.

As predicted, Sherman did split his forces and Johnston prepared to spring his trap on May 19. With the recent arrival of Leonidas Polk's troops from Mississippi and Alabama, Johnston now had nearly seventy-four thousand men— the largest force ever assembled by the Confederacy in the West. In contrast, the lone Union wing approaching Cassville under Schofield and Joseph Hooker comprised fewer than thirty-five thousand men. For once Johnston would have numerical superiority. But he had only a narrow window of time in which to operate before Sherman would be able to consolidate his two wings.[7]

Johnston assigned Polk's corps to directly confront the Union wing approaching Cassville on the Adairsville Road. As these troops engaged, Hood would be in a concealed position to savagely assault the Union's left flank, rolling it up and forcing a quick surrender. Simultaneously, Hardee's corps, including Mercer's brigade, would be retreating westward, as Sherman's second wing approached on the western side of Cassville. Hardee would delay Sherman's second wing long enough for Johnston to spring his trap and crush the first wing.

Initially, all went as planned. Polk and Hood were in battle position and ready to spring their trap when Hood became aware of Yankee cavalry behind him. In reality, a small Union cavalry detachment had wandered several miles east from Hooker's main line on reconnaissance.[8] Fearing an attack from the rear, Hood called off the attack. An angry and dejected Johnston had no choice but to pull Hood and Polk back and place them in a better defensive position southeast of Cassville on a wooded ridge.[9]

Johnston had lost a rare opportunity. By now Sherman's second wing was bearing down on Cassville, heavily engaging Hardee. As Hardee fell back toward Cassville, Mercer's brigade was closest to the Union troops, with the Sixty-third Georgia in advance position. As heavy artillery pounded the Sixty-third Georgia, it narrowly escaped being surrounded and captured.[10]

Johnston had lost his best chance of the Atlanta campaign to seriously maim or defeat Sherman. As the sun set, Sherman had united his two wings and was raining a heavy artillery barrage down on Confederate troops. By midnight the

Confederates again were retreating south, following the railroad nine miles to Cartersville. The officers and men shouldered bitter disappointment. A feeling of futility settled in. Could Sherman and his blue horde be stopped?

The next day, May 20, 1864, Johnston's Army of Tennessee crossed the Etowah River and took up strong defensive positions around Allatoona Pass. At this low moment a troop train wound through the thousand-foot-high Allatoona Mountains and delivered the Fifty-seventh Georgia to Allatoona Station. Still reeling from their sickening twenty-three days at Andersonville, the men now linked up with Mercer's brigade and prepared to fight a desperate war.

18

The Hell Hole!

As Robert Braswell stepped from the crowded troop train at Allatoona Station and shouldered his rifle and haversack, he was accompanied by his uncle, Seaborn Mims. After six months' medical furlough in Fort Valley, Mims's leg had finally healed from the gunshot wound at Champion Hill.

The Fifty-seventh Georgia collected its gear and marched to General William H. T. Walker's divisional camp. The men found Mercer's brigade and began to dig in and get organized. In the confusion Robert Braswell heard his name called and turned to stare in joyful disbelief at his two brothers, William and Samuel. Robert did not know that while he was isolated at Andersonville, his brothers had been transferred from Mobile with the First Confederate Regiment to join Johnston's army. As fate would have it, the First Confederate had also been assigned to John Jackson's brigade, which also was in Walker's division.[1]

After warmly greeting his brothers, Robert stared in amazement at William and Samuel. He had not seen them since the summer of 1862. His brothers no longer had their fresh parade-dress look. The last twenty days of constant marching and skirmishing had left them muddy and haggard. William's duties as a master sergeant had weighed heavily on him. Only five days earlier General Walker had ordered Jackson's brigade to assault General Thomas Sweeny's division, which was seeking to make a bridgehead across the Oostanaula River at Lay's Ferry, Georgia. The brigade attacked and scored initial success but was soon riddled by Union artillery. Falling back, many men of the First Confederate were killed and scores more wounded and captured.[2] This was the first heavy combat that William and Samuel had seen.

After nearly three years of service in the Confederate army, the Braswell brothers and Seaborn Mims were at last united in the same division within their native state. Fighting Sherman was now a family matter.

During its first three days in north Georgia, the Fifty-seventh Georgia stayed quietly in camp while Sherman rested his army and Johnston licked his wounds. Walker's division had lost 28 men, and 269 had been wounded in the first two weeks of the Atlanta campaign. Mercer's brigade had seen 4 die and 41 wounded. The tally would quickly grow.[3]

In these same two weeks Sherman had accomplished the unthinkable and had marched more than halfway to Atlanta. If Union forces now forded the

Etowah River, only one more river, the Chattahoochee, would separate Sherman from Atlanta. Even more impressive, Sherman's engineers had quickly repaired ripped-up railroad track and rebuilt burned bridges. And the Union general was far from being overextended with a tenuous supply line: Yankee locomotives were now steaming right up to Union camps. Because Jefferson Davis had hesitated to allow Nathan Bedford Forrest's cavalry to sweep out of Tennessee and sever Sherman's supply line, Sherman was as strong as he was on his first day of advance.

On Monday, May 23, 1864, Sherman crossed the Etowah in yet another flanking motion, avoiding Johnston's strong defensive position at Allatoona Pass. To do so Sherman briefly left the railroad, taking twenty days of supplies with him. He skirted south of the mountainous Confederate stronghold, intending to cut back and reconnect with the railroad behind Johnston's lines.

Alerted by his cavalry to Sherman's movement, Johnston abandoned Allatoona Pass and skillfully moved fourteen miles southwest to the hamlet of Dallas to intersect with the Union army. The terrain around Dallas was densely wooded, virtually unmapped, and had few roads. Johnston's troops hastily dug a new line into low wooded ridges that extended on a five-mile front from Dallas northeast to a rural crossroad at New Hope Methodist Church. John Bell Hood's corps—and Mercer's brigade—lay directly in the path of the advancing armies of Brigadier General George Thomas and Major General John M. Schofield.

Late in the afternoon of May 25 the forward elements of Major General Joseph Hooker's corps made contact with Hood's. Sherman ordered a frontal assault. As dark thunderclouds formed ominously overhead and rain pelted down, three of Hooker's divisions advanced straight at Alexander Stewart's division of Hood's corps. Stewart's entrenched infantry unsheathed a murderous fire, and a sixteen-gun artillery battalion belched forth canister.[4] Within minutes the Union line was mutilated. By dark 1,665 Union soldiers lay dead or wounded in front of New Hope Church. The Confederates lost less than half that number.[5]

During the night the Union army regrouped and took up positions facing the entire six-mile Confederate line. Sickened by the waste and carnage of the frontal assault at New Hope Church, a chastened Sherman was again convinced that his best offensive weapon was a flanking maneuver. While his huge army held Johnston firmly in place, he secretly sent elements of General Oliver Howard's corps two miles northeast of the church toward Pickett's Mill.

As Howard approached Pickett's Mill, he thought that he had exceeded the end of the Confederate line and began to turn the flank. He did not know that he was marching straight into the gunsights of perhaps the most formidable fighting unit in Joe Johnston's army, Patrick Cleburne's entrenched and camouflaged brigade. Howard's flanking effort was shredded as emplaced infantry fire exploded at point-blank range and artillery belched forth body-ripping canister. In minutes sixteen hundred Yanks lay dead or wounded but fewer than five hundred Rebs had fallen.

Sherman never spoke of Pickett's Mill in either his official reports or in his later *Memoirs*. It was a tragic memory that he chose to forget. But he learned the lessons of that disaster well. Although the battles of New Hope Church and Pickett's Mill were relatively limited engagements, they changed the entire nature of the Atlanta campaign. Both battles demonstrated that a small, well-armed, and disciplined defensive unit could mangle a much larger offensive force if the smaller unit was entrenched behind even minor fortifications. Generals Sherman and Johnston would be forced to adapt to these realities.

While Cleburne was blunting the Union thrust at Pickett's Mill, Mercer's brigade was also in combat. Mercer's brigade had been temporarily detached from Walker's Georgia division to serve with General Benjamin Franklin "Frank" Cheatham's Tennessee division to assist Cheatham in clearing Union forces from the strategic heights of Elsberry Mountain. Mercer's brigade lined up on Cheatham's far right, adjoining Brigadier General Alfred Vaughn Jr.'s brigade. The Confederate advance met fierce resistance but was able to sweep over the Union lines and clear the ridge. However, the Tennesseeans and Georgians incurred mounting casualties for the next twenty-four hours as they attempted to secure the ridge.[6]

By the morning of June 1 the staff officers of Mercer's brigade could look from the heights of Elsberry Mountain and see Union troops gradually pulling out of line and moving eastward. Sherman was short on rations and was once more flanking and driving for the rail line at Acworth, well south of the Confederate stronghold at Allatoona.

Marching away, the blue troops soon forgot the names of Dallas, New Hope Church, and Pickett's Mill. They simply called the whole bloody mess the Hell Hole.

As Johnston prepared to move once more to parry Sherman's thrust, Mercer's brigade had been reinforced by the arrival from Savannah on May 29 of the First Georgia Volunteers under the twenty-seven-year-old colonel Charles Olmstead. This was the regiment that had defended and surrendered Fort Pulaski in Savannah during the initial months of the war. Now Mercer's brigade was complete, the largest in the Army of Tennessee.[7]

During the first week of June, Johnston again sought a defensible position to punish Sherman's 112,000 troops. Johnston chose a range of low mountains ten miles southeast of Dallas and five miles north of Marietta. Johnston now had his back pressed dangerously close to Atlanta. His thin gray line would stretch in a semicircle across Lost, Pine, and Brush mountains on an east-west axis.

As the Confederates fell back from the Dallas–New Hope line on June 4, they marched under cover of darkness and incessant rain for ten miles, slogging through knee-deep mud. Colonel Olmstead recounted this night of dark misery:

> The roads too were particularly bad, there had been a great deal of rain and the constant passage of artillery and transportation trains had cut them up most abominably. . . . The memory of the night marches over these roads is like a night mare to me as I think of them; horses and men wearied and exhausted, stumbling along, through red clay, mud and darkness—prolonged waiting every few hundred yards when somewhere in front a stalled wagon or broken down caisson would block the road. . . .
>
> These night tramps were generally made in moody silence. I remember to have fallen asleep in the saddle often, waking with a start and wondering where I was when the order came to move on. This is a side of war that histories do not lay much stress upon but every old soldier bears it in mind.[8]

Upon arrival at his mountainous line, Johnston positioned his three corps along a ten-mile front, with Polk on the right, Hardee in the center, and Hood on the left. Unfortunately, Johnston's line would have to shift constantly to the east to correspond to Sherman's movement, causing exhaustion among the troops as they again dug mud for new trenches and rifle pits.

For two weeks Sherman probed Johnston's line. Each day brought unrelenting rain, artillery duels, and deadly sniping. Mercer's brigade, on constant picket duty since June 8, began to accrue serious casualties for the first time.

On June 15 Mercer's brigade served as part of the advance line for Hardee's corps in the vicinity of Gilgal Church. Suddenly, around noon the sporadic fire of Union artillery increased to a furious roar, and infantry units of Hooker's corps attacked Hardee's advance troops. Soon the Yanks sent Rebel cavalry scouts scurrying back to Confederate lines. By 1:30 P.M. Mercer's heavily engaged brigade also received orders to fall back. While retreating under fire, twenty men were killed or wounded.[9]

As the sun set, the brigade established a new line, and the Fifty-seventh Georgia and six companies of the First Volunteers pulled picket duty. The next morning, June 16, the Union attack continued, pounding the zone held by the First Volunteers. The First Volunteers held on until nightfall, suffering seventy-three casualties. In the darkness Mercer's troops withdrew behind the lines of Walker's and Major General William B. Bate's divisions to regroup.[10]

By June 18 Mercer's brigade was again on the front lines near Mud Creek and endured heavy fire. On this day Johnston began to withdraw his army into a new defensive perimeter aligned across three more mountains, Big Kennesaw, Little Kennesaw, and Pigeon Hill. As Walker's division quietly retreated in the dark, Mercer's brigade held the brittle picket line, protecting the exposed retrograde action.

Late that night disaster struck. Olmstead recorded the moment:

Major Allen of the 63rd was the officer in command of the picket and his orders were to remain in position for a certain time after the Brigade had retired and then to withdraw quietly and follow it without attracting the attention of the enemy. When Allen joined us about day break he brought in the details of the 54th, the 57th, and the 63rd Regiments but not that of the 1st. On being asked about them he expressed great sorrow and chagrin and said that in some way he had lost touch with them in the black darkness of the night and had not been able to communicate the order for withdrawal. He also said that the orders given to him to preserve quiet, had prevented any loud calling to locate the detail and that failing to find Captain Levy he had to come in without him when the time was up. . . . Captain Levy wrote to me some time afterward from the Federal prison on Johnson's Island, Lake Erie, to which he [and his men] had been taken after his capture.[11]

As Mercer's brigade staggered onto the slopes of Kennesaw Mountain in June 1864, its units were undergoing a great transformation. For the first time they were becoming a battle-hardened brigade. The Fifty-seventh Georgia was no longer its only veteran regiment. Indeed, since the beginning of the campaign against Sherman's army, Mercer's brigade had suffered 435 casualties: 29 killed, 224 wounded, and 182 missing in action. Now Mercer's Georgia boys would need all the courage and stamina they could muster.[12]

19

Kennesaw Mountain

After slipping and stumbling through dense darkness and deep mud for more than two miles, Mercer's brigade arrived on the southwest flank of the Kennesaw Mountain range at 2:30 A.M. on June 19, 1864. Amid rain and thunder, the exhausted men collapsed, huddling under trees and rubber ponchos. No sooner had they fallen asleep than the engineer wagons creaked up the slope, and the brigade received orders to dig trenches and earthworks immediately.

The men cursed and grumbled, responding only when prodded. Suddenly, Sherman's artillery boomed, flashing fire in the night. Tree branches shattered and fell as shells screamed overhead. An instant urgency came over Mercer's troops, and they began to dig in frantically. Colonel Olmstead chuckled years later when he recalled that a young lieutenant in the Fifty-seventh Georgia, James Everett, wryly remarked in the middle of the chaos, "Boys, I'm going to get a cannon on my plantation when the war ends, there's nothing like it to make lazy people work!"[1]

With morning light Captain George Mercer scribbled in his journal, "Slept in heavy rain; cold, wet, and uncomfortable: formed line of battle at 7 A.M. and constructed works and sent out picket; men broken down and completely exhausted, with constant work and no rest. I slept for the first time in five nights. Very heavy rain during day."[2]

For several days Johnston shifted his line to match Sherman's deployment of troops. Johnston keenly missed General Polk, who had been killed the week before by a direct hit from an artillery shell while surveying the Union line with Hardee and Johnston. Johnston had cradled Polk's mangled body in his arms and wept openly. Polk, a West Point graduate turned Episcopalian bishop, had baptized Johnston, Hardee, and Hood a few weeks before his own death.[3]

Johnston now temporarily assigned General William Loring to Polk's corps. Johnston placed the untried corps commander in the most defensible position on the heights of Kennesaw Mountain, holding down the Confederate right flank. Hardee's corps held the center of the gray line, and Hood's corps shifted to the left side of the line. Johnston's Army of Tennessee covered an eight-mile front with only forty-three thousand effective troops.[4]

Mercer's brigade was positioned on the extreme right of Hardee's corps on a raised spur that jutted off the southern base of Pigeon Hill. Mercer's brigade adjoined Samuel Gibbs French's division of Loring's corps at the Burnt Hick-

Captain George A. Mercer
(From Northern, ed., Men of Mark, *108)*

ory Road. They were surrounded by beautiful, lush countryside and were entrenched on a steep hillside under a forest of hardwood trees with thick, shadowed canopy. Kennesaw Mountain loomed to their immediate right, rising to seven hundred feet. A broad expanse of sloping, open meadow lay before them at the base of the hillside. Any Union advance would have to cross this wide, exposed killing ground.

For several days Sherman and Johnston probed each other's lines. Finally, Sherman—seemingly oblivious to the lessons of the Hell Hole—again decided on a major frontal attack. Why did Sherman make such a decision?

In his *Memoirs* Sherman does not give a clear explanation for his actions. However, he alludes to impassable quagmires caused by nineteen days of constant rain; these had made it impossible to maneuver for flanking operations. He was also concerned that if he extended his line beyond the eight-mile Confederate line, he would be stretched too thin and would be too far removed from his base of supply on the railroad.[5]

Most important, Sherman believed that the Confederate line was so overextended that he would be able to punch through its thin width and roll it up. Sherman wrote, "I reasoned, if we could make a breach anywhere near the rebel center, and thrust in a strong head of column, that with the one moiety of our army we could hold in check the corresponding wing of the enemy, and with the other sweep in flank and overwhelm the other half."[6]

Sherman issued orders for two major attacks to be made simultaneously

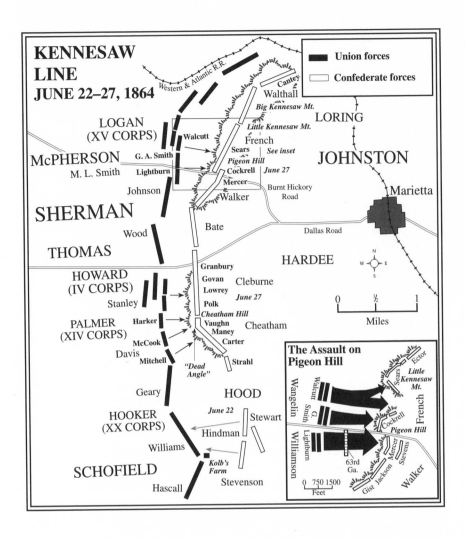

KENNESAW LINE
JUNE 22–27, 1864

Union forces
Confederate forces

Western & Atlantic R.R.

Cantey
Walthall
Big Kennesaw Mt.

LOGAN (XV CORPS)
Walcutt
Little Kennesaw Mt.

LORING

McPHERSON
G. A. Smith
M. L. Smith
Lightburn
French
Sears | See inset
Pigeon Hill
Cockrell | June 27

JOHNSTON

Johnson
Mercer
Walker
Burnt Hickory Road

Marietta

SHERMAN
Wood
Bate
Dallas Road

THOMAS
Granbury

HARDEE

N
W — E
S

HOWARD (IV CORPS)
Stanley
Govan
Lowrey
Cleburne
June 27
Polk

PALMER (XIV CORPS)
Harker
McCook
Davis
Mitchell
Cheatham Hill
Vaughn
Maney
Carter
Cheatham

0   ½   1
Miles

"Dead Angle"
Strahl

Geary

HOOD

HOOKER (XX CORPS)
June 22
Stewart
Hindman

Williams

SCHOFIELD
Hascall
Kolb's Farm
Stevenson

The Assault on Pigeon Hill

Wangelin
Walcutt
G. Smith
Lightburn
Williamson
63rd Ga.
Sears
Little Kennesaw Mt.
Ector
Cockrell
Pigeon Hill
French
Mercer
Stevens
Gist
Jackson
Walker

0   750 1500
Feet

against the Confederate line on June 27. The primary attack would be against the brigades of generals Frank Cheatham and Patrick Cleburne in Hardee's corps in the center of the Confederate line. The secondary attack would be where Hardee's and Loring's corps met at the base of Little Kennesaw Mountain and Pigeon Hill. Mercer's brigade would be the bull's-eye of Sherman's secondary target.

Before Sherman attacked, Johnston received news from Richmond that greatly upset him. Three days earlier, on June 24, Johnston's good friend, the Confederate senator Louis T. Wigfall of Texas, had visited Johnston at his Marietta headquarters. Wigfall had told Johnston of a persistent rumor that Jefferson Davis was so tired of Johnston's continual retreats and lack of battlefield victory that the Confederate president was considering relieving Johnston of his command and replacing him with John Bell Hood. Wigfall had stressed that Johnston could avert this only by defeating Sherman at Kennesaw or stopping him north of the Chattahoochee.[7]

Johnston had responded that the only way to whip Sherman was to unleash the cavalry of either Nathan Bedford Forrest or Stephen Lee to destroy Sherman's supply line. However, Davis had been consistently unwilling to weaken his forces in Alabama and Mississippi by transferring cavalry units, even if the fate of the Confederacy hinged on the defeat of Sherman in Georgia. Johnston was caught in a quandary that he could not resolve.[8] As long as Sherman had vastly superior troop strength, he could outflank Johnston all the way to the Gulf of Mexico. And, as long as Sherman had an uninterrupted supply line, he could maintain his superior numbers.[9]

Johnston had little time to mull Wigfall's news, for early on June 27 Sherman unleashed his blue horde against the Rebel line. As the sun rose, the men of the Fifty-seventh Georgia awoke grateful that it was not their turn to man the picket line of Mercer's brigade. As eight o'clock approached and breakfast was concluded, the formerly sporadic Union artillery fire swelled to a constant and ominous din, usually the sign of an impending infantry attack.

All eyes in Mercer's brigade peered intently from their elevated trenches on the southern spur of Pigeon Hill across a wide sloping meadow to their vulnerable picket lines, which were manned by the Sixty-third Georgia. Normally, a picket line was a quarter mile in front of the main line. A series of rifle pits were then dug ten to fifteen yards apart about 150 yards in front of the picket line. The rifle pits were big enough to hold four to six men and were usually positioned one hundred to two hundreds yards from the foremost enemy line. Everyone knew that a sudden attack could easily overrun these exposed positions.

On this day six companies of the Sixty-third Georgia were posted in the rifle pits, which were only twenty yards from the edge of dense woods. The remaining four companies of the Sixty-third were held in reserve on the main picket line. As the artillery barrage ceased at 8:15 A.M. the hot, humid morning became deathly silent. The pickets of the Sixty-third Georgia grew uneasy and strained to see enemy troop movement. Hidden from the view of Mercer's brigade by thick foliage were fifty-five hundred Union soldiers of James Birdseye McPherson's Army of the Tennessee who now began to advance down the Burnt Hickory Road.

McPherson had assigned Brigadier General Morgan L. Smith to command this wing of Sherman's two-pronged attack. Using the Burnt Hickory Road for his approach, Morgan Smith directed his younger brother, Brigadier General Giles A. Smith, to veer off to the left side of the road and attack Loring's corps, which was entrenched on Pigeon Hill. Brigadier General Andrew A. J. Lightburn would veer to the right side of the Burnt Hickory Road and attack Walker's division of Hardee's corps—specifically targeting Mercer's brigade.

As Lightburn's troops marched forward, finally leaving the road and filtering into the cover of deep woods, six Union regiments advanced in two horizontal lines. The first line consisted of the Thirtieth Ohio, the Eighty-third Indiana, and the Fifty-third Ohio. The supporting second line was manned by the Fifty-fourth Ohio, the Thirty-seventh Ohio, and the Forty-seventh Ohio. Although they had to fight through dense brush and wade through a knee-deep swamp, the Union soldiers approached the Sixty-third Georgia's picket line undetected.[10]

When the first of Lightburn's troops reached the edge of the forest and peered across the broad sloping pasture toward Mercer's brigade, they were surprised to find that the Confederate rifle pits were only twenty paces in front of them. The Fifty-third Ohio immediately charged out of the woods, followed by the Eighty-third Indiana and Forty-seventh Ohio. The inexperienced men of the Sixty-third Georgia never had a chance. Suddenly, they had to decide whether to stay put or scramble back to their lines. If they ran, they would face the fire of their own troops, and the Yanks would be firing at their back. But to remain in position was suicidal.

Major Joseph H. V. Allen was in command of the Sixty-third Georgia picket. Only days before, many had blamed him for the capture of the pickets of the First Georgia Volunteers during a night withdrawal. Now, standing with the four reserve companies of the Sixty-third Georgia, he stared horrified at the plight of his men in the rifle pits. Desperately seeking to avoid another disaster, he ordered the four reserve companies to advance and reinforce the men in the rifle pits. It was a foolish decision—wasting the lives of good men to try to save a hopeless situation.

In the midst of the panic and confusion the three Union regiments quickly overran the six companies of Georgians in the rifle pits. Violent hand-to-hand combat broke out. In one rifle pit alone nine Confederates were bayoneted and clubbed to death.

A young Irish soldier from Savannah, John Smith, stubbornly fired his weapon and was reloading when a Yankee grabbed his rifle by the barrel. A furious tug-of-war ensued until the plucky Rebel shoved the Yankee backward, turned tail, and ran, yelling, "To hell with you and the gun too."

Another Southern boy, Lieutenant George A. Bailie, winced as a minié ball grazed his ear. He looked up and found himself staring down the barrel of a Yankee rifle. Bailie had only a sword to defend himself. Picking up a rock, he hurled it at the enemy soldier. The Yankee was knocked senseless, and Bailie beat a hasty retreat up the hill toward Mercer's line.

Above the din a Confederate officer shouted, "Save yourselves, boys!" and the survivors of the Sixty-third Georgia looked wild eyed for any place of safety. "They had picked up something too hot to hold," recalled Orderly Sergeant Walter Clark.[11]

If the desperate men of the Sixty-third ran toward their own lines, they would be caught in a crossfire. Already, French's artillery on Pigeon Hill was zeroing in on Lightburn's Union advance. Shells crashed among the fleeing survivors of the Sixty-third Georgia. And Mercer's brigade was now shooting at any moving target. Rather than be caught in the slaughter, many Rebs turned and ran toward the Union-infested woods, and most were captured immediately. Others took their chances and ran the gauntlet across the meadow. Will Clark described the scene: "With the first volley as they entered the open field, Lieut. Blanchard was wounded and W. J. Steed fell by his side with a ball through his lungs. A moment later A. M. Hilzheim, who had joined us only a day before, had received a fatal wound, and Wyatt Chamblin had fallen with a shattered leg. . . . A little way off Charlie Bayliss lay dead and John Weigle had fallen with a broken thigh."

Finding temporary shelter, Steed and Weigle grimaced in pain and surveyed their situation. It became clear that to escape capture their only option was to crawl toward Confederate lines. Walter Clark continued:

> Steed and Weigle took advantage of a temporary lull in the firing and renewed their efforts to escape. Steed was so weakened by loss of blood from his four wounds that he could only rise, stagger a little way and fall, then rest for a time and renew the effort, while Weigle was forced to crawl and drag his wounded limb. In the effort he was shot in the other leg, but was finally reached by the litter bearers and taken to the rear, one of them being fatally wounded as they bore him off. After repeated efforts, occupying an hour or more, Steed reached the haven and swooned away. In this condition he was found and rescued. He still lives, but an armless sleeve furnishes constant reminder of the terrible experience of that June day. Weigle, poor fellow, a model soldier and a brave, true man, died from his wounds.[12]

As the survivors of the Sixty-third Georgia bolted toward Mercer's lines, Lightburn's Union troops looked with fear toward the elevated Confederate breastworks. Forming ranks, the Yanks charged across the meadow, hoping to use the fleeing Confederates as a moving shield from Rebel fire. The men of Mercer's brigade, trying desperately to miss their own, filled the air with minié balls. Exploding shells and mutilating case shot from French's artillery, as well as the raking fire of a Confederate Missouri regiment posted on Pigeon Hill, tore the Union ranks apart. Major T. T. Taylor of the Forty-seventh Ohio recorded their agony: "Sheets of flame baptize them; plunging shot strike comrades on every hand, and they fall unnoticed by your side. The advance is climbing under tree trunks, jumping over hacked saplings, tearing through the sharpened brush, stepping over fallen comrades . . . facing the sheeted flame filled with missiles, giving forth ten thousand shrieks and tones, intensified by the cries of agony and the torture of the wounded."[13]

In only a few minutes the Union advance faltered and the blue troops hugged the ground. Major Taylor described the terror of being pinned down under Confederate fire: "I laid down behind a small rock from which I could see the greater portion of the material part of the line [Mercer's brigade]. The rebs soon got the range of the rock & every time I opened my mouth or gave an order *Zip* came a bullet against the stone. At various points I sheltered myself behind the trees and had the infinite [terror,] time and again of hearing balls intended expressly for my body strike the tree behind which I stood or sat, and more than once the dirt & bark was knocked in my face."[14]

Within ten minutes General Lightburn decided that Mercer's position could not be taken, so he directed his troops to withdraw to the woods at the foot of the meadow, leaving many wounded on the field. Later in the day Major James Williams, Mercer's brigade inspector, led a Confederate counterattack, and any remaining Union troops were driven from the captured rifle pits.

When the last of the wounded were brought into Mercer's lines and casualties tallied, the novice Sixty-third Georgia regiment had lost 88 of 265 men who began the day. Company A of the Sixty-third Georgia had taken 47 men into action and only 24 had returned. Though the Sixty-third had stubbornly tried to hold its ground, it had been brutalized.[15]

Lightburn's Union troops paid a high price as well. Though they captured 40 prisoners of the Sixty-third Georgia, they did so at a cost of 171 killed and wounded.[16]

That night General Walker visited Mercer's camp and spoke to the battered Sixty-third Georgia. Sergeant Clark recalled Walker's remarks: "Gen W. H. T. Walker complimented the regiment on its gallantry, but suggested that it be tempered with a little more discretion."[17] But only time and experience could teach battlefield wisdom.

While Mercer's troops blunted Lightburn's advance, the larger Union assault was taking a beating a mile and a half to the south. Two Yankee divisions comprising eight thousand men—Major General John Newton's division on the right and Major General Jefferson C. Davis's division on the left—assaulted the center of the Rebel line in an ill-fated charge that pitted them against the entrenched troops of Patrick Cleburne and Frank Cheatham. In some of the most intense fighting that these soldiers experienced, the Union forces displayed a courage and fanatical determination that almost broke the Confederate line. But Cleburne's and Cheatham's soldiers were some of the best that the South could offer, and they hung on. Private Sam Watkins of the First Tennessee recorded a graphic description:

My pen is unable to describe the scene of carnage and death that ensued in the next two hours. Column after column of Federal soldiers were crowded upon that line. . . . Yet still the Yankees came. It seemed impossible to check the onslaught, but every man was true to his trust, and seemed to think that at that moment the whole responsibility of the Confederate government was rested upon his shoulders. Talk about battles, victories, shouts, cheers, and triumphs, but in comparison with this day's fight, all others dwarf into insignificance. The sun beaming down on our uncovered heads, the thermometer being one hundred and ten degrees in the shade, and a solid line of blazing fire right from the muzzles of the Yankee guns being poured right into our very faces, singeing our hair and clothes, the hot blood of our dead and wounded spurting on us, the blinding smoke and stifling atmosphere filling our eyes and mouths, and the awful concussion causing the blood to gush out of our noses and ears, and above all, the roar of battle, made it a perfect pandemonium.[18]

In reflecting on the slaughter of that day, Watkins wrote:

I have heard men say that if they ever killed a Yankee during the war they were not aware of it. I am satisfied that on this memorable day, every man in our regiment killed from one score to four score, yea, five score men. I mean from twenty to one hundred each. All that was necessary was to load and shoot. In fact, I will ever think that the reason they did not capture our works was the impossibility of their living men passing over the bodies of their dead. The ground was piled up with one solid mass of dead and wounded Yankees. I learned afterwards from the burying squad that in some places they were piled up like cord wood, twelve deep.[19]

Despite the carnage, Union regiments continued to charge Confederate lines with a bravery that won the admiration of the most hardened Reb. Yet Sherman ultimately was forced to call off the attack. Watching the broken blue tide recede, Sam Watkins wrote:

When the Yankees fell back, and the firing ceased, I never saw so many broken down and exhausted men in my life. I was sick as a horse, and as wet with blood and sweat as I could be, and many of our men were vomiting with excessive fatigue, over exhaustion, and sunstroke; our tongues were parched and cracked for water, and our faces blackened with powder and smoke, and our dead and wounded were piled indiscriminately in the trenches. There was not a single man in the company who was not wounded, or had holes shot through his hat and clothing. . . .
On coming to a little stream of water, I undressed for the purpose of bathing, and after undressing found my arm all battered and bruised and bloodshot from my wrist to my shoulder, and as sore as a blister. I had shot one hundred and twenty times that day. My gun became so hot that frequently the

Private Samuel Watkins
(National Park Service)

powder would flash before I could ram home the ball, and I had frequently to
exchange my gun for that of a dead comrade. . . . Afterward I heard a soldier
express himself by saying that he thought "Hell had broke loose in Georgia,
sure enough."[20]

Sherman had ordered a needless and wasteful assault. Shortly before the
Union troops charged, General Schofield, on the southern flank, was able to
move two brigades across Olley's Creek, successfully flanking Johnston and de-
stabilizing the Confederate line. This movement alone was enough to force
Johnston to retreat again toward Atlanta. The loss of life by Sherman's "go for
broke" assault was a travesty.

The oft-repeated lesson of Kennesaw Mountain was that even the most courageous troops could not succeed with an assault against well-entrenched and
-controlled defensive positions. Rapid mobility was proving superior to brute
force. And both Union and Confederate generals would break their hearts and
commands while learning this new reality.

Ironically, Johnston could bask in the most one-sided victory of his military
career. But though Johnston had won the battle, he was losing the war. Sherman
could easily absorb three thousand casualties. He could stoically bury his dead
and move on, with the prize of Atlanta still before him.

Kennesaw Mountain was a major Confederate victory. Johnston had fought
his kind of battle and had mauled superior forces. President Jefferson Davis
could at last be assured that Johnston would fight and could win. But Sherman
was still bearing down upon Atlanta.

20

On the Banks of the Chattahoochee

Neither side left Kennesaw Mountain immediately. For the next few days Johnston's and Sherman's exhausted troops remained in their trenches and fortifications along the Kennesaw line, while Sherman waited for the muddy roads to dry and planned his next thrust to the Chattahoochee River, just over ten miles away. Johnston already had hundreds of slaves working on a massive defensive line, centered on the bridge where the Western and Atlantic Railroad crossed the Chattahoochee. Johnston now prepared to move his Army of Tennessee once more.[1] Once he withdrew across the Chattahoochee, the center of downtown Atlanta was a scant seven miles to his rear.

As common soldiers waited for orders to disengage from the Kennesaw line and move toward Atlanta, sniper fire and artillery duels continued to take their murderous toll. On General Mercer's front, the opposing skirmish lines were about two hundred yards apart and peppering each other with accurate rifle fire. Charles Henry Thiot was a forty-two-year-old private serving with the First Georgia Volunteers. He was a rice farmer and owned a plantation named Roseville twenty miles from Savannah. About a week before, he had written to his wife, Anna, describing the close quarters of trench warfare: "You do not know my dear Wife, what a struggle it is for me to write to you this morning. Here it is the glorious Sabbath, and I would that I could commune with you aright, but here I am in the trenches, crowded with men sheltered by blankets stretched over poles, and they all jabbering and talking. And I am not sure if the one at my elbow is not reading as I write. We are not permitted to go away from the trenches except by express permission, and were I to obtain it to hunt a shade, there is no knowing how soon a shell would come screaming about me."

As Thiot continued his letter and looked at his filthy messmates, he reflected on the poor hygiene, diet, and health that were depleting the Confederate army:

> A good many have broken down by attacks of diarrhea occasioned by so much exposure. We have no chance to keep clean, for we have no soap, and having left our knapsacks, the shirt and drawers I carry in my haversack are constantly wet. I dry them every chance I get, and this morning put on a clean shirt—the first in two weeks. We never take off our clothes at all, but have orders to even sleep with our harness on, and at our pieces, for we never know when we will be ordered to "fall in." . . .

*Private Charles Thiot and Anna Thiot
(Special Collections and Archives,
Robert W. Woodruff Library, Emory
University, Atlanta, Ga.)*

Well now, I think that for my own amusement I will shock your fastidious-
ness a little, just a little by informing you that I have *lice* on me—caught two
the first search and three this morning!! But I have many to bear me company,
and among them Genl. Mercer who I understand caught *forty-two*. It is a
common thing to see a fellow seated down with his shirt in his lap hunting
game. It is horrible, but is one of the inconveniences there is no avoiding.

Continuing his Sabbath reverie, Thiot grew serious and reflected on how
warfare was changing him, making him into a far more callous individual, increasingly impervious to the pain of others:

It is singular how easily a man may become accustomed to the sights and
sounds of battle. I am already accustomed to seeing the poor fellows borne
along upon the litters, or as on yesterday, while on picket, seeing a poor
sufferer moving feebly, supported by a comrade, with the ragged rent in his
coat showing where the messenger of death had touched his vitals. I feel
sympathy always, but my feelings are not shocked as at first. And then the
continued "pit-pat and zip" of minie balls as they trim the leaves or sink into
the earth have scarcely a terror in them.[2]

Yet despite the necessity of combat veterans' becoming hardened to human
suffering, examples of mercy and generosity were plentiful. On June 28, the day
after the Sixty-third Georgia had been mauled and Lightburn's Union troops

repulsed, elements of the Fifty-fourth and Fifty-seventh Georgia were on the picket line when they heard a wounded Yankee pleading for help. Lieutenant Hamilton Branch of the Fifty-fourth Georgia saw what happened: "Capt. Shinholster of the 57th [Company K] got up, and ran out to him with a canteen of water and telling him to try and crawl into our lines, ran back to his post, the enemy firing at him all the time. After getting back one of the men said that if anyone would go with him that he would go out and bring the man in. So Capt S. [Shinholster] goes out again and with the help of this man brought the wounded man in."[3]

The act of mercy by Captain Shinholster, who died three weeks later from chronic diarrhea and acute dehydration, was not rare among the blue or gray. Yet the overwhelming evidence of inhumanity was appalling. For two full days the Union wounded were left between the lines to slowly broil and die in the hot Georgia sun, while the corpses next to them putrefied. Finally, on June 29 neither side could tolerate the terrible stench of decaying corpses. They called a seven-hour truce. Union and Confederate troops worked together to drag the bloated bodies into mass graves.

While they carried on their grisly work, soldiers conducted much trading between the lines. Conversations broke out while Rebs and Yanks merged amiably together. A few admiring Yanks who had tried to break General Frank Cheatham's stubborn line even asked him for his autograph. Yet, as soon as the truce ended, men who had grasped hands in friendship returned to their trenches and again sighted rifles at each other.

As the men of Mercer's brigade hunkered in their Kennesaw trenches and waited to retreat toward Atlanta, they became preoccupied by hunger. Long after the war Colonel Olmstead described the Confederate menu for his grandchildren:

> The ration as prescribed by regulations is varied and ample, but with us it consisted of corn bread, meat, (generally bacon and sometimes stringy beef) with a little salt; the coffee, sugar, molasses, beans, flour etc. that are so alluring in the printed list of rations, were conspicuous by their absence.
>
> From every Regiment men were detailed to form what was known as the "cooking brigade" who performed these ministrations in camp well to the rear. Corn bread was all they cooked, the meat being issued raw for each man in each mess to treat as taste and opportunity might permit. The bread was prepared in dutch ovens and each individual "pone" bore the sign manual of the cook who had pressed it into shape; the finger prints were plainly to be seen, with transverse ridges between, on every one of them. I reflected some times upon the degree of cleanliness of these fingers, but it was just as well not to let the mind dwell upon that theme too particularly.

The ability to preserve food from day to day was also limited, resulting in stale rations and frequent food poisoning. Olmstead recalled:

> The rations were usually brought up in the Commissary wagons to the main line in the dusk of the evening, to avoid the fire of the enemy; then what the men did not eat at once was stored away for the next days consumption in the haversacks, or "war bags" to be brought forth, when needed, encrusted with the stale crumbs, fragments of tobacco and sand, always to be found in the bottom of these receptacles.
>
> "Pretty poor fare" you will say, and I am ready to agree with you, but in that campaign there was enough of it and the most of us attacked it with appetites and digestions that regarded quantity more than quality.[4]

Thiot was even more critical of the food situation, telling his wife, "The bread is baked a day before we get it . . . and the bacon is rather old and sometimes rancid. . . . It deranges the bowels and in my case it gives me heartburn. I went to [Dr.] Elliott this morning and fortunately he had some soda of which I got a little. . . . You do not know how I long for some vegetables. This constant diet of cornbread and bacon tells upon us."[5]

While men in the trenches endured long miserable days, Sherman and Johnston pondered their strategies. Aware that Sherman was preparing to flank him again, Johnston beat him to the punch and moved his entire army from the Kennesaw line during the night of July 2. Previously, Johnston had ordered Brigadier General Francis Shoup, his chief military engineer, to prepare two lines of field fortifications between Kennesaw and Atlanta: the first at Smyrna Camp Ground and the second on the northern bank of the Chattahoochee River. Johnston now retreated four miles south from Kennesaw along the railroad to Smyrna Camp Ground.

At 10 P.M. Loring's corps slipped silently down from the heights of the Kennesaw ridge line. An hour later Hardee's and Hood's corps evacuated their trenches, leaving behind their pickets to keep up a lively fire to shield and muffle the withdrawal. For the first time a significant number of Rebs lagged behind, seizing the opportunity to desert to the Federals. Confederate morale was taking a beating as they withdrew yet again and Atlanta drew closer. At least one soldier in Mercer's brigade noted the increase in desertions. Private Celathiel Helms of the Sixty-third Georgia wrote to his wife, "The men are going over to the Yankees by the tens and twenties and hundreds almost every night. . . . [They are] all out of heart."[6]

The night was unusually dark as Mercer's brigade withdrew from alongside the Burnt Hickory Road. There was the typical chaos of packing quickly and quietly. In the process Captain Robert Harris, commander of Company A, Fifty-seventh Georgia, realized that he had left behind the company's ink supply, a rare commodity. He asked for a volunteer to slip back and recover the ink. Sergeant Sidney Williams stepped forward and disappeared into the night. Soon a shot rang out and they heard a scream. Fifteen-year-old William Bibb stole back through the woods and returned carrying Williams. He had been shot in the leg, a wound that resulted in amputation. It was a high price to pay for ink.[7]

As Mercer's brigade marched along, the men found that they were stiff and winded from being confined to trenches for many days. Lacking sleep, they fought to put one foot in front of the other. It was a night that Colonel Olmstead never forgot.

Charles Olmstead had grown up in Savannah. In 1852, when he was fifteen, he was sent to the Georgia Military Institute in the small north Georgia community of Marietta. Located three miles from Kennesaw Mountain, this military college served as young Olmstead's home for four years and became one of the greatest influences on his life.[8] As a senior, Olmstead rose to become the adjutant of the corps. Later he wrote, "It is not possible for me to overestimate the benefits I derived from the four years of training at the Military Institute. . . . I was taught how to yield implicit obedience to rightful authority and how to accept responsibility if it were placed upon me, how to command as well as to obey."[9]

On the gloomy night that Mercer's brigade retreated with Johnston's army from their Kennesaw Mountain lines, they marched directly across the campus of the Georgia Military Institute. Olmstead recalled the poignancy of the moment:

> The night was dark and the little country road narrow, so progress was exceedingly slow. . . . I sat on my horse taking little "cat naps", indifferent to surroundings, when suddenly the sense of being in a familiar spot aroused me; we were marching up the rear of the hill on which the old Georgia Military Institute was located. It was the school in which I had been educated and in which I had spent four happy years.
>
> Many had been my dreams of the future while there but never had there been forecast of such an event as marching with an army corps at midnight through this beloved spot. Every inch of its soil every brick of its buildings was dear to me and it saddened my soul to believe that its destruction was near. It had furnished too many officers to the Confederate Army to be spared and Sherman ordered it to be burned on the following day.

Perhaps the most haunting aspect of the surrealistic visit was Olmstead's realization of the tragic deaths of many of his classmates:

> You may be sure that memory was busy and that my mind was full of the associations so strangely awakened. My dearest friend at the Institute had been John Patton of the Class of 1857. . . . He had been the best man at my

wedding, and I had looked forward to the enjoyment of his friendship while my life lasted. And now riding there in the dark there came, with a bitter pang, the thought that for nearly two years he had slept in a soldiers grave. He was killed in the Battle of South Mountain in Lee's invasion of Maryland in 1862.

There were recollections too of many of the old Cadet Corps who had laid down their lives for the South, (in almost every battle of the War some of them had perished,) and their faces haunted me as I rode through the familiar grounds.[10]

It took seven hours to cover four miles, and by 6 A.M. on July 3 Mercer's brigade had filed into Smyrna Camp Ground, a brush arbor Methodist revival center. Johnston's line was six miles south of Marietta, and it now stretched along a six-mile front from Nickajack Creek on the left to Rottenwood Creek on the right. The Chattahoochee River was only a few miles to the rear.

At Smyrna Camp Ground Walker's division held a well-fortified and commanding position that was threatened only by a small hill two hundred yards in front of Mercer's brigade. General Hardee was concerned about the hill, believing that it could become a crucial site for a Union artillery battery. Hardee ordered Walker to take the hill, and Walker then rode down the line to give the order to Mercer.

General Mercer's age and the stress of command were beginning to show. On this day he was ill and had given command of the brigade to Colonel Olmstead. Olmstead later wrote that he strongly objected to Hardee's order to occupy the exposed hill:

> During the day General Walker . . . ordered me to send a Regiment out to seize and hold the hill, saying that General Hardee feared the enemy would take it for an artillery position. Of course there was no such thing as demurring but I took the liberty of pointing out to General Walker that any troops sent out there would be isolated and, moreover that should the enemy put a battery upon the hill he could not use it since the summit was within range of the musketry fire of our main line. The General said he was aware of these facts but that the orders to him were imperative and must be obeyed.[11]

Fuming, Olmstead sent eighty men of the First Volunteers and 130 men of the Fifty-seventh Georgia out to occupy the hill, including Company E, the Fort Valley Infantry. That afternoon Captain George Mercer inspected the site and wrote, "[I] found it too weak to resist shell."[12] As Olmstead had predicted, calamity struck a few hours later when Sherman caught up with Johnston. Olmstead wrote:

> [I ordered them out] with full realization that the duty before [them] was perilous in the extreme and believing, in spite of Division and Corps Commanders that it was a needless risk. The Regiment had scarcely reached

its post and begun to fortify when a heavy artillery fire was opened upon it and in a very few minutes a number of the men were killed and wounded.

Then there was an abundance of the enemys skirmish lines upon either flank and to avoid being cut off and surrounded there was nothing for the Regiment to do save to retire to the main line. When this was done the enemy rushed a battery to the top of the hill as had been anticipated, but we opened upon the gunners at once with rifle fire and drove them rapidly away. They left the guns standing without a man near them and there they remained harmless and silent all the rest of the day and were removed under the cover of the night.

My judgment in the premises had been justified but that did not bring back the lives that were lost nor heal the grievous wounds that had been inflicted. How many instances of this kind there must have been during these long four years of war; how many lives recklessly squandered through insufficient consideration before the giving of orders.[13]

One private who agreed with Olmstead was Robert Braswell. In the confusion of the Union shelling of the hill and the infantry attacks by skirmishers, Braswell was separated from Seaborn Mims. Now, as he frantically searched the faces of the men of the Fifty-seventh Georgia as they crawled back over the Confederate earthworks, he soon realized that Mims had not returned. No one remembered his being wounded. He had simply disappeared. Shattered and weeping, Braswell prayed that his uncle had been captured—captured and not killed.[14]

When the final cost of the fiasco was tallied, 40 men from Mercer's brigade had been killed, wounded, or captured: 23 from the First Volunteers and 17 from the Fifty-seventh. Many a soldier cursed Hardee and Walker.[15]

July 4, 1864, dawned and both sides reflected on the national day of independence. Sherman was well aware that the presidential election was only a few months away. Grant was making little progress against Lee in Virginia. Now the outcome of the election might depend on Sherman's ability to capture Atlanta quickly. If the general was stalled outside Atlanta, embroiled in a siege when November rolled around, Lincoln probably would be thrown out of office, and the new administration would hammer out a negotiated peace. Haunted by such thoughts, Sherman's adrenaline surged and his rapid flanking instincts were revived.

The men of the Fifty-seventh Georgia would not have forgotten that one year ago they had marched out of the Vicksburg lines, stacked their rifles, and surrendered their regimental flag. Now they faced the same armies, but the stakes were much higher, the war closer to home, and their future bleak. Fighting fear and fatigue, most of these veterans felt their resolve grow.

Johnston correctly detected that Sherman would once more flank his Smyrna Camp Ground lines. Johnston again moved first and on July 5 retreated to his impregnable lines on the northern banks of the Chattahoochee.

As Walker's division filed into Johnston's river line, the men took up a position near Bolton Station, defending the center of the six-mile front. The fortifications that they occupied were stronger than any that they had seen before. Log-enforced earthworks formed wedge-shaped bastions twelve feet thick and spaced at eighty-yard intervals. The earthworks were connected by log stockades ten to fifteen feet high. Powerful siege cannons, brought up from Mobile, Alabama, could pound an attacking army into the ground. Even a bulldog like Sherman would not attack this line. He had no choice but to flank Johnston one more time and this he did.

Reflecting the Southern desire for Sherman to engage the Rebs in a frontal assault, Lieutenant Hamilton Branch, twenty-one, of the Fifty-fourth Georgia wrote, "If Sherman would only charge Johnston, where he now is, the Yankee army of Tennessee would only exist in name, but Old Joe will have to attack him I am afraid. Afraid because we will lose so many of our precious men's lives doing it. We are all quite well and in good spirits, although we do want this falling back to stop."[16]

Branch was right. Sherman would have no trouble forcing the Confederates to come out and fight. And Southerners from Jefferson Davis to the lowliest private did "want this falling back to stop." As Thiot succinctly stated to his wife, Anna, "Our men are buoyant and long for the fight, that we may have it over *and go home.*"[17]

As he viewed the Confederate defensive position on the Chattahoochee, Sherman exclaimed that they are "one of the strongest pieces of field fortification I ever saw."[18] Having finally learned his lesson at Kennesaw, Sherman declined to attack. Instead, he quietly slipped Major General Schofield's smaller Army of the Ohio, accompanied by a Union cavalry division under Brigadier General Kenner Garrard, upstream to find a crossing to use to flank Johnston.

Schofield found a lightly defended ford on July 8. Years later Sherman reflected on this critical moment with great glee: "Schofield effected his crossing at Soap's Creek very handsomely on the 9th, capturing the small guard that was watching the crossing. By night he was on the high ground beyond, strongly entrenched, with two good pontoon-bridges finished, and was prepared, if necessary, for an assault by the whole Confederate army. . . . I have always thought Johnston neglected his opportunity there, for he had lain comparatively idle while we got control of both banks of the river above him."[19]

Without losing a man, Sherman was able to render the massive Confederate defensive works untenable by placing a firm Union bridgehead at Johnston's rear. Sherman was correct in stating that if Johnston made a major blunder in the north Georgia campaign, he did so on the banks of the Chattahoochee.

On the night of July 9 Johnston's Army of Tennessee retreated to the south bank of the Chattahoochee on pontoon bridges, fully protected by the earthworks. As Mercer's brigade filed past him, Colonel Olmstead engaged an officer in conversation:

> I observed Capt. Wallace Howard of the 63rd Ga. watching the crossing of the troops and gazing with melancholy earnestness upon the hills on the opposite side. I made some remark to him about our nearing the point, Atlanta, where the great battle must be fought. "I don't know", he replied, "I don't like giving up so much territory, it looks to me like the beginning of the end and as though we were going right straight down to the Gulf of Mexico." . . .
> Hearing his pessimistic talk gave me the first real doubts that had ever entered my mind as to the ultimate success of the Southern Cause. I reflected however that his home was in the country occupied by the enemy—a fact that would naturally explain his low spirits, and the thought cheered me, but he was not very far from the truth.[20]

After the crossing, the men took up the pontoon bridges and burned the trestle bridge and railroad bridge. While the bulk of the army fell back to form a defensive line on the northern perimeter of Atlanta near Peachtree Creek, Mercer's brigade and five other brigades were left on the south bank of the river as an outpost.[21]

As the Confederates withdrew, Sherman settled on a plan to take Atlanta. He had revealed his hand in a dispatch of July 6 to General Halleck in Washington: "We shall cross [the Chattahoochee] in due time, and, instead of attacking Atlanta direct, or any of its forts, I propose to make a circuit, destroying all its railroads."[22]

As the Confederates withdrew into the Atlanta line to face a possible siege, Sherman knew that the jugular of the Army of Tennessee was the railroad supply line. Accordingly, he sent Major General Lovell H. Rousseau's cavalry through Alabama to destroy the direct rail line between Montgomery and Atlanta. He dispatched Major General George Stoneman's cavalry forty miles southwest of Atlanta to Newnan to destroy the Atlanta and West Point Railroad. McPherson's Army of the Tennessee then swung northeast around the outskirts of Atlanta to Stone Mountain and Decatur to cut the rail line between Atlanta, Augusta, and Richmond, also blocking Johnston's line of retreat to the east. Only the southern rail line to Macon—the Macon and Western—remained open to the Confederates. Only this lifeline connected them to Savannah and to Richmond.

July 10–17, 1864, were quiet days as Sherman maneuvered his army. Mercer's brigade—and much of Walker's division—remained on the south banks of the Chattahoochee. Hamilton Branch of the Fifty-fourth Georgia described the scene in a letter to his mother:

We are now in bivouac about 400 yards from the river and the enemy are in plain view on the other side. . . . We have been left here as rear guard to keep them from crossing for awhile. Our brigade is here and Polks and another. It has been raining for the last hour or two. Much to our surprise the enemy have not planted their batterys opposite to us, nor have they fired a shell at us yet. . . .

We are in pits about ten yards from the river. This morning we made an agreement with the enemy not to fire on one another, and so our boys have been amusing themselves all day talking with the enemy. The troops immediately opposed to us belong to the 20th Army Corps, Genl. Hooker, and are detachments from the 123 NY, 5th Conn, & 141 NY & 46 Penn which compose Genl. Knights Brigade. The Yanks are very anxious to trade for tobacco. They say that they will give Indian rubber cloths, knifes, coffee or anything for tobacco.[23]

It did not take long for both Sherman and Johnston to put a stop to such friendly exchanges between armies. Colonel Olmstead, ordered to see that Johnston's instructions were carried out, recorded an early morning moment:

I was detailed as division officer of the day with instructions to see to the maintenance of this order. The duty involved a constant oversight of a long section of the river bank; a miserable, cold Northeast rain storm set in during the night and the early mornings found me soaking wet, chilled to the bone and fagged out from want of sleep, just the conditions to make a man willing to give his head for a cup of coffee, (a stimulant that we knew nothing of in our Army.)

Looking across the river I saw two Yankee soldiers walking along with a pole, stretching from the shoulders of one to those of the other from which was suspended a smoking caldron of hot coffee. They were on their way to give a little mornings refreshment to their line of pickets. I could almost smell the delightful aroma, and a green eyed envy took possession of my soul. . . . It would have been a great relief to put a bullet through that caldron, though I have often thought how mean it was to harbor such a feeling. None of us know however how mean we can be until an occasion arises for the development of the "Old Adam" in us.[24]

Mercer's brigade guarded the Chattahoochee River for eight days of relative calm and much-needed rest. But while the troops relaxed, Jefferson Davis and Joseph Johnston were engaged in a feud that would shape the future of the Army of Tennessee.

21

Hood Has Gone Up Like a Rocket

General Johnston was a private person, seldom sharing his personal thoughts or strategic plans, even with his most trusted corps commanders. This totally military man had about him an air of reserve and mystery. Such reticence was magnified with people Johnston did not like or trust. Unfortunately, his supreme commander, Jefferson Davis, was one of those people. And Davis wanted—and needed—to know what was going on in Georgia.

When Johnston fell back across the Chattahoochee, Davis yearned to immediately relieve the general of his command. Yet Davis could not turn to anyone else who would inspire confidence based on military experience. More important, a moment of acute crisis was the worst time to change command. Davis faced a complex dilemma.

He unwisely dispatched Braxton Bragg to investigate matters in Atlanta and report back. He could have found no more biased an individual. Relieved of command of the Army of Tennessee only six months before and replaced by Johnston, Bragg neither liked Johnston nor desired for him to succeed.

To deepen the intrigue, Johnston's corps commander John Bell Hood had breached military protocol by carrying on a private correspondence with Davis, a personal friend. In his letters Hood spoke harshly of Johnston, especially criticizing his reluctance to wage offensive war. Hood implied that a more aggressive general—meaning himself—could quickly turn the tables on Sherman in Georgia. Now Hood and Bragg conspired in Atlanta to secure a change of command.[1]

Davis decided to give Johnston one last chance. If Johnston would only reveal to Davis his battle plans and take him into his confidence, Davis would stick with Old Joe. Accordingly, on July 16 Davis sent Johnston a very clear and direct message: "A telegram from Atlanta of yesterday announces that the enemy is extending entrenchments from river toward railroad to Augusta. I wish to hear from you as to present situation, and your plan of operations so specifically as will enable me to anticipate events."[2]

Johnston could read between the lines. He had not only been asked for specific battle plans, he had been issued an ultimatum. However, Johnston's response to Davis was as vague and noncommittal as ever: "Your dispatch of today received. . . . As the enemy had double our number, we must be on the defensive. My plan of operations must, therefore, depend on that of the enemy. It is mainly to watch for an opportunity to fight to advantage."[3]

Johnston's evasive response was the last straw. It was vague and it was defiant. Davis made the hard decision to replace Johnston. But with whom?

Davis had two options, Hardee and Hood. Although Hardee was the army's senior lieutenant general and unquestionably capable, he had refused an opportunity to command the Army of Tennessee six months earlier when Bragg had been relieved. Davis now doubted Hardee's desire to lead amid severe crisis.[4]

Hood, on the other hand, spoke with great self-confidence that bordered on unbridled ambition. He was also erratic and inexperienced. Davis turned to Robert E. Lee for advice. Lee responded by telegram: "Hood is a bold fighter. I am doubtful as to the other qualities necessary. . . . [He is] very industrious on the battlefield, careless off, & I have had no opportunity of judging his action, when the whole responsibility rested upon him. I have a very high opinion of his gallantry, earnestness & zeal. Genl Hardee has more experience in managing an army."[5]

Clearly, Lee favored Hardee. However, goaded by Bragg, Davis gambled on Hood. On the evening of July 17 Davis instructed General Samuel Cooper, adjutant of the Confederate army, to send a telegram to Johnston, relieving him of command and replacing him with Hood.[6]

Mercer's brigade heard the news early on the morning of July 18. At the time the brigade was being relieved from outpost duty on the Chattahoochee by one of Frank Cheatham's brigades and was preparing to move into the defensive perimeter along Peachtree Creek. Mercer's brigade and Walker's entire division—indeed, the whole Army of Tennessee—reacted with shock, anger, and grief.

Writing to his mother a day later, Lieutenant Hamilton Branch of the Fifty-fourth Georgia expressed his disgust:

> We learned yesterday to our great surprise and sorrow that our beloved gallant commander had been relieved from the command of this army. I never have seen or heard of an army so wrapped up in a commander as this army proved itself to be on yesterday. When it was announced everyone seemed to feel as if they had lost their best friend and the general remark was, well this army is lost, and everyone seemed to be whipped.
>
> As for myself I have never felt so downhearted in my life as I did on yesterday, and if we had not have been ordered off, I know that I could not have helped from crying. Genl Johnston had the love and confidence of every man in his army, and not one doubted but that he would annihilate Sherman before he had finished the campaign.
>
> Genl. Hood the present commander of this army is a fighting man and no doubt a fine officer and under him we will gain the victory, but he is not Genl Johnston.[7]

General Walker also expressed his personal feelings in a letter to his wife, providing keen insight into the process of Hood's elevation to command:

> I was handed early this morning before I got out of blanket (I won't say bed) an order of Genl. Johnston turning over the command of the army to Lt. Genl. Hood. I thought when I saw Bragg come that he had come to relieve him but I knew he had something on hand.
>
> I have feared this all along. Now that it is all over, I tell you . . . that I never have approved of our falling back but have been in favor of a fight and I have felt satisfied in my own mind that if Johnston fell back behind the Chattahoochee he would be relieved and when I saw Bragg I jumped at the conclusion that he had come to relieve him.

Then, in a moment of tenderness, Walker allowed his wife to know his true fondness for Johnston and her husband's fears for the future:

> Johnston and I have always been friends. For over a quarter of a century we have known each other. . . . I admire him and am fond of him and dislike exceedingly to see him leave us.
>
> Hood has "gone up like a rocket." It is to be hoped . . . that "he will not come down like the stick" [the stick attached to a sky rocket]. He is brave. Whether he has the capacity to command armies (for it requires a high order of talent) time will develop. I will express no opinion.
>
> A fight now is obliged to come off for if Johnston has been relieved for falling back (as I take it for granted he was), it is as much as to say to Hood, don't you try the same game.[8]

In 1912, when Colonel Olmstead was seventy-five, he looked back on this pivotal moment in the life of the Army of Tennessee and summarized the dominant view of the Confederate soldier:

> The removal of Genl. Johnston at the crisis of the Campaign was one of the most lamentable events of the entire war. Its effect upon the morale of the Army was immediately disastrous; it took the heart out of the men for he was their idol and they believed in him in spite of the long retreat from Dalton to Atlanta. They knew that Sherman's Army was much larger than our own and that the falling back had been unavoidable. . . . But they had seen every assault of Sherman's repulsed with bloody loss and realized that every mile of advance brought him that much farther from his base and would add to his discomfiture in the event of defeat. . . . They were prepared to follow him to the death and I believe to this day that but for his removal Atlanta would not have fallen.[9]

Olmstead also reflected on the complex relationship between Johnston, Davis, and Hood:

The causes, or rather, the *cause* that led to this most unhappy action was a difference between President Davis and General Johnston that might almost be considered a personal enmity; the two men were both high spirited, quick tempered and stubborn in holding to their own views, while neither understood the other nor gave him credit for the virtues and high qualities that he really possessed. Gen Johnston had a grievance from the beginning of the war in relation to his rank in the Confederate Army. . . . It so embittered him as entirely to prevent his giving to Mr. Davis the frank confidence that always existed between the latter and Genl Lee. There was probably fault on both sides and it is difficult now to say who was most to blame though it is quite sure that had friendly good will been present between them, no distrust and suspicion in one, nor haughty reserve in the other, the battles around Atlanta would not have been fought under the leadership of General Hood. Of General Johnstons abilities as a military man there was but one opinion in the Confederacy, and time has not altered the judgement of his contemporaries. In every thing save, *courage,* where they stood as equals, he was head and shoulders above Genl Hood upon whom his mantle was about to fall.[10]

Sherman and his senior officers were delighted by Davis's decision. Howard, Schofield, and McPherson had been classmates of Hood's at West Point, where Hood had finished forty-fourth in a class of fifty-two. Indeed, he might not have graduated, if his roommate, Schofield, had not tutored him in mathematics. Though Hood had a reputation for bravery, his classmates knew him to be less than brilliant.

Hood was also reckless and at times foolhardy. At West Point he had accumulated 196 demerits when two hundred demerits resulted in expulsion from the academy. He was impetuous and loved nothing more than a fight; and he was passionate and burning with ambition.

Sherman first heard the news of Hood's elevation to command from Schofield, who had found an Atlanta newspaper. Handing Sherman the paper, Sherman hurriedly read the headline and asked, "Schofield, do you know Hood? What sort of fellow is he?"

"Yes, I know him well," Schofield replied, "and I will tell you the sort of man he is. He'll hit you like hell before you know it."[11]

Later, in recounting this exchange, Sherman wrote, "I inferred that the change of commanders meant 'fight.' . . . This was just what we wanted, viz., to fight in open ground, on any thing like equal terms, instead of being forced to run up against prepared entrenchments."[12]

As the men of Walker's division broke camp on July 18 and made their way toward the Confederate lines on Peachtree Creek, their route took them directly past Johnston's headquarters at the Niles house. Colonel James C. Nisbet of the Sixty-sixth Georgia remembered the moment: "We passed his headquarters. He stood with head uncovered. We lifted our hats. There was no cheering! We simply passed silently, with heads uncovered. Some of the officers broke ranks and grasped his hand, as the tears poured down their cheeks."[13]

As Walker's division assembled along Peachtree Creek, the reunited Braswell brothers engaged in tense conversation, savoring the moments of being together. William, Samuel, and Robert realized that they were developing the hardened eyes of much older men. Their laughter was mostly hollow, only a diversion from a life that had lost joy and promise. The present moment was urgent and grim. Sherman was a hundred miles from their mother's front door in Fort Valley. They knew that the Union advance must be stopped now. With Hood in command everyone sensed that a decisive battle was imminent.

When Sherman aligned his troops around the outskirts of Atlanta, Hood saw his chance. There is strong evidence that Johnston had already perceived the same opportunity and had put the battle plan in motion before he was relieved of command. If so, Hood recognized the plan's merit and pressed on.[14]

What the Confederate command discovered was that Sherman, in seeking to simultaneously sever all railroads leading into Atlanta, had momentarily divided his army. McPherson's Army of the Tennessee and Schofield's Army of the Ohio had been sent northeast, near the outlying village of Decatur, to destroy the railroad lines leading to Augusta. At the same time Brigadier General George Thomas's large Army of the Cumberland was approaching from the north and would soon be crossing Peachtree Creek. For a brief period a two-mile gap would separate Thomas from McPherson and Schofield. Not since Cassville had the Confederates had such an opportunity to divide the Union forces and confront one Union army at a time.

Though the opportunity was great, the Confederate command structure was in shambles. Hood had never commanded an entire army and now would lead the Army of Tennessee into battle within forty-eight hours of assuming command. Of his three corps commanders, only Hardee had previously commanded a corps, and he was seething, angry that Johnston had been removed from command. But Hardee was also incensed that he had been passed over for command of the Army of Tennessee by a younger, less experienced, officer.

Only the day before Alexander Stewart had been given permanent command of Polk's corps and Frank Cheatham had been assigned to Hood's corps. Now these two officers—tried and proved at division level—must be tested at corps level. The Confederate senior command structure had not a single steady, stable, proven presence. The result would soon show.

By July 19 Hood had decided to attack Thomas's Army of the Cumberland. Yet he delayed calling a council of war until early on the morning of July 20, the very day of the attack.[15] This gave his senior officers little time to consider their assignments and required that the attack be late in the day, giving Thomas critical extra hours to move across Peachtree Creek and entrench.

Hood's plan called for seven Confederate divisions to face seven Union divisions on an uneven three-mile front roughly parallel to Peachtree Creek. Hood hoped that the Union forces would still be en route and not dug in. Hardee's corps, comprising four Confederate divisions, would be on the right and Stewart's corps, comprising three divisions, would be on the left. Cheatham's corps would not attack Thomas but would face east to block McPherson and Schofield, should they attempt to reinforce Thomas by rapid march from Decatur.

Facing Peachtree Creek, Hardee chose to arrange his battle line with William Bate's division on the right, William Walker's division in the middle, and George Maney's division on the left, connecting with Stewart's corps. Cleburne's division was kept in reserve. General Walker, in turn, aligned his division front by placing Mercer's brigade on the right, Clement Stevens's brigade in the middle, and States Rights Gist's brigade on the left.

As Robert Braswell took his place with the Fifty-seventh Georgia, he was able to look to his left and see the regimental flag of his brothers' First Confederate Georgia, waving among Stevens's brigade, which was adjacent to his. It seemed strange and dangerous to be going into battle so close to his brothers. When William and Samuel were at a distance, they were not in his thoughts. But now that they were only a few hundred yards apart, Robert was filled with fear for their safety and a dark sense of foreboding.

Hardee's and Stewart's troops were in line by 1 P.M., the jump-off time. But things immediately began to fall apart. To the east Union troops under McPherson and Schofield were moving closer to Atlanta, requiring Cheatham's corps to move farther to the right to block them. For two hours the entire Confederate line lurched to the right, seeking cohesion with Cheatham's troops and giving Union troops time to dig in on the south side of Peachtree Creek.

Shortly before 3 P.M. the Confederate line was finally in place. Hardee was approximately one mile from his original position, and his line now extended beyond Peachtree Road. According to Hood's battle plan, Hardee's corps was to initiate the Confederate assault, followed by Stewart's corps. However, before Hardee's corps could advance, a portion of Stewart's corps shrieked the Rebel yell and prematurely bolted forward with colors flying. Hood's plan for a carefully coordinated attack fell into disarray.

By the time Hardee's division advanced, it was almost 4 P.M. Nothing had gone as planned. Hood, confined by his injuries to his headquarters, was not present to make crucial decisions, and a furious Hardee had not attempted to stay in communication with Hood. The Confederate charge was bedlam.

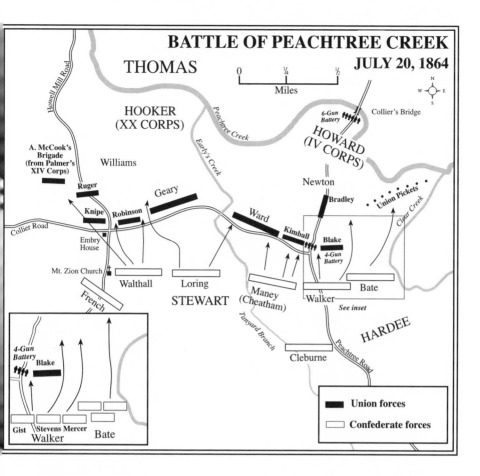

BATTLE OF PEACHTREE CREEK
THOMAS
JULY 20, 1864

HOOKER
(XX CORPS)

A. McCook's
Brigade
(from Palmer's
XIV Corps)

Williams

Ruger

Geary

Knipe   Robinson

Collier Road

Embry
House

Mt. Zion Church

Walthall   Loring

STEWART

French

Peachtree Creek

Early's Creek

6-Gun
Battery

Collier's Bridge

HOWARD
(IV CORPS)

Newton

Bradley

Union Pickets

Clear Creek

Ward

Kimball

Blake
4-Gun
Battery

Maney
(Cheatham)

Walker

Bate

See inset

Tanyard Branch

Cleburne

Peachtree Road

HARDEE

4-Gun
Battery
Blake

Gist   Stevens Mercer
Walker   Bate

Union forces

Confederate forces

0   ¼   ½
Miles

Yet, despite Confederate command weakness, the Union forces were caught
by surprise.

Because of the Confederate realignment to the right, most of Mercer's brigade charged into a morass of wooded, vine-entangled swamp, only to find no
Union troops in front of them. They had unknowingly flanked the left end of
the Union line.[16] Colonel Charles Olmstead described the confusion: "Our own
Division advanced over very difficult ground, first through a thick wood, then
across a boggy valley through which a small water course meandered tortuously.
It turned and twisted so much that we had to wade it two or three times in
pressing forward. Indeed we never got fairly into action as the attack had failed
in other parts of the field and the Division was withdrawn before it reached a
point of close touch with the enemy."[17]

However, notes made by Lieutenant Hamilton Branch of the Fifty-fourth
Georgia confirm that another segment of Mercer's brigade did make solid and

violent contact with the Yankee line as it blended into the advance of Stevens's brigade. Branch wrote, "We then found that a line of battle from our division, composed of Steven's *and a part of Mercer's brigade* had already advanced and was charging the enemy."[18]

The confusion of the Confederate charge fragmented Mercer's brigade. Most of the brigade saw little combat that afternoon. However, some of Mercer's troops—including the Fifty-seventh Georgia—shared in the intense fighting encountered by Stevens's brigade.[19]

Stevens's brigade, Gist's brigade, and a portion of Mercer's brigade charged into a hornet's nest. They collided with the troops of John Newton's division of the Fourth Corps who had thrown up temporary earthworks. The First Georgia Confederate and the Sixty-sixth Georgia were in the middle of Stevens's assault against the dug-in Yanks. The colonel of the Sixty-sixth Georgia, James Cooper Nisbet, described the fierce fighting:

> We were told that the enemy had just crossed Peachtree Creek that morning and were unfortified. My regiment formed into line of battle on the left of the Brigade with my left resting on the Peachtree Road.
>
> We advanced, and drove in the enemy's skirmishers. . . . My regiment and that on my right, the 1st Georgia Confederate Infantry, captured the works in our front. But we were not supported. The enemy on my left, not being assaulted, continued to enfilade [rake] my line. Seeing fresh troops being rushed up against us, I was certain we could not hold the position. . . . Our brigade commander, General Stevens, rode in and ordered me to fall back and was killed as he gave the order. I ordered the regiment to fall back. . . .
>
> Never was I under a heavier fire than there—for a brief time. I thought I would certainly see my "Valhalla" that day. I lost one-fourth of all my officers and men engaged. The firing from both the front and flank was terrific. We abandoned the works and fell back a short distance, as ordered.[20]

Two of the dead abandoned on the field by the First Georgia Confederate were William and Samuel Braswell. There is no record of how they died, whether they died together, or where their bodies were buried. They simply vanished in the midst of fire and smoke, never to be seen again. They fell with more than one-third of the men of the First Georgia Confederate Regiment.[21]

The story was the same up and down the Confederate lines. Men in blue and gray fought with desperate will and ferocity. But the Confederates never presented a unified and coordinated front. While George Thomas was in the thick of combat, making crucial, on-the-scene decisions, John Bell Hood was shackled by his crippling wounds in Stewart's headquarters, removed from the immediacy of command. The result was Confederate defeat.

Hood's first experience at commanding the Army of Tennessee in battle was a disaster. Rather than taking responsibility, he blamed Hardee, and Hardee blamed Hood. But the blame game made little difference. Confederate casualties totaled twenty-five hundred to the Union's nineteen hundred.[22] Young Southern soldiers like William and Samuel Braswell had given their lives in a battle that had barely fazed the Union advance.

22

The Battle of Atlanta

As the sun sank below the tree line, an exhausted Robert Braswell clambered up the overgrown banks of Peachtree Creek and slipped back into the safety of the Confederate lines. For more than three hours he had floundered through dense woods without being struck by Yankee fire. At least sixteen other men in the Fifty-seventh Georgia were not so lucky. Now tired, wet, and muddy, Braswell probably felt nothing more than relief at surviving one more battle.

When his temples quit pounding and adrenaline receded, Robert naturally grew anxious about his two brothers in Stevens's brigade. Word was already buzzing through the lines that General Stevens had been killed—shot through the head while crawling from his dead horse—and that the Sixty-sixth Georgia and First Georgia Confederate had caught hell. These moments of dusk probably were when Robert Braswell slipped through the bedlam and smoke of battle to locate Stevens's brigade and find William and Samuel.

How Robert Braswell received the news that his brothers were dead is lost in that dark night of history. However, that William's and Samuel's violent deaths seared and scarred his soul forever is cold fact. July 20, 1864, would now be the day from which this seventeen-year-old man would forever measure time—the "before and after" event of his life.

Nor do we know how Braswell spent those first painful hours. Who consoled him and how he coped with his anguish have long been forgotten. But the dawn of July 21 mercifully wrenched Robert and hundreds of others out of their grief and into the frenzied activity of yet one more retreat. The early morning gloom found Hardee's and Stewart's corps moving away from Peachtree Creek and into the final defensive line tightly encircling Atlanta.

Once Mercer's brigade entered the Atlanta defenses, Second Lieutenant William Reed of the Sixty-third Georgia dropped down to rest. He was thinking of his sister, Bessie, who was living forty miles away in the small town of Madison, and he found a rare piece of paper and a pencil stub. Bessie was engaged to be married to Captain Briggs Napier, who was also fighting in Hardee's corps. In his letter William recounted a harrowing moment that he had experienced the night before, after the disaster at Peachtree Creek.

Mercer's brigade had not yet pulled back from the creek and was facing Thomas's troops through the darkness. Reed was assigned to picket duty and was keeping his head low, respectful of the continual sniper fire. That very afternoon a spent minié ball had ricocheted off his leg, leaving him badly bruised. In the dark night Reed heard a wounded soldier in front calling for help. Reed wrote, "I not knowing who it was but for the sake of humanity had one of the litter bearers of our brigade to bear him off the field. I never thought anymore of it; wounded men were all too common then."

Later, after he was relieved on the picket line, Reed passed by the wounded soldier whom he had rescued. The poor man had just had his leg amputated. Peering down into his face by lantern light, Reed suddenly recognized his sister's fiancé, Captain Napier. Aghast, he knelt down, placed Napier's head against his chest, and "brushed the hair off his forehead and made him as comfortable as possible."

Then, concluding, Reed admonished his sister, "The Captain though now with one leg is worth a dozen two legged ones and you must answer his letter without fail to cheer him up as much as possible. . . . Briggs acted like a man [and] stood up to his post with credit."

Suddenly seized by pangs of worry for his family, Reed finished his letter: "I can not realize that we are cut off from home though it troubles me more than anything else in the world. Oh Sister were this in Madison I should be miserable. Such may be but do not remain in the lines if it can be avoided. Hourly in danger I can stand to be, but for my very own loved ones to be in similar danger, I could not stand it."[1]

The bone-weary Georgians of Mercer's brigade were now energized by desperation. If Sherman were to capture Atlanta, he would soon be marching through their own hometowns, burning their houses, plundering their farms, and endangering their families.

Throughout July 21 Hood's battered Army of Tennessee continued its retreat into Atlanta. As it did, Cleburne's infantry brigade and Wheeler's cavalry were locked in one of the fiercest struggles of the Atlanta campaign, slowing Schofield's and McPherson's advance eastward from Decatur to Atlanta. Dug in on the summit of a mound called Bald Hill, Cleburne and Wheeler fiercely repelled wave after wave of Yankee assaults, often in hand-to-hand combat, giving Hood time to position his army inside the Atlanta defenses.[2]

By that night the Army of Tennessee had completed its retreat into Atlanta. Remaining civilians were fleeing the city. Now the threat was that they would repeat Vicksburg: a large Rebel army surrounded and besieged by a superior Union force with little hope that reinforcements would arrive to aid the Confederates.

Hood had other plans, however. Unlike John Pemberton, he refused to be surrounded or to allow Sherman to consolidate his forces. Hood determined that he would boldly return to the offensive and counterattack Sherman. He set his plan into motion that very night.

Hood still held one trump card: Sherman's blue horde remained a divided army. George Thomas, fearing a renewed attack, had spent July 21 digging in and reinforcing his lines along Peachtree Creek to the northwest. To the east McPherson and Schofield had bloodied their heads while throwing Cleburne's Rebs off Bald Hill. As a result Sherman's two wings still were separated. If Hood hurried, he could smash one wing and then regroup to take on the other.

Though a formidable fighter, Thomas always moved slowly and with deliberation. Hood gambled that he might still have time to crush McPherson and Schofield before "Old Slow Trot" Thomas could advance the Army of the Cumberland to their rescue. In addition, Wheeler's scouts had discovered that McPherson's left flank was exposed and unprotected. Sherman had recklessly dispatched the cavalry to destroy the railroad between Atlanta and Augusta when it should have been protecting McPherson's flank. If Hood could strike McPherson's exposed flank with sufficient force and surprise, McPherson's entire line might collapse like a row of dominoes.

But attacking McPherson's left flank would require a superhuman effort by Hood's troops. Hood's assault force, already physically and emotionally exhausted, would have to endure a fifteen-mile forced march throughout the night of July 21 and smash into McPherson's targeted flank at first dawn of July 22. It was a gamble but it was Hood's best option. The cornered young general gripped his crutch and went for broke.

Hood tapped Hardee's corps—his largest corps with the most experienced leadership—to undertake the difficult journey. Stewart's shattered corps would remain behind to pin down Thomas. Cheatham's corps would face the center of McPherson's line and await Hardee to roll up the Union's left flank. Once Hardee began the rout of the Army of the Tennessee from the southeast, Cheatham would surge forward and smash into the blue line from the west, crushing them in a pincer movement. It was a brilliant scheme on paper and smacked of Lee's tactics at Chancellorsville.

Hardee's corps, positioned at what today is the corner of Peachtree and Spring streets, was drenched by a hard rain as the sun set. Though the rain eased the heat, steam rose from the wet ground and the humidity grew thicker as the corps prepared to march.

Bate's and Walker's divisions moved out first, at 8 P.M., and advanced down Peachtree Street through Atlanta, heading east toward the McDonough Road. Entering Five Points in the heart of Atlanta, they found much drunken looting taking place in the glare of burning buildings. With Union shells whistling overhead and vandals shattering store windows, a feeling of lawlessness and violence pervaded the city.

Still, the soldiers retained their sense of humor. Colonel James Cooper Nisbet of the Sixty-sixth Georgia remembered that as his troops moved through Five Points, the intensity of the Yankee shelling increased. As Nisbet and his men paused for a quick rest, he heard a loud squawking and looked up to see a large colorful parrot perched high in a tree, freed from his cage by a fleeing owner. Nisbet also noticed a country bumpkin from north Georgia walking under the tree:

> We were resting, the men lying about on the streets and sidewalks. One of the men, a tall, lanky "rube", was stalking up and down the sidewalk, oblivious to bursting shells, eating hard-tack. A voice from one of the trees said: " Give poor Polly a cracker!" The country youth stopped, and looked around. Again, "Give poor Polly a cracker," came from the tree. Finally he spied the parrot and said: "Gee Whilkens, boys, damned if the world hain't coming to an end! Even the birds are talking and begging for bread." Looking up he addressed the parrot: "Sure you are a mighty smart bird, and I'm sorry for you, but you go to hell! This is the first cracker I've seen for two days!"[3]

Bate's and Walker's divisions continued down Peachtree Street to where the state capitol sits today, then exited the city via the McDonough Road.[4] By dawn only Bate and Walker of Hardee's corps had reached the staging ground at Widow Parker's farm, about three miles southwest of Decatur. Any hope of a surprise attack was lost. As Hardee's remaining two divisions gradually stumbled into the assembly point, they were formed into assault columns. Soldiers were literally asleep on their feet. Hundreds more had dropped out along the road from Atlanta. Hood's expectations of a forced march of fifteen miles in one night by exhausted and fragmented troops had proved unrealistic. Hardee would have to make the best of a bad situation.

It was almost noon when Hardee finally had his divisions aligned. Because time was so short, he had not reconnoitered the land in front of him to discern the position and strength of enemy lines. He could only hope that he had advanced far enough to flank the end of McPherson's line. The debacle of Peachtree Creek haunted him as time slipped away.

Hardee formed his corps with Maney and Cleburne on the left, followed by Walker and Bate on the right. Each division was formed into double lines. As Hardee blindly began his final northwest approach, he faced nearly two miles of extremely thick woods and undergrowth, bisected by a large millpond, before it would be possible to glimpse the first Union troops.[5]

As Hardee's men stepped toward battle, General Walker was in an unusually irascible mood. The night before he had swallowed his pride and made his peace with Hood. Though a staunch Johnston supporter, Walker had dropped by Hood's headquarters only minutes before embarking upon Hardee's flanking movement. As Hood later recounted the moment, Walker "rode by my head-quarters, called me aside, and, with characteristic frankness, expressed his appreciation of the grave responsibilities attached to the position in which I had been placed. . . . [He] wished me to know, before he entered battle, that he was with me in heart and purpose, and intended to abide by me through all emergencies."[6]

His peace mission completed, Walker strode out into the night to face the bedlam and confusion of troop movement. As he rode through the destruction in Atlanta, the forty-seven-year-old Walker must have wondered where his life was heading. In recent weeks he had been repeatedly passed over for higher command. The youthful Hood's ascendancy was only the latest affront. And now his own home state of Georgia was in its death throes. As Atlanta fell around him, Walker could see his life's two great ambitions—high military command and the restoration of his family fortune—crumbling as well. It was a bitter night of self-reflection.[7]

With dawn the impossibility of a surprise attack became apparent. Walker's melancholy kindled into smoldering anger. As Hardee struggled to align his division fronts, Walker's tired eyes flashed. He moved his division out from the staging ground and followed the left bank of Sugar Creek, but his troops soon were fragmented by thick woods and undergrowth. Walker could not keep in close contact with Bate's division on the right bank of the creek or Cleburne's division, which was concealed in the dense woods on his left. As they neared Terry's millpond, which they found to be wide and unfordable, a disgusted Walker rode over to Hardee and proposed a change in direction. Hardee, who was under intense pressure, exploded, addressing Walker as rudely as he would a private: "No, Sir! This movement has been delayed too long already. Go, and obey my orders!"

This was more than Walker could stomach. Swinging into his saddle and riding furiously back to his division, Walker screamed at his aide, Joseph B. Cumming, "Major, did you hear that? . . . I shall make him remember this insult. If I survive this battle, he shall answer me for it."[8]

When Walker reached his division, his troops were stalled before Terry's millpond. Blinded by rage—and rumored to be fueled by a few nips of peach brandy—Walker found the local man that his troops had forced to act as a guide and put a pistol to his head. Walker threatened to shoot the man for deliberately leading the troops into a trap and had to be restrained.

In the middle of all this a courier arrived with a written apology from Hardee. Somewhat appeased, Walker pulled himself together and directed his division around the west end of the millpond. In readying his troops for their final approach to the edge of the woods and the battlefield clearing, Walker placed Gist's brigade on the left and Stevens's brigade on the right. Mercer's brigade formed the second line and would be held in reserve.

As Walker's division proceeded toward battle, an eighteen-year-old Alabaman, Phil Stephenson, caught a glimpse of Walker. The lad later recalled:

> We passed close to Walker himself, "Fighting Billy," as he was called, a hero of the Mexican War. One of the thinnest men I ever saw. Imagine a fence rail, dressed in complete uniform, closely buttoned up warm as it was, topped by a long pale face, almost hidden, however, by a bushy black beard, and above all a huge black felt hat with a big black feather curling around it. I saw him "full front" as we went by, and there seemed hardly space enough on his attenuated body for the double row of buttons of his general's uniform coat. Long and tall as he looked, as he sat on his horse, straight as a ram rod, evidently waiting with his staff around him to "go in."[9]

As Walker's division left the ravine and pushed up a slope, Walker spurred his horse ahead of his troops and raised his field glasses at the summit of the hill. At that moment a Union picket squeezed off a single shot and Walker toppled from his horse, killed instantly, his gloved hand frozen around his field glasses. Clearly, the Rebs were not going to be surprising the Yanks that morning.[10]

The Confederate predicament was not Hardee's fault. He had done his part against all odds. He had force-marched his troops over fifteen miles through darkness and positioned them beyond the left end of the Union line. Indeed, when Hardee notified Hood of his position before his attack, Hood pointed to his map and shouted, "Hardee is just where I wanted him!"[11]

But an apprehensive McPherson had awakened at dawn, worried about his exposed left flank. With much effort the Union general had immediately reinforced and extended his line, which was why Hardee now faced a frontal assault against a full Union corps supported by artillery. A stroke of intuition had saved Sherman's army.

After Walker was killed, Hardee ordered General Hugh Mercer to take command of Walker's division and shifted command of Mercer's brigade to Colonel Charles Olmstead of the First Georgia Volunteers.[12] Mercer was fifty-five, in chronic poor health, and exhausted by the physical demands of the Atlanta campaign. Nevertheless, Mercer gamely assumed command and struggled to prepare the brigades of Gist and Stevens for the initial attack, placing Olmstead's in reserve.

As Bate's and Walker's divisions lined up at the edge of the woods, they gaped up a hill at the Union line facing them three hundred yards away. Brigadier General Grenville Dodge's Sixteenth Corps was composed of two divisions: Brigadier General Thomas Sweeny's Second Division on the Union left and Brigadier General John Fuller's Fourth Division on the right. Dodge's Sixteenth Corps was understrength, with only five thousand soldiers stretched in a single line, and had not had time to entrench or build earthworks. However, the thin blue line was supported by artillery—the Fourteenth Ohio Battery and Battery H of the First Missouri. Together these twelve guns would fire more than one thousand rounds of shell, case, and canister into the attacking Confederates. Bate's and Mercer's divisions had no artillery with which to respond and neutralize the Union firepower.[13]

What was essential to Confederate success against superior numbers was a carefully coordinated attack. Hardee's divisions had to advance as one, keeping constant pressure on the Union line. Even more crucial, as soon as Dodge's Sixteenth Corps and, it was hoped, Major General Francis Preston Blair Jr.'s Seventeenth Corps, began to collapse and retreat, Hood would have to immediately send Cheatham's corps in with a smashing frontal assault against Major General John Logan's Fifteenth Corps. The Union Goliath could be felled only by a swift and coordinated one-two punch. But the Confederate offensive failed to deliver it.

Bate's division, on the far right of the Confederate line, led the Confederate assault at approximately 12:15 P.M.[14] Rather than kicking off the offensive with confidence, Bate found himself totally unsure and confused. His division was significantly depleted, reduced to twelve hundred troops, the size of a small brigade. Even worse, Bate's orders did not fit the situation that he now faced. On paper Bate and Mercer were to move forward together unopposed, veer to the west, and attack the *rear* of Blair's unsuspecting Seventeenth Corps. In reality Bate had to frontally attack Dodge's very alert and fresh Sixteenth Corps, which was only three hundred yards away through a torrent of shot and canister. Bate sent a courier to Hardee for clarification of his orders but received no further word. Time ran out and Bate was forced to advance.

Bate's division bore down against the right side of Dodge's Sixteenth Corps, focusing its attack on Sweeny's division.[15] As the Confederate troops emerged from the shelter of the woods, they had to descend a long open hill, cross a waist-high creek at the bottom, and charge up another slope with the Union line positioned at the summit. "The enemy emerged from the woods in heavy charging column with battle flags proudly flaunting in the breeze," according to the Union general Elliott W. Rice. "They burst forth from the woods in truly magnificent style in front of my right. . . . Yet still my thin line stood like a fence of iron, not a man deserting his colors, which were all the time being proudly and defiantly waved in the very teeth of the enemy."[16]

As the Confederates charged down the hill, the Union artillery opened up with shell fire. Halfway across the valley, the Rebs paused to fire a volley. Sweeny's troops squeezed their triggers first, dropping Bate's men. A fierce open-ground firefight ensued.

In a few minutes Bate's division grimly resumed its charge into concentrated

BATTLE OF ATLANTA
JULY 22, 1862

Union works
Confederate works
Confederate troops

SCHOFIELD
(XXIII CORPS)

DeGress Battery
Troup Hurt House
Georgia R.R.
To Decatur

Gibson
Baker
Clayton
Holtzclaw
Sharp
Stovall
Manigault
Deas
Brantly
M. L. Smith

To Atlanta

Brown

McPHERSON

LOGAN
(XV CORPS)

CHEATHAM

Stevenson
Cumming
Palmer
Pettus
Reynolds

Harrow

Sweeny
DODGE
(XVI CORPS)
Fuller

Tyler
Lewis
Finley
Bate

G. W. Smith

Leggett's Hill
Leggett

BLAIR
(XVII CORPS)

McPherson
killed here

Gist
Mercer
Nisbet

W. H. T. Walker

Atlanta
defenses

F. M. Walker

G. A. Smith

J. A. Smith

Lowrey

Carter

Maney

Strahl

Magevney

Govan

Cleburne

HARDEE

canister fire. Because Walker's division had not yet engaged Fuller's Union division to its left, Fuller's troops were free to pour raking fire into Bate's left flank. They quickly shredded Bate's line, and his men broke and retreated to the woods. Bate's mauled division was through for the day.[17]

Rather than charging in concert with Bate's division, Walker's division, now led by Mercer, was waiting for Gist's brigade to emerge from the dense woods and form the left side of its division front. By the time Gist's troops had trickled in and lined up with the rest of Walker's division, Bate's division had been smashed and routed. The front line of Walker's division did not deploy until Bate's division was in full retreat.

Yet when Mercer finally sent Gist's and Stevens's brigades into battle, Gist's brigade again lagged far behind, and they lost whatever advantage might have accrued from presenting a united front. Stevens's brigade bore down on the gap between Sweeny's right and Fuller's left. Stevens's men crossed a field covered with underbrush, forded a shallow stream, and double-timed up a sloping field, straight into the murderous cannon fire of the six Rodman guns of the Fourteenth Ohio Battery. As the Rodmans blasted gaping holes in the line of Stevens's brigade, the Yanks had a clear shot at Stevens's left flank because of the absence of Gist's brigade, and raked Stevens's brigade with murderous rifle fire. Although Stevens's men twice drew close to the blue line, they were mutilated and driven back. Many were captured.[18]

As Stevens's brigade retreated, Gist's brigade was finally engaging the Union line on the left, charging straight for the gap between Fuller's right and the exposed rear of Giles Smith's division. Fuller quickly saw that if Gist's charge succeeded, it would destabilize the Union line. Brigadier General Fuller himself seized the flag of the Twenty-seventh Ohio, which ignited his troops.

Gist's Georgians and South Carolinians soon found themselves in the same predicament as Stevens's retreating brigade. Both flanks were exposed and they were being raked by gunfire. With Stevens's brigade in full retreat, the Fourteenth Ohio Battery now shifted the fire of its Rodman guns toward Gist. In an attempt to rally his faltering charge, Gist rode to the front waving his hat and was severely wounded.

Writing about the charge of Walker's division many years later, Major William H. Chamberlin of the Eighty-first Ohio offered "a tribute to the bravery of the enemy. . . . They came tearing wildly through the woods with the yells of demons. We had an advantage in artillery; they in numbers. Their assaults were repulsed only to be fearlessly renewed, until the sight of dead and wounded lying in their way, as they charged again and again to break our lines, must have appalled the stoutest hearts. So persistent were their onslaughts that numbers were made prisoners by rushing directly into our lines."[19] Gist's troops retreated in scattered clumps of blood-splattered men.

Mercer's brigade, held in reserve under Olmstead, was all that was left of Walker's division, now led by Mercer. These men had watched Stevens's and Gist's brigades being pulverized and were helping the survivors reach Confederate lines. Now they waited to see if they too would be sent alone and unsupported against the firepower of the thin Union line.

While Mercer fretted about whether to send his lone brigade against the Union line, Colonel Olmstead aligned the brigade front. Suddenly, a Union shell exploded, and shrapnel struck Olmstead in the head, knocking him senseless. The chronically ill colonel William Barkuloo of the Fifty-seventh Georgia was quickly placed in command, and Mercer foolishly sent the lone brigade against two Union divisions.[20]

Once again leaving the woods and charging down the hill toward the creek, the Georgia brigade screamed its Rebel yell as the Union artillery zeroed in on it. The men of Mercer's brigade reached the creek. Now they faced the final advance up toward the Union lines. Barkuloo ordered his brigade to halt and hunker down beside the creek bed. In his battle report he wrote:

> I ordered a halt as soon as the brigade reached the fringe of bushes along
> the branch and proceeded to reconnoiter the position of the enemy. . . .
> In this I was ably seconded by Captains [George] Mercer and Gordon, of
> Brigadier General Mercer's staff. We found the enemy drawn up in three lines
> of battle on the crest of the hill and supported by two batteries. . . . Their
> lines outflanked ours both to the right and left. Having ascertained these facts,
> I determined to withdraw the brigade at once from under the heavy fire of
> artillery then pouring into our ranks. Having given the command, the troops
> fell back in good order to about their former position, having lost about 15
> killed and wounded.[21]

Whether Barkuloo's decision was cowardly or wise can be debated, but with the retreat of Mercer's brigade, fighting on the right side of Hardee's corps was effectively over. Albert Castel ably summarizes the moment:

> Less than forty-five minutes after they have begun, Bate's and Walker's
> assaults [led by Mercer] end in dismal failure. Nowhere did they get within
> a hundred yards of the Union line. On the surface it would seem that six
> Confederate brigades were unable even to reach, much less breach, an
> unfortified position held by three Union brigades. Actually, owing to straggling,
> skulking, and the small size of Bate's force, the number of Rebel combatants
> probably did not exceed Sweeny's and Fuller's combined strength of 5,000;
> perhaps, indeed, it was smaller. In addition the Federals were rested, skillfully
> commanded, and enjoyed the enormous advantage of artillery support,
> whereas Bate's and Walker's troops were weak from fatigue, their attacks were
> uncoordinated, and of necessity they had to rely solely on small arms. They
> stood so little chance of success that it would have been remarkable had they
> achieved it.[22]

The Confederates were faring much better on the left side of Hardee's corps. At approximately 12:45 P.M., about the time that Barkuloo was hunkering down in the creek bed, Patrick Cleburne's division plowed into the Union line with characteristic ferocity, joined with the good fortune of finding a vulnerable chink in the Union armor. Spearheaded by Daniel Govan's and James Smith's brigades, Cleburne drove a wedge between Blair's Seventeenth Corps and Dodge's Sixteenth Corps.[23]

General Hardee saw a sudden chance for victory and sought to give Cleburne all the reinforcement he could. As he gazed across Walker's and Bate's spent divisions, Hardee realized that Mercer's brigade, led by Barkuloo, had barely been touched by the Confederate charge. Hardee ordered Mercer to detach Mercer's brigade from his division and send it to support Cleburne.[24]

Upon reaching Cleburne's rear lines, Barkuloo had a sudden change of heart. In his battle report he stated:

[Mercer] ordered me to report to Brigadier-General [Mark] Lowrey [of Cleburne's division], on our left. As soon as I reached the place designated I was directed to march the brigade around to near General Hardee's quarters, from where, by direction of a staff officer, I advanced some 500 or 600 yards up the road. . . . While forming this line the report reached me that General Cleburne had carried the enemy's works, capturing several pieces of artillery and 2,000 prisoners, and had no use for us. Being but recently from a sick bed, and exhausted by the fatigues of the day, I here turned over the command to Lieutenant-Colonel Rawls, Fifty-fourth Georgia, and reported to the brigade hospital.

With Cleburne up against the entire Union Army of the Tennessee, Barkuloo's assertion that he was not needed is weak. Barkuloo's retreat to a hospital bed would effectively end his hopes of a command in the future. Now Mercer's brigade adjusted to its fourth commander within a few hours.

Throughout the morning Hood was ensconced in the James E. Williams house, two and a half miles from where Bate and Mercer first attacked and a mile west of the nearest Union line. Removed from the action and peering through field glasses, he had fretted and cursed the morning away as the Yanks shredded the advance of Bate's and Walker's divisions. Then, shortly before 1 P.M., when Cleburne advanced and successfully drove the Union line, Hood—confused and lacking information—hesitated. He had planned to unleash Cheatham's corps the minute that the Union flank was destabilized, but now he was not sure. Would Cleburne bog down too? Was this a false start? Hood's vacillation became the fatal mistake of the day. The Confederate offensive depended on precise timing and coordination, a narrow window of opportunity. And Hood, removed from the immediacy of battle, was frozen in indecision.

By 2 P.M. Cleburne's plucky troops were wilting with exhaustion. With no rest in nearly forty-eight hours, they were still fighting the entire Union Army of the Tennessee alone with no other Confederate units to so much as distract the Union army. Yet Cleburne was still succeeding. By 3 P.M. Cleburne's troops had driven to the base of Bald Hill—the pivot of the Union line—and now faced the incredible irony that they must capture the very hill that they had defended the day before.

Finally, after the battle had been in progress for more than three hours, Hood unleashed Cheatham's corps against the Union's Fifteenth Corps, focusing on Mortimer Leggett's division, the weak link in the line. After Cleburne learned that Cheatham was at last in action, Cleburne was free to reinforce his battered men with Lowrey's reserve division, which was hunkered down in the forest five hundred yards south of the battlefield. Mercer's brigade, under the command of Lieutenant Colonel Rawls of the Fifty-fourth Georgia, would now reenter the battle with Lowrey's other troops.[25]

Cheatham's corps encountered initial success. Carter Stevenson's division, advancing at about 3:30 P.M., drove toward Bald Hill to strengthen Cleburne's offensive. While Cleburne continued to advance from the southeast, Stevenson would drive the Yanks from the northwest, opening a two-directional front. Farther north, Arthur Manigault's Alabama and South Carolina brigade of Brown's division successfully attacked the Fifteenth Corps, which was positioned in stout breastworks astride the Georgia Railroad. Enduring strong Union artillery fire, Manigault's troops drove the Yanks out of their entrenchments and tore a hole in the Union line.[26]

As Cheatham's corps advanced, General Sherman received news that General James McPherson, commander of the Army of the Tennessee, had been killed. A grieving Sherman himself now swung into battle and personally directed a seven-brigade counterattack that soon blunted Cheatham's offensive.[27]

By 5 P.M. the Confederate army was in desperate straits. Cheatham's corps was stalled. Cleburne alone was able to muster the strength for a final assault. Pulling together Govan's, Smith's, and Lowrey's brigades, joined with Maney's brigade and Mercer's brigade of Walker's division, Cleburne led a desperate last-gasp charge against Bald Hill. Cleburne's brigades advanced from the southeast, Maney's brigade from the southwest, and Mercer's brigade from the south.[28]

The advance of Mercer's brigade initially went well under Rawls, rolling over two lines of Union troops. However, as the men surged over the earthworks and trenches of the second line, Rawls was wounded and Lieutenant Colonel Guyton of the Fifty-seventh Georgia took command. In his battlefield report Guyton related:

> We assaulted the enemy's works carrying two lines. . . . The enemy was at this
> time occupying a third line of works distant from the line occupied by us about
> thirty paces, both sides firing rapidly. The brigade was in the utmost state of
> confusion as regarded its organization, the regiments being intermingled with
> each other and the right of Maney's brigade. On assuming command, I imme-
> diately ordered an advance, but the men could be induced to go no farther,
> which I think was owing in part, if not altogether, to want of organization,
> officers being unable to form their commands under so close and deadly fire.[29]

In a letter to his mother the next day, Lieutenant Hamilton Branch of Mercer's brigade remembered this moment with bitterness:

> [W]e charged one line and drove them from it. We then jumped over this line
> and charged the second and drove them from that also. Here the big mistake

was made, for we were ordered to halt. The enemy were now behind another line about ten yards in front of us and pouring a galling fire into us, for the line that we had taken had three gaps in it and through these they fired on us. It was here that Lt. Col. Rawls was wounded. . . . If we had not been halted in the second line we could have taken the third line and thus cut two corps of the enemy off, but as it was we had to remain behind the second line and keep firing at the enemy and they at us, both behind breastworks and only 20 yds. apart.[30]

While Mercer's brigade, now under Guyton, bogged down, the rest of Cleburne's troops fought furiously. For forty-five minutes Yanks and Rebs fired at each other from close quarters, often pinned against both sides of defensive breastworks. Although some of the Confederate units had brief success, the Yanks were still in possession of Bald Hill as darkness fell. Cleburne and Maney grudgingly fell back to the second line of captured entrenchments and hunkered down for the night.

Although the battle was over, fierce Union fire pinned down the advance elements of the Confederate line. Captain George Mercer of Mercer's brigade scribbled in his field journal, "We remained all night in the work greatly exposed to fire of sharp shooters. The position being raked by the enemy's artillery."[31] Shortly before dawn all Confederate units were ordered to pull back and a new line established to face another day.

As July 23 dawned, neither the Union nor Confederate troops renewed the offensive. Like two broken and exhausted boxers, each kept to its own corner. Near noon a truce was called to remove the dead and wounded from between the lines. The Battle of Atlanta was over.

The toll was tremendous. Confederate casualties numbered between 5,500 and 8,000. Union losses were 3,800, most captured by Cleburne from the Seventeenth Corps. Hardee's corps reported losses of 3,299, of which 1,388 (40 percent) were from Cleburne's division. Mercer's brigade sustained 168 casualties: First Georgia Volunteers, 28; Fifty-fourth Georgia, 61; Fifty-seventh, 26; and the Sixty-third, 53.[32]

As gunfire receded, many reflected on Hood's five short days of command. In this brief time he had engaged in two major battles and had lost almost as many men as Johnston had lost in ten weeks. Jefferson Davis had wanted a commander who would fight. If nothing else, he got his wish.

On the evening of July 23, 1864, as the sky grew dark on the field of battle, Atlanta was not yet occupied by Union forces. But as Sherman smugly summarized the situation in his *Memoirs,* "The enemy had retired during the night inside of Atlanta, and we remained masters of the situation outside."[33]

23

Sell the Cotton If You Can!

During the night of July 22 and the early dawn of July 23, 1864, Hardee's corps withdrew to the southwest and dug in along Intrenchment Creek, seeking to form a shield for the Macon and Western Railroad.[1] For the next four days Hardee's troops tended their wounds, fortified their new position, and constructed defenses from felled trees. These were quiet days with little troop movement and no renewed offensives.[2]

For Robert Braswell it was a time of grief and tragedy. His uncle, Seaborn Mims, was either dead or captured. His brothers lay in a mass grave along Peachtree Creek. Braswell was now profoundly alone.

Other members of the Fifty-seventh Georgia were adapting. Sergeant John M. Davis of Company K had been wounded and left for dead at Peachtree Creek. Later found and evacuated by train to the S. P. Moore Hospital in Griffin, Georgia, Davis described his ordeal in a letter to his wife:

> I was wounded in a charge on the 20th. The ball entered my left side just below the ribs and ranged down, struck the hip bone, glanced round to the back bone, there loged [lodged]. I was picked up in a few hours by friends I shall never forget and toted a mile and half to the Dr. He probed after the ball. Could not get it. Said it had entered my hollow [abdominal cavity]. He could do nothing for me and left me to die.
>
> I lay without any attention two days and nights. I could not be moved without fainting. I was brought to this place Friday at night in a dying condition to all appearance. I was as helpless as an infant and maggots in my wound by thousands. The Dr. went to work with me. He got them all out. On Saturday evening he put me under the influance of cloriform and cut the ball out. It never entered my hollow. I am now mending as fast as can be, though I cant walk yet.
>
> . . . I hear disturbing news about the raiders [Union cavalry]. The papers say they have burnt the Circle [the town of Social Circle] and Madison. I fear they past too clost to you. Distruction is in there hands. I cannot tell you what to do. I think you and Father had better sell the cotton if you can. . . .
>
> While [I] was writing the Dr. come to me laughing. Asked me if I was writing home. I told him I was. He told me to tell you he thought I would be able in 10 days to start home. . . . Tell Black George to fix up the carriage.

Take out the big seat out of the carriage and put a mattress in so I can lie down in it.[3]

Other men were attempting to put a positive light on a grim situation. John Bell Hood and Braxton Bragg tried to convince Richmond that a clear Confederate defeat had indeed been a victory. In the deceptive words of Bragg, Sherman had been "badly defeated and completely failed [foiled] in one of his bold flank movements, heretofore so successful." Bragg knew better and so did Jefferson Davis.[4]

Edwin T. Davis, the young Mercer University student in the Fifty-seventh Georgia, also tried to whitewash a grim situation. On July 26 he sent a glowing report of the Battle of Atlanta to the Savannah newspaper, the *Republican:*

> The onsets of Hardee's Veterans were too terrific for mortals to withstand. As the enemy's artillery cut great chasms in their ranks they closed up in a splendid style, though thronging the road to death, as if to a festival. The conduct of all the troops was splendid; but none, history will attest, was superior to that of Mercer's Georgians!
>
> . . . When night brought a truce and an end to the conflict, victory being in no uneven balance, near two thousand prisoners, twenty-three pieces of fine artillery, five stands of colors, and much baggage and plunder attested the skill of our Generals and the impetuous valor of subordinate officers and men. The enemy had been driven nearly two miles and stormed from their entrenched positions.
>
> . . . Of the spirit and morale of the army I need say but little. It is large-spirited, determined, well-appointed, and fond of their new and great Commander-in-chief (Hood). Under him, the pride of Texans and the hope of Georgians, they expect to be led to new fields of imperishable glory and renown.[5]

The truth was that the diehard optimists in the Confederate army were locked in a state of delusion and denial. Yet many common soldiers had little idea of the true Confederate predicament. In a letter to his wife, Anna, a month after the Battle of Atlanta, Private Charles Thiot of the First Georgia Volunteers reflected: "I hear that Genl. Hood has said that he give Sherman *seven days* to fight or retreat. But we hear so many rumors in camp, that we hardly believe anything that is not read out before us as a special order. . . . You all at distant points know more about us than we do ourselves. And even in a fight we only know what happens immediately before us. And when you hear soldiers telling their marvelous tales about what was done on the right or on the left, they are telling what they *heard* and not what they *saw.*"[6]

Unsure of what was really happening, the men of Mercer's brigade took one day at a time. They let the generals wrestle with strategy, while they worried about the next meal and their wives and children at home.

On July 25 Walker's men received news that their division would be dissolved. With Confederate combat units severely depleted and understrength, it was decided to reinforce three of Hardee's divisions by dissolving a fourth division. The natural choice was Walker's division because Walker was dead. Mercer's brigade was assigned to General Patrick Cleburne, Gist's brigade to Cheatham (now returned to his old division from temporary corps command), and Stevens's brigade to Bate. Later in the day General Mercer also received orders relieving him of command and directing him to report to Savannah. His advancing age and deteriorating health now removed him from frontline combat.[7]

Brigadier General James Argyle Smith, a West Point graduate and experienced combat officer, was given command of Mercer's brigade. Wounded during the Battle of Atlanta, Smith was on medical furlough and did not report to the brigade until September 24.[8] In the interim a dispute erupted over who should assume temporary command of the brigade.

The two candidates were Colonel William Barkuloo of the Fifty-seventh Georgia and Colonel Charles Olmstead of the First Georgia Volunteers. Olmstead had been second in command under Mercer. However, Olmstead had been hit in the head by a shell fragment early in the Battle of Atlanta, resulting in a serious concussion. Barkuloo had then assumed command of the brigade.

When Olmstead returned from medical leave on July 31, he considered himself to be the "Senior Colonel."[9] Although Barkuloo's commission dated to March 1862, Olmstead had been elected colonel of the First Volunteers in December 1861, making him one of the first senior active colonels in the Confederacy.[10] Olmstead insisted that he should be reinstated to temporary brigade command. Barkuloo resisted and a fierce letter-writing campaign commenced, with each colonel stating his case to his superiors and soliciting letters of recommendation from fellow officers. Ultimately, Olmstead received the nod for temporary command. However, a dangerous rift had developed within the brigade, as each officer had his supporters.[11]

After this contest for command, nothing further was seen or heard from Colonel William Barkuloo. He simply disappeared from the record, and the command of the Fifty-seventh Georgia devolved upon Lieutenant Colonel Cincinnatus Guyton. Barkuloo probably spent the last year of the war on medical leave.[12]

Despite the internal conflict, the men of Mercer's brigade were proud to be assigned to Cleburne's command. In a letter to the editor of the *(Savannah) Republican,* Edwin Davis crowed, "Mercer's [brigade] was assigned to Cleburne's Division. . . . It is said that after witnessing the repeated charges of Mercer's brigade, General Cleburne made a special request for it, saying that he was willing to risk them on any field by the side of his Alabamans, Texans, and Arkansans—men who knew no such word as fail."[13] Olmstead echoed this pride in his memoirs: "General Cleburne was a distinguished soldier, one of the finest that the war produced upon our side and I have always felt that it was a privilege to serve under him."[14]

The admiration did not go both ways, however. Cleburne doubted that he was receiving a combat-proven brigade. In a letter to Hardee, Cleburne immediately warned, "[If Mercer's brigade is] to do any good, a brigade commander is immediately necessary. Its present commander [Olmstead] is not efficient."[15] The implication was that Cleburne trusted neither Olmstead nor Mercer's brigade and believed that the men must be whipped into shape by new leadership.

The Georgians had been greatly reduced in numbers during the Atlanta campaign. Captain George Mercer jotted in his diary on July 31 that although the brigade had started in north Georgia in May with twenty-eight hundred troops, 929 (or one-third) of the men had been killed, wounded, captured, or were missing in action.[16] Still, Mercer's brigade remained the largest brigade in Hardee's corps. By contrast, during the Battle of Atlanta, Cleburne had lost more than 40 percent of his men, including half of his sixty senior officers. Now Cleburne welcomed any able-bodied men he could find.

From July 23 until August 31 Mercer's brigade experienced no major combat. The Georgians remained positioned within the interior lines of Atlanta, guarding the vulnerable southern perimeter of the city.[17] During this same period the Battle of Ezra Church was fought, hundreds of Sherman's cavalry were captured near Macon attempting to rescue Union prisoners in Andersonville, and the Confederate cavalry under General Joe Wheeler ventured north to attempt to cut Sherman's supply lines. For Hardee's corps, however, the greatest challenge was to endure sniper fire and the incessant bombardment of Atlanta, which Sherman commenced in full fury on August 9. Not until August 30 was Mercer's brigade again engaged in heavy combat at the railroad village of Jonesboro.

For more than a month after the Battle of Atlanta, Sherman tried unsuccessfully to pulverize the city with artillery fire and to destroy the lone Confederate supply line, the Macon and Western Railroad. Finally, Sherman abandoned his own railroad supply line, packed fifteen days of rations in wagons, and moved his entire army during the nights of August 25 and 26, marching in a large wheeling arc to the west and south of Atlanta. Only the Twentieth Corps was left to guard the railroad bridge over the Chattahoochee. Sherman was determined that he would destroy the Macon and Western Railroad, threaten the soft underbelly of south Atlanta, and force Hood into a decisive battle.

Major General Patrick Cleburne
(Courtesy of the Library of Congress)

Surprised to find the Union lines empty the next day, George Mercer wrote, "At day-light our Scouts discovered that the enemy had abandoned his works in our front. Our skirmish line went forward and occupied them. I found them much heavier and stronger than our own—badly policed and very filthy."[18]

Hood was initially perplexed by what Sherman was up to. However, on the evening of August 30 Hood received cavalry reports that Union general Oliver Howard's Army of the Tennessee was closing fast on the Macon and Western rail line at Jonesboro, twenty miles south of Atlanta and nestled beside the Flint River. Now Hood knew where the confrontation would be.

Deciding that he would remain in Atlanta with Stewart's corps and the Georgia Militia, Hood ordered Hardee to immediately take command of a two-corps task force and march to defeat Sherman's forces at Jonesboro. Hardee's task force consisted of Hardee's corps, now under the temporary command of General Cleburne, and Hood's former corps, now under the permanent command of Lieutenant General Stephen D. Lee, recently transferred from the command of the Department of Alabama, Mississippi, and East Louisiana.[19] Hood instructed Hardee to push Howard aggressively back across the headwaters of the Flint River and crush him. If he were successful, Lee would then return immediately to Atlanta, join forces with Stewart, and attack the rest of Sherman's army—Thomas and Schofield—from the north while Hardee struck from the south.

Howard's Union troops beat Hardee to Jonesboro. As the sun was setting on August 30, the advance units of Howard's army had marched within sight of Jonesboro, and the ever-prudent Howard called a halt for the night. He knew that a Confederate force was defending Jonesboro, and he had not been able to ascertain its strength. Because he expected to find Hardee's entire corps, he pulled back a half mile from the town and dug in along a line of low hills. Howard did not know that Jonesboro was weakly defended, mostly by cavalry units, and that he could have seized the railroad before darkness fell.

Shortly before dawn on August 31, Hardee's advance units filtered into Jonesboro after marching all night. As at the Battle of Atlanta, Hood's orders emphatically instructed Hardee to attack at dawn. However, all of Hardee's corps, now led by Cleburne, did not arrive until after 9 A.M., and Lee's units were not in place until 1:30 P.M. By the time Hardee's twenty thousand troops were aligned, they formed a front that was a mile and a half long. Howard's force was about the same size.

There were other haunting similarities to Peachtree Creek and the Battle of Atlanta. Again, Hardee wanted his line to move in a wheeling, stair-step progression (*en echelon*), with Cleburne kicking the offensive off on the far left of the Confederate line. As soon as Cleburne hit the extreme right flank of the Union line and had it destabilized, Lee was to unleash his corps directly at the center of the Union line and drive Howard back across the Flint River. It was the same strategy that had failed on July 20 and 22. And the Confederate strategy would fail again for the same reasons: lack of communication, coordination, and timing, as well as unrealistic expectations of exhausted troops.

Mirroring Peachtree Creek, by the time Hardee was ready to begin the battle, Howard had had precious hours for his troops to dig in and build earthworks. The Union line was composed of three full divisions supported by artillery and entrenched in a semicircle with both flanks securely anchored to the Flint River. The Yanks were experienced, rested, well fed, and spoiling for a fight.

As planned, Cleburne prepared to begin the Confederate advance on the left at 3 P.M. However, Lee mistook nervous skirmish fire near Cleburne for a major engagement, and at 2:30 P.M. Lee prematurely sent his corps charging the center of the Union line. The concept of a coordinated *en echelon* approach again failed before the battle began.

Only by sheer luck was Mercer's brigade spared major loss in the Confederate charge. The brigade was positioned on the extreme left of the Confederate line, adjacent to Hiram Granbury's veteran brigade in Cleburne's division, which was now under the temporary command of Lowrey. As the Confederate line sputtered forward, Granbury's brigade came under fire from the dismounted troopers of Judson Kilpatrick's cavalry division. Veering to attack Kilpatrick's men, Granbury's brigade soon ran off the dismounted horse soldiers. Caught up in their good fortune, Granbury's and Mercer's brigades pursued the fleeing Union troops across the Flint River, which removed the two Confederate brigades from the main Union line of fire.

As the Rebel brigades gave chase, Private John Methvin of the Fifty-seventh Georgia ran beside his brother, Sergeant Thomas Methvin. Splashing across the Flint River, they encountered a humorous sight. Even when he was eighty-four, John Methvin clearly recollected the moment:

> We charged upon the federal forces and they retreated across the Flint River, and in their hurry to get away, many of them plunged into the river and waded or swam through. One big fat Irishman, or German, who had on a pair of heavy boots, had struggled through the deep water, but his clothes and boots were so water-soaked and heavy that he could run no further, so he dropped in his tracks, threw up his hands and cried out in broken English his surrender. I think he was the biggest heap of helpless humanity I have ever seen. We sent him to Andersonville to dry out and wait the crossing of another river.[20]

Few men were laughing in the Confederate lines, however. The Rebs were attacking entrenched Union positions defended by artillery. The Confederates suffered horrendous losses and never penetrated the Union line. The Confederate charge became a slaughter and resulted in one of the most lopsided battles of the Civil War. By the end of the day the Confederates had suffered 1,725 casualties, the Union only 179.

As night fell on the evening of August 30, Hood was anxious and secluded in Atlanta. Railroad crews attempting to go south on the Macon and Western Railroad had collided with George Thomas's Union soldiers, who were tearing up track north of Jonesboro near Rough and Ready. This meant that the enormous Army of the Cumberland had moved between Atlanta and Hardee's Army of Tennessee in Jonesboro. Late in the afternoon Union troops cut the telegraph wires between Hardee's and Hood's headquarters, and Hood feared the worst.

Unaware of what had transpired in Jonesboro, Hood became convinced that Howard's attack was only a Union feint and that Sherman's true objective now was to go after the weakened southern defenses of Atlanta. Alarmed, Hood sent a courier to Jonesboro at 6 P.M. on August 30 with a message directing Lee's corps to immediately return to Atlanta. Hood ordered Hardee to remain in Jonesboro in order "to protect Macon and communication in rear."

Hood was mistaken. Sherman had no intention of attacking Atlanta. Instead, Sherman had six corps poised to attack Hardee's single corps on September 1. Thomas and Schofield were in position to rapidly move south along the railroad and crush Hardee's exposed right flank, should Howard's Army of the Tennessee need assistance.

Sherman—if he knew all the facts, which he didn't—now had the opportunity to totally destroy Hood. As Lee secretly trekked back to Atlanta, all three of Hood's corps were separated from each other and could be crushed one at a time. Fortunately, Sherman did not realize until late on September 1 that Lee was not in Jonesboro.

All through the night of August 31, Hardee was preparing his isolated corps for the defensive stand of his career. He now had no more than twelve thousand men and had to cover a two-mile line that once had been held by two corps. The major sector of his thin line faced north to south and confronted Howard's Army of the Tennessee. But Hardee also knew that Thomas and Schofield were free to advance due south and crush his northern, or right, flank. He therefore angled the north end of his line eastward to cross the railroad and confront Thomas. The result was a vertical line that curved like a fish hook at the top. The most vulnerable position was in the curve of the hook.

The last of Lee's corps pulled out after midnight. In the dark early hours of September 1, Hardee aligned his troops. Cleburne's division, led by Lowrey, would hold down the right, or northern, end of the line, including the vulnerable fish hook. Brown's small division would be in the center, and Cheatham's division, now under John Carter, would hold the left end of the line.

Cleburne's division was stretched especially thin, covering the length of a line previously held by Lee's entire corps. The men were spread out in single rank spaced six feet apart. Mercer's brigade, under Olmstead, was on the division left, connecting with the right end of Brown's division, placing them close to the middle of Hardee's line. Lowrey's brigade, now led by John Weir, was in the center of Cleburne's division, followed by the tough and tested brigades of Hiram Granbury and Daniel Govan. Govan's Arkansans held the curve in the fish hook, aware that the Yanks would be seeking to exploit their obvious vulnerability. Six artillery batteries supported the Confederate line. Two were positioned to give Govan extra strength.[21]

As Mercer's brigade stumbled through the darkness and found its new position, the men realized that Lee's corps had built flimsy earthworks and that they were close to the Yankee forward skirmishers. Captain George Mercer jotted in his field diary, "Up at $2\frac{1}{2}$ A.M. moved to right of our force at Jonesboro, and relieved Lee's corps before day break: Our line very close to enemy's skirmishers who annoy us very greatly."[22]

Shortly before the sun rose, the men of Mercer's brigade found out how close the Yanks truly were. On this day a detachment of the Fifty-seventh Georgia drew skirmish duty. As the men crept out of their lines and edged toward their forward positions, the Georgians were suddenly surrounded by the Union troops of William Hazen's Second Division. Many years later John Methvin wrote two separate accounts of the carnage and confusion that ensued:

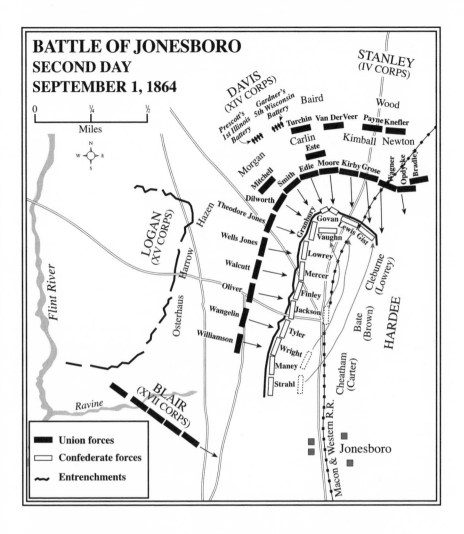

BATTLE OF JONESBORO
SECOND DAY
SEPTEMBER 1, 1864

STANLEY
(IV CORPS)

DAVIS
(XIV CORPS)

Prescott's 1st Illinois Battery
Gardner's 5th Wisconsin Battery
Baird
Wood

Turchin Van Der Veer Payne Knefler

Carlin Kimball Newton

Morgan Este
Mitchell Smith Edie Moore Kirby Grose Wagner Opdyke Bradley

Dilworth

Theodore Jones
Hazen
Govan

Wells Jones
Granbury
Lewis Gist
Vaughn

LOGAN
(XV CORPS)
Harrow
Walcutt
Lowrey
Mercer

Osterhaus
Oliver
Finley
Jackson
Cleburne
(Lowrey)

Wangelin
Williamson
Tyler
Bate
(Brown)
HARDEE

Wright
Maney
Cheatham
(Carter)

Strahl

Flint River

0   ¼   ½
Miles

N
W   E
S

Ravine

BLAIR
(XVII CORPS)

Macon & Western R.R.

Jonesboro

■ Union forces
□ Confederate forces
~ Entrenchments

Early next morning in the heavy gloaming, my regiment was called out to the advanced picket line. It was a fearful strain upon our courage, for we knew what it meant, but all was quiet. My brother, Thomas, as his office required, was adjusting the line and placing videttes [sentinels], when suddenly the shriek of battle broke loose and the federals who were concealed in ambush close by, were upon us. Here a wild and bloody scene, hard to describe, took place. My brother was shot down by my side. Most of the regiment was either killed or wounded or captured, but we fought through and held the line till night.[23]

After the skirmish John Methvin returned to find his brother's body and bury him:

My brother, T. J. Methvin, fell, shot through the head; his blood splattered on me as he fell. Oh! The cruelty and wickedness of war! We buried his body close to where he fell in a coffinless grave, wrapped in his martial cloak about him. The martial cloak consisted of a "tent fly" which we had been using for sleeping upon when the weather was fair, but as a covering for raining. All that bloody death scene comes fresh this morning and breaks my heart as I think of the death of that noble brother.[24]

As the survivors of the picket detachment made their way back to Mercer's brigade, they learned that thirty-three men of the Fifty-seventh Georgia had been captured or killed, the greatest single loss by the regiment since the Battle of Champion Hill.[25]

As September 1 wore on, Sherman was a confident man, taking his time about matters. Consumed with tearing up railroad track between Atlanta and Jonesboro, he did not know that Lee's corps had returned to Atlanta. He did not find out until 3 P.M. that Howard's Army of the Tennessee faced only Hardee's corps. Suddenly seeing his opportunity, Sherman ordered an immediate attack.

As the sun was setting, Sherman ordered the bulk of Howard's Army of the Tennessee to demonstrate—put on a good show of firepower as a subterfuge— along the main north-south line, holding Hardee's line in place. Then Sherman unleashed John C. Davis's Fourteenth Corps from the Army of the Cumberland to descend down the railroad tracks from the north and attack the vulnerable angle in the Confederate line. In one of the most fierce and concentrated battles of the Civil War, the Union troops assaulted Cleburne's division. As Confederate artillery blew holes in the advancing lines, Davis's men fell by the droves. Still, the Union mounted the only successful large-scale frontal assault of the Atlanta campaign.

Orderly Sergeant Walter Clark of the Sixty-third Georgia remembered the Union charge: "At 3 P.M. the enemy massed heavily in front of Lewis' Ky. [Orphan Brigade] and Govan's Ark. brigades and assaulted in three lines of battle, but were repulsed. They then formed in column of companies, making ten lines of battle, and renewed the attack. Our breastworks at this point were inferior and were manned only by a line in single rank. With such odds the issue could not long remain in doubt."[26]

When the Union forces reached the Confederate earthworks near the angle, the fighting quickly became hand to hand and the bayonet—rarely used— became the weapon of choice. In Brigadier General Absalom Baird's Tenth Kentucky Regiment, the three Noe brothers clambered over the earthworks together, and soon two of them had pinned two Confederates to the ground with their bayonets. After the war General Baird remarked, "On no occasion within my knowledge has the use of the bayonet been so general or so well authenticated."[27]

Yet despite the intensity of the battle, Hardee was able to beat off initial attacks and reinforce his right by transferring troops from the center of his line. However, Govan's crack troops—reduced to fighting with Bowie knives and bayonets and using their guns as clubs—were finally crushed by sheer numbers. Private Stan C. Harvey remembered, "They ran over us like a drove of Texas beeves, by sheer force of numbers."[28] Nearly six hundred members of Govan's brigade were captured, including Govan himself (he was later released in a prisoner exchange).

With great skill Hardee was able to temporarily close the gap and seal off the break caused by the collapse of the angle. Fortunately for Hardee, Howard's demonstrating Army of the Tennessee made no major advance before sunset. Had the Union attack come earlier in the day, Hardee's corps would have been crushed. However, darkness forced Sherman to break off the engagement. Hardee successfully fought one of the most desperate defensive battles of the war. And Sherman lost an opportunity to destroy or capture Hardee's entire corps.

As for the men of Mercer's brigade, they missed much of the direct action of the day.[29] Dug in and facing Howard's Army of the Tennessee, they did not receive the direct assault of the Yanks. However, the action was only yards away, close enough to keep them under fire and in constant tension. Captain Mercer recorded in his diary that the brigade lost sixty-one men that day, more than half taken as prisoners of war from the Fifty-seventh Georgia.[30]

Hardee knew that he must immediately retreat. And Hood had decided to abandon Atlanta. Remaining in Atlanta could result only in Union siege and Confederate starvation. If there were to be any chance of survival, the three corps of the Army of Tennessee had to be reunited in a defensible position.

The only direction that the Confederate army could go was south of Jonesboro. The hamlet of Lovejoy's Station was six miles below Jonesboro on the Macon and Western line and offered defensible terrain and earthworks. The three separated corps of the Army of Tennessee would attempt to meet at Lovejoy's Station.

By 5 P.M. on September 1, while Hardee was fighting for his life, Hood marched out of Atlanta with Stewart's corps and the Georgia Militia. Stephen D. Lee's corps was already moving toward Lovejoy's Station, separated from Hood. As Hood left Atlanta, he gave instructions to his rearguard cavalry to destroy all stockpiles of ammunition and supplies—supplies that the Confederate army desperately needed. The horse soldiers torched eighty-one freight cars of ammunition and seven locomotives, setting off explosions that could be heard for miles.

Hardee's task was more difficult. He had to disengage and retreat without Sherman's knowledge. Hardee's troops began to withdraw at about 10 P.M. Colonel Olmstead of Mercer's brigade recorded these moments:

The order to march came about 10 o'clock and the men moved out as silently as possible. A certain amount of noise could not be avoided, and that was accounted for to the enemy by sundry calls to the various Regiments to come and draw their rations.

We got away from the trenches without molestation and marching all night reached Lovejoy's Station on the Macon and Western Railroad about daylight. The memory of that night's march is like a horrible dream. I was so tired physically as scarcely to be able to sit on my horse, and the mental depression, deep enough because of our own failure, was the more profound as the red glare in the Northern sky and the sullen rumble of distant explosions told that Hood was burning his stores and abandoning Atlanta to Sherman. The long campaign had ended in defeat and disaster.[31]

September 2 found Hardee's corps exhausted but safely near Lovejoy's Station. Because Stewart's and Lee's corps would not arrive at Lovejoy's Station until evening on September 3, Hardee was again isolated, with only three divisions to face Sherman's pursuing twelve divisions. Hardee's men dug in furiously, knowing that only stout earthworks could save them.

At about 2 P.M. the Federals caught up with Hardee. Hardee had chosen a defensive position a mile north of Lovejoy's Station along a low ridge called Cedar Bluffs. He established a single line of battle that ran east to west. Sherman surveyed the scene, noting the strong Confederate earthworks, and decided to be cautious until he received definitive word from Atlanta and could better understand the disposition of Hood's troops. Sherman instructed his artillery to pound the Confederate entrenchments.

George Mercer surveyed the Union lines and reflected on Hardee's predicament:

> Hardee's Corps in position of great danger unless the rest of the Army forms a junction. Yesterday our army was completely dislocated; stated today that Atlanta has been abandoned, and the rest of the Army near enough to form a junction. From the level nature of the Country, our men on the main line and in rear of it, are greatly exposed to random bullets from the skirmish line; already some have been killed and wounded. . . . Prisoners report five Corps opposite to us. Heavy shelling all afternoon. Shrapnel, shell, and grape fall around our [headquarters] in profusion.[32]

On September 3—the same day that Stewart's and Lee's corps successfully joined up with Hardee's corps—Sherman received definitive word that Slocum's Twentieth Corps had occupied Atlanta. Sherman celebrated and, to the Confederates' utter surprise, decided to end the long and bloody campaign. Although he had an opportunity to press on and defeat Hood's Army of Tennessee once and for all, Sherman was aware that he was in the heart of enemy territory and dependent on a tenuous supply line. Now that he had gained his primary objective—the symbolic city of Atlanta—it was time to regroup. As Sherman later wrote, "[A]fter due reflection, I resolved not to attempt at that time a further pursuit of Hood's army, but slowly and deliberately to move back, occupy Atlanta, enjoy a short period of rest, and to think well over the next step required in the progress of events."[33]

On the night of September 5, 1864, Sherman's forces withdrew in triumph to Atlanta, leaving Hood's battered army thankful to be able to fight another day. Sherman telegraphed the War Department in Washington: "Atlanta is ours, and fairly won."[34]

The Tennessee Campaign

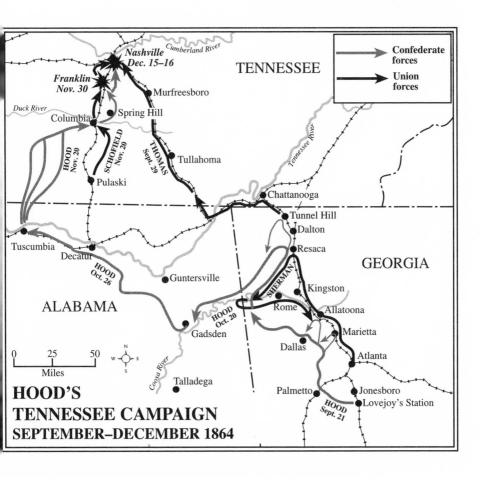

Confederate forces

Union forces

Cumberland River

Nashville
Dec. 15–16

TENNESSEE

Franklin
Nov. 30

Murfreesboro

Duck River

Columbia

Spring Hill

HOOD Nov. 20

SCHOFIELD Nov. 20

THOMAS Sept. 29

Tullahoma

Pulaski

Chattanooga

Tennessee River

Tunnel Hill

Dalton

Tuscumbia

Decatur

HOOD Oct. 26

Resaca

GEORGIA

Guntersville

SHERMAN

Kingston

ALABAMA

HOOD Oct. 20

Rome

Allatoona

Gadsden

Marietta

Dallas

Atlanta

0   25   50

N
W   E
S

Miles

Talladega

Palmetto

Jonesboro

Lovejoy's Station

HOOD Sept. 21

HOOD'S
TENNESSEE CAMPAIGN
SEPTEMBER–DECEMBER 1864

Coosa River

24

Crossing into Tennessee

It was a time of soul searching. Nine of the ten companies comprising the Fifty-seventh Georgia were from middle Georgia.[1] Some men had not been home in nearly a year. And now none of them was more than eighty miles from his family, a short train ride away. As Sherman's blue legions faded into the distance toward Atlanta and battlefields grew quiet, most men took stock of their situation.

Only fools and diehards refused to recognize that the Confederacy was in its death throes. The fall of Atlanta had broken its back. But its stubborn heart still beat. Now Rebs looked sullenly at each other, talked quietly, angrily, and asked the questions, "Why? Why continue on? Is prolonged defeat worth losing your life for? Why not go home?"

Pride, hate, and the refusal to let one's buddies down still had much power, although reason had lost its compass and purpose its allure. Although many men deserted, most did not because they could not face themselves if they did.

Robert Braswell must have had such thoughts. Now seventeen he was a dirty, ragged, gaunt rail. He had learned many things in three years of war. And one of them was to hate Yankees. He hated them for killing his brothers. And though he would not have known how to say it, he hated them for stealing his youth and robbing his innocence. As his later photographs so clearly show, his hawkish eyes would burn until his dying day. He yearned to go home, but he could not and would not.

The men had time to rest from September 6 through September 29, 1864. The blue stayed in Atlanta and the gray at Lovejoy's Station and, later, Palmetto, Georgia. It was as if a truce had been called and each side was catching up, preparing for another day. But turmoil wracked the Confederate command.

Hood was through with Hardee—repeatedly blaming Hardee, his most experienced and able corps commander, for the fall of Atlanta—and Hardee had had more of Hood than he could stomach. On September 8 Hood requested that Hardee be transferred and replaced by General Richard Taylor. Jefferson Davis decided to visit Hood's headquarters and check the volatile situation himself.[2]

What Davis found was that all three corps commanders—Hardee, Stewart, and Lee—believed that Hood should be replaced by Johnston or P. G. T. Beauregard. The old power triangle had reemerged, and Davis could not bring himself to consider that he had been wrong in removing Johnston from command or relegating Beauregard, who was recovering from an illness, to the defense of Charleston. Though Hood offered to resign, Davis turned him down. Davis then transferred Hardee to Charleston to take command of the Department of South Carolina, Georgia, and Florida.[3]

Davis also made a major structural change. He created a new organization called the Military Division of the West. Beauregard would command this new structure, which would be comprised of Hood's Department of Tennessee and Richard Taylor's Department of Alabama, Mississippi, and East Louisiana. Theoretically, this would place Beauregard in command of Hood and Taylor. In effect, however, Beauregard could serve as little more than a distant adviser. Bound by administrative duties at his headquarters offices, Beauregard would seldom be physically with the troops. And Beauregard's orders specifically stated that he would take immediate command of Hood's or Taylor's armies *only* if he were personally present with an army and only in time of extreme peril. In an age of slow communications and limited transportation, Beauregard was hamstrung from the beginning by his inability to direct Hood or Taylor from a distance. In short, Beauregard was given a promotion with little authority and nebulous lines of command. Such confusion only exacerbated Davis's command problem with Hood.[4]

While the generals squabbled, some Georgia boys were pleased to receive visits from family members. Colonel Charles Olmstead, still in temporary command of Mercer's brigade, was delighted when his wife and sister-in-law suddenly appeared in camp. However, all officers had been ordered to remain with their commands in anticipation of immediate troop movement. Unable to get a brief furlough so that he could spend some private time with his wife, Florence, Olmstead grew depressed. But Florence Olmstead used her charms in an all-out attack upon Olmstead's superiors. Olmstead later described for his children what happened:

> It looked blue enough for us until your Aunt Fan and mother went to put the matter before Gen Hardee, (whom they both knew,) carrying with them, for purposes of bribery, some of the good things they had brought up with them to reinforce our commissariat. The General was complaisant enough but said, "Ladies, this matter rests with Gen'l Cleburne who is here now; let me introduce him."
>
> The introduction was made and then Gen. Cleburne, who was a shy man, found himself in a tight place. He started to explain how essential it was to have all officers with the Division on that day, but every word of explanation and argument was met by gifts of peaches, apples, cakes and other appetizing things that were piled up in his arms while Gen Hardee stood by roaring with laughter. Of course, there was only one ending to the situation, the General surrendered at discretion for the first time in his life.[5]

The lull in warfare could not last, and the question was whether Hood or Sherman would make the first offensive move. On September 21, fifteen days after the final shot was fired at Lovejoy's Station, Hood moved his army twenty-four miles southwest of Atlanta to the small town of Palmetto and informed Richmond the next day that he had decided on an offensive plan. During this transition Brigadier General James Argyle Smith returned from medical furlough on September 24 to take command of Mercer's brigade, transferring Olmstead back to the command of the First Georgia Volunteers.[6]

Clearly, Sherman could not stay in Atlanta indefinitely. His only hope for permanent stability and resupply was to create a path to the sea, so that he could be supplied by the Union navy. As Sherman told Grant:

> It will be a physical impossibility to protect the railroads, now that Hood,
> Forrest, Wheeler, and the whole batch of devils, are turned loose without
> home or habitation. . . . I propose that we break up the railroad from Chat-
> tanooga forward, and that we strike out with our wagons for Milledgeville,
> Millen, and Savannah. Until we can repopulate Georgia, it is useless for us to
> occupy it; but the utter destruction of its roads, houses, and people, will
> cripple their military resources. By attempting to hold the roads, we will lose
> a thousand men each month, and will gain no result. I can make this march,
> and make Georgia howl![7]

If Sherman chose to march to the sea, he could go southeast to Savannah or southwest to Mobile. Hood's intelligence mistakenly predicted that Sherman was leaning toward Mobile, which would take him slashing through the munitions industry in the heart of Alabama. To do so Sherman would have to follow the West Point Railroad.[8]

However, if Hood could move first, he could slip northwest of Sherman and destroy the Nashville and Chattanooga Railroad, which had been supplying Atlanta. Sherman would then have no choice but to follow Hood and fight in the mountainous terrain that favored the Confederates.

For these reasons Hood beat Sherman to the draw and moved to Palmetto, next to the West Point Railroad and near the Chattahoochee River. From this point Hood could try to block any move that Sherman made toward Alabama, or Hood could move north and cut the Union supply line from Tennessee, drawing Sherman after him.

When Jefferson Davis visited Hood at Palmetto, they further revised the offensive plans. If Sherman pursued Hood into north Georgia and Hood found Sherman too strong to engage in battle, Hood would retreat through the mountains to Gadsden, Alabama, where he could be supplied by the Alabama and Tennessee Rivers Railroad. If Sherman refused to leave Georgia and moved toward the Gulf of Mexico or the Atlantic, Hood and Davis agreed that Hood would pursue Sherman. Their strategy was that Hood would do whatever he could to impede Sherman's progress, because the Southerner did not have enough troops to defeat Sherman's large army. But Hood could tie Sherman down until after the presidential election in November, moves that might help to defeat Lincoln and make the initiation of peace talks politically palatable.[9]

Hood's army left Palmetto on September 29, crossed the Chattahoochee over a pontoon bridge near Campbellton, and headed north. His combined force was nearly 40,000 men and moved rapidly. Sherman immediately pursued Hood, taking with him a force of five corps totaling 55,000 troops. He left only the 12,000 men of Slocum's Twentieth Corps to guard Atlanta. Sherman also detached George Thomas with two divisions to garrison Chattanooga and guard the back door of Tennessee.[10]

For the next two weeks Hood and Sherman played cat and mouse. Hood's forces repeatedly inflicted serious damage to the Western and Atlantic Railroad, but Sherman's wizardly engineers always made quick repairs. By marching twelve to eighteen miles most days, Hood's main force was able to elude Sherman, and Sherman was able to avoid the traps set by Hood.

Now they made two crucial decisions. Sherman made the first one. He was tired of chasing Hood. He was ready to get on with his plan to march to the sea and open up a port of supply for the navy. He wanted to demonstrate to Northern voters that a Union army could move at will through the heart of Dixie. And he wanted to "make Georgia howl," unleashing a new form of psychological warfare designed to crush the civilian population's will to fight. With Hood retreating across the Alabama border, Sherman decided to return to his own agenda.

When Sherman communicated his desires to Grant, Grant was dubious. Hood could not simply be left alone to raise havoc. Sherman countered by assuring Grant that Thomas would be supplied with enough troops to protect Tennessee and keep Hood off-balance and penned up. Should Hood follow Sherman toward Savannah, Thomas would cut in behind Hood, destroy his supply line from Selma, Alabama, and leave Hood's army vulnerable and helpless, sandwiched between two Union armies. Grant gave in, and ten days later Sherman returned to Atlanta, sending the Fourth and Twenty-third Corps to reinforce Thomas.[11]

Hood's decision was a fateful one. He and Jefferson Davis had agreed that if Sherman reversed fields and headed for salt water, Hood would follow closely behind, destroying Sherman's supply line and impeding his progress. Now, without consulting Davis, Hood decided not to follow Sherman. Instead, he would cross the Tennessee River, try to cut Sherman's rail line, then head toward Nashville and defeat Thomas before reinforcements could reach the Yanks. Hood had fanciful dreams that if he succeeded, he could invade Kentucky and force Sherman to withdraw from the South to fight Hood along the Ohio River.[12]

Although Beauregard was skeptical, he reluctantly acquiesced to Hood's plans, as did Jefferson Davis.[13]

On November 13 Hood began to cross the Tennessee River at Florence, Alabama, with Cheatham's corps crossing first.[14] Olmstead, commanding the First Georgia Volunteers, remembered the crossing clearly:

> The whole army was massed at this point in large open fields, preparatory to crossing the river on a pontoon bridge that had been laid there. The various Brigades and Divisions were all in column of fours side by side with only a few paces separating the columns—they made a very impressive sight for it is not often that one sees an entire army in such close masses. It was a bright autumnal Sunday morning, the church bells were ringing in the little town and as the commands moved down in succession to the bridge, with colors fluttering in the sun light there was a sense of exhilaration in being a part of the brilliant spectacle. The pontoons were deep in the water as we crossed and the current of the mighty river chafed and fretted against them, but all held safely to their mooring and there were no mishaps that came to my knowledge.[15]

As Hood's army crossed the Tennessee River, the hundreds of Tennessee veterans were greatly excited. But it was an ominous time for Georgia troops as they turned their backs on Sherman, who was now set loose to terrorize their state.

On November 15 Sherman, aware that Hood had crossed the Tennessee River, left Atlanta and began his march toward Savannah and the sea. The crusty old cuss was heard to say of Hood, "Damn him! If he will go to the Ohio River, I'll give him rations. . . . My business is down south." Sherman then destroyed the Atlanta railroad terminus and burned all structures of military importance. His rampaging troops soon got out of hand, burning and pillaging civilian homes as well. Ultimately, more than 40 percent of Atlanta was left in ruin. Hood's Georgia troops soon heard of the plundering of Atlanta and feared for their families, many of whom lived along Sherman's eighty-mile-wide path to the sea.[16]

Soldiers of the Fifty-seventh Georgia had special reason to be concerned. As Sherman split his army into two wings and began to burn, loot, and pillage his way across middle Georgia, most of the Georgians knew that their families and farms would be directly in Sherman's line of advance. The families of men from four of the Fifty-seventh's companies were spared by a margin of less than thirty miles. But those men serving in the five companies from Baldwin County (Milledgeville), Wilkinson County (Gordon, Irwinton), and Washington County (Sandersville) soon learned that Sherman was laying waste to their homes, farms, and towns.[17]

On November 21, as the men of the Fifty-seventh Georgia were preparing to march farther into Tennessee, one of the most ironic scenes of the Civil War was playing out in Milledgeville, Georgia, home of Company H, the Independent Volunteers. When this company was first formed in May 1862, a young man named David Snelling enlisted.[18] Though considered an intelligent and stable young man, Snelling had experienced a difficult and tragic boyhood. In 1842, when he was six years old, his father, William B. Snelling, and three of the boy's siblings died of typhoid fever while living in Crawford County. David's mother, Elizabeth Lester Snelling, then moved with her three surviving children near Milledgeville to live close to her three prosperous brothers, who together owned more than four thousand acres and 150 slaves. Her brothers provided her with a small house between their plantations, along with means of support.

Twelve years later, in 1854, Elizabeth Snelling and her only daughter died, leaving David, then eighteen, and his brother, William, twelve. Their uncles sent William to New Orleans to live with an aunt, while David remained in Milledgeville with his uncle David Lester. Although he was adequately supported by his uncle, David felt that he was not treated as well as his cousins. He grew particularly bitter when his cousins were allowed to go away to college, and he was sent into the fields to supervise the slaves.

While working as a plantation manager, he developed a hatred of slavery. He also yearned to be freed from his own sense of indentured captivity and begin a new life. When Captain Richard Bonner recruited a company of soldiers in Milledgeville for Confederate service, David Snelling, then twenty-six, saw his chance and volunteered in May 1862. The soldiers comprised Company H of the Fifty-seventh Georgia and were soon shipped to Tennessee to be part of the Kentucky campaign. Less than three months later, while on picket duty, Snelling slipped off into the night and crossed Union lines near Bridgeport, Alabama. On August 5, 1862, he enlisted in the Union army.

In November 1862 Snelling was promoted to first lieutenant and placed in command of Company I of the First Alabama Regiment of Union Cavalry. During the Atlanta and Carolina campaigns of 1864 and 1865 this regiment served as part of Kilpatrick's cavalry corps. More important, Company I was specifically assigned to be part of Sherman's escort, and Snelling came to know General Sherman personally.

On the night before Sherman entered Milledgeville, the Union general spent the evening in a log cabin on the deserted plantation of the stalwart Confederate leader general Howell Cobb, a former governor of Georgia. David Snelling was with Sherman and found himself back at home in a blue uniform. During the night an old slave appeared and asked to see General Sherman to assure himself that this really was Sherman and that the Union army had come to bring freedom to his people. Sherman recorded the moment in his *Memoirs:*

> The old man became convinced that the "Yankees" had come at last, about
> whom he had been dreaming all his life; and some of the staff-officers gave

*First Lieutenant David Snelling
(Special Collections, Ina Dillard Russell
Library, Georgia College & State University,
Milledgeville, Ga.)*

him a strong drink of whiskey, which set his tongue going. Lieutenant Snelling, who commanded my escort, was a Georgian and recognized in this old negro a favorite slave of his uncle, who resided about six miles off; but the old slave did not at first recognize his young master in our uniform. . . . [The slave's] attention was then drawn to Snelling's face, when he fell on his knees and thanked God that he had found his young master alive and along with the Yankees. Snelling inquired all about his uncle and the family, asked my permission to go and pay his uncle a visit, which I granted, of course. The uncle was not cordial, by any means, to find his nephew in the ranks of the host that was desolating the land.[19]

Actually, Lieutenant Snelling arrived at his uncle's plantation late that night with a raiding party. He stole fresh horses from his uncle's stable, took several hundred dollars' worth of property, and set fire to the gin house before leaving. It was not a pleasant encounter.[20]

The next day David Snelling was by Sherman's side as he entered Milledgeville, then the capital of Georgia. No greater irony—or disgrace—could have been perceived by Snelling's former comrades in the Fifty-seventh Georgia as Hood's army tramped across the Alabama border into Tennessee.

On November 21 Hood at last gave orders for his army to break camp and march north into Tennessee. However, Mercer's brigade, now under James Argyle

Smith's command, was detached from Cleburne's division and remained behind to help ferry supplies across the Tennessee River. The supply train primarily carried vital foodstuffs and salt to preserve meat. Olmstead recalled:

> The orders finally came for the army to go forward into Tennessee but to our great disappointment Smith's Brigade did not march with it. We were detached and sent to a place called Cheatham's Ferry some twelve miles or so from Florence to aid in getting a supply train across the River. I learned that we were chosen for this service because being men from the coast we were supposed to have some knowledge of the management of boats.[21] We waited for two days at the Ferry before the train arrived on the other side of the river and then getting the wagons over gave pretty strenuous work for four or five days more, (though there was no let up at night)—for the river was a mile broad, the current was strong, and two or three old flat boats were the only means of transportation. At last the job was completed and we were on the march once more, but a full week behind the rest of the army.[22]

The weeklong detachment spared Mercer's brigade from the bloodletting that was soon to occur near the small Tennessee town of Franklin. Sergeant Walter Clark of the Sixty-third Georgia later quipped that Hood's "salt had literally saved our bacon."[23]

25
Cold-Blooded Murder

Upon arriving from Atlanta to take command of Union forces in Tennessee in early October 1864, General George Thomas faced the task of pulling together far-flung detachments of soldiers. With reinforcements sent by Sherman from Georgia, Thomas soon commanded an army of seventy thousand troops.[1] In contrast, Hood had a tattered army of thirty-eight thousand soldiers—including Nathan Bedford Forrest's crack cavalry—organized into three corps and twelve divisions and supported by 108 pieces of artillery. Hood could not take on the combined force of Thomas's army with much hope of victory.[2]

As the Rebel army stepped across the Tennessee border on November 21, 1864, and headed north, Hood was wedded to a hazy plan that was reasonable only if all the pieces fell into place. Hood was aware that two Union corps—nearly thirty thousand men under the command of Major General John Schofield—were temporarily camped at Pulaski, Tennessee. Recently arrived from Atlanta, they were separated by seventy miles from Thomas's main force, which was due north in Nashville. Hood determined to slip between Thomas and Schofield and pounce on Schofield before Thomas could come to his aid. If Hood could reach the strategic town of Columbia, Tennessee, thirty miles north of Pulaski, he would block Schofield's path to Nashville and trap him south of the Duck River. But to do so Hood had to move his army quickly and quietly.

The weather in Tennessee was cold, sleeting, and miserable. Both armies would soon endure one of the worst winters of the century. As they marched north through ice and slush, at least one-fourth of the Confederates were barefoot and few owned overcoats or adequate clothing.[3] Most relied on a single blanket for warmth and protection. The suffering from frostbite, hunger, and exhaustion would soon be severe.

To hasten his progress Hood divided his army into three columns and had them advance along parallel paths. The three corps were to link up at the hamlet of Mount Pleasant, Tennessee, and then move a dozen miles eastward to slam the back door on Schofield at Columbia. But Hood would have to reach Columbia before Schofield moved north to join Thomas in Nashville.

Schofield was blind to Hood's movement until Union cavalry scouts found Alexander Stewart's corps due west of Pulaski—parallel to Schofield—and halfway to Columbia. Schofield reacted instantly and ordered his troops to double-time to Nashville. Schofield recognized what Hood was up to and knew that he was in a race for his life.

Forrest's cavalry immediately harassed Schofield's troop movement. However, the able Union general Jacob D. Cox slipped his five-thousand-man advance division into Columbia on November 24, shortly before the Confederates arrived. Had Cox not won the race to Columbia, the bridges across the Duck River would have been in Hood's possession and Schofield caught en route and crushed.[4]

Schofield soon realized that his position at Columbia was impossible to defend. His back was pressed against the Duck River, and Forrest's cavalry could easily bypass Schofield's flanks, leaving him open to attack from the rear. Schofield abandoned his untenable position on the night of November 27 and crossed to the more defensible northern side of the Duck River, destroying the bridges behind him. The Yanks dug in and waited for Hood to attack. North and South had roughly equal troop strength for this fight, but Schofield knew that he had the defensive advantage.

Taking a lesson from Sherman, Hood decided not to attack Schofield but to secretly flank him, sending Cheatham's and Stewart's corps to Spring Hill, twelve miles north of Columbia and astride the Nashville Turnpike. If Hood could reach Spring Hill and entrench, he would have Schofield bagged and separated from Thomas.[5]

To keep Schofield confused and pinned down, Hood left most of his artillery and his wagon trains with Stephen Lee's corps in Columbia. Hood ordered Lee to commence a concentrated fire on the Union force in a subterfuge that would force Schofield to prepare for an imminent attack. As a result Hood's flanking forces, which were racing toward Springfield, moved without artillery support or resupply.[6]

Schofield was initially confused by Hood's covert maneuvers. Although he refused to move the bulk of his entrenched force until he understood the situation better, he did send Major General David Stanley with two divisions directly up the Nashville Turnpike toward Spring Hill to guard the back door for Schofield and secure his immediate line of retreat. Schofield also sent some of his wagon trains and his reserve artillery with Stanley to give them a head start toward his ultimate objective of Nashville.

What neither Stanley nor Hood knew was that they were dashing toward Spring Hill on parallel roads only a few miles apart. The Union force won the race by a whisker. Upon entering Spring Hill, General Stanley quickly consolidated and positioned his brigades, as Stewart's and Cheatham's Confederate corps came over the horizon with battle flags flying. Stanley now realized that his five thousand soldiers faced two-thirds of the Army of Tennessee—seven divisions and more than twenty-thousand veteran Rebs. But he also knew that he must hold open Schofield's primary line of retreat to Nashville at all hazards.

Grimly, Stanley arranged his men in a thin semicircle around Spring Hill and frantically threw together breastworks. Now thankful that Schofield had burdened him with the reserve artillery, he positioned his thirty-four guns to mow down advancing Rebel infantry. The plucky general then squinted toward his greatest ally, the rapidly setting sun.

As Hood approached Spring Hill with Cheatham's corps, he was fatigued and gripped by pain. He had strapped himself to his saddle early that morning and ridden at the front of his advancing army for long hours. Now the raw stub of his amputated thigh burned and his pelvis ached. His artificial cork leg stuck out stiffly from his saddle at an unnatural angle, and the black boot and spur wedged on his false foot looked ludicrous. It was past time for the poor man to dismount and rest.[7]

Pat Cleburne's division was in the point position of Cheatham's corps as they approached Spring Hill and was the first to engage Stanley's Union force. At 4 P.M. Cleburne's three thousand men surged forward and were soon ripped by raking fire from concealed Federals on their flank. Cleburne's troops fought fiercely and would have routed Stanley if the Union commander had not played his trump card—the reserve artillery that Schofield had entrusted to him. With no Confederate artillery to counteract the Union firepower, Cleburne's attack was blunted by three Union batteries, and he was forced to withdraw and regroup.[8]

As Cleburne's men engaged the Federals, Hood finally gave in to his pain and exhaustion. The foggy-headed general retreated to the comfort of Absalom Thompson's nearby farmhouse, where Hood would remain for the rest of the day and night. Cheatham became the on-scene commander of Confederate troops. Incredibly, Cheatham and Hood shared no common vision or plan for the rapidly accelerating battle. The deterioration that was beginning to infect the Confederate command structure perhaps has no equal in the annals of the Civil War.

As Cleburne realigned his bloodied soldiers, he needed the troops from the detached Mercer's brigade, which was still detained on the Tennessee River. Cleburne soon received orders from Cheatham to wait until he could be reinforced by other Confederate units. As time ticked away and the sun dropped lower in the darkening winter sky, chaos developed as arriving brigades tried to coordinate and get into position. Night fell without another Confederate assault. General Govan of Cleburne's division bitterly summarized the day: "We could have in twenty minutes captured or destroyed Stanley." But it was not to be.[9]

Darkness was complete by 6:15 P.M., and confusion among Confederate commanders was great. Hood and Cheatham each gave orders and then countermanded each other's orders, until no one had a clear picture of the positioning of Confederate troops. This situation was made more difficult because Hood's mind was no longer on the battle.

After darkness had fallen, Hood enjoyed a sumptuous dinner given by his hosts, the Thompsons, that was accompanied by much toasting. The weary and weakened general, who had arisen at 3 that morning, fell into bed at 9 P.M. and was lost in a deep—and perhaps drugged—sleep. He assumed that the Nashville Turnpike was adequately blocked, preventing any advance northward by Union troops. He was mistaken. Through a series of events that were bitterly disputed for years after the war and are just as obscure today, the turnpike was left wide open. Indeed, instead of bisecting the turnpike, the slumbering Confederate camps were positioned parallel to it. The road was open for the Union armies to advance if they dared. And Schofield had no choice but to dare. [10]

As Hood slept, Schofield was retreating from Columbia and praying for deliverance. By early that afternoon he had become aware that the bulk of Hood's troops were north of him and that his only hope of survival was to break through the tightening Rebel noose and join Thomas in Nashville. Leaving enough men in Columbia to keep Stephen Lee's demonstrating corps at bay until nightfall, Schofield prodded his divisions up the turnpike toward Spring Hill. The approaching darkness—and the diminished ammunition supply of Forrest's cavalry—would prove Schofield's salvation.

Around 7 P.M. Schofield entered Spring Hill virtually undetected. He assumed, of course, that the Confederates had blocked the Nashville Turnpike north of Spring Hill and determined that his only chance was to burst through the blockade in the middle of the night. As the lead elements of the Union force slipped out of Spring Hill to walk into the mouth of the lion, they literally tiptoed past the edges of the Confederate camps. According to Captain James A. Sexton of the Seventy-second Illinois, "We were in such close proximity to the Confederates, that we could see their long line of campfires as they burned brightly; could hear the rattle of their canteens; see the officers and men standing around the fires; while the rumbling of our wagon train on the pike, and the beating of our own hearts were the only sounds we could hear on our side." [11]

Incredibly, Schofield's force was not detected. By dawn the last of the straggling Union wagons had cleared the Confederate lines, and by midmorning the Union forces had arrived in the picturesque town of Franklin, Tennessee, nestled on the Harpeth River eight miles north of Spring Hill. Scarcely believing that they had made it, a Union officer wrote that a single Confederate brigade, "planted squarely across the pike, either south or north of Spring Hill, would have effectually prevented Schofield's retreat, and daylight would have found his whole force cut off from every avenue of escape by more than twice its numbers, to assault whom would have been madness, and to avoid whom would have been impossible." [12]

Hood awoke in a groggy stupor, only to learn that fate and incompetence had dealt him a terrible hand. As his commanding officers gathered for an early breakfast briefing and the Confederate folly became clear, Hood exploded. As Major General John Brown recalled, Hood was as "wrathy as a rattlesnake," full of venom and pent-up anger.[13] A sense of shame descended on the Confederate command in a chivalric age when shame could not be borne. Shame could be relieved only by retribution, revenge, or penance. Hood would see to it that his army repented deeply for its sins. Honor must be restored.

Painfully strapping himself to his saddle once more, Hood pursued Schofield with vengeance. Nearing Franklin, he seethed, loathing his commanding officers. As was his pattern, Hood convinced himself that his disgrace was their fault. If Cleburne had pressed the initial charge at Spring Hill, the Yankees would have been crushed. If only Cheatham had led competently while his commander slept, today would be the dawn of bright promise. But his officers and his men had become cowards, Hood irrationally concluded. Atlanta had placed in their hearts an intolerable fear of frontal assaults against breastworks. Now they must be chastened and taught a lesson. Now they must learn that the only way to win battles is by heroic charges at the point of the bayonet. Such were Hood's dark thoughts and mood as he drew close to Franklin.[14]

Around noon Hood came within sight of Franklin while he was riding in front with Stewart's advance corps. The Columbia Pike approached Franklin from the south by passing between two low hills, Breezy Hill and Winstead Hill, and opening out upon the broad, flat, and treeless plain that led to Franklin two miles away. Franklin, cradled in a horseshoe bend of the Harpeth River, was a bridgehead for commerce crossing the Harpeth and traveling to Nashville, eighteen miles away. Its strategic bridges now had Schofield stalled. Earlier, they had been partially destroyed, and Schofield's engineers were working feverishly to repair them so that Union troops and the supply train could join Thomas in Nashville.

Hood rode to the top of Winstead Hill, where he met his senior officers and surveyed the scene. In previous months Forrest had engaged in cavalry operations around Franklin and knew the lay of the land. As the Confederate officers looked through their field glasses, they saw a chilling sight: permanent breastworks, deep ditches, and a battery of long-range rifled cannon sited on the broad plain. The Union army had recognized Franklin's strategic importance and had strongly fortified the town since 1862. Pat Cleburne, comprehending the Union strength, lowered his field glasses and quietly muttered, "They are very formidable."[15] Cheatham and Forrest were more forceful. Cheatham addressed Hood directly, saying, "I don't like the looks of this fight. The Federals have an excellent position, and are well fortified. . . . [We] would take a desperate chance if we attempted to dislodge them."[16]

Forrest used a different tack and presented an alternative offensive plan.

After apprising Hood that he thought a head-on assault would be disastrous, he said, "General Hood, if you will give me one strong division of infantry with my cavalry, I will agree to flank the Federals from their works within two hours time."[17]

Hood did not listen. In fact, his blood boiled. He was tired of an army—and generals—afraid of earthworks. Timid talk of flanking rankled him. In his memoir he was frank about his frustration that afternoon:

> The best move in my career as a soldier, I was thus destined to behold come to naught [at Spring Hill]. The discovery that the Army, after a forward march of one hundred and eighty miles, was still, seemingly, unwilling to accept battle unless under the protection of breastworks, caused me to experience grave concern. In my inmost heart I questioned whether or not I would ever succeed in eradicating this evil. It seemed to me I had exhausted every means in the power of one man to remove this stumbling block to the Army of Tennessee. . . . I hereupon decided, before the enemy would be able to reach his stronghold at Nashville, to make that same afternoon another and final effort to overtake and rout him, and drive him in the Big Harpeth river at Franklin, since I could no longer hope to get between him and Nashville, by reason of the short distance from Franklin to that city, and the advantage which the Federals enjoyed in the possession of the direct road.[18]

The anger and disgust in Hood's tone were evident even fifteen years later, when he wrote this apologia shortly before his death. On Winstead Hill these emotions pushed Hood beyond reason. Lowering his field glasses, he belligerently ordered an immediate frontal assault.

Hood's decision was tragically ironic. A devotee of Robert E. Lee's, Hood often fashioned his offensive plans after the example of his hero. Only this time, the example he chose to emulate was Pickett's Charge at Gettysburg on July 3, 1863. There, against the strongest protests of James Longstreet, Lee had also stubbornly ordered a frontal assault across a wide pastureland.

Yet Robert E. Lee's chances of success in that debacle were so much greater than Hood's. Lee's advancing infantry had to cover only one mile of open plain, whereas Hood faced two miles. Lee's assault was preceded by nearly two hours of Confederate artillery bombardment from 170 guns with 130 to 150 rounds each, the greatest concentration of artillery fire ever unleashed on American soil until that day.[19] Hood, in contrast, would send the Army of Tennessee against the Union line with no artillery support. Finally, at Gettysburg the Union soldiers were not shielded by strong earthworks, only a low stone wall and flimsy barricades of fence rails. Union forces at Franklin were powerfully and professionally entrenched.

If Hood had learned from Gettysburg, he would not have attempted this frontal assault. But Hood did not think or remember. He reacted in anger and sickness. The result was wanton murder. Hood would lose seven thousand men, nearly a quarter of his attacking force.

Quickly snapping orders, Hood aligned the Army of Tennessee for the offensive. He would shove off before Stephen Lee's corps, which was escorting the artillery and ammunition trains, could arrive and lend support. With vengeance he directed the divisions of Cleburne and Brown to spearhead the assault and drive right up the middle of the Yankee gauntlet. Brown would advance on the left side of the Columbia Pike and Cleburne on the right. These generals may have faltered and hesitated at Spring Hill but they would not on this day, thought Hood. Now they would look directly down the barrels of Union cannon and face the strongest point of the Yankee entrenchment.[20]

As Cleburne prepared his men for their advance, he must have sorely missed Mercer's Georgia brigade, which was still detached on the Tennessee River, ferrying supplies. He desperately needed their manpower. Now he would depend on the three brigades that had been with him all the way: Govan's Arkansans, Hiram Granbury's Texans, and Lowrey's Alabama-Mississippi boys.

Govan remembered Cleburne's briefing even many years later:

Looking over and beyond the bare common over which we had to move, you could see behind the heavy earthworks the bristling bayonets of the enemy, and glitter of Napoleon guns, as they peeped through the embrasures. . . . [Cleburne] seemed greatly depressed and fully realized, as did every officer present, the desperate nature of the assault we were about to make. He informed us that by the direction of Gen. Hood he had called us together to impress upon us the importance of carrying the works of the enemy at all hazards; that we were to move forward at the sound of the bugle, moving on the flank until we came under fire, then change front, form into line, fix bayonets and take the works at the point of the bayonet.[21]

As Cleburne dismissed his officers, Govan saluted and gravely said to Cleburne, "Well, General, few of us will ever return to Arkansas to tell the story of this battle." Cleburne, perhaps smiling, replied, "Well, Govan, if we are to die, let us die like men." The reference to honor was appropriate. Hood had questioned and challenged Cleburne's honor and professionalism, and Cleburne would seek vindication at all costs.[22]

At four o'clock, a half-hour before sunset, Hood's Army of Tennessee formed a front that was a mile and a half long, unfurled its regimental battle flags, and marched to battle as bands played "Dixie" and "The Bonnie Blue Flag." With parade ground precision Cheatham's corps advanced on the left and Stewart's corps on the right, with Forrest's cavalry screening both flanks. Union soldiers gazed across their breastworks and were awed by the martial beauty of the sight. Then the first shot was fired, and frozen winter fields became gory slaughter grounds.

The Battle of Franklin, Tennessee, became one of the most fierce and tragic battles of the Civil War. Although the Confederates were able to bravely penetrate a solid wall of minié balls and canister and reach the Union breastworks, they could not sustain the attack in the absence of supporting artillery fire or the assistance that could have come from Stephen Lee's missing corps. In the midst of intense hand-to-hand combat, some of Hood's units were able to breach the Union line. However, Union reserve forces poured into the fight and pushed the Southerners back. As darkness fell, hundreds of Rebels lay helplessly plastered against the south side of the Union breastworks, unable to retreat or go forward. They refused to give up, blindly holding their rifles over the very top of the trench wall and then pulling the trigger. Indeed, sporadic and uncoordinated Confederate charges continued until late in the night. But the Union had broken the back of the Army of Tennessee by dusk. Darkness only shielded the immensity of the slaughter.

During the night Schofield successfully disengaged his Union forces, crossed the Harpeth, and continued on to Nashville. At sunrise Hood awoke to the extent of his losses. Most grievously, he had decimated his officer corps. Hood had lost twelve generals and fifty-five regimental commanders. Among the dead were Major General Patrick Cleburne and brigadiers general Hiram Granbury, John Carter, John Adams, States Rights Gist, and Otho Strahl. This was by far the worst loss of general officers by either side in a single attack during the war. Such experienced leadership could not be replaced and shattered the heart of Hood's army.

As the wounded were carried away and the dead buried, grizzled veterans agreed that Franklin was a scene of unmatched horror. Although a precise count of Confederate casualties was never made, Hood lost as many as seven thousand men, whereas the Yanks lost 2,326. On the morning after the battle a Confederate soldier saw "Gen. Hood and part of his staff coming up the pike road on horseback. Gen. Hood stopped close to where I was standing and took a long view of the arena of the awful contest. His sturdy visage assumed a melancholy appearance, and for a considerable time he sat on his horse and wept like a child."[23]

Hood's tears, though authentic, could not change the bitterness that now clutched the hearts of Confederate soldiers who had witnessed first his incompetence at Spring Hill and now his butchering of Confederate troops at Franklin. A surviving captain from Texas in Cleburne's decimated division spoke plainly:

Our Brigade [Granbury's Texans] and the Arkansas Brigade [Govan's] are so badly cut up that we can't move. Some officers have no men, and some companies have [no] officers. So we have to reorganize and consolidate. A Captain has to command the brigade. . . .

Gen. Hood has betrayed us. This is not the kind of fighting he promised us at Tuscumbia and Florence, Alabama, when we started into Tennessee. This was not a "fight with equal numbers and choice of the ground" by no means. . . . The wails and cries of widows and orphans made at Franklin will heat up the fires of the bottomless pit to burn the soul of Gen. J. B. Hood for Murdering their husbands and fathers. . . . It can't be called anything else but cold blooded murder.[24]

With far fewer generals to consult, John Bell Hood buried his dead, abandoned his wounded, and trudged on toward Nashville. What he would do when he arrived and faced Thomas's overpowering force eluded his muddled mind. But to retreat was to admit defeat. And to advance was to face annihilation. The crippled general limped blindly on.[25]

26

The Destruction of an Army

Two days before the Battle of Franklin, Mercer's brigade had completed the ferrying of supplies across the mile-wide Tennessee River and loaded everything on 140 wagons. On November 28 the unit left Cheatham's Ferry with the supply train and proceeded north to rejoin Hood's army.[1] The brigade would not hear of the catastrophe at Franklin until December 2, 1864, two days after the battle.

On December 3 Mercer's brigade passed through the beautiful village of Columbia and learned that its division commander, General Cleburne, had been buried nearby at Ashwood the day before. On his way toward Spring Hill on November 26, Cleburne had stopped to rest at the Lucius Polk plantation (home of the brother of the slain bishop-general Leonidas Polk) and had been enamored of the ivy-draped gothic chapel, St. John's. While walking through the lovely chapel cemetery, reading tombstones and breathing in the lush beauty, Cleburne had remarked to a staff member, Captain Hill, "It would not be hard to die if one could be buried in such a beautiful spot." When he was killed four days later, his men remembered his words. A small detachment brought the general's body back to the quiet cemetery and fulfilled his wish. Now Mercer's brigade, in shock and grief, paid its respects to its fallen hero.[2]

As they passed through Spring Hill, the Georgians ran into the first grisly evacuation sites for Confederate wounded. On December 4 their wagons rumbled along the Columbia Pike below Winstead Hill, and they marched down the attack route that led to Franklin. Remembering the moment, Charles Olmstead wrote:

> We arrived at Franklin on the third day after the battle and I had opportunity to examine the ground. . . . Every field officer in [Cleburne's] Division was either killed or wounded while the loss of the rank and file was awful. . . . I saw several of the enemys dead still lying in the field and all along the front of the works there were little pools of congealed blood in the frozen earth where our poor Southern boys had died. In one place the horse of a Confederate General lay astride of the parapet where he and his rider had been killed. I learned that this was General Adams the commander of a Mississippi Brigade.
> . . . It was impossible to avoid the thought that but for the detail that sent

202

us to Cheathams Ferry we too would in all probability have shared the same fate.[3]

Stunned by the decimation of their division, the men of Mercer's brigade did not have long to dwell on the debacle at Franklin. They pushed on eighteen miles to the outskirts of Nashville, rejoining Cleburne's shattered division on December 5. With the death of Cleburne, James Argyle Smith was promoted to division commander, and Charles Olmstead again returned to command Mercer's brigade, a position he would retain until the end of the war. Mercer's brigade joined Daniel Govan's and Mark Lowrey's brigades on the extreme right flank of the Confederate line near Brentwood, two and a half miles from Nashville. Granbury's brigade—which had been reduced from eleven hundred to 460 men at Franklin—was held in reserve.[4]

As the Fifty-seventh Georgia fell into line, Edwin Tralona Davis felt a new weight of responsibility on his young shoulders. He had left Mercer University only three years before as a naive fraternity boy, marching north as a second sergeant to participate in Bragg's invasion of Kentucky. Now, in the wake of the decimation of the officer corps at Atlanta and Franklin, the more seasoned Edwin Davis suddenly was promoted to captain of Company B of the Fifty-seventh Georgia. His college education and speaking ability had propelled him through the ranks. Now he would have to do more than speak well and look good. He would have to lead.[5]

Robert Braswell had walked step by step with Edwin Davis, enduring the same hardships and learning the same lessons. But Braswell was still a private and would remain such. After three years of military service he was still only seventeen. His youth and lack of formal education kept him in the ranks. And the tall, skinny boy probably was comfortable there. Still stunned by the death of his brothers in Atlanta, he could barely cope with the stress of combat.

The Georgians shivered as they arrived on the Confederate line at dusk and tried to dig in. Many cursed as their shovel blades bent, and they wished that they could use explosives to blast holes in the frozen clay. They suffered even more as the weather grew worse.[6]

As his troops agonized, Hood tried to break through his mental fog to concoct a coherent plan. Hood may or may not have known that Brigadier General George Thomas now had an army of seventy thousand well-supplied and rested troops, making Nashville one of the most fortified and defensible cities under Union control. Against this strength Hood could muster, at most, twenty-three thousand debilitated men, including cavalry. Why was Hood placing his army against such odds?[7]

Hood later explained that he believed that if he retreated from Tennessee, he had no way to avoid leaving his rear vulnerable to attack. He also acknowledged that he could not go on the offensive against Thomas because of his lack of strength. His only hope, Hood reasoned, was to place himself in a strong defensive position and dare Thomas to attack him. Only by such defensive tactics could Hood reduce Thomas's numerical advantage.[8]

Even if Hood's reasoning had been sound, he selected a poor location to fight a defensive battle. With a thin Confederate line four miles long, he faced a fortified Union line that extended for ten miles. Both ends of the Confederate line were exposed and could be flanked with ease.[9]

The ever-prudent George Thomas watched Hood from the warmth of his hotel room in Nashville. He would not play cat and mouse with Hood. When he struck Hood, he would do so with such brutal force and careful planning that he would crush the Army of Tennessee and remove its presence from the war. Only one thing worried Thomas. He had manpower and provisions enough to shatter Hood. But he lacked cavalry or, more specifically, cavalry horses. Thomas knew that once he cracked Hood's line, the Confederate force would flee for the safety of Alabama and Georgia. Only with adequate cavalry could Thomas mop up and capture Hood's fragmented army, completely subduing it.[10]

As a result Thomas and Hood sat and stared at each other. Hood was paralyzed. And Thomas would not advance until he had procured horses and everything was in perfect order for complete victory. Thomas was slow. But he was methodically cocking the hammer of an incredibly powerful weapon.

The men of Mercer's brigade had to endure the Nashville trenches for only two days. During this brief stay they skirmished with the first black Union soldiers that they had encountered. On December 6 General James Steedman's black troops drove in the Georgia pickets and instilled some respect among Olmstead's troops. The next day the Rebs retook the ground they had lost.[11] On December 8 Olmstead received unexpected orders to march his brigade twenty-eight miles southeast to Murfreesboro to reinforce Forrest's detached cavalry.

As Olmstead's troops pulled out of line at daybreak on December 9 and moved toward Murfreesboro, the weather grew even worse. The temperature dropped below ten degrees, and a mixture of sleet, rain, and snow began to fall. As the Georgia troops neared Forrest's headquarters in the late afternoon, they encountered an icy stream. To avoid wading through it, they found a high railroad trestle that spanned the stream. The slippery trestle had no flooring or handrail, but conquering their fear of heights was not half as bad as walking through freezing water. As Olmstead later described the scene, "Some of the leading files started [across] in an upright position, but did not keep it up more than a few steps. [They soon began] 'cooning it,' on their hands and knees over the ice coated cross-ties. It was rather a funny sight and there was much laughing and joking over it."[12]

As night descended, Olmstead's four regiments approached Forrest's head-quarters and were ordered to bivouac. Many troops were drained by the journey and were in danger of suffering frostbite. More than two hundred men in Mercer's brigade had no shoes.[13] Private Walter Clark of the Sixty-third Georgia was dressed better than most, and he noted that he "wore a thin fatigue jacket, with no overcoat and slept under a single blanket with the thermometer at nine degrees above zero."[14] Private John Methvin of the Fifty-seventh Georgia noted that "[t]hrough all this campaign in winter sleet and snow, my clothing consisted of a suit of thin cotton underwear, a pair of mixed wool and cotton pants, two threadbare round jackets, a slouch hat from the Franklin battlefield, shoes which had lost their heels, and no blanket to cover me when I slept."[15] The Georgia boys, who had been unable to light fires to warm themselves while they were in the Nashville trenches, now were in for a pleasant surprise.

They were directed "into bivouac in a thick cedar thicket at that point where there was perfect shelter from the icy wind, good water, and unlimited supply of cord wood that had been cut and piled for the Railroad near by," Olmstead wrote.[16] The wood instantly disappeared, and blazing fires soon illuminated the night sky. Many Rebs scorched the frayed backs of their butternut jackets and patched britches as they hovered close to the flames. Private Methvin remembered, "I slept between a meager fire and a board set up edgeways to keep off the wind. Sleeping thus one night, too close to the fire, my jackets were scorched out on the back till there was nothing at that spot between my skin and the outside world and weather except my thin cotton shirt."[17] For a brief moment Olmstead's men were snug and safe.

The next day, December 9, Olmstead awoke in an apprehensive state. After breakfast he was to report to his new commander, Major General Nathan Bedford Forrest. By now no Confederate officer in the western theater garnered more respect and mystique than the "Wizard of the Saddle." Olmstead approached his interview with a reverential fear, and he later recorded the occasion for his grandchildren:

> I left the Brigade in its comfortable camp and went to find Genl Forrest to
> report to him in person. A sleet storm had sprung up during the night, driven
> by a fierce gale and I rode right in the teeth of it, unable to see more than a
> few yards ahead. Poor Lady Gray's mane and tail were frozen stiff and my own
> hair and beard and every fold of my clothing were encrusted with ice. When
> the General's Head Quarters were finally reached I had to be helped from
> the saddle, but a blazing fire of great logs, by which the General was standing,
> quickly restored circulation, which was assisted also by a "nip" from his flask
> which he considerately handed me.

As Olmstead felt the reviving warmth of Forrest's own brandy, he could not help but stare at the living Confederate legend. Olmstead had never dreamed that he would serve under Forrest's command. Even decades later his initial impressions of Forrest remained indelible:

> The first look at him as he stood there, fully satisfied my preconceptions of the man; he appeared the born soldier that he was, Six feet and over in height, straight as an arrow, black hair, and piercing black eyes, a ruddy complexion and an indefinable something in his bearing that stamped him as a leader of men. That he had no education to speak of was currently reported and a little order, written by himself, that I received from him later on, gave demonstration of the truth of this; there was scarcely a word of it that was up to the dictionary standard. But what a *man* he was in all that makes manhood.[18]

Within six months the men of Mercer's brigade had experienced leadership under two of the finest combat officers in the Confederacy—Cleburne and Forrest. Even in the chaos of war, such leadership was transforming the brigade's self-image.

While Olmstead met with Forrest, Mercer's Georgians were sent out in the sleet storm to destroy track on the Nashville and Chattanooga Railroad. Long after the war Walter Clark of the Sixty-third Georgia grimaced when he remembered how painful it was to handle the rails without gloves.[19]

Finally, on December 10 the weather grew so severe that both Yanks and Rebs suspended all unnecessary tasks. Two days later Hamilton Branch of the Fifty-fourth Georgia scrawled a note to his mother: "As we had nothing to eat yesterday we did not work, nor have we worked today, but have been in bivouac about ½ mile from the rail road. We have been hearing heavy fireing the last two days in the direction of Nashville. I have just taken a good wash and put on good clean cloths and am therefore free from lice."[20]

On December 13 and 14 Mercer's brigade was back at work ripping up railroad track. Fortunately, the weather was gradually improving. As the grinding work continued, Branch wrote in his journal, "At Dr. Coleman's request Capt. Moody and myself accompanied him to a little sociable at Mr. Goodmans, about 2 miles from here. We had quite a nice time, there were 8 ladies and 8 gentleman. We danced until 1 o'clock, and also eat a very find [*sic*] supper." Presumably, Branch had bathed again and was once more louse free.[21]

On December 15 the artillery fire more than twenty miles away in Nashville intensified. Everyone knew that the long-anticipated battle had begun. Forrest, who was preparing to attack Murfreesboro, now waited for new orders.

In Nashville, George "Old Slow Trot" Thomas had finally located enough horses—his troops had even raided a circus tent—and pulled himself together.

*First Lieutenant Hamilton Branch
(Courtesy of the Kenan Research Center
at the Atlanta History Center)*

He had so tried the patience of the War Department and enraged General Grant that he had come within a breath of being removed from command for not attacking Hood. When he did, the Southern line caved in. Within two days the shattered Army of Tennessee was fleeing south toward Columbia, where Hood hoped to reorganize and make a stand on the Duck River.[22]

On the afternoon of December 16 a courier reached Forrest with orders to begin a forced march to link up with Hood in Columbia. Olmstead captured the moment in his memoirs, recalling that the retreat began five minutes later:

> Then began a march that had few parallels in the war for downright hardship and suffering—every circumstance conspired to make it such. The country was covered with sleet and snow, the weather was bitter. Many of the men of the brigade were absolutely barefooted, while all of them were clad in worn clothing that was three fourths cotton; not one in a hundred had an overcoat and added to all this was a knowledge of disaster and of the fact that the Federal army was between us and Hood. Everything combined to weigh down heart and soul with a deep sense of depression.
>
> I can not remember how late we marched that night but by crack of dawn on the following morning we were on the road again. And what a day that was! I saw with my own eyes, again and again, the print of bloody feet in the snow and men fell out of the column from whom we never heard again.[23]

On the night of December 18, 1864, Forrest's vanguard reached Columbia about midnight. His men had marched sixty miles in forty-eight hours in bitter cold. The cost was high. Hamilton Branch noted that Mercer's brigade lost three hundred to four hundred weakened men who had dropped out of line to die or be captured by Union cavalry. Those who survived the march would have little time to rest.[24]

27

Forrest's Rear Guard

While Forrest's troops fought bitter cold and rain en route to their rendezvous with John Bell Hood's forces in Columbia, Hood found the weather to be his ally. Indeed, his ability to survive the next twelve days of retreat would owe more to the elements of nature than his own strategy or the ability of either army. Two climatological factors became significant.

The first was swollen and unfordable rivers. The country through which Hood was retreating from Nashville was laced with rivers and streams. After torrential rains they were at full flood. If Hood crossed the major rivers ahead of the Union, he could destroy the bridges as he went and leave the Union cavalry stranded.

The second factor was soggy ground. Because of the rains Union cavalry units could not leave the major roads and dash across country. The result was that the Union cavalry, led by Major General James Wilson, was unable to surround Hood's army and draw the noose tight. Without nature on his side Hood would not have been able to retreat for one hundred miles and reach the sanctuary of Alabama.

The dawn of December 17, 1864, found Lieutenant General Stephen D. Lee's Confederate rear guard only seven miles north of Franklin, Tennessee. Wilson's Union cavalry skirmished with elements of General James Chalmers's Confederate horse soldiers, but Lee's infantry was able to cross the pontoon bridge over the Harpeth River and dash into Franklin. Despite intense Union fire Confederate engineers destroyed the bridge and toppled the railroad trestle, allowing Hood's army a five-hour head start south toward Columbia.[1]

Throughout December 17 and 18 Wilson's and Lee's troops collided in vicious rearguard action. The rain and flooding continued unabated. As Wilson pursued Hood, the distance between the Union cavalry and its supply line grew. Finally, by the afternoon of the second day, Wilson's horse soldiers were out of ammunition, rations, and forage. Wilson halted until he could resupply.[2]

By dawn on December 19 Hood had crossed the Duck River at Columbia and destroyed the bridges. Forrest had completed his forced march from Murfreesboro, joined Hood, and was assuming responsibility for fighting the rearguard action. The Union's hounds were now chasing a wily new fox. And in Forrest, Wilson was facing a determined and skillful foe.

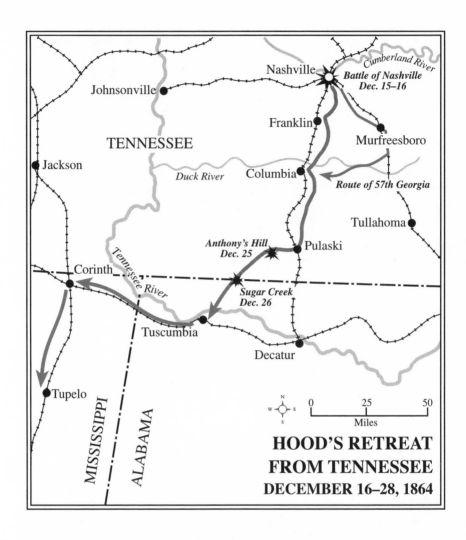

Johnsonville

Nashville · ☀ Battle of Nashville
Dec. 15–16

Cumberland River

TENNESSEE

Franklin●

Murfreesboro●

Jackson●

Duck River Columbia●

Route of 57th Georgia

Tullahoma●

Anthony's Hill
Dec. 25 ✶ ● Pulaski

Corinth●

Tennessee River

✶ *Sugar Creek*
Dec. 26

Tuscumbia●

Decatur●

●Tupelo

MISSISSIPPI

ALABAMA

N
W ⊕ E
S

0   25   50
Miles

HOOD'S RETREAT
FROM TENNESSEE
DECEMBER 16–28, 1864

When Forrest joined Hood, he found Hood considering a battle against George Thomas at the Duck River. Forrest was adamant that if the Army of Tennessee were to survive, it would have to move south of the Tennessee River and into Alabama immediately. Hood sullenly concurred, and the retreat became the single focus of the army.[3]

On December 19 Hood sent the wagon trains and artillery south in advance of the infantry. Forrest then organized his rear guard. His cavalry units totaled three thousand troops, and he requested a division of infantry to support his horsemen. He insisted that he be able to organize the new division with troops of his own choice. Forrest selected eight brigades—nineteen hundred men in all—and asked that Hood make Major General Edward Walthall, a tried and true combat leader, the new division's commander.[4]

In selecting the brigades, Forrest was looking for units that had not taken the brunt of the action at Franklin and Nashville. Mercer's brigade fit this criterion. With Forrest's choice of Mercer's brigade, and in its performance under his command, the Georgians would reach their finest hour.

In organizing his new infantry brigade Walthall made the following report:

> I reported accordingly with the following brigades: Brig. Gen. W. S. Featherston's; Col. J. B. Palmer's; Strahl's, commanded by Col. C. W. Heiskell; Smith's [Mercer's], commanded by Col. C. H. Olmstead; Maney's, commanded by Col. H. R. Field; Brig. Gen. D. H. Reynolds; Ector's, commanded by Col. D. Coleman; and Carlist's [Brigadier General William Quarles's], commanded by Brig. Gen. George D. Johnston—the last three belonging to my own division. These brigades were all greatly reduced in numbers, and deeming it expedient to consolidate them, that the command might be more wieldy and compact, I organized them thus; Palmer's and Smith's [Mercer's] brigades, under Colonel Palmer; Maney's and Strahl's, under Colonel Field; Reynolds' and Ector's, under Brigadier General Reynolds; and Featherston's and Carlist's [Quarles's], under Brigadier General Featherston.[5]

Now Mercer's brigade would be consolidated for the first time with Colonel J. B. Palmer's Tennessee brigade under Palmer's command. This organization would last throughout the remainder of the retreat.

The rain stopped during the night of December 19; the next morning emerged clear and cold. With the supply train and artillery a day ahead, leaving the turnpike clear, Hood's main army moved out of Columbia toward Pulaski, thirty miles away.

As Hood turned south in defeat toward Alabama that day, General Hardee was preparing to evacuate the besieged Savannah that night. News of Savannah's evacuation would mortify Olmstead's Georgians, especially the regiments of the First Georgia Volunteers and the Sixty-third Georgia, both of which were made up of men from the Georgia coast. The same news would electrify and galvanize the Union army. Within a few days Sherman would offer Savannah to President Lincoln as a Christmas present.

Now, trotting along in the middle of his army, Hood made the mistake of trying to be chummy with some of the disgruntled troops. As he passed some privates who were trudging along, he remarked, "Boys, the cards were fairly dealt at Nashville, and Thomas beat the game." One old Reb shot back, "Yes, General, but the cards were damned badly shuffled!" Hood spurred his horse on in dismayed silence, the loneliness of defeat growing deeper.[6]

As Hood's divisions left Columbia behind, Forrest's cavalry and his four consolidated infantry brigades—forty-nine hundred troops in all—remained in

Columbia to serve as rear guard and slow down Thomas's advancing legions. During the afternoon of December 20 Brigadier General Edward Hatch's advance units of Union cavalry were able to cross Rutherford Creek and arrived on the north bank of the Duck River. Hatch promptly began shelling Columbia. Forrest rode under a flag of truce to the river bank. Standing at the ruins of the bridge that Hood had destroyed, he asked Hatch to stop shelling the village because most of the Confederate army had already left. Forrest argued that the only result would be the loss of civilian life and property. The shelling ceased.[7]

Snow fell that night, deepening the Union's predicament. The Duck River was now cresting at fifteen feet and could be crossed only by pontoon bridge. Thomas had had such a bridge ready in Nashville, but someone had sent it to Murfreesboro by mistake. This error now delayed Thomas's pursuit.

The Tennessee countryside around Columbia was coated with ice on the morning of December 21, which would turn out to be a day of anger and frustration for Lieutenant Hamilton Branch of the Fifty-fourth Georgia. One of his hometown buddies, Frank Bourquin, had been huddled asleep in the darkness when the regimental cooks cut down a tree for firewood. The tree had landed on Bourquin, killing him instantly. For a young man to survive months of combat and be killed in this careless manner was more than Branch could bear. Now a detail of soldiers was in the local cemetery, trying to dig a hole in the frozen earth deep enough to bury Bourquin.[8]

The usually calm Colonel Olmstead was also furious. As he later wrote, "All of the baggage was sent to the rear and through the stupidity of my orderly, Linsky, my two blankets went with the rest; so I was left with no other protection in the bitter nights that followed, than a worn over-coat that was almost threadbare."

To solve his problem temporarily, the colonel rented a room from a nearby homeowner, a Mrs. Voght. Olmstead recalled, "I had a warm room with comfortable beds. . . . I can remember feeling as I snuggled down in the blankets on the first night and listened to the fierce winter wind howling outside, that I would be quite willing to have the war come to an end right then and there."[9]

The Federals were angry as well. The pontoon bridge had still not arrived, and assembly would not begin until December 22. Wilson's cavalry would not cross the Duck River and resume its pursuit of Hood until December 24.[10]

Nonetheless, on the morning of December 22 a small detachment of Union infantry forded the Duck River two miles north of Columbia. Although Forrest wanted to stay in place as long as he could in order to shield Hood's retreat, he knew that it was time to protect his rear guard by withdrawing from Columbia and moving south toward Pulaski.[11] By now Hood's army had reached Pulaski, and the division of Carter L. Stevenson, who was leading Hood's retreating infantry, was already several miles beyond the town. But Hood faced new problems. Beyond Pulaski the clay roads grew more rugged and rutted. The forty-nine miles that separated him from the Tennessee River would be a slow and arduous trip.

The weather was terrible as Forrest slipped out of Columbia. Because more than four hundred of his men had no shoes, he emptied wagons for them to ride in. When he needed the "barefoot brigade" for action, the men would get out of the wagons and engage the enemy. And when the rear guard was on the move, they would ride. For once it was an advantage to be barefoot.[12]

As Olmstead watched the shoeless soldiers, he witnessed an event that he would never forget:

> Allie Shellman [was] standing on the frozen turnpike without shoes, his feet tied up in a lot of old rags. The column filled the road and while we were waiting for the order to march a cavalry man rode by through the bushes at the side of the road. Passing, he happened to notice Shellman's condition and in an instant had one foot after another up at the saddle bow, took off his shoes and threw them at Allies feet with the remark, "Friend you need them more than I do," then galloped away without waiting to be thanked. *One* such incident as this goes a long way toward giving a firm faith in the good that is in human nature.[13]

As Robert Braswell toted his rifle and hustled out of Columbia, he and his comrades in the Fifty-seventh Georgia were participating in their fourth retreat from a major campaign in three years—Kentucky, Vicksburg, Atlanta, and now Nashville. They had endured continual marching and painful defeats. Never had the Fifty-seventh Georgia shared in a major victory. Yet they kept on marching. Braswell focused only on the next step in front of him. He had learned not to think about tomorrow.

As Thomas's infantry and cavalry finally crossed the wayward pontoon bridge on the morning of December 23 and resumed their chase after Hood, Forrest was gazing ahead, well aware that the bulk of Hood's army was near Lexington, Alabama, two-thirds of the way between Pulaski, Tennessee, and the Tennessee River to the southwest. However, Hood's progress was slowing. His wagons were breaking down on the abominable roads, and his troops were having particular difficulty with the wagons carrying the Confederate pontoon bridge. If the bridge did not arrive at the river, all was lost.

Because Hood needed to buy more time, Forrest doubled back toward Columbia and attacked Wilson before he could gain momentum. Olmstead described the delaying tactic: "We marched very slowly and whenever the enemy came too near [we] would form line of battle faced to the rear. This would oblige him [the enemy] also to deploy from column into line and feel his way by throwing out skirmishers, all of which took time and caused delay, the thing we aimed at."[14] December 24 was filled with such delays, giving Hood time to pull his wagons through the fields of mud.

As the night before Christmas arrived, Forrest's exhausted rear guard occupied Pulaski. Remembering that night, Walter Clark of the Sixty-third Georgia noted wryly, "Coiled up in a single blanket on the cold, bare ground, no visions of Santa Claus nor hopes of a Christmas menu on the morrow brightened our dreams."[15] For as long as these men lived, they would never experience another Christmas Eve without remembering that frigid and melancholy night.

During the predawn hours of Christmas Day, Forrest woke up his troops and ordered them to burn the large stores of supplies that Hood had abandoned in Pulaski. Olmstead noted, "All of the stores were being fed to a huge bonfire in the public square—bacon, clothing, boxes of ammunition, etc., all went into the blaze. I noticed women and children in their night dresses at the windows of some of the houses—many of the former sadly weeping and wringing their hands. So the day of 'Peace on earth and good will to man' was ushered in for us; God grant that none whom I love may ever see another like it."[16]

The night before, Forrest and Walthall had stayed up late, planning a special Christmas present for Wilson: a well-staged ambush. Forrest knew that Hood had finally reached the Tennessee River and was assembling the pontoon bridge, and Forrest needed to delay Thomas's advance. So on Christmas morning Forrest left a small rear guard in Pulaski to block Wilson's cavalry, while Forrest rapidly moved his main force seven miles south of Pulaski. Forrest was familiar with the region and remembered a narrow wooded ravine flanked by two high ridges that came together to form the ascent to a knoll called Anthony's Hill. It was natural terrain for an ambush.[17]

Forrest posted two brigades of Walthall's infantry—as well as three camouflaged field guns loaded with double canister—behind very visible rail barricades along the narrow lane leading through the ravine and up the slope of Anthony's Hill. These men were decoys to lure Wilson's cavalry up the steep trail. On both sides of the path leading to the barricades Forrest concealed two brigades of cavalry in the thick woods. Now the Confederates waited.

As the Union cavalry approached, Thomas J. Harrison's brigade was on point. When he spied the Rebs behind the barricades, Harrison ordered three regiments to dismount and attack. As the Yanks ran up the hill and pulled within yards of the barricades, Forrest's hidden field guns exploded in fury.[18]

Walter Clark of the Sixty-third Georgia was directly behind the artillery:

> Our regiment is placed as a support for the battery and as we line up,
> Forrest passes us on foot going to the front in a half bent position. Reaching

the trenches he watches the advance of the enemy for a few minutes and then hurries to the rear. In a moment we hear the clatter of a horse's feet and the "Wizard of the Saddle" [Forrest] dashes by at half speed, riding magnificently, his martial figure as straight as an arrow and looking six inches taller than his wont, a very god of war, yelling as he reaches the waiting ranks: "Charge! Charge! CHARGE!"

Over the breastworks flashes a line of grey and down the slope they sweep, yelling at every step. The captain commanding our regiment is undecided as to his duty, but finally orders us to retain our position in the rear of the battery. Just then Gen. Featherston rides up:

"What regiment is this?"

"63rd Ga."

"What are you doing here?"

"Supporting this battery!".

"Battery the devil! Get over them breastworks and get quick!"

And we "get". But the skirmish is soon over. The Yankees have fled, leaving a piece of artillery and a number of horses in our possession.[19]

The successful ambush was a much-needed boost to the Rebs' morale. Mercer's brigade was fully involved in the rout and reveled in the revenge. Two Union cavalry brigades were put to flight, suffering 150 casualties, 50 troops taken prisoner, 300 horses captured, and the loss of a twelve-pound Napoleon field piece, complete with carriage team. Wilson called for infantry support and deployed his men to attack Forrest's flanks. Seeing the threat, Forrest disengaged his men and started southward again. He had lost only fifteen men, with forty wounded.[20]

As Forrest and his troops left Anthony's Hill, he knew that he would have to use the impending darkness to escape Wilson and again find terrain that would work to his advantage. That night he pushed his troops fourteen miles to Sugar Creek. Walter Clark recalled,

Night comes on and if there was ever a darker or more starless one I can not place it. Tramping, tramping in the cold and mud and darkness, companies and regiments are all commingled and no one knows where he is, or where he ought to be. Too dark to see the file next in front, we walk by faith and not by sight. Elmore Dunbar was carrying the colors and but for his occasional whistling imitation of the bugle call in order to let us know "where he was at," our regiment would have lost in the darkness all semblance of its organization. I can not well conceive how a larger share of unadulterated physical discomfort could have been compressed into the five solid hours for which we kept it up.[21]

Olmstead also wrote of the night march:

> Gen. Forrest continued the retreat. That afternoon a thaw commenced and a cold rain set in; the roads were rivers of slush as the snow melted, but on we went in the black darkness, stumbling along, cold, weary to exhaustion, dead for sleep, but the march kept up until midnight when we came up with the other half of the rear guard where they had gone into bivouac.
>
> Our men filed off into the fields to the right and left of the road but there was sorry comfort for them—it was cultivated land and the furrows were filled with water—they slept as they could on the ridges between. . . .
>
> After the men were placed, Matthew and I looked around forlornly for some more attractive bed than a corn hill in which to sleep. . . . We discovered an ambulance standing on the side of the road which no one seemed to have claimed. Into this we crept. . . . So ended our Christmas![22]

On December 26 Forrest divided his force, sending the troops involved in the Christmas ambush, including Mercer's brigade, ahead with his supply train. With the rest of his troops he set up another ambush just south of Sugar Creek. Again using the thick foliage of a deep ravine for cover, Forrest and his troops charged down the hillsides and drove John Hammond's cavalry back a half mile, inflicting 150 casualties.[23]

Because he was low on ammunition and rations, Wilson ended his active pursuit of Forrest. Thomas now knew that he would not reach the Tennessee River in time to trap Hood. Earlier, he had ordered Admiral S. P. Lee to advance up the Tennessee River from the west with a flotilla of Union gunboats to destroy Hood's pontoon bridge. When Lee got within a mile of the bridge, he encountered natural obstructions and artillery fire. He withdrew, allowing the bridge to stand.[24]

The Rebel corps of Stephen Lee and Frank Cheatham crossed the Tennessee River on December 26. It was a slow process. The Rebs' rickety pontoon bridge bulged downstream against the rapid current, taking on the shape of a floating crescent. Only a few field guns or a single wagon could cross at one time. The infantry traversed single file and three paces apart. With the raging water wetting their feet, everyone held his breath. But the bridge stayed together.[25]

On December 27 Alexander Stewart's corps crossed the river, and the Army of Tennessee waited for Forrest's rear guard to catch up. After a march of twelve miles Forrest's lead units arrived in the afternoon, and his haggard horsemen crossed to safety that night. Only Walthall's infantry division remained. On December 28 Walthall's eight brigades arrived and crossed the groaning pontoon bridge. Mercer's brigade was the next to last to cross, followed by Matthew Ector's brigade.[26]

The hellish retreat was over. George Thomas remained on the north side of the river, and Hood disappeared from sight, marching his troops west to Tuscumbia, Alabama, and crossing into Mississippi through Iuka to Corinth. On January 10, 1865, he set up camp in Tupelo. In just thirty-eight days Hood had marched nearly five hundred miles, lost two major battles, suffered 23,500 casualties, survived a murderous retreat, and decimated the Army of Tennessee.

The North Carolina Campaign

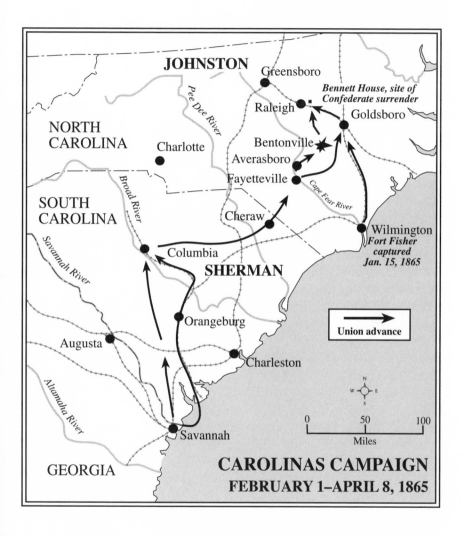

JOHNSTON

Greensboro

Bennett House, site of Confederate surrender

Raleigh

Goldsboro

NORTH CAROLINA

Pee Dee River

Charlotte

Bentonville

Averasboro

Fayetteville

Cape Fear River

SOUTH CAROLINA

Broad River

Cheraw

Savannah River

Wilmington

Fort Fisher captured Jan. 15, 1865

Columbia

SHERMAN

Orangeburg

Union advance

Augusta

Charleston

N
W ⊕ E
S

0   50   100
Miles

Altamaha River

Savannah

GEORGIA

CAROLINAS CAMPAIGN
FEBRUARY 1–APRIL 8, 1865

28

Going to Carolina

The last official record of all the men present and accounted for in Mercer's brigade is dated December 21, 1864. On that icy morning in Columbia, Tennessee, before beginning their rearguard action, the Georgians stood at attention in the snow and sounded off. The numbers were shocking:

First Georgia Volunteers	41 effective	52 present
Fifty-fourth Georgia	111 effective	168 present
Fifty-seventh Georgia	65 effective	120 present
Sixty-third Georgia	102 effective	143 present
TOTAL	319	483

The brigade's effective strength was one-third that of a regiment. The total strength of the brigade upon reaching Tupelo, Mississippi, was doubtless even lower.[1]

Now that they were finally able to collapse and rest, men succumbed to sickness. Robert Braswell was evacuated to a military hospital in Meridian, Mississippi. Hamilton Branch was so ill that upon returning to Georgia on furlough en route to the North Carolina campaign, he was hospitalized and did not return to military service. John Methvin was sent to Montgomery, Alabama, "where I was examined by a board of physicians who, judging that I would never be able to do any more service, gave me a long furlough, ninety days." Sergeant Walter Clark found that "after tramping eight hundred miles in absolute health I lay down and had an old-fashioned Burke County chill." And Colonel Olmstead "did nothing but sleep and rest by big fires from morning until morning again—happy to be united to my precious blankets again."[2]

Indeed, the losses of the Army of Tennessee were staggering. Hood's army, which had entered Tennessee with a combined strength of 38,000 men, had suffered 23,500 casualties in thirty-eight days. Hood had slaughtered his army.[3]

The survivors were disgusted and angry. Although still loyal to their regiments and brigades, they knew that the command leadership had failed them. Even a lowly sergeant like Walter Clark could boil it down to one sentence: "General John B. Hood's strategy in this campaign was apparently conspicuous only by its absence!"[4]

Hood's superiors knew this to be true as well, and Beauregard was en route to investigate. One day before Beauregard arrived, Hood sent a terse message to James Seddon, the Confederate secretary of war: "I respectfully request to be relieved from the command of this army." Seddon granted the request and on January 23 issued orders transferring command of the Army of Tennessee to General Richard Taylor. Hood boarded a train for Richmond the same day.

George "Old Slow Trot" Thomas remained on the other side of the Tennessee River. Although he would be criticized for his decision not to pursue the Rebs, he knew that the Army of Tennessee was no longer an effective fighting force. Yet even Thomas would tip his hat in respect for the rearguard efforts of Forrest's men. In his official report of January 20, 1865, Thomas wrote: "He [Hood] had formed a powerful rearguard, made up of detachments from all his organized force, numbering about 4,000 infantry, under General Walthall, and all his available cavalry, under Forrest. With the exception of his rearguard, his army had become a disheartened rabble of half-armed and barefooted men, who sought every opportunity to fall out by the wayside and desert their cause to put an end to sufferings. The rearguard, however was undaunted and firm, and did its work bravely to the last."[5]

As the men of Mercer's brigade tried to put the past behind them, they worried about the future. Sherman had terrorized and razed many of their communities, homes, and farms, causing families to flee to other parts of the state. Most men had not received word from their loved ones in weeks, and they were anxious.

Charles Henry Thiot of the First Georgia Volunteers owned a plantation twenty miles from Savannah named Roseville. He cultivated mainly rice and owned numerous slaves. He was distraught because he had received word in early December that his family was fleeing from Sherman's army. Thiot was trying to find his family any way that he could. From Tupelo he wrote to a friend:

Dear Grafton,
    . . . I hear today that Sherman has issued an order for the women and children to leave the city [Savannah]. Now then, do the lines extend up to Roseville? And will my family return *home,* or will they be compelled to seek an asylum elsewhere? I am very anxious about them.
    I got a letter from Anna of 4th Dec. From Savannah whither she and the children had fled on the approach of the enemy, but since then I have not heard a word. And I have not been able to get a letter to *her* in more than two months.
    I know she must be very anxious about me, as *Cleburne's Division* was cut all to pieces and Genl. Cleburne himself killed at the terrible battle of Franklin. Of this affair she must have heard, but not hearing from *me,* she

must have been filled with fears for my safety. If you know any way of getting a letter to her, please write to her, and say that I am well, and very anxious to get home.[6]

Two days later he tried writing to his wife, Anna, again and sent the letter with a comrade who had been granted furlough:

My dear Anna,

Lt. Elkins having made application for furlough, I prepare a line for you in the hope he may get it to you. I received two letters from you, one in the latter part of November and one on 4th Dec., but since then I have not heard a word, and am all anxiety about you and our home. Do get me a letter if you can, and tell me *all* that has happened to you. Don't hesitate to tell me *all,* because I now fear the worst. . . .

I did not know how things are in Effingham, nor where you and the children are at this time. But I am all anxiety about you, and know that you [are] full of anxiety about me. . . .

Love to all. Oh if you could only have staid at Roseville! But God guides and directs us.

Yours Husband[7]

During this time in camp in Tupelo, the men attended to other tasks as well, especially washing their clothes. Many men had not changed their clothes or uniforms in weeks. Walter Clark described how the situation had deteriorated:

In the bitter cold and constant marching of the Nashville campaign, I am satisfied that some of the boys did not wash their faces nor comb their hair at less than weekly intervals. As evidence of the infrequency of "bath tub nights" for reasons stated, I recall the fact that I lost a calico handkerchief and thought I had dropped it on the march. Some weeks afterwards in removing my outer clothing for the first time after its disappearance, I found it hidden away underneath the back of my vest.

On our return to Corinth, Miss., my mess took their underclothing to a lady to be washed and as they had been wearing it a month or more without change, they apologized for its condition. "No apology is necessary," she said. "I have washed some for Forrest's cavalry that was so stiffened with dirt that they were able to stand alone."[8]

While the Army of Tennessee recuperated, war raged in the east. Robert E. Lee's Army of Northern Virginia was under siege along the Richmond-Petersburg line, slowly strangled by Grant's 180,000-man army. Sherman would soon break out of Georgia with eighty-five thousand Union troops and burn a path through the Carolinas on his way to attack Lee's rear. What remained of the

Army of Tennessee now was urgently needed in North Carolina to help oppose Sherman.

How many soldiers remained in the Army of Tennessee to be transferred east? Although official reports on January 20, 1865, showed an effective total of 17,709 infantry and artillery troops, 4,000 were sent to reinforce Mobile, 3,500 were furloughed, and hundreds of others deserted and drifted away during the next several weeks. According to General Joseph E. Johnston, only five thousand troops from the Army of Tennessee eventually reached North Carolina.[9]

As Mercer's brigade prepared to leave Mississippi, the men were transferred from Forrest's command back to Cleburne's division in Cheatham's corps. Stephen Lee's corps left first for Augusta, Georgia, followed by Cheatham's corps on January 25, and Stewart's corps on January 30. Separated from Cheatham's main troop movement, Mercer's brigade traveled to Meridian, Mobile, and Montgomery before arriving in Columbus, Georgia, around February 1. In Columbus the brigade waited for several days for a train to Macon and then rode to the hamlet of Midway, several miles from Milledgeville. At Midway the soldiers received new blankets and fresh clothing. From there the brigade marched to Camack and caught a train to Augusta. From Augusta some units of Mercer's brigade joined Cheatham's corps near Salisbury, North Carolina. Other units of the brigade marched eastward to join Joseph Johnston's gathering army near Smithfield, North Carolina.[10]

As Mercer's brigade slowly made its way across middle Georgia, many of its members slipped quietly away into the night. They were so close to their families that they felt compelled to see their loved ones. Well aware that the defeat of the Confederacy was inevitable, some never returned to the army. Others, after a few weeks at home, made their way to rejoin their regiments in North Carolina.

John Methvin of the Fifty-seventh Georgia "reached home [in Jeffersonville] with skeleton-like proportions. My father had not heard from me since we first started on that march to Tennessee in September, and it was now far into the spring. And so, believing I was dead, heart broken, he went out of the back door, weeping, as I going in at the front gate. His sorrow was turned into joy as we embraced each other once more. It was a time of rejoicing, but tinged with a sense of bereavement as we remembered Tommie's tragic death at Jonesboro, and William's imprisonment at Johnston's Island."[11]

Colonel Olmstead eagerly looked forward to seeing his wife when his brigade detrained near Milledgeville. He knew that she had left Savannah and fled to her mother's Milledgeville home. But while he was waiting for the troop train in Columbus, Georgia, he learned from a relative that his wife had returned to Savannah. He was devastated.

Later, as Olmstead moved through Milledgeville near midnight with a column of troops, he decided to visit his mother-in-law. He later told his children:

[A]s soon as the men were detrained and in bivouac I set out for your grandmother's house. A man in a cart who was driving that way gave me a lift and in due time the familiar corner was reached. Everything looked sombre enough, there was not a ray of light from that house or any other and not a sound broke the stillness of the night—a forlorn sort of homecoming it seemed.

I felt some anxiety in going up the front step lest "Boss" the old mastiff that guarded the premises might mistake me for a marauder: he was a dog to be afraid of but on this occasion made no sign. I knocked several times on the front door without getting any response but finally heard some one moving about in the hall. . . .

I went at once to your grandmothers room. The dear old lady was sitting up in bed with a big shawl around her, and as I came up to her she threw her arms about my neck and wept over me. I sat by the bed side a long while talking of your dear mother and the children. . . .

It made my heart very heavy for the clouds seemed dark above me: I could see no prospect of being with my dear ones at any time in the near future and it was impossible to avoid the reflection that there was little hope for the Confederate cause and that I was about to enter another campaign from which there might be no return.

As his mother-in-law drifted back to sleep, Olmstead sat by the fireside in her room and reflected upon the cost of the war to this dear lady: "she was alone, with only servants about her, in that great house that I had always associated with bright, happy gatherings of a large and loving family. Three of her sons had died since the beginning of the war, two from the hardships incidental to army life in Virginia and a third from exposure in Railroad service, while yet a fourth had been desperately wounded at Malvern Hill and was even then, (more than two years after,) in a precarious state of health."

Olmstead's luck was not all bad, however. Early the next morning, before joining his command, he found a trunk that his wife had left for safekeeping with her mother. Olmstead described his delight: "It was a trunk full of clothing that your mother had sent out from Savannah as soon as she arrived there, while communications were still open. There was in it a good uniform suit comparatively new and never was a suit more needed. My old one had become disreputable to the last degree; it was threadbare throughout and there was a broad band of scorched cloth from the back of the collar to the tail of the coat, and down each leg of the trousers to the heels, the result of my snuggling up to the fires during the hard nights of the retreat from Tennessee."[12]

As Mercer's brigade moved through Milledgeville, Lieutenant Archibald McKinley and the slave Scott probably also returned home, however briefly. A native of Milledgeville, McKinley later affirmed that Scott remained with him through "Genl. Hood's advance on & disasterous retreat from Nashville. And lastly through the North Carolina campaign of 1865."[13] Both men yearned for home and the comfort of their families.

From Milledgeville Mercer's brigade marched on to Augusta, where Sergeant Walter Clark slipped away for ten days to "rest at home." His homecoming was one of sadness:

> Sixteen miles away [from Augusta], embowered in a grove of oak and elm, lay the home I had left, holding within the sacred shadow of its walls all that I loved best on earth. For nearly two months no tiding had come to me from them. We had been so constantly on the move that the letters written had never reached me. The latest message received had told me of my father's illness, but its tone gave me hope of his early recovery.
>
> Our passage through Augusta gave me the privilege of revisiting the old homestead, but it was a sad home-coming. Twice since I had left it last the family circle had been broken and the shadow of death had fallen on its hearthstone. A few short months before in the autumnal haze of a September day, as sweet a sister as brother ever owned had breathed out her young life just as she was budding into womanhood. And now only a week before I entered its portals again my father [a doctor], worn out by the added burdens imposed by the absorption of younger physicians in the military service, had been laid away beneath the shadow of the trees in the city of the dead. . . . Beyond and above any partial judgment born of the love I bore him, I have always thought him the best and purest man I have ever known. . . .
>
> After ten days rest at home, in company with eight comrades of the Oglethorpes, I left Augusta Feb. 20 to rejoin my command in upper South Carolina, reaching it after six days' tramp, near Pomaria.[14]

Clark's small band of loyal deserters caught up with their regiment near Chester, South Carolina. Clark reports that they remained in Chester until March 10, then "left by rail for Charlotte, but by reason of an accident, failed to arrive at our destination until the evening of the 11th. On the 12th we moved on to Salisbury, remained there until the 17th, when the train took us to Smith-field. A march of 16 miles on the 18th enabled us to rejoin our corps near Bentonville."[15]

As Mercer's brigade neared the North Carolina border, General Cheatham became aware of how many of Olmstead's Georgians had taken "French leave" to see their families. The brigade now probably comprised less than three hundred men. Cheatham requested an interview with Olmstead to inquire about the problem, and Olmstead recorded his impressions:

> It distressed me to see how many of our men had slipped away from the ranks during the passage through Georgia, though I quite well understood

and sympathized with them for going. When we were nearly up to the North Carolina line, Gen Cheatham, who then commanded the corps, sent for me to ask an explanation of this falling off in the Brigade numbers.

I told him that the men had no intention of deserting the colors, but that as husbands and fathers they had felt obliged to go to look after their families most of whom had lived on the line of Sherman's March and were now homeless and destitute. I further said that if he would send me back to Georgia I felt confident of being able to return to the army with most of the missing ones. The proposition met with his approval and he at once instructed his Adjutant General to prepare an order detailing me for this service. The paper was handed me and I started off the same day.

This was the first time I had ever been brought in contact with Genl Cheatham and it can not be said that he made a very favorable impression upon me. He was known as a man of great personal bravery, an indomitable fighter and with a fine record upon many bloody fields. But he was also reputed to be a hard drinker . . . It is certainly true that during my interview with him there was decided evidence of his being under the influence of liquor. As he handed me the order he said with a gravity that was ludicrous, "Colonel you go and bring those men back and if you want anybody shot just wink your eye."[16]

Olmstead did not want anyone shot. He returned to Georgia and advertised in the Augusta, Macon, and Columbus newspapers for members of Mercer's brigade to return to duty. In two weeks he returned with more than five hundred men. But by then the Battle of Bentonville had been fought, and the Army of Tennessee had fired its last shot. Only those members of Mercer's brigade who had proceeded directly to Bentonville and arrived by mid-March participated in the battle.[17]

29

The Battle of Bentonville

As soldiers from Mercer's brigade slowly made their way back to their regiments in North Carolina from their unofficial leave, much was changing in the Confederacy. As the primary defense of the Confederacy collapsed into the confined region of Virginia and the Carolinas, the Confederate congress pressured Jefferson Davis to establish a unified military command. On January 31, 1865, Robert E. Lee reluctantly agreed to serve as general in chief of all Confederate armies.

On February 21, 1865, Lee assigned Joseph E. Johnston to again command the Army of Tennessee and all troops in the Department of South Carolina, Georgia, and Florida. Johnston was to "concentrate all available forces and drive back Sherman."[1]

Johnston had no illusions. He frankly informed Lee, "It is too late to expect me to concentrate troops capable of driving back Sherman. The remnant of the Army of Tennessee is much divided. So are other troops." In his postwar memoir he wrote, "Even if united before the powerful Federal army, the Confederate forces were utterly inadequate to the exploit of driving it back, being less than a fourth of its number." Johnston knew that his army could not achieve a military victory.[2]

Why, then, did Johnston accept the command? What did he hope to accomplish? Johnston stated his objective clearly in his memoir: "[My acceptance of command] was done with a full consciousness on my part, however, that we could have no other object, in continuing the war, than to obtain fair terms of peace; for the Southern cause must have appeared hopeless then, to all intelligent and dispassionate Southern men. I therefore resumed the duties of my military grade with no hope beyond that of contributing to obtain peace on such conditions as, under the circumstance, ought to satisfy the Southern people and their Government."[3]

Soldiers in the Army of Tennessee reacted with joy and celebration to the news that "Old Joe" would again be leading them. His return to command renewed their confidence in leadership at a critical time.

As the Confederate military struggled for life, ominous political events were unfolding. On January 31, 1865, the U.S. House of Representatives passed by two-thirds vote the Thirteenth Amendment to the Constitution, abolishing slavery. Although it would not be ratified until December 1865, its approval was certain. And without slavery the Southern agrarian economy would require a radical restructuring and diversification that would take a century to accomplish. The South faced economic disaster.

President Lincoln was inaugurated for a second term on March 4. This was both good and bad news for the Confederacy. The good news was that Lincoln held moderate and gracious views concerning what should be done with the "conquered" South and its citizen-soldiers. The bad news was that Lincoln's election signaled that there would be no negotiated peace. Lincoln would demand unconditional surrender and a return to a unified central government.

In the midst of this rapid political change, a Yankee military juggernaut bore down on North Carolina. From the north Grant and a force of 180,000 well-equipped troops were wearing down Robert E. Lee's Richmond-Petersburg line. Lee knew that he could not endure much longer. Soon he would be forced to retreat south, perhaps linking up with Johnston's army for a final stand in North Carolina.

From the southwest Sherman was sweeping toward North Carolina with a force of ninety thousand confident soldiers to confront Johnston's army of twenty-three thousand dispersed and weakened troops. Sherman's objective was to reach the railhead of Goldsboro, North Carolina, while Grant drove Lee south. As Sherman later wrote, "Being at Goldsboro, with its railroads finished back to Morehead City and Wilmington, I can easily take Raleigh, when it seems that Lee must come out."[4] It was clear that Sherman was headed toward Lee's back door. The best that Johnston could hope for was to delay and harass Sherman.

On March 7 Sherman's army crossed into North Carolina, skirmishing at Rockingham and Southwest Creek. Johnston's most pressing task was to consolidate his far-flung army.[5] A Confederate contingent under Braxton Bragg was reeling back from the coast of North Carolina, after the final fall of Wilmington. Hardee's troops were making their way from Savannah, skirmishing with Sherman as he advanced. The three greatly reduced corps of the Army of Tennessee—Lee's, Cheatham's, and Stewart's—were slowly filtering into North Carolina in the general direction of Charlotte. As General Wade Hampton growled, "It would scarcely have been possible to disperse a force more effectually."[6]

Johnston was determined to be aggressive and on the offensive against Sherman. As in the Atlanta campaign, Johnston faced a numerically superior foe—four Yanks to every Reb. His only hope was to lure Sherman into separating the two wings of his army and defeat one wing at a time. Johnston had tried this strategy repeatedly in Georgia and failed. Perhaps now he would succeed.

Sherman soon cooperated with Johnston's scheme. Advancing with confidence, Sherman split his massive army into two wings on parallel paths that were roughly a day's march apart. Major General Henry W. Slocum commanded the left wing, and Major General O. O. Howard commanded the right. As Sherman drew close to Goldsboro, Johnston had little time in which to strike. Once Grant's two wings united and merged with Schofield's army, which was advancing from the coast to Goldsboro, Johnston would have no chance.

Johnston was lacking vital information, however. He was not sure whether Sherman was advancing toward Goldsboro or Raleigh. Johnston's intelligence reports pointed toward Goldsboro. But if Sherman captured Raleigh instead, he would control the Raleigh and Gaston Railroad, a move that would starve Lee's Army of Northern Virginia. Therefore on March 15 Johnston established his headquarters at Smithfield, midway between Raleigh and Goldsboro, ready to move in either direction.[7]

Lieutenant General Wade Hampton, recently transferred from the Army of Northern Virginia, was now the cavalry commander of Johnston's army. As this experienced and competent officer scouted Sherman's advance, he arrived on March 17 at the Willis Cole farmhouse near the junction of the Averasboro and Smithfield roads. This location placed Hampton three miles southwest of Bentonville, eighteen miles south of Johnston at Smithfield, and within twenty-five miles of Sherman's destination of Goldsboro. Hampton also stood squarely in the path of Slocum's approaching left wing. Howard's right wing was a full day's march removed. Hampton knew that if Johnston were going to strike, he must do it now.[8]

Reconnoitering the countryside, Hampton found perfect topography for the type of surprise attack that the Confederates would have to fight. And Hampton was spoiling for a fight. While in Virginia, Hampton had lost a brother, Frank Hampton, and a son, Preston Hampton, in violent combat.[9] Only a month before, Sherman had burned Hampton's fine home and plantation near Columbia, South Carolina, reducing the great library to ashes. As Hampton pondered his losses, his oldest son, Wade Jr., galloped in from Smithfield with a note from Johnston. Johnston wanted to know whether the Confederates should strike Sherman south of the Neuse River near where Hampton stood. Hampton replied that they should attack immediately and that he had found the perfect place for battle. Upon reading Hampton's message, Johnston responded, "We will go to the place at which your dispatch was written. The scheme mentioned in my note, which you pronounce practicable, will be attempted."[10] The modest hamlet of Bentonville now became the locus for the last great battle of the Civil War.

On Saturday, March 18, the day before the Battle of Bentonville, Johnston directed his converging Confederate forces to the site that Hampton had scouted. It was now obvious that many divisions of the Army of Tennessee would not arrive in time for battle. Although Major General William B. Bate managed to get half of Cheatham's corps to Smithfield, Cheatham remained with the other half, stuck in a transportation bottleneck in Salisbury, North Carolina.[11]

As Johnston collected his troops, the senior Hampton attempted to delay Slocum's progress. Hampton reported that by afternoon "I was pressed back by force of numbers to the crest of a wooded hill which overlooked a very large field that I had selected as a proper place for the battle."[12] He threw up rail barricades and placed two artillery batteries on a commanding hill north of the road. Hampton later remarked, "I knew that if a serious attack was made on me the guns would be lost but I determined to run this risk in the hope of checking the Federal advance."[13] Hampton's gamble paid off. After Slocum's troops made "a rather feeble demonstration against us at sunset, we were thus left in possession of the ground chosen for the fight."[14]

Sherman happened to be riding with Slocum's wing that afternoon. When he looked through his field glasses, Sherman did not believe that the Confederates' blocking action was the prelude to a major battle; he figured it for only a cavalry skirmish. Sherman instructed both his wings to bivouac at 4 P.M. and left Slocum's wing early the next morning so that he could confer with Howard's right wing.[15]

Meanwhile, during the predawn hours of Sunday, March 19, Johnston had quietly positioned his army for battle. Stewart's and Bragg's troops were present, but Hardee's were still missing. Hardee had camped six miles north of Bentonville after a hard twenty-mile march from Elevation. He had his tired troops back on the road by 3 A.M. However, his map was inaccurate, and Hardee had farther to march than he had anticipated.[16]

Johnston placed Bragg's troops perpendicular to, and bisecting, the Goldsboro Road, obstructing Slocum's advance. Major General Robert Hoke's division, recently transferred from the Army of Northern Virginia, would serve as the immediate blocking force and would be the first Confederate soldiers visible to the Federals as they broke camp and advanced down the road. Bragg would have to withstand the initial brunt of the battle alone.[17]

The rest of the Confederate line would be concealed in thick woods on Bragg's right, curving like a crescent until it ran parallel down the left side of the Goldsboro Road. Hardee's troops would adjoin Bragg's at a forty-five-degree angle and become the hidden center of the Confederate line. Stewart's remnant corps of the Army of Tennessee would adjoin Hardee's forces, becoming the right side of the line, facing the exposed flank of the Union army as it advanced up the Goldsboro highway. Hampton's cavalry, after initially engaging the approaching Federals and falling back through Hoke's blocking screen, would circle behind Hardee's and Stewart's lines, taking a position to the far right of Stewart's. If the Union line crumbled, Hampton's cavalry would be in position to fall on the Yankee rear, blocking its retreat.[18]

Johnston's and Hampton's plan was simple. After Slocum's lead elements had engaged Bragg's troops positioned across the road, Hardee and Stewart would charge from the woods and attack the vulnerable left flank of the extended Union

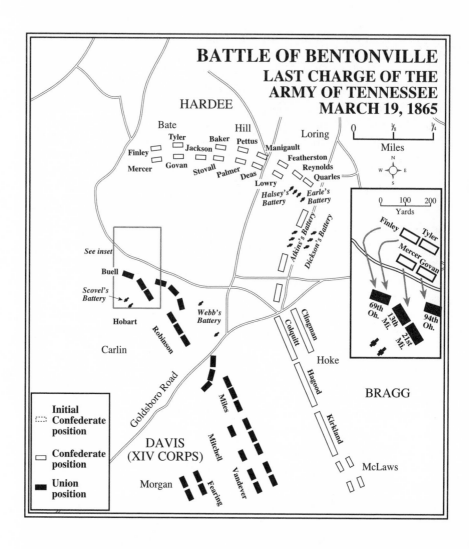

BATTLE OF BENTONVILLE
LAST CHARGE OF THE
ARMY OF TENNESSEE
MARCH 19, 1865

HARDEE

Bate   Hill   Loring
Tyler   Baker Pettus
Finley   Jackson   Manigault
Mercer Govan Stovall Palmer Featherston
                        Deas   Reynolds
                        Lowry   Quarles
                  Halsey's   Earle's
                  Battery   Battery
                      Atkins's Battery
                      Dickson's Battery
See inset
Buell
Scovel's
Battery
Hobart   Webb's
              Battery
Robinson
Carlin   Clingman   Hoke
                  Colquitt
                          Hagood   BRAGG
Goldsboro Road   Miles
                              Kirkland
DAVIS   Mitchell
(XIV CORPS)   Vandever   McLaws
Morgan   Fearing

Initial
Confederate
position

Confederate
position

Union
position

Miles

N
W   E
S

Finley   Tyler
Mercer Govan
69th 13th 21st 94th
Oh.   Mi.   Mi.   Oh.

column. If this could be done while the column was in transit and not dug in, Johnston could surprise and overwhelm the confused Union line.

As the men trekked through the thick, shadowed woods in the early morning light to find their place in the line of the Army of Tennessee, Mercer's brigade was in Cheatham's corps, temporarily commanded by Bate. Cheatham's corps would anchor the extreme right end of the Confederate line. The corps was now reduced to nine hundred men and was smaller than an average regiment at the beginning of the war. On this first day of battle Cheatham's corps consisted of two incomplete divisions: Cleburne's, led by Brigadier General James A. Smith, and Bate's, led by Captain Daniel L. Kenan.[19]

As Bate positioned Cheatham's corps, he assigned Cleburne's division to the front line: Daniel Govan's Arkansas brigade on the left and Mercer's Georgia brigade on the right. Bate left Kenan's division in reserve, with Tyler's Tennessee brigade supporting Govan, and Finley's Florida brigade backing Mercer.

Lying flat in the shelter of the woods, the four regiments of Mercer's brigade probably totaled fewer than three hundred men. In the Atlanta campaign it had been the largest brigade in the Army of Tennessee. Now Olmstead and the five hundred men he had corralled on his trip to Georgia were stuck with Cheatham on troop trains. They would never see this battle, and they would never fire another shot.

The officer corps of Mercer's brigade was also severely depleted. The brigade was temporarily commanded by the young captain John Richard Bonner of Milledgeville, Georgia. For the last three years Bonner had faithfully led Company H, the Baldwin County Independent Volunteers, of the Fifty-seventh Georgia Regiment. He had been wounded at Champion Hill and in the Atlanta campaign. Although he was commanding a brigade for the first time, it was now not much larger than Bonner's original company.[20]

As the Georgians peered through the woods on that Sunday morning, prayers crossed many lips. To their right were nothing but quiet, empty woods that were strangely peaceful. The Georgians were the very last brigade on the far end of the Confederate line that had formed for the final grand charge of the Army of Tennessee.[21]

Private Frank Stone of the First Georgia Volunteers carried the distinctive blue and white flag of Cleburne's division to the front ranks (Cleburne's was the only infantry division in the Army of Tennessee that was permitted to carry its own colors instead of the Confederate battle flag).[22] With Govan's veterans on their left, the Georgians knew they were in good company. They were proud, but they were also filled with fear, doubt, and confusion. To have come this far, survived this long, only to be killed in a last-gasp battle made little sense.

While Johnston aligned his troops, Slocum's Union troops stirred and began to advance. Slocum's wing was comprised of two corps: the Thirteenth Corps under Major General Jefferson C. Davis and the Twentieth Corps under Major General Alpheus S. Williams. Davis's was the advance corps and had camped three miles from Johnston's skirmishers. Five months before, the Thirteenth Corps had fought violently, bloodying Cleburne's division at "the angle" in the Battle of Jonesboro, Georgia.

The lead division of the Thirteenth Corps was the First Division commanded by Brigadier General William Carlin. As Carlin's three brigades trudged down the Goldsboro Road in the early morning sunlight, they soon came under fire from advanced Confederate soldiers. Certain that it was only Confederate cavalry and not positioned infantry, Carlin continued his advance. As the fire grew

Lieutenant Archibald McKinley, Captain John Bonner, Sergeant William S. Stetson, and the slave Scott, all of Company H, Fifty-seventh Georgia (Special Collections, Ina Dillard Russell Library, Georgia College & State University, Milledgeville, Ga.)

stronger, he deployed his three brigades to ascertain the strength and character of the enemy fire. By 1 P.M., after several sharp and bloody encounters, Carlin was convinced that he was facing a major Confederate force.[23]

Meanwhile, Johnston was fuming. Hardee, whose corps was to be the center of Johnston's line, had not arrived. To temporarily fill the space between Stewart's Army of Tennessee troops on the right and Bragg's Department of North Carolina troops on the left, Johnston could post only two batteries of Hampton's horse artillery and hope that they were not pressed.[24]

Hardee finally arrived by midday but was not in position to attack until 3 P.M. By then the element of surprise was lost. During the interval that Johnston waited on Hardee, Slocum was able to rush the entire Thirteenth Corps forward and entrench in a semicircle with the Goldsboro Road bisecting its perimeter. He had directed the Twentieth Corps to advance immediately and reinforce the Thirteenth Corps. Finally, at 2:30 P.M. Slocum wrote Sherman a terse dispatch: "I have met [the enemy] in strong force on the road from Bentonville to Cox's Bridge. It is reported by prisoners that Johnston and Hardee are here. I think a portion of the Right Wing should be brought forward at once."[25]

The Army of Tennessee still waited tensely in the woods. Earlier in the morning it had beaten back Carlin's probing attack, leaving scattered Union dead in front of its line. With its position revealed, its charge would be a much more brutal affair.

Shortly after 3 P.M. the Confederates were ready to forge out of the woods and attack the Thirteenth Corps's left flank. Both Hardee's and Stewart's corps would advance, with Hardee in charge of the assault. Once Hardee's charge had destabilized the Union's left flank, Bragg would aggressively attack the center or front of the Union line.[26] The Confederate strategy was to move in stages from right to left. Cleburne's division would take the first step, its final charge, toward the enemy.[27]

Walter Clark of the Sixty-third Georgia described the terrain that Cleburne's division would cross: "In our front and gently sloping upwards for three hundred yards was an old field dotted with second growth pines, and two hundred and fifty yards beyond its highest point on the descending slope lay the Federal breastworks."[28] Once the Rebs crested the low ridge, they would face concentrated fire.

When Hardee trotted forth on horseback and gave the order to advance, Cleburne's division stepped out. Mercer's brigade was briefly slowed by crossing its own defenses, and Govan's brigade surged ahead.[29] Soon Rebel yells split the air. Those who looked on marveled at the parade ground precision by which the Army of Tennessee advanced. Colonel Charles Broadfoot wrote,

> It looked like a picture and at our distance was truly beautiful. Several officers led the charge on horseback across an open field in full view, with colors flying and line of battle in such perfect order as to be able to distinguish the several field officers in proper place and followed by a battery which dashed at full gallop, wheeled, unlimbered, and opened fire. It was gallantly done, but it was painful to see how close their battle flags were together, regiments being scarcely larger than companies and division[s] not much larger than a regiment should be.[30]

The Army of Tennessee forces moved up the three-hundred-yard slope, marching at double time. Clark remembered that, "as we advanced, we passed over the bodies of the enemy who had been killed in the assault and whose faces, from exposure to the sun, had turned almost black." As the Rebs crested the hill, they could see the Union entrenchments 250 yards away. Instantly, the air was filled with whistling minié balls. With yells and cheers the Rebs poured down the hill, losing themselves in increasing momentum.[31]

Cleburne's division attacked Buell's entrenched brigade. Cleburne's troops bore directly down on the Thirteenth and Twenty-first Michigan Regiments, with the Sixty-ninth Ohio slightly to their right. The terrain that Govan's brigade traversed was more thickly wooded than the nearly open plain that Mercer's brigade crossed. As enemy fire increased, Mercer's brigade veered toward the shelter of the timber, mingling with Govan's line.[32] In the middle of this confusion, the Yanks unleashed a volley that almost broke Mercer's brigade. Clark clearly remembered the moment:

> Down the slope we charged until half the distance had been covered and the enemy's line is only a hundred yards away. The "zips" of the minies get thicker and thicker and the line partially demoralized by the heavy fire suddenly halts.
>
> Frank Stone is carrying the colors (Cleburne's division flag—a blue field with white circle in the center) and he and I jump for the same pine. It is only six inches thick and will cover neither of us fully, but we divide its protective capacity fairly. Fifteen or twenty feet to my left there is an exclamation of pain and as I turn to look Jim Beasley clasps his hand to his face as the blood spurts from his cheek.
>
> My cartridge box has been drawn to the front of my body for convenience in loading as well as for protection and as I look to the front again a ball strikes it, and strikes so hard that it forces from me an involuntary grunt. Frank hears it and turns to me quickly, "Are you hurt?" I said I believed not and proceed to investigate. The ball passing through the leather and tin had struck the leaden end of a cartridge and being in that way deflected had passed out the right side of the box instead of through my body.[33]

As Mercer's brigade hit the ground, the Sixty-ninth Ohio was to the right of the Georgians and raked them with fire. Bate called up his two reserve regiments (Finley and Tyler) to fill in on the right of Mercer's brigade and directly assault the Sixty-ninth Ohio.[34]

As the reserve line came up, General Hardee galloped boldly down the line of the Army of Tennessee, fully exposed to enemy fire, and exhorted the men to follow him. Spurring his horse, he jumped a ditch where many men were huddled and waved the troops forward. Inspired by his example, they jumped up and resumed the charge.[35]

At this moment Clark looked over at the Florida brigade (Finley) that had attached to Mercer's right and saw its color-bearer "making his way alone towards the breastworks at half speed, with his flag held aloft, fifty yards in front of the halted ranks. Inspired by his example or recovering from the temporary panic, the line moves forward again."[36]

Stewart's Army of Tennessee surged ahead. Within minutes these battered veterans had overrun Carlin's division, smashing his brigades and hurling them from their entrenchments. The Rebs captured three guns and several hundred prisoners. As Carlin's survivors fled south down the Goldsboro Road toward the reinforcements of the advancing Twentieth Corps, Johnston and Hardee were ecstatic.

As always, the hungry Rebs had one eye open for food, even in the middle of battle. A man in Brigadier General William Taliaferro's division recalled that one Yankee picket was eating dinner when he was overrun. He dropped his tin bucket of rice and peas to surrender, but a Rebel lieutenant grabbed the bucket in midflight and carried it off, spoon still in the rice.[37]

Clark also remembered a lucky find: "The enemy desert their breastworks and make for the rear at a double-quick. Leaping the entrenchments, a hatchet, frying pan and Enfield rifle lie right in my path. Sticking the pan and hatchet in my belt, I drop my Austrian gun and seizing the Enfield I see across the ravine a group of enemy running up the hill. Aiming at the center of the squad I send one of their own balls after them, but the cartridge is faulty and fails to reach its mark. We pursue them for half a mile and the disordered ranks are halted to be re-formed."[38]

By now the Army of Tennessee needed reorganization. Regiments had become mixed, orders were confused, and men were winded. Hardee ordered a temporary halt and as a result lost the offensive momentum.[39]

As the Army of Tennessee destabilized the Union flank and routed Carlin's division, Bragg failed to advance against the front—or center—of the Union line. Only as the Army of Tennessee stopped to regroup did Bragg make a belated and disjointed charge. Unlike Hardee, who was with the troops in the field, Bragg was behind the lines at his command post, and the charge was not effective.[40] Bragg's inexcusable delay and lax performance saved the Union's Thirteenth Corps from destruction or capture.

As Bragg's attack foundered, the Army of Tennessee finished its reorganization and pursued Carlin's division down the Goldsboro Road. Soon they were joined by Taliaferro's division. However, as the sun set, the retreating Union Thirteenth Corps was reinforced by fresh brigades from the Twentieth Corps. The Yanks also positioned four artillery batteries to crisscross the Confederate advance. When Bate's corps and Mercer's brigade reached the lines of the Union Twentieth Corps, Bate deployed his corps for its second charge of the afternoon.[41] With his crutches strapped to his saddle, Bate led his men forward.[42] As they advanced, Walter Clark was sent out as a skirmisher, and he later recorded the intensity of the Confederate charge:

The line of battle follows in our [the skirmishers'] wake. But before it reaches us a ball strikes John Miller, passing directly through his body, and he turned to the color-bearer and said, "Frank, I'm killed." Frank replied, "I hope not John". The line presses on and John lies down under the pines to die.

In a little while Frank is disabled by a wound in the side and the colors are turned over to Billy Morris. The regiment reaches the position occupied by the skirmish line and under heavy fire we are ordered to lie down. Sam Woods and [I] seek the shelter of a large pine and while kneeling together behind it a minie passes through Sam's hand and thigh and he limps to the rear.

Advancing again, we are halted just before night by a pond or lagoon in our front. A friendly log lies near its edge and we lie down behind it. A Federal battery opens on us and the color-bearer of Olmstead's 1st Ga. regiment is knocked six or eight feet and disemboweled by a solid shot as it plows through the ranks.[43]

Though Bate's attack was repulsed, Hardee was not ready to give up. He sent Taliaferro's two brigades against the Union line with the same bloody result. Then, in desperation, Hardee ordered Lafayette McClaws's brigades forward. The Confederates fought long into the night—launching a total of seven assaults—without breaking the Union line. Near midnight Johnston finally ordered his troops to withdraw to the positions that they had occupied that morning.[44]

At best the first day of the Battle of Bentonville had been a stalemate. Johnston had not isolated and defeated a Union wing. By dawn Sherman would arrive with the lead elements of his right wing, and Johnston would have no chance of victory.

As Mercer's brigade retreated with Cleburne's spent division, the men took stock of their losses. Clark reflected on his own company, the Oglethorpes of the Sixty-third Georgia, and reported:

> Night comes on, the firing ceases and the fight is ended. . . . Of the 19
> Oglethorpes only one has been killed and three wounded, though thirteen
> others bear on their bodies, clothing or equipment marks of the enemy's fire,
> some of them in three or four places. Frank Stone, in addition to the wound
> in his side and a hole through his sleeve, has a chew of tobacco taken off by a
> ball that passes through his pocket. John Kirkpatrick has his canteen ventilated,
> Sol Foreman and Will Dabney find the meal in their haversacks seasoned with
> minies instead of salt, and the writer, in addition to the demoralization of his
> cartridge box, finds a hole in his haversack and thirteen in his folded blanket,
> all probably made by a single ball. . . .
>
> By the aid of torches we find John Miller's body and near it a naked arm
> taken off at the elbow by a cannon ball. Placing them on a blanket, John
> Kirkpatrick, Will Dabney, the writer and another comrade carry them nearly
> half a mile to an open field and give them as decent burial as we can.[45]

Throughout the night Johnston's forces retreated and by dawn of Monday, March 20, the Confederates had dug in on favorable terrain and established a defensive perimeter. Johnston established his headquarters on the John Benton farm just east of Bentonville and sought to evacuate his wounded.

When Sherman arrived outside Bentonville early on March 20, he was surprised to see that Johnston had not ordered a full retreat during the night. Now Sherman had three times as many troops on the field as Johnston did, and the offensive initiative was in Sherman's hand.[46] Facing such odds, why didn't Johnston retreat to fight another day? Perhaps there were several reasons.

First, there might not be another day. The war was clearly winding down and if Johnston were to make an impact, it would be now or never. Second, Johnston had pulled back into a good defensive position. Only by forcing Sherman into a bloody assault—such as at Kennesaw—could Johnston have any hope of equalizing the numerical advantage that Sherman held. It was a long shot. But it was the best shot Johnston had.[47]

Third, Johnston was worried about his many wounded. His only avenue of retreat was across the Mill Creek bridge. With no ambulances, transfer of the wounded was slow. Johnston was giving his medical corps every minute he could.[48]

And what about Sherman? He had Johnston in the palm of his hand. Why didn't he destroy him? Again, there were several reasons.

The war was drawing to a rapid conclusion, and even Sherman was tired of bloodshed. To frontally assault Johnston would extract high casualties on both sides. As Sherman told Schofield, "[Johnston's] position is in the swamps, difficult of approach, and I don't like to assail his parapets."[49] Sherman sensed that there was a more economical way to bring the war to an end without undue loss of time or life.

Also, Sherman wanted to stick to his grand strategy and not be distracted by Johnston's ploy. In a dispatch to Schofield on March 21, Sherman stated, "The moment Johnston gives ground I propose to fall back on Goldsborough and wait the completion of our railroad and re-equipment of my army."[50] Sherman never intended to attack Johnston and hoped that he would retreat.

On the night of March 21, 1865, Johnston withdrew from Bentonville to Smithfield. Sherman did not pursue, and three days later the Union army entered Goldsboro, joining forces with Schofield. When casualties for the Battle of Bentonville were tallied, Johnston's army had lost 2,606 men, Sherman's 1,527. It was the last major battle for Johnston's shattered army and the final combat for Mercer's brigade.

30

Going Home

During the last week of March 1865, Johnston's men shuffled into Smithfield, North Carolina, and Sherman advanced to Goldsboro, North Carolina, linking up with Schofield's reinforcements as they arrived from the coast. Sherman immediately prepared to move north to join forces with Grant in Virginia.[1]

Robert E. Lee's army had been mired throughout the winter in brutal trench warfare along the Richmond-Petersburg line in Virginia. The Army of Northern Virginia was slowly starving and losing hope. Grant was determined to shatter this deadlock when he unleashed his spring campaign.

To the south Johnston was licking his wounds and wondering what to do next. He was already reorganizing his army. His divisions, brigades, and regiments were so depleted that he had to consolidate and form them into new units.

Within Mercer's brigade the First Georgia Volunteers, the Fifty-seventh Georgia, and the Sixty-third Georgia became the First Volunteer Regiment of Georgia. Olmstead was retained as colonel, Cincinnatus Guyton of the Fifty-seventh Georgia was made lieutenant colonel, and Joseph V. H. Allen of the Sixty-third Georgia was made major. Olmstead estimated that the new regiment had eight hundred men.[2]

The Fifty-fourth Georgia was separated from Mercer's brigade and consolidated with the Thirty-seventh Georgia and the Fourth Battalion Georgia Sharpshooters to form the Fifty-fourth Georgia Regiment. Both new consolidated regiments were placed in Hardee's corps, John C. Brown's division, and James A. Smith's brigade. Johnston's newly organized army inherited the proud mantle of the Army of Tennessee.[3]

"Old Joe" Johnston was convinced that Lee would soon break loose from the Richmond-Petersburg siege and move south to rendezvous with the Army of Tennessee for a final stand. What this would accomplish neither general made clear. But merging the Rebel armies seems to have been an attempt to prolong the inevitable.[4]

Grant soon wrenched the tactical initiative from Lee. On April 1–2 Grant's army won the Battle of Five Forks, snapping the Confederate line and forcing Lee to abandon Richmond and Petersburg on April 3. The Confederate government fled south from Richmond toward Greensboro, North Carolina, while Lee's Army of Northern Virginia began a rapid retreat toward Johnston's Army of Tennessee. Soon, however, Lee's army was desperately in search of food and hounded by Grant's pursuing cavalry. Recognizing that he could no longer retreat and that battle was futile, Lee met with Grant on Palm Sunday, April 9, in the small village of Appomattox Court House to discuss terms of surrender. On April 12 the Army of Northern Virginia stacked its arms and formally surrendered.

By April 10 Sherman, aware that Lee's surrender was imminent, reversed course and set his army in motion to corral Johnston.[5] The Yanks were wild with excitement. They knew they would soon be going home, the saviors of the Union.[6]

Meanwhile, Johnston had been unable to communicate directly with Lee for more than a week. Johnston still hoped that Lee was retreating in a deliberate effort to combine forces with his Army of Tennessee; Johnston did not know that Lee was surrendering.[7] Frustrated by his unanswered requests for information, Johnston moved his army from Smithfield to Raleigh, hoping to expedite his rendezvous with Lee. Johnston was camped fourteen miles east of Raleigh on April 10 and aware of Sherman's approach when he received a telegram from Jefferson Davis in Greensboro. Davis floored Johnston by disclosing unofficial reports that Lee had surrendered the Army of Northern Virginia at Appomattox Court House. Davis asked Johnston to come to Greensboro immediately for consultation.[8]

Johnston arrived in Greensboro by rail on April 11, still with no confirmation that Lee had surrendered. As Johnston met with Davis and members of his cabinet, the general was shocked by the president's talk of continuing the war effort. Davis believed that the army could be rebuilt and a successful war waged, perhaps west of the Mississippi with reinforcement from Kirby Smith. Johnston knew that his small army of twenty-two thousand troops would soon be surrounded by the combined armies of Grant and Sherman, which exceeded 290,000 men. To continue the war was absurd, and Johnston and General P. G. T. Beauregard, who again served under Johnston in the closing weeks of the war, clearly told Davis so.[9]

On the night of April 12 John C. Breckinridge, the Confederate secretary of war, brought official confirmation that Lee had surrendered his army. The next day Johnston and Beauregard were invited to join Davis's cabinet for its final meeting. Davis asked Johnston to express his views. Johnston was firm and to the point, saying that to continue the war would be "the greatest of human crimes."[10] Beauregard agreed, as did Davis's entire cabinet, with the exception of Judah Benjamin. Finally, the belligerent Davis gave in and consented to seek a truce for the purpose of negotiation. Johnston may have won his greatest victory in his firm debate with Jefferson Davis.[11]

On April 14 Johnston sent Sherman a dispatch requesting a cease-fire. That night Abraham Lincoln was assassinated, sending a seismic shock through both armies. Union soldiers were furious, suspecting that the retreating Confederate government had orchestrated the assassination. A lynch mob of two thousand Yankee soldiers moved toward Raleigh to raze the city. Only the efforts of Major General John Logan and his battery of Union field artillery turned the angry soldiers away.[12] The country needed the Confederacy to surrender immediately.

Accompanied by Secretary of War Breckinridge, Johnston met Sherman on April 17 between the opposing lines at the rustic Bennett farmhouse near Durham, North Carolina. Because of his schedule and constant travel, Johnston still did not know that Lincoln was dead. Sherman shared with Johnston a confidential dispatch that he had received concerning the assassination. A clerk observed, "The perspiration came out in large drops on his [Johnston's] forehead and he did not attempt to conceal his distress." Johnston remarked that this was the "greatest possible calamity" that could confront the South.[13] Lincoln would have treated the encircled South with clemency and compassion.

As Johnston recovered from his shock, he and Sherman began their deliberations. On April 18 they drafted a peace document that was more sweeping and liberal than the surrender terms at Appomattox. To his dismay, Johnston was not able to discuss the proposed terms with Jefferson Davis because the Confederate president had suddenly fled toward Charlotte. However, President Andrew Johnson then rejected the proposal, stating that Sherman had exceeded his authority as a military commander.

On April 25 the downcast and confused Johnston was astounded to receive a communiqué from Jefferson Davis ordering him *not* to surrender but to disperse his army in multiple directions with orders to reassemble at a new location to fight again. In a determined act of insubordination, Johnston disregarded Davis's orders. In his memoirs he wrote, "The belief that . . . it would be a great crime to prolong the war, prompted me to disobey these instructions—the last that I received from the Confederate Government. . . . In that belief, I determined to do all in my power to bring about a termination of hostilities."[14]

On April 26 Sherman and Johnston met again to negotiate a modified document of surrender. "We met at noon in Mr. Bennett's house, as before," Johnston recalled. "I found General Sherman, as he appeared in our previous conversation, anxious to prevent further bloodshed, so we agreed without difficulty upon terms putting an end to the war within the limits of our commands." President Johnson accepted this peace document, and General Johnston surrendered the Army of Tennessee on terms similar to those at Appomattox.[15]

Although smaller Confederate armies in the West would surrender later, the stroke of Johnston's pen effectively ended the bloodiest war that Americans have ever fought. In four short years North and South waged 2,261 battles that caused one million military casualties. A total of 360,000 Yankees and at least 260,000 Rebels were killed. Indeed, more Americans died in this war between brothers than in all the nation's other wars combined, through the Vietnam War.[16]

General John Gordon had surrendered the Army of Northern Virginia in a formal ceremony at Appomattox, but Sherman saw no need for this. Instead, he permitted the Rebs to furl their battle flags and stack their arms in the privacy of their own camps.[17]

Most Southern veterans experienced great relief in the midst of wrenching sorrow. A Tennessee soldier wrote, "All phases of human feeling were exhibited. Some raved and swore that they would never submit to it. Some paced back and forth like caged lions. Some seated themselves on logs and buried their faces in their hands."[18] Olmstead was among the more introspective:

> You will readily understand the mingled emotions that were in my heart.
> I was weary of war and of the long separation from my wife and children; my
> eyes yearned for a sight of the dear little boy who had been born in my absence
> and the thought of returning home to face no more perils and hardships of
> a soldier's calling filled my soul with gratitude to the Giver of all good. I was
> thankful too that life had been spared and that a new career could be begun,
> while I was yet young, and blessed with a vigorous and unmutilated body.
>
> Yet, nevertheless, it was impossible to avoid a deep feeling of depression as
> memory brought back the high hope and courage with which we had entered
> the war and contrasted also the brilliant successes that had marked the earlier
> stages of the conflict, with the ruin and desolation that had finally come upon
> the South. The faces of many dear friends who had laid down their lives for the
> Cause, were present with me too. I can not think of them even now without a
> pang of sorrowful emotion.[19]

As soldiers came to terms with their raw feelings and began to think of home, they were paid a small stipend. Olmstead recalled, "We were paid off, too, in genuine 'coin of the realm'—two silver dollars to each officer and man from Confederate Treasury money that had been hurried out of Richmond when the fall of that city seemed inevitable. It was the only pay I received for the whole of my last year of service and I have often wished that these two coins had been kept as mementos. Many did so keep theirs, but my needs prevented me from so doing."[20]

Small groups of men immediately drifted off toward home without waiting to obtain their official paroles. Members of Mercer's old brigade received their paroles on May 2, and the next day many began the march out of North Carolina as a unit, including the sick and wounded.[21] Forty-three-year-old Charles Thiot of the First Georgia Volunteers had seen continual combat since the north Georgia campaign had begun more than a year earlier. He had spent much of March and April 1865 in hospitals in Charlotte and Raleigh. Now he was weak and desperately ill. He longed to see his wife, Anna, and return to his plantation, Roseville, near Savannah. Finally, overcome with exhaustion, he could march no longer and dropped out of line somewhere in North Carolina. His messmates in the Oglethorpe Light Infantry did not realize how weak he was and left him on the side of the road to catch his breath and join them later.[22]

Many years afterward, Thiot's grandson, Charles T. Winship, continued the story: "That was the last that was ever seen of him by anyone who knew him. The best guess as to his fate is that he went for shelter to some farm house, died there and was buried without notification being given to the army. I have heard my grandmother tell how for months after the end of the war she would lie awake at night listening for footsteps hoping that her husband might not yet return."[23]

The 230-mile trip from North Carolina to Augusta, Georgia, took eleven days. Sergeant Clark remembered, "In evidence of South Carolina's loyalty to the cause, even in its dying hours, I recall the fact that while passing through its territory, on our homeward march, no man or woman refused to accept Confederate money for any purchase made by us."[24] From Augusta the First Volunteers and the Sixty-third Georgia turned toward Savannah and the coast. The Fifty-seventh Georgia headed toward middle and south Georgia. Many of these men would not see each other again. But they would never forget each other's faces and how their lives had been forged, refined, and bonded together in the heat of combat.[25]

Olmstead did not return to Savannah with the First Volunteers. When he reached Augusta, he received tragic news. Years later he wrote his three daughters, "I learned with deep grief of the banishment of officer's families from Savannah and the death of your little brother. It was a bitter blow. I felt glad however to know that your mother had gone back to your grandmother's house at Milledgeville."[26] Olmstead never saw his only son.

Olmstead probably traveled with the men of the Fifty-seventh Georgia, leaving Augusta the next day by train through Atlanta, Macon, and on to Milledgeville. "It was a tedious journey," he recalled, "one that tired me far more than the marching had done. We rode in ramshackle old cattle cars seated on boards that were stuck through from side to side, and the dust and heat were dreadful. But Milledgeville was reached at last and I held my beloved wife and blessed little 'Daughter' in my arms. God had been good to me and I acknowledged it from the depth of my soul."[27]

Much had happened since twenty-four-year-old Charles Olmstead had surrendered Fort Pulaski in April 1862. Then a novice, he now returned a sensitive but hardened combat officer who had served under Walker, Cleburne, and Forrest.

Upon arrival in Milledgeville, Olmstead probably was accompanied by survivors of Company H of the Fifty-seventh Georgia, "The Independent Volunteers." Most of these men were from Milledgeville, and their captain, John Richard Bonner, had led Mercer's brigade at Bentonville. They returned to a joyous homecoming. But many who had left with them in 1862 were dead or maimed. Captain Bonner's descendant, James C. Bonner, recounted the toll of war on this company: "Two of its twelve officers had been killed and six wounded. Of fifty-six privates only eleven returned home without wounds. Twenty-seven were dead, including Thomas, Charles, and James Martin. Of the seven Russell boys—brothers and cousins—five were dead, three of them from battle wounds. The two survivors, Joseph and Samuel, were seriously wounded."[28]

Among those who returned to Milledgeville, although he was not on Bonner's list of veterans, was Scott, the slave. Yet he had faithfully marched with Company H every step of the way, from Kentucky to North Carolina. Returning with Lieutenant Archibald McKinley, Scott came home a legally free man. Yet his battle was just beginning. Scott and his descendants would continue to fight poverty, illiteracy, prejudice, and racial enmity into the twentieth century and beyond.

Yet there appear to have been authentic affection and commitment between McKinley and Scott, despite the scourge of slavery. During the Vicksburg campaign it was reported in error that McKinley had been killed in battle. Scott was overcome with grief and tears. McKinley reported that after Scott found him to be alive, he "nursed me with the greatest care and tenderness until I recovered." McKinley's family was among those that would act compassionately toward so courageous a former slave as Scott. Within weeks the McKinleys would give Scott a house and twenty acres to farm. Until the day Scott died in 1870, he and McKinley remained devoted to each other.[29]

The horrific losses and suffering evidenced by Company H of Milledgeville typified the ten companies of the Fifty-seventh Georgia. All told, the Confederacy had mobilized 80 percent or more of its military-age white males, and a third had died. The South's war effort, along with the property destroyed by the Union armies, had cost two-thirds of all assessed wealth as of 1860. Families had been destroyed and left destitute.[30]

As Olmstead and Company H departed from the Macon railroad station for Milledgeville, Company E, the Fort Valley Infantry, boarded a freight train from Macon for the thirty-mile ride south to Fort Valley. Robert Braswell rode with the two dozen men of his company who had surrendered in Greensboro. They now were members of an exclusive fraternity of survivors. In their later years they would recount their war stories again and again, becoming white-haired legends to big-eyed little boys.[31]

Braswell was fourteen when he left home in 1861, and now he was a tall, brawny eighteen-year-old who towered above his companions at six-four. Broad shouldered but gaunt, he had reached manhood on a near-starvation diet. For many months Robert had not dared to hope that he would ever see adulthood. He undoubtedly had endured by organizing his life into daylong chapters. Now that the guns had stopped firing, the future beckoned. A hardened young soldier would have to adapt to a new type of life.

As the train neared Fort Valley, it steamed directly across the Braswell family land, just as it had on the journey to Andersonville in 1864. As he looked across the vacant fields, Braswell suddenly recognized that everything had changed. His grandfather Mims had been dead for nearly two years. Robert's older brothers, William and Samuel, lay in a mass grave along Peachtree Creek. And the fate of his uncle, Seaborn Mims, remained unknown—he was either dead in North Georgia or a prisoner of war. Robert Braswell returned home as the only living male in his immediate family.

Surely, his thoughts also focused on Laura Love. How many times had he wondered whether he would ever see her pretty face again? Would she still love him now that the romance and urgency of war had waned? Was he so changed and hardened by battle that she would not recognize him as the boy she once loved?

Rocking along in the dusty cattle car, Robert Braswell was sure of only one thing: he would never leave Fort Valley again. And he didn't.

Epilogue

The Future of Their Lives

After the Civil War, what became of the men and women who are depicted in this book? How did they continue their lives? What were their achievements and contributions? Did the future bring them peace and fulfillment? Or did the conflict of war continue to haunt their days?

Colonel William Barkuloo, Fifty-seventh Georgia Regiment

After the Battle of Atlanta, Barkuloo voluntarily relinquished command of the Fifty-seventh Georgia. Those who have researched Barkuloo assume that he was granted medical leave to return to his home in Brunswick, Georgia, where he was living at the end of the war. In 1866 he was elected clerk and treasurer of the Brunswick City Council. He designed the Brunswick city seal that is still in use today.

Barkuloo was fifty-one when he died in 1873. He was buried at Oak Grove Cemetery in an unmarked grave. He was survived by four children.[1]

Lieutenant Hamilton Branch, Fifty-fourth Georgia Regiment

After Hood's retreat from Tennessee, twenty-two-year-old Hamilton Branch was hospitalized in Augusta, Georgia, and was not able to join the Fifty-fourth Georgia for the North Carolina campaign. Hamilton returned to his home in Savannah after the Confederacy surrendered. In 1867 he married Marie Eugenia Dickerson and worked for her father at the Central Railroad wharf. They had three children.

In 1879 Savannah erected a Confederate monument in Forsyth Park. A marble statue of a soldier in a tattered frock coat and slouch hat stands atop the monument. Branch served as the sculptor's model, and the finished sculpture bears a striking resemblance to him, including the hole in his trousers where he was wounded.

In 1899, when he was fifty-six, Hamilton Branch died of a stroke while on an evening stroll.[2] His marble visage still peers down from the heights of the memorial.

The Confederate monument in Forsyth Park, Savannah. Hamilton Branch was the model for the figure of the soldier. (Courtesy of the Hargrett Rare Book and Manuscript Library, University of Georgia Libraries)

Private Robert L. Braswell, Fifty-seventh Georgia Regiment

Upon his return to Fort Valley, eighteen-year-old Braswell was delighted to find that fourteen-year-old Laura Love was still infatuated with him. They were married on June 25, 1866. They had four sons and three daughters. Laura was only thirty-nine when she died on April 6, 1890. Although he was only in his early forties, Braswell never remarried.[3]

Throughout his life he tried to continue farming. However, by the time his four sons were grown, much of the old Mims land had been sold, and none of his sons became a farmer.

Braswell attended local Confederate reunions and became known around Fort Valley as a Confederate warrior and local historian. Robert Braswell died on January 12, 1920, having lived to what was then a ripe old age, seventy-three. Much of his obituary was devoted to his Civil War record.[4]

Of greatest importance to me is that Robert Braswell is my great-great-grandfather.

Orderly Sergeant Walter A. Clark, Sixty-third Georgia Regiment

In the final days of the war twenty-three-year-old Walter A. Clark was promoted to first lieutenant of the consolidated First Volunteer Regiment of Georgia. Although he was wounded four times by rifle fire during the war, he was never seriously injured. After the surrender in Greensboro he returned to his home in Richmond County, Georgia, near Augusta.

Clark's postwar life was primarily devoted to public service. In 1870 he was elected to the state legislature and won reelection twice. In 1897 he was elected treasurer of Richmond County.[5] Three years later he wrote a graphic account of his four years of service with the Oglethorpes of Augusta, *Under the Stars and Bars.*

Captain Edwin T. Davis, Fifty-seventh Georgia Regiment

Instead of returning to his hometown of Riddleville or to Mercer University after the war, twenty-three-year-old Edwin Davis settled in Thomasville, Georgia, the home of his comrades in Company A, the Dixie Boys. There, amid some of the largest and finest plantations in Georgia, he met Martha Tallulah Jones of the historic Greenwood Plantation. They were married one year later on May 2, 1866, and had two daughters, Martha and Marion.

Davis was only thirty-seven when he died. He was buried at Greenwood Plantation. His widow, Mattie, lived to be eighty-eight.[6]

Lieutenant Colonel Cincinnatus Guyton, Fifty-seventh Georgia Regiment

Guyton was perhaps the most able combat officer in the Fifty-seventh Georgia Regiment. He was thirty-one when he returned to his wife, Mary Blackshear Guyton, and to the responsibilities of a very large agricultural enterprise in Laurens County, Georgia. Cincinnatus and Mary had five children, all of whom died very young. Mary also succumbed to illness, dying in middle age.

Guyton was forty-one when he remarried, taking the hand of Caroline Boisfeuillet of Macon. They had four children who lived to maturity. During these years Guyton continued to represent the Sixteenth District in the Georgia legislature. He served in the state House of Representatives in 1877 and was a state senator in 1882–83. He was particularly known for opposing the political policies of Republican carpetbaggers.

He contracted Bright's disease (an inflammation of the kidneys) and died in 1884 at the age of fifty-two, leaving his wife, Carrie, with four children younger than ten. Carrie later married Reverend George C. Thompson and lived until 1916.[7]

Lieutenant Jim Kuglar, Fifty-sixth Georgia Regiment

Kuglar was twenty-five when he returned to his hometown of Bowden in Carrol County, Georgia. He married Frances Alexander on November 16, 1865.

He lived into his nineties and left a large and impressive family: nine children, forty-one grandchildren, thirty-one great-grandchildren, and one great-great-grandchild. When he was ninety-one, "Uncle Jim" Kuglar dictated a lucid and valuable memoir of his experiences in the Civil War.[8]

Lieutenant Archibald C. McKinley, Fifty-seventh Georgia Regiment

McKinley returned to his family's plantation, Walnut Level, in Milledgeville and married Sarah Elizabeth Spalding on November 19, 1866. In 1869 the McKinleys moved to Sapelo Island to pursue agriculture.[9] Eight years later he returned to Milledgeville to help his father with his law practice and farming. In 1880 the McKinleys returned to Sapelo Island to live out their lives. Archibald died in 1917 and was buried in Memory Hill cemetery in Milledgeville.

Captain George A. Mercer, First Georgia Volunteer Regiment

Mercer married Nannie Maury Herndon of Virginia during the early days of the war. Throughout the conflict he remained on the staff of his father, Brigadier General Hugh Mercer. After the surrender the younger Mercer returned to his law practice in Savannah. He and his wife had seven children.

A graduate of Princeton University and the University of Virginia, Mercer was president of the board of education in Savannah for many years. He also served as president of the Savannah Medical College and of the Georgia Historical Society. He was seventy-two when he died on October 23, 1907.[10]

Brigadier General Hugh Weedon Mercer

After the Battle of Atlanta, General Mercer was transferred to Savannah and served on the staff of General Hardee. When Savannah fell to Sherman, Mercer retreated with Hardee to Charleston. Mercer then joined the staff of General Howel Cobb in Macon, Georgia. He was fifty-seven when he returned to Savannah at the end of the war and resumed his prewar career as a banker. In 1869 he moved to Baltimore, where he was a commission merchant (today he would have been a stockbroker). As his health deteriorated, he moved in 1872 to Baden-Baden, Germany, site of mineral springs that were used by the Romans. Mercer died on June 9, 1877, at the age of sixty-nine.[11]

Private John J. Methvin, Fifty-seventh Georgia Regiment

Methvin returned to his home in Jeffersonville, enrolled in school, and became a practicing attorney in 1869. Two years later he moved to Cleveland, Georgia, where he practiced law, was a schoolteacher, and soon became the county school commissioner. Also in 1871 Methvin was licensed to preach by the Georgia Conference of the Methodist Church. On May 6, 1874, he married Emma L. Beall of Irwinton, Georgia.

Methvin became president of Gainesville College in 1880 and in 1883 was elected president of Butler Female College. In 1885 the Methodist Church appointed Methvin to be superintendent of New Hope Seminary in the "Indian Territory" of Oklahoma. Methvin served as a Methodist minister to Native Americans for fifty-six years. He was ninety-four when he died in 1941.[12]

Sergeant Seaborn Mims, Fifty-seventh Georgia Regiment

Mims delighted his family by returning home to Fort Valley after the surrender; for the last year of the war his relatives did not know whether he was dead or alive. He had been captured near Marietta, Georgia, on July 3, 1864, and was sent to the prisoner-of-war camp at Camp Douglas, Illinois. The 1870 federal census shows that Mims was then living in Perry, Georgia.[13]

Colonel Charles H. Olmstead, First Georgia Volunteer Regiment

Olmstead was twenty-eight when he rejoined his wife, Florence, at their home in Savannah, where they raised three daughters, Susan, Sarah, and Florence. Olmstead engaged successfully in shipping, life insurance, and banking. Later he was employed in the statistical department of Wanamaker's in New York City.

He wrote his *Memoirs* in 1912 when he was seventy-six. He was eighty-nine when he died in Savannah on August 17, 1926. Before his death he wrote, "I gratefully acknowledge that 'goodness and mercy' *have* followed me 'all the days of my life.'"[14]

Scott

After accompanying Archibald McKinley through three years of combat, Scott returned to Milledgeville with McKinley. When he died on April 17, 1870, five years after the end of the war, Scott was still farming the land that the grateful McKinleys had given him. He was forty-five.[15]

The longest account in McKinley's journey was written on the day that Scott died: "[Scott] . . . was an old family servant, his father (Peter) having been a slave of my Mother's father. . . . [Scott was] apparently in perfect health. After eating very largely during this morning, he smoked his pipe & laid down on his bed to take a nap—in a few minutes had a spasm & died in a few minutes more without speaking."[16]

Lieutenant David Snelling, Fifty-seventh Georgia Regiment

Snelling continued to ride with Sherman during his march through Georgia and the Carolinas. Upon the Confederate surrender, Snelling was discharged from the Union army in Nashville and found the courage to return to his home in Milledgeville, Georgia. Because he was estranged from his immediate family, the Lesters, he found lodging with an old friend who had helped raise him, Colonel John Singleton. Within a few days Snelling visited Captain John Bonner, who had recruited him into the local company from which he had deserted in 1862. Surprisingly, Bonner received him cordially.

However, within a few days of arriving in Milledgeville, Snelling received several death threats and fled in the middle of the night, leaving his few possessions behind. He gradually made his way across the South until he settled in Arkansas, where he married Margaret Nelson in 1880. They had seven children.

Never happy, Snelling drifted from job to job and struggled with alcoholism. Finally, he settled near Ozark, Arkansas, cultivated a small farm, and worked as a house painter. He died on April 23, 1901.[17]

Private Wright Vinson, Fifty-seventh Georgia Regiment

After Wright Vinson died of smallpox in Jackson, Mississippi, in 1862, his wife, Christiana, raised their infant son, Charley, in Crawford County, Georgia. Christiana was still a young woman when she died, and Charley was raised by relatives.

As an adult, Charley E. Vinson moved near Macon, Georgia, and became a successful farmer and plantation owner. He was instrumental in starting a high school and served on the board of directors of a bank in Macon. He married Florede Olds, and they had four sons and two daughters. His youngest daughter, Nell Oldham, recalled that her father often held a picture of Wright and Christiana in his hands as tears flowed silently down his cheeks.

One of Charley's sons, Lamar Vinson, was killed on the beaches of Normandy on D-day during World War II.[18]

Afterword

Lessons of a Great-Great-Grandson

This historical journey began for me in 1991 when I discovered my great-great-grandfather's name, Robert Braswell, in the index of a Civil War veterans book and decided to investigate his regiment. This quest has resulted in the experience of a lifetime and has taught me much. As I reflect on my pilgrimage, I conclude with six insights.

Human Endurance

Learning my great-great-grandfather's story and that of the men with whom he served has left me in awe of the strength and endurance of the human soul. As the Japanese proverb says, "To endure what is unendurable is true endurance." The men whose stories fill these pages had true endurance.

Several years ago, as I was researching this book, I paused and looked at my seventeen-year-old son, Drew, and my fourteen-year-old son, Luke. Drew was rushing off on a date—neat, dressed to the nines, radiating health and innocence. I realized that he was the same age as Robert Braswell when his brothers were killed beside him at Peachtree Creek, and I tried to imagine Drew as a thin, hollow-eyed veteran of three years of warfare: Kentucky, Vicksburg, Andersonville, Atlanta, Tennessee, Bentonville.

Then I looked at Luke, who had a Pony League baseball cap perched on his red hair—an inheritance from the Braswells—and wondered how I could ever send him off to war. He was still a child who had not yet conquered the traumas of middle school, yet he was the same age that Robert Braswell was when he left with the Everett Guards for Savannah. I shook my head and sat in silence. How could it happen? How could it be?

Recently, I asked an eighty-four-year-old veteran of World War II how, as an eighteen-year-old, he made it through two years of fierce combat in Europe, from Omaha Beach to the Elbe River. He replied, "When I couldn't go any further, I thought of home. Thought of Mom and Dad. My girlfriend. Somehow I kept on going. There was no other choice."

Though the human spirit can be shattered, many have discovered that, when they have to, they can endure what they imagined to be unendurable. The first lesson that my great-great-grandfather has taught me is that people are made of hardy stuff.

One afternoon I found Williamson Mims's will in the courthouse of Houston County, Georgia. I had only recently learned that Mims was my great-great-great-grandfather, and now I was turning the dusty and faded pages of the oldest *Record of Wills* book in Houston County.

As I held my breath and turned to page 139, my eyes fell on these words:

> I give and bequeath to my beloved wife, Synthia Mims, the place and planta-
> tion on which I live in Houston County including my mills on Mossy Creek
> amounting to some fifteen hundred acres. . . . All my farming utensils, horses,
> mules, hogs, cattle and sheep. . . . Also my man Carter (a miller) and his wife
> Biddy and their children, Ribbin, Georgia, Ann and Fred. My negro woman
> Caroline and her four children, Laura, Cruso, Anna, Victoria. My man John (a
> carpenter), my negro woman Harriet (called Harriet Hall), my man Alexander
> (my sawyer), my boy Arnold, my boy Anthony, my man Jack (stock hauler), my
> man big Ben and his wife Roda and their children George and Anderson, and
> my negro woman Martha (Jack's wife). And my old negros to be taken care of
> by my wife.[1]

Old Man Mims went on to assign all eighty-five of his slaves to his wife and eight children, along with his livestock and farm implements. Seated beside me at the courthouse was a young African American woman who was also tracing her family history. I quietly turned away in shame, unable to look her in the eye, aggrieved by a family truth that I had never known. Not even my mother knew that her family had owned slaves. As I write these words, it has been only 142 years since the ink dried on Williamson Mims's will—a mere six generations removed. Yet I never knew or suspected this historical fact.

I do not believe that my ignorance of the past is unique, however. Do you know the names of your ancestors, much less their stories? Those who left their native lands of Europe, Africa, and Asia and were transported to the United States were courageous souls whose journey changed the course of their family history forever. Yet their names and history are often erased from memory, their stories lost in time.

Despite the sadness that I feel because my family owned slaves, I have gained immeasurably from discovering the past. Knowing the stories of Robert Braswell, Wright Vinson, Charles Olmstead, Scott, and the other men and women in this saga has enriched my life. But most of all I have learned that the difficult and painful lessons of the past must not be suppressed. History shines a light of truth and guidance on our present day. If we forget the struggles, trials, and mistakes of the past, we endanger our future.

Forgiveness and Healing

For both the North and the South the questions came: "How do you forgive? How do you forgive the bloodshed, the cruelty, the vengeance, the willful destruction, the loss of life and innocence of a razed generation?"

Perhaps a testimony to human goodness is that 140 years after the Civil War, much forgiveness has taken place. For many in my generation the Civil War is all but blotted out. Unlike many cultures in which wounds fester, hatred lingers for centuries, and revenge is a finely honed art, American society has somehow absorbed this tragic war of fratricide.

The spirit of African Americans can only be admired and revered. Although the war ended slavery, African Americans suffered in poverty for another century, subjected to laws and customs of segregation and racial prejudice. And yet the spirit of black Americans has proved unbroken, magnanimous, adaptable, and irrepressibly free.

As the great-great-grandson of a Civil War veteran, I have learned that we must continue our quest for equality and mutual forgiveness. For only forgiveness brings health and healing to the human heart.

Friendship and Camaraderie

As so many students of the American Civil War have observed, the one element that kept soldiers loyal to their cause and faithful to the bitter end was not so much ideology as it was friendship. Friends would not desert each other.

I was reminded of this truth while doing research in a small county library in middle Georgia. An elderly librarian fumbled through an old file and gave me a yellowed newspaper clipping about a trial that took place in Wilkinson County, Georgia, a few years after the Civil War. An Irishman, James Kirkpatrick, had enlisted in Company I, the Barkuloo Rifles, of the Fifty-seventh Georgia Regiment when he was twenty-six. He returned from the war a depressed thirty-year-old and numbed his grief and pain with alcohol. One night in a drunken rage he assaulted William Smallwood with a butcher knife. Smallwood recovered from his injuries. Kirkpatrick was charged with assault and stood trial.

As Kirkpatrick faced the jury, most of its members were people he knew. In fact, most of the men on the panel were veterans of the Fifty-seventh Georgia Regiment. Friendship or no, the case was airtight and Kirkpatrick was obviously guilty. However, just before the jury was to render its verdict, a very sober James Kirkpatrick stood and asked if he might address the panel. The judge consented, and a reporter preserved much of what the defendant had to say, often referring to himself in the third person, by his nickname, "Kirk":

Gentlemen of the jury . . . some of the best blood in the country flows in
Kirk's veins, and it would be a disgrace for such good people as he is related
to have a kinsman in the penitentiary. Besides I have a little boy named Tom,
six-years old at home sick. . . .

Now, Dick Hatfield, you remember the night after the battle at Baker's
Creek [Champion Hill] you do, you was sent out on picket when you had
nothing to eat. Kirk took your gun and stood at your post, he did, while you
stepped aside to eat the corn. When you had eaten the second ear and dropped
the cob, the noise you made attracted the enemy's picket and he cut down on
the sound and came near hitting Kirk, when it should have been you, Dick,
instead of Kirk. You were in a tight [spot] then, Dick, you were, and Kirk stood
by you. Now, Dick, remember that Kirk is in a tight [spot]. He wants you to
stick, he does. . . .

Jim Jones, you remember when we were camped near Dalton in the winter
of 1863, you do, you had missed your luck and gone broke in a game. You went
to Kirk and begged him for a stake, ye did, and he loaned you one, and ye went
away and came back with plenty and paid me and said, "Kirk, that loan did me
more good than any favor I have ever received and I shall always remember
you for it." Now, Jim, you were in a tight [spot] then and broke, and Kirk stuck.
Remember that Kirk is in a tight [spot] now and wants you to stick sure. . . .

Alfred Hall, you were always a good praying fellow. . . . [Y]ou remember
the night after the battle of Resaca, you came to Kirk, after our line had fallen
back, and said, "Kirk, my brother is left behind, either wounded or killed." You
were wounded so that you could not go and you requested Kirk to do you the
favor to go back and look after your brother. Then it was that Kirk told you he
would do it. At risk of his life Kirk went and found him, and he was mortally
wounded, and took him on his shoulders and carried him for a mile or more
and brought him into our lines and layed him down and we saw him die. Now,
Alfred, you thanked Kirk then for the kindness and said you always would
remember it and if you could ever do him a favor you would. Alfred, now Kirk
is in a tight, and he wants you to stick.

Bart Stevens, you remember the night the army fell back from Kennesaw
Mountain across the Chattahoochee river, you were sick, you begged Kirk to
stay with you and take care of you, you did. Kirk did so and carried your gun
and knapsack all night for you, he did, and the next morning you thanked Kirk
and told the Captain what had been done for you and you promised that you
would always stick to Kirk, you did. Now, Bart, the time is at hand to stick to
Kirk, and if you think well of what he has done for you, stick. . . .

Jesse Arrington, you remember me on the return after the bloody battle of
Nashville in 1864, that it was sleeting and snowing and freezing and you were
barefooted, you were. It was a terrible day, you and another soldier of some

other command got into a scrap over a pair of shoes lying by the roadside, and about that time Kirk came up, the other fellow was about to get the better of you, he was, Jess, but Kirk reenforced you and we soon put him to route, and held to the shoes, we did. . . . Now, Jess, Kirk has never called on you before but he seems to be in a tight and is calling on you, and begorra!, he wants you to stick!

Now, if you gentlemen of the jury who know Kirk and for whom he has done something are willing to stick him and relieve him and his good kinfolks and above all his bright little fellow from disgrace, then stand for Kirk and stick to him![2]

Needless to say, Kirkpatrick was acquitted. Men who have gone through hell together are forged into a brotherhood that stands above law and reason. In the words of Kirk, "They stick!"

As a great-great-grandson of a Civil War veteran I have learned that the pivotal events of history are shaped far more by relationships and regional loyalty than by reason and ideology.

Evil and Consequence

Above all else I have learned that where there is radical evil, there is radical consequence. The forces that converged to incite the American Civil War were, of course, multiple and complex. Slavery was not the primary issue that caused Northern boys to sign up to preserve the Union and Southern boys to fire on Fort Sumter. But to push the issue of slavery to the side and say that it was not at the heart of the conflict is a distortion of reality.

In truth, slavery was an insidious evil within the United States, an evil based on economic dependence that muted and negated the innate voice of ethics and morality. As a great-great-grandson of a Civil War Rebel, I have learned that every form of human abuse and enslavement is evil. And the consequence of a "necessary evil" for financial gain or political expediency is paid for by blood, tragedy, and the fall of nations. Where there is toleration of radical evil, there is radical consequence.

Goodness and Transformation

Finally, I have come to reaffirm that even the worst human tragedy can ultimately be transformed into good. I was reminded of this while reading the final paragraph of Charles H. Olmstead's memoirs. Olmstead was seventy-six years old, forty-seven years removed from the Civil War, when he wrote the conclusion of the journal that he penned for his children in 1912:

Here my dear children these rambling reminiscences are brought to an end; I am glad to have written them for your sakes, for the writing has awakened many happy recollections as well as those of more sombre hue. I find though that time has softened all pain and made brighter the pleasant things of life. I have lived long enough since those four years of strife to learn to believe that the failure of the South to establish a separate independence was not an evil. As a section we had to pass through deep waters after open warfare ended but those unhappy days likewise have passed away, and now we are an integral part of a great nation honored and respected around the whole world.[3]

This is a magnificent statement by a man who knew bitter defeat, personal loss, and haunting memories. Yet Olmstead was wise enough to understand that within every nation—as within every family—foundations sometimes must be shaken and the hardened soil of our hearts plowed under before new chapters of health and stability can be written. In the Civil War, American soil was forever broken and tilled, the resultant growth still unfolding.

I have often laughed and said that it has taken me four times as long to write this saga as it did for the North and South to fight the Civil War. However, at some point in this slow and enjoyable process I promised myself that I would place a copy of this book in a small wooden box and bury it at the foot of Robert Braswell's grave. In so doing, I simply want to say that his great-great-grandson has not forgotten the sacrifice that he made to help the United States evolve into a great and wonderful nation. And I will wrap the wooden box in an American flag with fifty stars, a symbol of that new nation.

To Robert Braswell, Edwin Davis, Charles Olmstead, Wright Vinson, Patrick Cleburne, Hamilton Branch, Scott, and all the men and women I have come to know vicariously over the fourteen years that it took to research and write this book, I want to express gratitude for enriching my life in countless ways. May the telling of your story bring health, growth, and spiritual reflection to another generation.

Notes

Chapter 1. War Fever

1. "Braswell Family History," in author's possession.

2. In 1861 Fort Valley was located in Houston County. In 1924 Peach County was created, encompassing part of Houston County, and Fort Valley is now the county seat of Peach County.

3. Central Georgia Historical Society, *First Hundred and Ten Years*, 115, 125, 134. No extant records reflect the number of slaves in Fort Valley, but the 1860 census shows that Houston County had 4,828 whites, 28 "free coloreds," and 10,755 slaves.

4. Coleman, ed., *A History of Georgia*, 145–51.

5. Kersh, "Recollections," 79.

6. William L. Braswell veteran record.

7. Kersh, "Recollections," 163.

8. White, *Statistics;* "Fort Valley Progress," *(Fort Valley, Ga.) Leader Tribune,* August 13, 1880; *(Fort Valley, Ga.) Leader Tribune,* January 8, 1891. In 1849 Fort Valley had a white population of 250. By 1854 the white population of Fort Valley had grown to 500. In 1891 the white population was 1,500. It is estimated that the population in 1861 would have been between 800 and 1,000.

9. Central Georgia Historical Society, *First Hundred and Ten Years*, 217–19; Derry, *Georgia*, 26–27, 30.

10. Central Georgia Historical Society, *First Hundred and Ten Years*, 224.

11. Reggie Mullis Williams (descendant of William Holly Sr.), interview.

12. Young, Gholson, and Hargrove, eds., *History of Macon*, 251. The First Independent Battalion included the Everett Guards of Houston County, the Lamar Infantry of Bibb County, the Ross Volunteers of Bibb County, the Macon County Infantry, and the Columbus Minute Boys of Muscogee County.

Chapter 2. Savannah

1. Holland to Urban Rumble, Penfield, Georgia, 1861, "Rumble Family Letters," 194–95.

2. Spencer King, *Sound of Drums*, 242; Dowell, *History of Mercer University*, 110. Twenty-nine students from Mercer University died in the Civil War.

3. Edwin Tralona Davis, "Diary," December 12, 1861.

4. Governor Treutlin Chapter of the Daughters of the American Revolution, "Vinson-Vincent," *History of Peach County, Georgia*, 442–47.

5. Lawrence, *Present for Mr. Lincoln*, 104.

6. Ibid., 103.

7. Ibid.

8. McPherson, *Battle Cry of Freedom,* 485–89. The four major fatal diseases during the Civil War were, in order of lethality, diarrhea/dysentery, typhoid, pneumonia, and malaria.

9. Lawliss, *Civil War Source Book,* 150–51, 169. When the Civil War began, the North had ninety warships; the South had none.

10. Mercer, Diary, November 10, 1861.

11. Stephens Jr., ed., *Intrepid Warrior,* 77.

12. Emory M. Thomas, *Robert E. Lee,* 57.

13. Lawrence, *Present for Mr. Lincoln,* 51; Julian, "Siege of Fort Pulaski," 5–6, 10–14; U.S. War Department, *War of the Rebellion* (hereafter referred to as *O.R. [Official Records]*), 4:225–26—all references to *O.R.* are to series 1 unless otherwise noted; Lawliss, *Civil War Source Book,* 150–52.

14. The Confederate Conscription Act provided for substitution (repealed in December 1863) and for certain exemptions. The draft age was later raised to forty-five, then, toward the end of the war, to fifty.

Chapter 3. Birth of a Confederate Regiment

1. Cates, "From Santa Rosa Island to Bentonville," 42–54.

2. Lillian Henderson, "Mims, Seaborn S.," *Roster,* 1:767; U.S. Bureau of the Census, 1850 and 1860, Georgia, Houston County, City of Fort Valley, n.p.

3. Edwin Tralona Davis, "Diary," May 3, 1862.

4. U.S. Bureau of the Census, 1870, Georgia, Glynn County, City of Brunswick, 4; Gordon B. Smith, "The Fifty-seventh Regiment," 1.

5. Henry Cleveland to Jefferson Davis, February 15, 1862, Letters Received by the Confederate Secretary of War, 1861–65, RG 109, microfilm copy 437, roll 37, National Archives; Edwin Tralona Davis, "The Battle of Atlanta," *Savannah Republican,* July 26, 1864.

6. Gordon B. Smith, "Fifty-seventh Regiment," 1; U.S. Bureau of the Census, 1850, South Carolina.

7. Gordon B. Smith, "Fifty-seventh Regiment," 1.

8. Ibid.

9. William Barkuloo to Samuel Cooper, March 3, 1862, Letters Received by the Confederate Adjutant General, 1861–65, RG 109, microfilm copy 474, roll 6, National Archives.

10. Wright Vinson to Christiana Vinson, May 11, 1862, Civil War Letters.

11. William Barkuloo to George Randolph, May 28, 1862, Telegrams Received by the Confederate Secretary of War, 1861–65, RG 109, microcopy 474, roll 7, National Archives.

12. Hart, *Official History of Laurens County,* 1:390–92.

13. Olmstead, *Memoirs,* 135.

14. Spencer King, *Sound of Drums,* 246.

15. Edwin Tralona Davis, "Diary," May 31, 1862.

Chapter 4. In Sight of the Yankees

    1. Wright Vinson to Christiana Vinson, June 14, 20, and July 5, 1862, Civil War Letters.

    2. Edwin Tralona Davis, "Diary," July 1862; *O.R.* 16, pt. 2:717; Major John Dunwoody to General Samuel Cooper, June 25, 1862, Letters Received by the Confederate Adjutant General, 1861–1865, RG 109, microfilm copy 474, roll 14, National Archives.

    3. Edwin Tralona Davis, "Diary," July 5, 1862.

    4. Wright Vinson to Christiana Vinson, July 5, 1862, Civil War Letters. The Confederate Conscription Act of April 16, 1862, permitted a man of military age to provide an able-bodied man to replace him in military service. Such a legal replacement was called a "substitute." Substitutes were usually bought for a high price and originally were permissible for skilled craftsmen and professionals deemed crucial for the support of war industries. However, the substitute system was greatly abused in both North and South, and the Confederacy made it illegal during 1863.

    5. Edwin Tralona Davis, "Diary," July 6, 1862.

    6. Connelly, *Army of the Heartland,* 191.

    7. Wright Vinson to Mr. Gordon, July 11, 1862, Civil War Letters.

    8. Wright Vinson to Christiana Vinson, July 14, 20, 1862, Civil War Letters.

Chapter 5. Dreams of Kentucky

    1. By July 18, 1862, the Western Department (sometimes called Department No. 2) included Alabama, Mississippi, central and western Tennessee, eastern Louisiana, and western Florida. Boatner, "Department No. 2 (Confed)," *The Civil War Dictionary,* 236.

    2. Connelly, *Army of the Heartland,* 187–204.

    3. Ibid., 206.

Chapter 6. Crossing Big Creek Gap

    1. Wright Vinson to Christiana Vinson, August 2, 1862, Civil War Letters.

    2. Barrow, Segars, and Rosenburg, eds., *Forgotten Confederates,* 1–26. For a partial listing of black Americans serving in the Sixty-third Georgia and First Georgia of Mercer's brigade, see 51–52. Lawliss, *Civil War Source Book,* 15.

    3. Barrow, Segars, and Rosenburg, eds., *Forgotten Confederates,* 4–5, 25–26.

    4. McKinley, *Journal of Archibald C. McKinley,* xxxv–xxxvi.

    5. The Fifty-seventh Georgia was classified as the Fifty-fourth Georgia during the Kentucky campaign, roughly from August 1 to October 23, 1862. However, after the campaign the regiment was permanently reclassified as the Fifty-seventh Georgia Regiment, Army of Tennessee. To avoid confusion I will always refer to the regiment as the Fifty-seventh Georgia within this book.

    6. Edwin Tralona Davis, "Diary," August 6, 1862; Jim Kuglar, Reminiscences, 5. Following the Kentucky campaign, the Fifty-ninth Georgia Regiment was permanently reclassified as the Thirty-fourth Georgia Regiment, Army of Tennessee.

7. Kuglar, Reminiscences, 4.
8. Wright Vinson to Christiana Vinson, August 6, 1862, Civil War Letters.
9. *O.R.* 16, pt. 2:741.
10. Cuttino, ed., *Saddle Bag*, 109.
11. Wright Vinson to Christiana Vinson, August 12–13, 1862, Civil War Letters.
12. Edwin Tralona Davis, "Diary," August 14, 1862.
13. Kuglar, Reminiscences, 5.

Chapter 7. First Blood

1. Hammond, "Campaign of General E. Kirby Smith," 9:233.
2. Ibid.
3. Edwin Tralona Davis, "Diary," August 18, 1862.
4. Fuller, "Battle at Averysboro, N.C.," 68.
5. Wright Vinson to Christiana Vinson, April 21, 1862, Civil War Letters.
6. Kuglar, Reminiscences, 6.
7. *O.R.* 16, pt. 2:775–76, 778.
8. Cuttino, ed., *Saddle Bag*, 113.
9. Kuglar, Reminiscences, 7.

Chapter 8. By Marching, Not Fighting

1. Heth, "Memoirs of Henry Heth," 21.
2. Kuglar, Reminiscences, 9–10.
3. Wright Vinson to Christiana Vinson, September 1, 1862, Civil War Letters.
4. Kuglar, Reminiscences, 11.
5. Ibid., 11–12.
6. Cuttino, ed., *Saddle Bag*, 115–16.
7. Connelly, *Army of the Heartland*, 222.
8. Ibid., 217–18
9. Parks, *General Edmund Kirby Smith, C.S.A.*, 221; Kuglar, Reminiscences, 13–16; *O.R.* 16, pt. 2:799.
10. Foote, *The Civil War: A Narrative, Fort Sumter to Perryville*, 660.

Chapter 9. Winning the Battle and Losing the War

1. Kuglar, Reminiscences, 19.
2. Connelly, *Army of the Heartland*, 243.
3. Kuglar, Reminiscences, 20.
4. Horn, *The Army of Tennessee*, 180–86.
5. Connelly, *Army of the Heartland*, 267.
6. Kuglar, Reminiscences, 23.
7. Ibid.
8. Fuller, "Battle at Averysboro, N.C.," 68.
9. Hammond, "Campaign of General E. Kirby Smith," 10:75.

10. Ibid.

11. Daniel, *Soldiering in the Army of Tennessee,* 54.

12. Kuglar, Reminiscences, 25.

13. Street Jr., *The Struggle for Tennessee,* 82.

14. Horn, *The Army of Tennessee,* 189.

15. Kuglar, Reminiscences, 25.

16. Ibid., 26.

17. Henry, *Story of the Confederacy,* 191.

Chapter 10. Hard Decisions

1. Cuttino, ed., *Saddle Bag,* 123–24.

2. Lillian Henderson, *Roster,* 5:836–1023. When mortality and casualty records for individual Georgia regiments do not exist in the *O.R.,* it is possible to make an approximate count by reviewing the service records of the men in each regiment as listed in the *Roster of the Confederate Soldiers of Georgia, 1861–1865.* I used this method when I could not find official casualty records.

3. Street Jr., *The Struggle for Tennessee,* 84.

4. Daniel, *Soldiering in the Army of Tennessee,* 71.

5. Connelly, *Autumn of Glory,* 17.

6. Heth, "Memoirs of Henry Heth," 23–24.

7. Street Jr., *The Struggle for Tennessee,* 82.

8. *O.R.* 16, pt. 2:984.

9. Kuglar, Reminiscences, 26–27.

10. Wright Vinson to Christiana Vinson, November 6, 1862, Civil War Letters.

11. Ibid., November 11, 1862.

12. Ibid., November 13, 1862.

13. Ibid., December 1–2, 1862.

14. Ibid., December 15, 1862.

15. Phillips and Axelrod, eds., *My Brother's Face,* 79.

16. Service Record of James N. Mathews, Phillips' Legion Cavalry [Georgia], Co. E, Georgia Division of Archives and History.

17. Among Confederate regiments, the Fifty-seventh Georgia had one of the lowest desertion rates. See Weitz, *A Higher Duty,* 140.

Chapter 11. Dust to Dust

1. Connelly, *Autumn of Glory,* 38.

2. Woodworth, *Jefferson Davis and His Generals,* 182; Connelly, *Autumn of Glory,* 38.

3. Wright Vinson to Christiana Vinson, December 20, 1862, Civil War Letters.

4. William D. Vinson to Christiana Vinson, March 17, 1863, Civil War Letters.

5. Kuglar, Reminiscences, 28–29.

6. Ibid., 30–31.

7. Ibid., 32.

8. Ibid.

9. Wright Vinson to Christiana Vinson, January 6, 9, 1863, Civil War Letters.

10. N. W. Carswell to Christiana Vinson, January 18, 1863, Wright Vinson, Civil War Letters.

11. John B. Fowler to Christiana Vinson, January 21, 1863, Wright Vinson Civil War Letters.

12. William D. Vinson to Christiana Vinson, March 17, 1863, Wright Vinson Civil War Letters.

Chapter 12. The Battle of Champion Hill

1. Grant, *Ulysses S. Grant,* 332.

2. *O.R.* 24, pt. 3:814–15, 828, 835, 840, 842, 845.

3. Johnston, *Narrative of Military Operations,* 506.

4. *O.R.* 24, pt. 3:876, 882; *O.R.* 24, pt. 1:240.

5. Bearss, *The Campaign for Vicksburg,* 2:582.

6. Ibid., 2:587.

7. *O.R.* 24, pt. 2:104.

8. Alfred Cumming to Stephen D. Lee, November 3, 1899, Mississippi Dept. of Archives and History, RG 12, file folder 15, 12:8.

9. Bearss, *The Campaign for Vicksburg,* 2:596–97.

10. *O.R.* 24, pt. 2:104; Bearss, *The Campaign for Vicksburg,* 2:587, 597.

11. Alfred Cumming to Stephen D. Lee, November 3, 1889, 4.

12. *O.R.* 24, pt. 2:105.

13. Alfred Cumming to Stephen D. Lee, November 3, 1889, 4.

14. Bearss, *The Campaign for Vicksburg,* 2:601.

15. Ibid., 2:603.

16. "Battle of Champion Hill," *(Milledgeville, Ga.) Confederate Union,* June 16, 1863.

17. Spencer King, *Sound of Drums,* 243, 246.

18. Cantrell, *Sketches of the First Regiment Ga. Vols.,* 58.

19. Bearss, *The Campaign for Vicksburg,* 2:603.

20. Lillian Henderson, "Mims, Seaborn S.," *Roster,* 5:964.

21. Lillian Henderson, "Harris, Henry C.," *Roster* 5:964; Governor Treutlin Chapter of the Daughters of the American Revolution, *History of Peach County, Georgia,* 80.

22. Lillian Henderson, "Holly, William B.," *Roster,* 5:969.

23. Merrell, Biographical sketch.

24. T. J. Williams, "Battle of Champion Hill," in *Military Order of the Loyal Legion of the United States: Ohio,* 5:206.

25. Charles L. Longley, "Champion's Hill [sic]," in *Military Order of the Loyal Legion of the United States: Iowa,* 1:212–13.

26. Ritter, Diary, Archives of the Vicksburg National Military Park, Twenty-fourth Iowa.

27. Williams, "Battle of Champion Hill," 207.

28. Bearss, *The Campaign for Vicksburg,* 2:607.

29. Ibid., 2:611.

30. Ibid., 2:608.

31. *O.R.* 24, pt. 2:106; Bearss, *The Campaign for Vicksburg,* 2:603, 613.

32. *O.R.* 24, pt. 2:96, 106; Bearss, *The Campaign for Vicksburg,* 2:613, n. 15; Gottschalk, *In Deadly Earnest,* 254.

33. T. J. Williams, "Battle of Champion Hill," 208–9.

34. Longley, "Champion Hill," 213–14.

35. F. H. Ivey, "Report on the Battle of Champion Hill," *(Milledgeville, Ga.) Confederate Union,* June 2, 1863, 3.

36. Keen to Clement A. Evans, Brewton, Georgia, April 3, 1900, Civil War Miscellany, Personal Papers, RG 57-1-1, Georgia Division of Archives and History; Elizabeth F. Hopkins, "The 'Dixie Boys' Flag," AC3-2560, MF283, roll 59, Georgia Division of Archives and History.

37. Bearss, *The Campaign for Vicksburg,* 2:614–16.

38. Lillian Henderson, "Davis, Edwin Tralona," *Roster,* 5:920.

39. Ivey, "Report on the Battle of Champion Hill"; *O.R.* 24, pt. 2:96.

40. Bonner, *Milledgeville,* 172.

41. Ivey, "Report on the Battle of Champion Hill."

42. *O. R.* 24, pt. 2:99, 106–7.

43. According to the Internet site Words@Random, to "see the elephant" is a mid-nineteenth-century phrase that, in its specific military sense, means "to see combat, especially for the first time"—upon seeing the elephant, troops lose their innocence and become hardened veterans. See Words@Random, *The Mavens' Word of the Day,* July 14, 1998, www.randomhouse.com/wotd/index.pperl?date=19980714 (November 29, 2004).

44. McKinley, *Journal of Archibald C. McKinley,* 36; Ivey, "Report on the Battle of Champion Hill," 3.

45. Howell Jr., *Hill of Death,* 27.

46. Spencer King, *Sound of Drums,* 243.

47. Howell Jr., *Hill of Death,* 19.

Chapter 13. Siege and Surrender

1. *O.R.* 24, pt. 1:266.

2. Ibid., pt. 3:888.

3. Balfour, Diary, Mississippi Dept. of Archives and History, 3.

4. Keen to Clement A. Evans, Brewton, Georgia, April 3, 1900, Personal Papers.

5. Stevenson's division had four brigades. Brigadier General Seth Barton's Georgia troops held the extreme right of the division front and were positioned adjacent to the Mississippi River at South Fort, extending northeast. Colonel Alexander Reynold's Tennessee brigade adjoined Barton's left and extended to the Hall's Ferry Road. Brigadier General Alfred Cumming's Georgia brigade adjoined Reynold's left at the Hall's Ferry Road and extended to the Square Fort. Brigadier General Stephen D. Lee's Alabama brigade adjoined Cumming's left at the Square Fort and extended to the Railroad Redoubt, where they linked up with Major General John Forney's division. See Bearss, *The Campaign for Vicksburg,* 3:737; Clement A. Evans, ed., *Confederate Military History,* 9:149.

6. The location of the Fifty-seventh Georgia is not within the grounds of the Vicks-

burg National Military Park. It is found by following Interstate 20 southwest toward the Mississippi River. Get off the interstate at exit 1C and turn right onto the Halls Ferry Road. Travel approximately a half-mile. Before you reach the intersection with Confederate Drive, you will see a grassy knoll on the right with a red metal marker at its summit that specifies the location of the Fifty-seventh Georgia.

7. Sherman, *Memoirs*, 354.

8. Bearss, *The Campaign for Vicksburg*, 3:858.

9. Governor Treutlin Chapter of the Daughters of the American Revolution, *History of Peach County, Georgia*, 81.

10. *O.R.* 24, pt. 2:107.

11. Bearss, *The Campaign for Vicksburg*, 3:947–50.

12. Ibid., 942.

13. Mary Beaty Brown, "Reminiscences of the Sixties," 115–16.

14. Mattie Rowland Braswell (daughter-in-law of Robert L. Braswell), interview.

15. *(Vicksburg, Miss.) Daily Citizen*, July 2, 1863; transcription of "Order to Eat Mules, Vicksburg, June 28, 1863," United Daughters of the Confederacy, John B. Gordon Chapter, Historical Collections No. 8, Thomasville, Georgia, Public Library.

16. Waugh, *The Class of 1846*, x.

17. "Dr. Harris Tells of the Origin and Presentation of the 'Dixie Boy' Flag," *Thomasville (Ga.) Times-Enterprise*, May 24, 1920; Robert H. Harris, "The 'Dixie Boys' Flag," *(Thomaston, Ga.) Daily Times-Enterprise*, April 29, 1886.

18. McKinley, *Journal of Archibald C. McKinley*, 36.

19. Cantrell, *Sketches of the First Regiment Ga. Vols.*, 63.

20. Bearss, *The Campaign for Vicksburg*, 3:1308–10.

Chapter 14. The Changing of the Guard

1. Cantrell, *Sketches of the First Regiment Ga. Vols.*, 63–64.

2. Barkuloo veterans record.

3. Francis E. Fitzpatrick letters.

4. Kersh, "Recollections," 81.

5. Braswell Family History, n.d., in author's possession.

6. Williamson Mims, Will and Testament of Williamson Mims, will dated April 24, 1863, date of death September 8, 1863, Record of Wills, Book B, 139, Houston County Registry of Probate, Perry, Georgia.

7. *(Milledgeville, Ga.) Southern Recorder*, August 11, 1863, 3.

8. Kersh, "Recollections," 82.

9. Williamson Mims, Will and Testament, 139.

10. *O.R.* 28, pt. 2:385.

Chapter 15. Dishonor

1. *O.R.* 28, pt. 1:144.

2. *O.R.* 28, pt. 2:434.

3. *O.R.* 35, pt. 1:362.

4. Lawrence, *Present for Mr. Lincoln,* 75.

5. Muster Report for the Georgia 57th Regiment, February 3, 1863, National Archives, microfilm, box 131–139.

6. *O.R.* 35, pt. 1:530–31.

7. John J. Methvin, "The Autobiography of John Jasper Methvin," 14, in private collection; Lillian Henderson, "Methvin, William K.; Methvin, Thomas J.; Methvin, John J.," in *Roster,* 5:953, 954, 960.

8. *O.R.* 35, pt. 1:363.

9. *O.R.* 35, pt. 1:530–31.

10. Mercer, Diary, January 15, 1864, 217–18.

11. *O.R.* 35, pt. 1:531–32.

12. Lillian Henderson, *Roster,* 5:917–1023. Casualty records indicate that at least companies A, C, E, and F were involved in the skirmish on Whitemarsh Island.

13. *O.R.* 35, pt. 1:362.

14. Robert H. Harris to Mary Martha Love Harris, February 22, 1864, Elizabeth Hopkins Collection, "Miscellaneous Letters of Thomasville Families," vol. 194.

15. *O.R.* 35, pt. 1:363.

16. "Reinlistment of the 57th Georgia Regiment," *Savannah Republican,* March 7, 1864, p. 2. The reference to General Benjamin Franklin "Beast" Butler is puzzling because Butler was not near Savannah, but perhaps it is more of a political statement. Butler was the first to apply the term *contraband of war* to slaves who had fled into Union lines and gained freedom. Because they were contraband of war, Butler refused to return them to their former owners. Butler also was instrumental in the taking of New Orleans, where he served as a controversial military governor. The South loathed Butler, whom Jefferson Davis declared to be an outlaw (Benjamin F. Butler, *Butler's Book,* 256–64).

17. Marvel, *Andersonville,* 51.

Chapter 16. Andersonville

1. *O.R.* 35, pt. 1:531.

2. Futch, *History of Andersonville Prison,* 3.

3. *O.R.* series II, 7, pt. 1:13; Marvel, *Andersonville,* 51.

4. Marvel, *Andersonville,* 4.

5. McElroy, *This Was Andersonville,* 30–31. Also see Ransom's account of Hubbard's death in *John Ransom's Andersonville Diary,* 77–78.

6. Ransom, *John Ransom's Andersonville Diary,* 78–79.

7. Marvel, *Andersonville,* 65–66; Futch, *History of Andersonville Prison,* 24; Ransom, *John Ransom's Andersonville Diary,* 78–79.

Chapter 17. We Expect to Show Them the Elephant

1. Daniel, *Soldiering in the Army of Tennessee,* 5.

2. Ibid.

3. Richard Taylor is quoted by Mosser, "I Shall Make Him Remember," 24.

4. Castel, *Decision in the West,* 141.

5. McMurry, *Atlanta 1864*, 97–99.

6. Mercer, Diary, May 17, 1864, 4:41.

7. Castel, *Decision in the West*, 198.

8. Most scholars state that the cavalry force that Hood detected was only a scouting party detached from the cavalry division of Brigadier General Edward McCook. See Connelly, *Autumn of Glory*, 347. However, Albert Castel states in *Decision in the West*, 201, that the Union force that came upon Hood was McCook's entire cavalry division, followed by Major General George Stoneman's division. Both McCook and Stoneman reported to Schofield. See also McMurry, *Atlanta 1864*, 81.

9. Castel, *Decision in the West*, 201–2.

10. Russell K. Brown, *To the Manner Born*, 235.

Chapter 18. The Hell Hole!

1. The First Confederate Division was soon reassigned to Clement H. Steven's Georgia brigade.

2. Cates, "From Santa Rosa Island to Bentonville," 67; Castel, *Decision in the West*, 164–65.

3. Russell K. Brown, *To the Manner Born*, 235.

4. Castel, *Decision in the West*, 223–25.

5. During Sherman's assault on Stewart's division, Walker's division (and Mercer's brigade) was in reserve directly behind Stewart.

6. Russell K. Brown, *To the Manner Born*, 239.

7. House, "History of the First Volunteer Regiment," 17–23; Olmstead, *Memoirs*, 99–116. Five of the ten companies of the First Georgia Volunteers had experienced little combat. After Fort Pulaski surrendered on April 11, 1862, captured Confederate soldiers—including Olmstead—were imprisoned at Johnson's Island Prison, on Lake Erie in Ohio. Olmstead and his troops were included in a prisoner exchange in October 1862 and returned to Savannah.

8. Olmstead, *Memoirs*, 135.

9. Mercer, Diary, June 15–16, 1864, 4:47.

10. Ibid., June 16, 1864, 4:47; Russell K. Brown, *To the Manner Born*, 242.

11. Olmstead, *Memoirs*, 139.

12. Mercer, Diary, June 22, 1864, 4:49.

Chapter 19. Kennesaw Mountain

1. Olmstead, *Memoirs*, 140.

2. Mercer, Diary, June 19, 1864, 4:48.

3. Parks, *General Leonidas Polk, C.S.A.*, 374, 377–78, 382; Daniel, *Soldiering in the Army of Tennessee*, 122.

4. Castel, *Decision in the West*, 301.

5. Sherman, *Memoirs*, 527–30.

6. Ibid., 530.

7. Symonds, *Joseph E. Johnston*, 310.

8. Castel, *Decision in the West,* 302.

9. Ibid., 302–3.

10. Kelly, *Kennesaw Mountain,* 32–36.

11. Clark, *Under the Stars and Bars,* 132.

12. Ibid.

13. Thomas T. Taylor to Mrs. Thomas Taylor, June 29, 1864, Thomas T. Taylor Letters, Special Collections, Woodruff Library, Emory University.

14. Ibid.

15. Russell K. Brown, *To the Manner Born,* 246.

16. *O.R.* 38, pt. 3:222, 253.

17. Clark, *Under the Stars and Bars,* 136.

18. Watkins, *1861 vs 1882. "Co. Aytch,"* 142–45.

19. Ibid.

20. Ibid.

Chapter 20. On the Banks of the Chattahoochee

1. Castel, *Decision in the West,* 332–34.

2. Charles Thiot to Anna Thiot, June 20–22, 1864, Charles Thiot Papers, Emory University, Robert W. Woodruff Library, Special Collections Dept., Microfilm No. 497.

3. Joslyn, *Charlotte's Boys,* 258.

4. Olmstead, *Memoirs,* 141.

5. Charles Thiot to Anna Thiot, June 20, 1864, Thiot Papers.

6. Celathiel Helms to Evelina Mary A. E. Helms, July 6, 1864, "Letters from Confederate Soldiers." Helms died of measles in Macon, Georgia, one month later.

7. William Hilary Bibb and Maggie Bibb Gribben, "Sketches of Judge William Bibb."

8. In 1856 Georgia Military Institute had six faculty members who taught 140 cadets. Conrad, *The Young Lions,* 9.

9. Olmstead, *Memoirs,* 50.

10. Ibid., 143.

11. Ibid., 144.

12. Mercer, Diary, July 3, 1864, 4:50.

13. Olmstead, *Memoirs,* 144–45.

14. Lillian Henderson, "Mims, Seaborn S.," *Roster,* 5:964.

15. Russell K. Brown, *To the Manner Born,* 250; House, "History of the First Volunteer Regiment," 38.

16. Joslyn, *Charlotte's Boys,* 263.

17. Charles Thiot to Anna Thiot, June 20, 1864, Thiot Papers.

18. Sherman, *Memoirs,* 536.

19. Ibid., 541–42.

20. Olmstead, *Memoirs,* 145–46.

21. Mercer, Diary, July 9, 1864, 4:52.

22. Sherman, *Memoirs,* 540.

23. Joslyn, *Charlotte's Boys,* 265–66.

24. Olmstead, *Memoirs,* 146.

Chapter 21. Hood Has Gone Up Like a Rocket

1. Connelly, *Autumn of Glory,* 417; Castel, *Decision in the West,* 76–77, 355–56.
2. Castel, *Decision in the West,* 357–58.
3. Ibid., 358.
4. *O.R.* 38, pt. 3:765ff; Hughes Jr., *General William J. Hardee,* 179–86.
5. Castel, *Decision in the West,* 353.
6. Johnston, *Narrative of Military Operations,* 348–49.
7. Joslyn, *Charlotte's Boys,* 268.
8. Russell K. Brown, *To the Manner Born,* 257.
9. Olmstead, *Memoirs,* 147.
10. Ibid., 147–48.
11. David Evans, "The Atlanta Campaign," 28.
12. Sherman, *Memoirs,* 544.
13. Nisbet, *4 Years,* 206.
14. Johnston, *Narrative of Military Operations,* 350; Connelly, *Autumn of Glory,* 424–25.
15. Connelly, *Autumn of Glory,* 440; Castel, *Decision in the West,* 368.
16. Walker's division advanced into battle and made contact with the Union army near the present site of Piedmont Hospital on Peachtree Street.
17. Olmstead, *Memoirs,* 149.
18. Joslyn, *Charlotte's Boys,* 269, emphasis added.
19. Lillian Henderson, *Roster,* 5:917–1023. Henderson's data indicate that sixteen men of the Fifty-seventh Georgia were killed or wounded at the Battle of Peachtree Creek.
20. Nisbet, *4 Years,* 209–10.
21. Castel, *Decision in the West,* 381; Cates, "From Santa Rosa Island to Bentonville," 68. Cates states that seventy-three men of the First Confederate, or more than a third of the regiment, were killed, wounded, or captured.
22. Castel, *Decision in the West,* 381.

Chapter 22. The Battle of Atlanta

1. William Reed to Bessie Reed, Atlanta, July 21, 1864, "Confederate Letters, Diaries, and Reminiscences," 123–24.
2. Bald Hill was at the present-day intersection of Moreland Avenue and Memorial Drive.
3. Nisbet, *4 Years,* 211.
4. McDonough Road is now Capitol Avenue.
5. Hughes Jr., *General William J. Hardee,* 227.
6. Hood, *Advance and Retreat,* 181–82.
7. Russell K. Brown, *To the Manner Born,* 297.
8. Hughes Jr., *General William J. Hardee,* 229.
9. Hughes Jr., ed., *Civil War Memoir of Philip Daingerfield Stephenson,* 221.

10. Russell K. Brown, *To the Manner Born,* 266–67; Castel, *Decision in the West,* 394–95.

11. Ronald H. Bailey, *Battles for Atlanta,* 97.

12. *O.R.* 38, pt. 3:758.

13. Ronald H. Bailey, *Battles for Atlanta,* 99.

14. Leading authorities are in considerable disagreement regarding the exact sequence of charges by Hardee's division in the Battle of Atlanta. Thomas J. Connelly, in *Autumn of Glory,* 448–49, follows closely the sequence depicted by Nathaniel Cheairs Hughes Jr. in *General William J. Hardee: Old Reliable,* 229–30. In this scenario Cleburne began the offensive, joined later by Walker and finally by Bate. However, Albert Castel, in *Decision in the West,* 391, 397–99, states just the opposite, that Bate led the attack, followed by Walker and then Cleburne. William R. Scaife, *The Campaign for Atlanta,* 52–54, and Richard M. McMurry, *Atlanta 1864,* 154–55, agree. I concur with Castel, Scaife, and McMurry. Either way, Hardee's offensive was very fragmented and sporadic.

15. Sweeny's division was located where Memorial Drive and Clay Street intersect today.

16. Scaife, *The Campaign for Atlanta,* 53.

17. Castel, *Decision in the West,* 393, 397.

18. Nisbet, *4 Years,* 212–19.

19. Scaife, *The Campaign for Atlanta,* 53.

20. Olmstead, *Memoirs,* 150.

21. *O.R.* 38, pt. 3:759.

22. Castel, *Decision in the West,* 398.

23. Scaife, *The Campaign for Atlanta,* 54.

24. *O.R.* 38, pt. 3:754, 759; Russell K. Brown, *To the Manner Born,* 269.

25. *O.R.* 38, pt. 3:754; Russell K. Brown, *To the Manner Born,* 269–71; Castel, *Decision in the West,* 404, 409–10; Scaife, *The Campaign for Atlanta,* 56; Ronald H. Bailey, *Battles for Atlanta,* 105–6.

26. Manigault, *A Carolinian Goes to War,* 225–29.

27. McPherson was killed by lead elements of the Fifth Confederate Regiment of Cleburne's division that had penetrated Union lines. Ambushed while on a reconnaissance mission, McPherson refused to surrender and was shot while attempting to escape. McPherson was the only Union army commander killed in battle during the Civil War.

28. Purdue and Purdue, *Pat Cleburne,* 357.

29. *O.R.* 38, pt. 3:754.

30. Joslyn, *Charlotte's Boys,* 271.

31. Mercer, Diary, July 22, 1864, 4:54.

32. *O.R.* 38, pt. 3:756.

33. Sherman, *Memoirs,* 555.

Chapter 23. Sell the Cotton If You Can!

1. Castel, *Decision in the West,* 415.

2. Mercer, Diary, July 23–August 2, 1864, 4:55–56.

3. John Morgan Davis to Mary Davis and children, August 1, 1864, Letters.

4. Castel, *Decision in the West,* 423.

5. Edwin Tralona Davis to editor of *(Savannah, Ga.) Republican,* July 26, 1864, in *Diary.*

6. Charles Thiot to Anna Thiot, August 24, 1864, Thiot Papers.

7. Mercer, Diary, July 25–26, 1864, 4:55.

8. Ibid., September 24, 1864, 4:61.

9. Olmstead, *Memoirs,* 151.

10. House, "History of the First Volunteer Regiment," 50–51.

11. William Barkuloo and Charles H. Olmstead to Samuel Cooper, July 29–31, 1864, Letters received by the Confederate Adjutant General, 1861–65, RG 109, microfilm copy 474, roll 97, National Archives; *O.R.* 38, pt. 3:760.

12. House, "History of the First Volunteer Regiment," 51. Because Barkuloo had suffered increasingly poor health, I surmise that he obtained medical leave.

13. Davis to editor.

14. Olmstead, *Memoirs,* 151.

15. *O.R.* 38, pt. 5:949; Castel, *Decision in the West,* 450.

16. Mercer, Diary, July 31, 1864, 4:56–57. Mercer says that "the grand total" loss for "the Brigade" is 929 but then omits the Fifty-seventh Georgia from his accounting: First Georgia Volunteers, 265; Fifty-fourth Georgia, 138; and the Sixty-third Georgia, 316. If his other figures and total are reliable, the Fifty-seventh Georgia lost 210 men.

17. Ibid., July 27, 1864, 4:55.

18. Ibid., August 29, 1864, 4:58.

19. Castel, *Decision in the West,* 423.

20. Methvin, "Autobiography," 15–16.

21. Castel, *Decision in the West,* 510–11.

22. Mercer, Diary, September 1, 1864, 4:58–59.

23. Methvin, "Autobiography," 16.

24. John Methvin, "Hotch-Potch" (collection of handwritten notes of John Methvin), September 1, 1933, 12, private collection.

25. Mercer, Diary, September 1, 1864, 4:59; *O.R.* 38, pt. 3:758.

26. Clark, *Under the Stars and Bars,* 105–6. The First Kentucky ("Orphan") Brigade was composed primarily of men from Kentucky. However, because Kentucky remained a Union-controlled state throughout the war, the brigade was organized and trained in Tennessee in 1861. Later, after the Confederate army invaded Kentucky and then was forced out, the First Kentucky Brigade could not return to its home state, thus earning its name, the Orphan Brigade.

27. Ronald H. Bailey, *Battles for Atlanta,* 149.

28. Ibid., 150.

29. Clark, *Under the Stars and Bars,* 106.

30. Mercer, Diary, September 1, 1864, 4:59.

31. Olmstead, *Memoirs,* 156.

32. Mercer, Diary, September 3, 1864, 4:59.

33. Sherman, *Memoirs,* 584.

34. Ibid., 583–84.

Chapter 24. Crossing into Tennessee

1. The middle Georgia counties were Laurens, Wilkinson, Houston (now Peach), Crawford, Washington, and Baldwin. Company A was from Thomas County, which is in southwest Georgia, adjacent to the Florida border.
2. Hughes, *General William J. Hardee*, 243–49.
3. Connelly, *Autumn of Glory*, 472; Hood, *Advance and Retreat*, 248–55.
4. Connelly, *Autumn of Glory*, 472–73; Hood, *Advance and Retreat*, 255.
5. Olmstead, *Memoirs*, 158.
6. House, "History of the First Volunteer Regiment," 57.
7. Sherman, *Memoirs*, 627.
8. Connelly, *Autumn of Glory*, 478.
9. Ibid., 477–78.
10. Castel, *Decision in the West*, 552–54; Nevin, *Sherman's March*, 20.
11. Castel, *Decision in the West*, 553; Sherman, *Memoirs*, 639–41.
12. Connelly, *Autumn of Glory*, 483; Hood, *Advance and Retreat*, 264, 266–69.
13. Connelly, *Autumn of Glory*, 485; Sword, *Embrace an Angry Wind*, 64.
14. Cheatham now commanded Hardee's former corps.
15. Olmstead, *Memoirs*, 162.
16. Nevin, *Sherman's March*, 33.
17. The five companies in the Fifty-seventh Georgia that were from counties directly in the path of Sherman's march to the sea were Company D, the Smith Guards, Wilkinson County; Company G, the Mount Vernon Rifles, Washington County; Company H, the Independent Volunteers, Baldwin County; Company I, the Barkuloo Rifles, Wilkinson and Laurens counties; and Company K, the Oconee Grays, Wilkinson County.
18. Bonner, "David R. Snelling," 275–82.
19. Sherman, *Memoirs*, 602–3.
20. Bonner, "David R. Snelling," 276.
21. Fifteen of the forty companies in Mercer's brigade were from coastal Chatham County.
22. Olmstead, *Memoirs*, 163.
23. Clark, *Under the Stars and Bars*, 156.

Chapter 25. Cold-Blooded Murder

1. Nevin, *Sherman's March*, 34. Sherman dispatched Thomas to Tennessee on September 29, 1864.
2. Ibid., 83.
3. Daniel, *Soldiering in the Army of Tennessee*, 147.
4. Sword, *Embrace an Angry Wind*, 93; Horn, *The Army of Tennessee*, 384.
5. Sword, *Embrace an Angry Wind*, 95–98; Horn, *The Army of Tennessee*, 385; Nevin, *Sherman's March*, 88–89.
6. Nevin, *Sherman's March*, 85–89.
7. Sword, *Embrace an Angry Wind*, 113–14.
8. Nevin, *Sherman's March*, 92.

9. Sword, *Embrace an Angry Wind*, 126–35; Horn, *The Army of Tennessee*, 387–88; Nevin, *Sherman's March*, 92.

10. Sword, *Embrace an Angry Wind*, 136; Anne J. Bailey, *The Chessboard of War*, 83–87.

11. Nevin, *Sherman's March*, 94.

12. Ibid., 95.

13. Sword, *Embrace an Angry Wind*, 156–57; Nevin, *Sherman's March*, 95.

14. Hood, *Advance and Retreat*, 290.

15. Buck, *Cleburne and His Command*, 281.

16. Losson, *Tennessee's Forgotten Warrior*, 218.

17. Wyeth, *That Devil Forrest*, 480.

18. Hood, *Advance and Retreat*, 290–91.

19. Foote, *The Civil War: A Narrative, Fredericksburg to Meridian*, 530.

20. Sword, *Embrace an Angry Wind*, 179–80.

21. Purdue and Purdue, *Pat Cleburne*, 420.

22. Ibid.

23. Logsdon, ed., *Eyewitnesses*, 73.

24. Norman D. Brown, ed., *One of Cleburne's Command*, 150–51.

25. Sword, *Embrace an Angry Wind*, 280.

Chapter 26. The Destruction of an Army

1. Joslyn, *Charlotte's Boys*, 289.

2. Ibid., 290; Purdue and Purdue, *Pat Cleburne*, 392, 423; Symonds, *Stonewall of the West*, 259.

3. Olmstead, *Memoirs*, 164.

4. *O.R.* 45, pt. 1:739; Daniel, *Soldiering in the Army of Tennessee*, 160.

5. Lillian Henderson, "Davis, Edwin Tralona," *Roster*, 5:920.

6. Olmstead, *Memoirs*, 164–65; Nevin, *Sherman's March*, 123.

7. Sword, *Embrace an Angry Wind*, 287; Horn, *The Army of Tennessee*, 417; Hood, *Advance and Retreat*, 299.

8. Hood, *Advance and Retreat*, 299–300.

9. Nevin, *Sherman's March*, 121.

10. Sword, *Embrace an Angry Wind*, 289–90; Nevin, *Sherman's March*, 123.

11. Joslyn, *Charlotte's Boys*, 290.

12. Olmstead, *Memoirs*, 165.

13. Joslyn, *Charlotte's Boys*, 294.

14. Clark, *Under the Stars and Bars*, 156.

15. Methvin, "Autobiography," 17–18.

16. Olmstead, *Memoirs*, 165.

17. Methvin, "Autobiography," 18.

18. Olmstead, *Memoirs*, 166.

19. Clark, *Under the Stars and Bars*, 156. If bare hands became wet with perspiration, they stuck to the icy metal, tearing the skin away and blistering calloused palms.

20. Joslyn, *Charlotte's Boys*, 291.

21. Ibid., 293.

22. Sword, *Embrace an Angry Wind*, 290–93, 308–12, 319.

23. Olmstead, *Memoirs*, 168.

24. Joslyn, *Charlotte's Boys*, 295.

Chapter 27. Forrest's Rear Guard

1. Sword, *Embrace an Angry Wind*, 397.

2. Ibid., 401.

3. Horn, *The Army of Tennessee*, 420; Sword, *Embrace an Angry Wind*, 405–6.

4. Wyeth, *That Devil Forrest*, 502; Sword, *Embrace an Angry Wind*, 407.

5. *O.R.* 45, pt. 1:726; Sword, *Embrace an Angry Wind*, 407.

6. Sword, *Embrace an Angry Wind*, 408; Losson, *Tennessee's Forgotten Warrior*, 241, 324.

7. Jordan and Pryor, *Campaigns of General Forrest*, 646; Sword, *Embrace an Angry Wind*, 411.

8. Joslyn, *Charlotte's Boys*, 296.

9. Olmstead, *Memoirs*, 169–70.

10. Wyeth, *That Devil Forrest*, 504; Sword, *Embrace an Angry Wind*, 413.

11. Sword, *Embrace an Angry Wind*, 414–15.

12. Wyeth, *That Devil Forrest*, 502–3; Horn, *The Army of Tennessee*, 421.

13. Olmstead, *Memoirs*, 169.

14. Ibid., 170.

15. Clark, *Under the Stars and Bars*, 156.

16. Jordan and Pryor, *Campaigns of General Forrest*, 649; Olmstead, *Memoirs*, 171.

17. Jordan and Pryor, *Campaigns of General Forrest*, 649.

18. Ibid., 649–51; Sword, *Embrace an Angry Wind*, 417–18.

19. Clark, *Under the Stars and Bars*, 159–60.

20. Jordan and Pryor, *Campaigns of General Forrest*, 651; Sword, *Embrace an Angry Wind*, 417–18.

21. Clark, *Under the Stars and Bars*, 160–61.

22. Olmstead, *Memoirs*, 172.

23. Jordan and Pryor, *Campaigns of General Forrest*, 652–53; Sword, *Embrace an Angry Wind*, 419.

24. Sword, *Embrace an Angry Wind*, 420–21.

25. McMurry, *John Bell Hood*, 181.

26. Olmstead, *Memoirs*, 173; Sword, *Embrace an Angry Wind*, 421; Horne, *The Army of Tennessee*, 421.

Chapter 28. Going to Carolina

1. *O.R.* 45, pt. 1:729.

2. Military records of Robert L. Braswell, National Archives; Joslyn, *Charlotte's Boys*, 298; Clark, *Under the Stars and Bars*, 163; Methvin, "Autobiography," 18; Olmstead, *Memoirs*, 173.

3. Sword, *Embrace an Angry Wind,* 425.

4. Clark, *Under the Stars and Bars,* 169.

5. *O.R.* 45, pt. 1:42.

6. Charles Thiot to Grafton, January 17, 1865, Thiot Papers.

7. Charles Thiot to Anna Thiot, January 19, 1865, Thiot Papers.

8. Clark, *Under the Stars and Bars,* 176.

9. Horne, *The Army of Tennessee,* 422; Johnston, *Narrative of Military Operations,* 372.

10. Olmstead, *Memoirs,* 174–77; Clark, *Under the Stars and Bars,* 187. Olmstead's and Clark's travel itineraries were different, probably because Clark was separated from Mercer's brigade, as he describes on p. 186.

11. Methvin, "Autobiography," 18. Lieutenant William K. Methvin, John Methvin's oldest brother, also served in Company D of the Fifty-seventh Georgia. He was captured at the Battle of Champion Hill and imprisoned at Johnson's Island, Ohio, for the duration of the war. Methvin, "Autobiography," 14; Lillian Henderson, "Methvin, William K.," *Roster,* 5:953.

12. Olmstead, *Memoirs,* 175–76.

13. McKinley, *Journal of Archibald C. McKinley,* 36.

14. Clark, *Under the Stars and Bars,* 187–88.

15. Ibid., 190.

16. Olmstead, *Memoirs,* 177.

17. Ibid., 177; Clark, *Under the Stars and Bars,* 190. Olmstead states (p. 177) that Mercer's brigade was consolidated into a single regiment after the Battle of Bentonville and that approximately eight hundred troops were present at that point. This included the five hundred that Olmstead brought back from Georgia too late for the battle. Thus at least three hundred members of the brigade would have been present at the Battle of Bentonville.

Chapter 29. The Battle of Bentonville

1. Johnston, *Narrative of Military Operations,* 371; Symonds, *Joseph E. Johnston,* 342.

2. Johnston, *Narrative of Military Operations,* 373; *O.R.* 47, pt. 2:1247–48; Johnston, "My Negotiations," 183–97; Symonds, *Joseph E. Johnston,* 344.

3. Johnston, *Narrative of Military Operations,* 372.

4. Sherman, *Memoirs,* 2:257–59.

5. Connelly, *Autumn of Glory,* 525.

6. Hampton, "The Battle of Bentonville," 4:701.

7. Johnston, *Narrative of Military Operations,* 382.

8. Ibid., 384; Bradley, *Last Stand,* 141; Hughes Jr., *Bentonville,* 39.

9. Longacre, *Gentleman and Soldier,* 137, 219.

10. Hughes Jr., *Bentonville,* 39; Bradley, *Last Stand,* 142.

11. Hughes Jr., *Bentonville,* 42.

12. Hampton, "The Battle of Bentonville," 701–2.

13. Ibid., 702.

14. Ibid., 701–2.

15. Sherman, *Memoirs*, 785; Hughes Jr., *Bentonville*, 68.

16. Johnston, *Narrative of Military Operations*, 385.

17. Ibid., 386.

18. Hampton, "The Battle of Bentonville," 703; Hughes Jr., *Bentonville*, 54–56; Korn, *Pursuit to Appomattox*, 71.

19. Bradley, *Last Stand*, 177; Hughes Jr., *Bentonville*, 42–43.

20. Bonner, *Milledgeville*, 172.

21. Later in the day Brigadier General William Taliaferro's division of Hardee's army would move behind Bate and be positioned to the right of Mercer's brigade.

22. Woodhead, *Echoes of Glory: Confederacy*, 233; Clark, *Under the Stars and Bars*, 192.

23. Bradley, *Last Stand*, 182–89.

24. Hampton, "The Battle of Bentonville," 703; Connelly, *Autumn of Glory*, 526.

25. *O.R.* 47, pt. 1:903–4; Hughes Jr., *Bentonville*, 67–80; Connelly, *Autumn of Glory*, 526–27.

26. Connelly, *Autumn of Glory*, 527.

27. Hughes Jr., *Bentonville*, 120.

28. Clark, *Under the Stars and Bars*, 192.

29. Hughes Jr., *Bentonville*, 120; Bradley, *Last Stand*, 209.

30. Broadfoot is quoted in Walter Clark, ed., *Histories of the Several Regiments and Battalions from North Carolina in the Great War 1861–1865* (Raleigh, N.C.: E. M. Uzzell, 1901), 4:21, as cited in Bradley, *Last Stand*, 204.

31. Clark, *Under the Stars and Bars*, 192.

32. Bradley, *Last Stand*, 209.

33. Clark, *Under the Stars and Bars*, 193; Hughes Jr., *Bentonville*, 120–22.

34. Hughes Jr., *Bentonville*, 121; Bradley, *Last Stand*, 215.

35. Johnston, *Narrative of Military Operations*, 387–88; Hughes Jr., *Bentonville*, 122.

36. Clark, *Under the Stars and Bars*, 193.

37. Bradley, *Last Stand*, 213.

38. Clark, *Under the Stars and Bars*, 193.

39. Johnston, *Narrative of Military Operations*, 368; Hughes Jr., *Bentonville*, 124–25.

40. Bradley, *Last Stand*, 204–5.

41. Hughes Jr., *Bentonville*, 125, 138–40.

42. Bate was an officer in the Mexican War. He saw action in most of the major battles of the western theater of the Civil War, was wounded three times, and had six horses shot out from under him. The severe leg wound he suffered at Shiloh required him to use crutches.

43. Clark, *Under the Stars and Bars*, 194–95.

44. Glatthaar, *March to the Sea*, 172; Hughes Jr., *Bentonville*, 140–49.

45. Clark, *Under the Stars and Bars*, 195–96.

46. Glatthaar, *March to the Sea*, 172.

47. Bradley, *Last Stand*, 343.

48. Hughes Jr., *Bentonville*, 209.

49. *O.R.* 47, pt. 2:942; Sherman, *Memoirs*, 786.

50. *O.R.* 47, pt. 2:942.

Chapter 30. Going Home

1. Sherman, *Memoirs*, 818–19, 829.

2. Olmstead, *Memoirs*, 177.

3. *O.R.* 47, pt. 1:1061. The reorganization was made official on April 10.

4. Johnston, *Narrative of Military Operations*, 394–95.

5. Sherman, *Memoirs*, 831; Glatthaar, *March to the Sea*, 176.

6. Trudeau, *Out of the Storm*, 213.

7. Johnston, *Narrative of Military Operations*, 395; Connelly, *Autumn of Glory*, 530–32.

8. Johnston, *Narrative of Military Operations*, 396.

9. Ibid., 397–99; William C. Davis, *Jefferson Davis*, 614–15.

10. Johnston, *Narrative of Military Operations*, 398; Roman, *Military Operations*, 2:665.

11. Johnston, *Narrative of Military Operations*, 398–99; William C. Davis, *Jefferson Davis*, 615–17.

12. Glatthaar, *March to the Sea*, 176–77.

13. Johnston, *Narrative of Military Operations*, 401–2; Trudeau, *Out of the Storm*, 239.

14. Johnston, *Narrative of Military Operations*, 411–12; William C. Davis, *Jefferson Davis*, 622–26.

15. Johnston, *Narrative of Military Operations*, 411; Trudeau, *Out of the Storm*, 238.

16. McPherson, *Battle Cry of Freedom*, 854; Spencer King, *Sound of Drums*, 13.

17. Trudeau, *Out of the Storm*, 242.

18. Ibid., 243.

19. Olmstead, *Memoirs*, 179.

20. Johnston, *Narrative of Military Operations*, 408–9; Olmstead, *Memoirs*, 178.

21. Clark, *Under the Stars and Bars*, 199.

22. Lillian Henderson, "Thiot, Charles H.," *Roster*, 1:199.

23. Charles T. Winship to Bell I. Wiley, September 9, 1956, Thiot Papers, introduction.

24. Clark, *Under the Stars and Bars*, 199.

25. Ibid.

26. Olmstead, *Memoirs*, 179.

27. Ibid.

28. Bonner, *Milledgeville*, 173.

29. McKinley, *Journal of Archibald C. McKinley*, 36.

30. Gallagher, *The Confederate War*, 53.

31. Robert Braswell's fragmented and incomplete military records do not show that he was in the North Carolina campaign and fought at Bentonville. However, in applications for pensions for Confederate veterans made by the wife of H. P. Everett in 1910, the

wife of J. H. Branham in 1911, and the wife of James A. Everett in 1919, Braswell signed as a witness and stated that he was with these three men at both Bentonville and the surrender at Greensboro. The records of Company E of the Fort Valley Infantry reveal that twenty-four men surrendered at Greensboro; see Lillian Henderson, *Roster*, 5:917ff.

Epilogue. The Future of Their Lives

1. Though the grave is unmarked, records show that Mr. and Mrs. William D. Barkuloo were buried in Oak Grove Cemetery in lot 43, section B. See Herbert L. Joiner Sr., "History of Oak Grove Cemetery," 1977, manuscript collection of Brunswick–Glynn County (Ga.) Regional Library.

2. Joslyn, *Charlotte's Boys*, 323–37.

3. *Houston County, Georgia, Marriage Record: 1825–1898*, bk. C, 1:41; Governor Treutlin Chapter of the Daughters of the American Revolution, Fort Valley, Georgia, "Braswell-Love-Shipp," *History of Peach County, Georgia*, 199–201.

4. "Mr. R. L. Braswell Died Monday A.M.," *(Fort Valley, Ga.) Leader Tribune*, January 15, 1920.

5. Derry, *Georgia*, 565.

6. Felton, "The Young Family of Georgia," 147; Rosemary L. Henderson, "Greenwood Plantation Families," 8–9; Lillian Henderson, "Davis, Edwin Tralona," *Roster*, 5:920.

7. Hart, *Official History of Laurens County*, 1:391–92; *Hawkinsville (Ga.) Dispatch*, August 21, 1884; *Dublin (Ga.) Post*, August 20, 1884.

8. Kuglar, Reminiscences, 1, 47.

9. McKinley, *Journal of Archibald C. McKinley*, xiv–xv.

10. Northern, ed., *Men of Mark*, 4:108–12.

11. Warner, *Generals in Gray*, 216–17.

12. Methvin, "Autobiography."

13. Lillian Henderson, "Mims, Seaborn S.," *Roster*, 5:964.

14. Olmstead, *Memoirs*, 59.

15. McKinley, *Journal of Archibald C. McKinley*, 36.

16. Ibid., 35–36.

17. Bonner, "David R. Snelling," 175.

18. Nell Vinson-Oldham (daughter of Charlie Vinson), interview.

Afterword. Lessons of a Great-Great-Grandson

1. Williamson Mims, Will and Testament, 139.

2. Compiled and copied by Joseph T. Maddox, Irwington, Georgia, 1973, Historical Collection, Wilkinson County (Georgia) Library.

3. Olmstead, *Memoirs*, 129–30.

Bibliography

PRIMARY SOURCES

Manuscripts, Diaries, Journals, Letters, Memoirs, Wills

Armstrong, Henrietta A. Journal. Georgia Division of Archives and History.

Balfour, Emma. Diary. Mississippi Department of Archives and History.

Barkuloo, William. Letters. Georgia Division of Archives and History.

———. Letters. National Archives.

Bibb, William H., and Maggie Bibb Gribben. "Sketches of Judge William Bibb." United Daughters of the Confederacy Veterans Records, vol. 1. Thomasville (Ga.) Public Library.

Butler, Benjamin Franklin. Letter. Civil War Miscellany, Personal Papers, RG 57-1-1. Georgia Division of Archives and History.

Chunn, William A. Letters. Collection of Dr. A. J. Conyers, Waco, Tex.

Cleburne, Patrick. Letters. National Archives.

Cleveland, Henry. Letters. National Archives.

Crawford, Lewis. Letters. Georgia Division of Archives and History.

Cumming, Alfred. Letters. Mississippi Department of Archives and History.

Davis, John Morgan. Letters. Civil War Miscellany, Personal Papers, RG 57-1-1. Georgia Division of Archives and History.

Dunwoody, John. Letters. National Archives.

Featherston, Lewis H. Papers. Special Collections. Woodruff Library, Emory University.

Felton, A. C. "The Young Family of Georgia." Unpublished typescript dated April 1955. Thomasville (Ga.) Genealogical, History and Fine Arts Library.

Fiquers, Hardin. Fiquers Family Papers. Tennessee State Library, Nashville.

Fitzpatrick, Francis E. Letters. Collection of Emily Ship Stoll, Morganfield, Ky.

Hardee, William J. Letters. National Archives.

Harris, Robert H. Letters. Elizabeth Hopkins Collection. Thomasville (Ga.) Genealogical, History and Fine Arts Library.

Helms, Celathiel. Letters, August 13, 1863–July 18, 1864. In "Letters from Confederate Soldiers, 1860–1865." Collected and bound by the Georgia Division, United Daughters of the Confederacy. Vol. 2 of UDC Bound Typescripts. Georgia Division of Archives and History.

Hopkins, Elizabeth F. "The 'Dixie Boys' Flag." Georgia Division of Archives and History.

Houston County, Georgia. Marriage Records. Vol. 1, bk. C.

Ivey, F. H. Letters. Georgia Division of Archives and History.

Jefferson, Thomas E. Civil War Letters, 1862–1863. AC73-307. Georgia Division of Archives and History.

Joiner, Herbert L., Sr. "History of Oak Grove Cemetery." 1977. Manuscript Collection of Regional Library, Brunswick, Glynn County, Ga.

Keen, John L. Civil War Miscellany, Personal Papers, RG 57-1-1. Georgia Division of Archives and History.

———. Letters. Georgia Division of Archives and History.

King, Patrick Cleburn. "Reminiscences of Mr. Patrick Cleburn King." Georgia Division of Archives and History.

Kuglar, James M. Reminiscences originally published in the *Carrolton Free Press*, ca. 1933–36. Typescript in Civil War Miscellany, Personal Papers, RG 57-1-1. Georgia Division of Archives and History.

Maddox, Joseph T., ed. "Kirkpatrick Trial." Georgia Historical Collection. Wilkinson County Library, Irwinton, Ga.

Mercer, George A. Diary and Note Book of George A. Mercer. Southern Historical Collection. University of North Carolina Library, Chapel Hill.

Merrell, G. W. Biographical sketch of Philo H. Chandler. In "Carroll's Soldiers, Sketches by G. W. Merrell," Civil War Miscellany, Personal Papers, RG 57-1-1. Georgia Division of Archives and History.

Mims, Williamson. Will and Testament of Williamson Mims. Record of Wills, Book B, Houston County Registry of Probate, Perry, Ga.

Olmstead, Charles H. Letters. National Archives.

Reed, William Gibbons. "Confederate Letters, Diaries, and Reminiscences, 1860–1865." Collected and bound by Georgia Division, United Daughters of the Confederacy. Vol. 10 of UDC Bound Typescripts. Georgia Division of Archives and History.

Ritter, Israel. Diary. Archives of the Vicksburg National Military Park.

Sexton, Margaret Branch. Collection. Hargrett Library, University of Georgia, Athens.

Taylor, Thomas T. Letters. Special Collections. Woodruff Library, Emory University.

Thiot, Charles. Papers. Special Collections. Woodruff Library, Emory University.

United Daughters of the Confederacy, John B. Gordon Chapter, Historical Collections No. VIII, Thomasville (Ga.) Public Library.

Vinson, John Fletcher. Letters. Confederate Research Center, Hill College, Hillsboro, Tex.

Vinson, Wright. Civil War Letters, 1862–1863. AC63-107. Georgia Division of Archives and History.

Books and Pamphlets

Anderson, John Q., ed. *Campaigning with Parsons' Texas Cavalry C.S.A.: The War Journal and Letters of the Four Orr Brothers, 12th Texas Cavalry Regiment.* Hillsboro, Tex.: Texian Press, 1967.

Andrews, W. H. *Footprints of a Regiment: A Recollection of the 1st Georgia Regulars—1861–1865.* Annotated and with an introduction by Richard M. McMurray. Atlanta: Longstreet Press, 1992.

Banks, R. W. *The Battle of Franklin: November 30, 1864.* 1908. Reprint, Dayton, Ohio: Morningside House, 1988.

Benson, Susan Williams, ed. *Berry Benson's Civil War Book: Memoirs of a Confederate Scout and Sharpshooter.* 1878, 1962. Reprint, Athens: University of Georgia Press, 1992.

Bevens, William E. *Reminiscences of a Private.* 1914. Reprint, Daniel E. Sutherland, ed., Fayetteville: University of Arkansas Press, 1992.

Brooks, U. R. *Butler and His Cavalry in the War of Secession, 1861–1865.* 1909. Reprint, South Carolina Regimental Series, J. J. Fox, ed., Oxford, Miss.: Guild Bindery Press, 1989.

———. *Stories of the Confederacy.* 1912. Reprint, South Carolina Regimental Series, J. H. Fox, ed., Oxford, Miss.: Guild Bindery Press, 1991.

Brown, Norman D., ed. *One of Cleburne's Command: The Civil War Reminiscences and Diary of Capt. Samuel T. Foster, Granbury's Texas Brigade, CSA.* Austin: University of Texas Press, 1980.

Buck, Irving A. *Cleburne and His Command.* 1908. Reprint, Dayton, Ohio: Press of Morningside Bookshop, 1985.

Butler, Benjamin F. *Butler's Book.* Boston: A. M. Thayer, 1892.

Cantrell, Oscar A. *Sketches of the First Regiment Ga. Vols. Together with the History of the 56th Regiment, Georgia Vols., to January 1, 1864.* Atlanta: Intelligencer Steam Power Presses, 1864.

Castel, Albert. *Tom Taylor's Civil War.* Lawrence: University Press of Kansas, 2000.

Chesnut, Mary Boykin. *Mary Chesnut's Civil War.* Edited by C. Vann Woodward. New Haven, Conn., 1981.

Clark, Walter A. *Under the Stars and Bars.* 1900. Reprint, Jonesboro, Ga.: Freedom Hill Press, 1987.

Cox, Jacob D. *Atlanta.* Campaigns of the Civil War. 1882. Reprint, Dayton, Ohio: Morningside House, 1987.

———. *The March to the Sea: Franklin and Nashville.* Vol. 10 in *Campaigns of the Civil War.* New York: Charles Scribner's Sons, 1882.

Cuttino, George P., ed. *Saddle Bag and Spinning Wheel: Being the Civil War Letters of George W. Peddy, M.D. and His Wife Kate F. Peddy.* Macon, Ga.: Mercer University Press, 1981.

Davis, Jefferson. *The Rise and Fall of the Confederate Government.* 2 vols. New York: D. Appleton, 1881.

Davis, William C., ed. *Diary of a Confederate Soldier: John S. Jackman of the Orphan Brigade.* Columbia: University of South Carolina Press, 1990.

Douglas, Lucia Rutherford, ed. *Douglas's Texas Battery, C.S.A.* Waco, Tex.: Texian Press, 1966.

Dunaway, Sarah Owen, ed. *Confederate Reminiscences and Letters, 1861–1865.* 20 vols. Atlanta: Georgia Division, United Daughters of the Confederacy, 1995–.

Folsom, James M. *Heroes and Martyrs of Georgia: Georgia's Record in the Revolution of 1861.* 1864. Reprint, Baltimore: Butternut and Blue, 1995.

Grant, Ulysses S. *Ulysses S. Grant: Memoirs and Selected Letters.* 1885. Reprint, Mary Drake McFeely and William S. McFeely, eds., New York: Literary Classics of the United States, 1990.

Hallock, Judith Lee, ed. *The Civil War Letters of Joshua K. Callaway*. Athens: University of Georgia Press, 1997.

Hart, Bertha Sheppard. *The Official History of Laurens County, Georgia, 1807–1941*. 2 vols. Atlanta: Cherokee, 1978, ca. 1941–1988.

Hood, John Bell. *Advance and Retreat: Personal Experiences in the United States and Confederate States Armies*. 1880. Reprint, Bloomington: Indiana University Press, 1959.

Hughes, Nathaniel Cheairs, Jr., ed. *The Civil War Memoir of Philip Daingerfield Stephenson, D.D.* Conway, Ark.: UCA Press, 1995.

Johnston, Joseph E. *Narrative of Military Operations during the Civil War*. 1874. Reprint, New York: Da Capo Press, 1990.

Jordan, Thomas, and J. P. Pryor. *The Campaigns of General Nathan Bedford Forrest and of Forrest's Cavalry*. 1868. Reprint, New York: Da Capo Press, 1996.

Joslyn, Mauriel P., ed. *Charlotte's Boys: Civil War Letters of the Branch Family of Savannah*. Berryville, Va.: Rockbridge, 1996.

McElroy, John. *This Was Andersonville*. 1879. Reprint, Roy Meredith, ed., New York: McDowell, Obolensky, 1957.

McKinley, Archibald C. *The Journal of Archibald C. McKinley*. Edited by Robert L. Humphries. Athens: University of Georgia Press, 1991.

Manigault, Arthur M. *A Carolinian Goes to War: The Civil War Narrative of Arthur Middleton Manigault, Brigadier General, C.S.A*. Edited by R. Lockwood Tower. Columbia: University of South Carolina Press, 1983.

Nisbet, James C. *4 Years on the Firing Line*. 1914. Reprint, Bell Irvin Wiley, ed., Jackson, Miss.: McCowat-Mercer Press, 1963.

Olmstead, Charles H. *The Memoirs of Charles H. Olmstead*. Edited by Lilla M. Hawes. Collections of the Georgia Historical Society, vol. 14. Savannah: Georgia Historical Society, 1964.

Quintard, Charles T. *Doctor Quintard, Chaplain C.S.A. and Second Bishop of Tennessee: The Memoir and Civil War Diary of Charles Todd Quintard*. Edited by Sam Davis Elliott. Baton Rouge: Louisiana State University Press, 2003.

Ransom, John. *John Ransom's Andersonville Diary*. 1881. Reprint, New York: Berkley Books, 1994.

Ridley, Bromfield L., ed. *Battles and Sketches of the Army of Tennessee*. 1906. Reprint, Dayton, Ohio: Morningside Bookshop, 1978.

Roman, Alfred. *The Military Operations of General Beauregard*. 2 vols. New York: Harper, 1884.

Ross, Lawrence S. *Personal Civil War Letters of General Lawrence Sullivan Ross*. Edited by Shelly Morrison and Perry Wayne Shelton. Austin, Tex., privately printed, 1994.

Sherman, W. T. *Memoirs of General W. T. Sherman*. 1875. Reprint, Charles Royster, ed., New York: Literary Classics of the United States, 1990.

Simpson, Harold B., ed. *The Bugle Softly Blows: The Confederate Diary of Benjamin M. Seaton*. Waco, Tex.: Texian Press, 1965.

Sneden, Robert Knox. *Eye of the Storm: A Civil War Odyssey*. Edited by Charles F. Bryan Jr. and Nelson D. Lankford. New York: Free Press, 2000.

Stevenson, William G. *Thirteen Months in the Rebel Army: Impressions of a Northerner Forced into the Southern Army.* 1862. Reprint, New York: A. S. Barnes, 1959.

U.S. War Department. *The War of the Rebellion: A Compilation of the Official Records of the Union and Confederate Armies.* 127 vols. Washington, D.C.: GPO, 1880–1901.

Watkins, Sam R. *1861 vs 1882. "Co. Aytch," Maury Grays, First Tennessee Regiment; or, A Side Show of the Show.* 1882. Reprint, Dayton, Ohio: Morningside Bookshop, 1982.

White, George. *Statistics of the State of Georgia.* Savannah, Ga.: W. Thorns Williams, 1849.

Worsham, W. J. *The Old Nineteenth Tennessee Regiment C.S.A.: June, 1861–April 1865.* Knoxville, Tenn.: Paragon, 1902.

Articles and Parts of Books

Bragg, Braxton. "General Bragg's Report of the Kentucky Campaign." In Ridley, *Battles and Sketches of the Army of Tennessee,* 134–41.

Brown, Mary Beaty. "Reminiscences of the Sixties." In Dunaway, ed., *Confederate Reminiscences and Letters, 1861–1865,* 6:114–19.

"Civil War Flag of 'Dixie Boys' of Thomasville Was Never Given Up." *Thomasville (Ga.) Times-Enterprise,* May 19, 1920.

Crawford, Mrs. Martin J., and Mrs. Seaborn Jones. "They Endured and Conquered," AC3-2560, MF283, roll 59. Georgia Division of Archives and History.

Crenshaw, Laura O. Obituary of Thomas E. Etheridge. *Confederate Veteran* 38 (1931): 117.

Davis, Edwin Tralona. "The Battle of Atlanta." *Savannah Republican,* July 26, 1864.

———. "Diary and Official Correspondence Concerning Edwin Tralona Davis . . . December 12, 1861–October 17, 1862." In Dunaway, ed., *Confederate Reminiscences and Letters, 1861–1865,* 17:3–13.

"The 'Dixie Boy' Flag May Finally Find Its Way Back to Where It Was Presented." *Thomasville (Ga.) Times-Enterprise,* March 4, 1893.

"Dr. Harris Tells of the Origin and Presentation of the 'Dixie Boy' Flag." *Thomasville (Ga.) Times-Enterprise,* May 24, 1920.

Fuller, David F. "Battle at Averysboro, N.C." *Confederate Veteran* 5 (1897): 68.

Hammond, Paul F. "Campaign of General E. Kirby Smith, in Kentucky in 1862." *Southern Historical Society Papers* 9 (July–August 1881):225–33, 246–54, 289–97, 455–62; 10 (September–October 1881):70–76.

Hampton, Wade. "The Battle of Bentonville." In Johnson and Buel, *Battles and Leaders of the Civil War,* 4:700–5.

Heth, Henry. "The Memoirs of Henry Heth, Part 1." Edited by James L. Morrison Jr. *Civil War History* 8 (March 1962): 5–24.

"Historic Battle Flag in Hands of U.D.C. Chapter at Dublin, Georgia." *Thomasville (Ga.) Times-Enterprise,* December 2, 1924.

Holland, W. D. "Rumble Family Letters." In Dunaway, ed., *Confederate Reminiscences and Letters, 1861–1865,* 7:194–209.

Hopkins, Elizabeth F. "The 'Dixie Boy' Martyr." In vol. 5, United Daughters of the
Confederacy Bound Typescripts. Georgia Department of Archives and History.

Ivey, F. H. "Report on the Battle of Champion Hill." *Confederate Union,* June 2, 1863.

James, F. B. "McCook's Brigade at the Assault upon Kennesaw Mountain, Georgia,
June 27, 1864." In *Military Order of the Loyal Legion of the United States: Ohio,*
4:255–77. Wilmington, N.C.: Broadfoot, 1992.

Jeffares, John E. "John E. Jeffares Letters." In Dunaway, ed., *Confederate
Reminiscences and Letters, 1861–1865,* 8:250–53.

Johnston, Joseph E. "My Negotiations with General Sherman." *North American Review*
143 (1896): 183–97.

Jordan, Green Handley. "Letter to a Sister." In vol. 8, United Daughters of the
Confederacy Bound Typescripts. Georgia Department of Archives and History.

Kersh, Mariah Austin. "Recollections of the Days of 1861–65." In Governor Treutlin
Chapter of the Daughters of the American Revolution, *History of Peach County,
Georgia,* 79–83.

Lee, Stephen D. "The Campaign of Vicksburg, Mississippi, in 1863—from April 15, to
and Including the Battle of Champion Hills, or Baker's Creek, May 16, 1863." In
Franklin L. Riley, ed., *Publications of the Mississippi Historical Society.* Oxford:
Mississippi Historical Society, 1900, 3:21–53.

Longley, Charles L. "Champion Hill." In *Military Order of the Loyal Legion of the
United States: Iowa,* 1:208–14. Wilmington, N.C.: Broadfoot, 1992.

McNeel, John M. "Letters to a Wife." In vol. 3, United Daughters of the Confederacy
Bound Typescripts. Georgia Department of Archives and History.

Norrell, William O. "Journal of William O. Norrell, Co. B, 63rd Georgia Regiment
Volunteers." *Journal of Confederate History* 1, no. 1 (1988): 50–82.

Olmstead, Charles H. "Capt. Matthew H. Hopkins." *Confederate Veteran* 25 (1917):
132.

———. "Reminiscences of Service." In vol. 8, United Daughters of the Confederacy
Bound Typescripts. Georgia Department of Archives and History.

"Reinlistment of the 57th Georgia Regiment." *Savannah Republican,* March 7, 1864,
p. 2.

Ripple, Ezra H. "A Civil, and Sometimes Uncivil, War: A Union Veteran Talks of Life in
a Prison Camp." Edited by Bruce Catton. *American Heritage,* October 1964, 50–61.

Smith, Edwin Kirby. "Battle of Richmond Kentucky." In Ridley, *Battles and Sketches of
the Army of Tennessee,* 130–32.

Stiles, John. "Some 'Sure Enough' Confederates." *Confederate Veteran* 33 (1925): 143.

Strong, J. B. "Brown Family Letters." In Dunaway, ed., *Confederate Reminiscences and
Letters, 1861–1865,* 17:247–52.

Thrash, Ann. "Frederick Bruce Thigpen." In vol. 8, United Daughters of the
Confederacy Bound Typescripts. Georgia Department of Archives and History.

"To Restore the Flag." *Thomasville (Ga.) Times-Enterprise,* February 25, 1893.

Williams, T. J. "The Battle of Champion Hill." In *Military Order of the Loyal Legion of
the United States: Ohio,* 5:204–11. Wilmington, N.C.: Broadfoot, 1992.

Newspapers

Atlanta Journal
Dublin (Ga.) Post
(Fort Valley, Ga.) Leader
(Fort Valley, Ga.) Leader Tribune
(Fort Valley, Ga.) Leader Tribune and Peachland Journal
Hawkinsville (Ga.) Dispatch
Macon Telegraph
(Milledgeville, Ga.) Confederate Union
(Milledgeville, Ga.) Southern Recorder
(Savannah) Republican
Savannah Republican
(Thomasville, Ga.) Daily Times-Enterprise
Thomasville (Ga.) Times-Enterprise
(Thomasville, Ga.) Times
(Vicksburg, Miss.) Daily Citizen

Federal and State Government Records

U.S. Census, Georgia: 1840–1870
U.S. Census, South Carolina, 1850

Veterans' Records, National Archives Administration

Barkuloo, William, colonel, Fifty-seventh Regiment, Georgia Infantry, Confederate army.

Braswell, Robert L., private, Fifty-seventh Regiment, Georgia Infantry, Confederate army.

Braswell, Samuel W., private, First Confederate Regiment, Georgia Volunteers, Confederate army.

Braswell, William L., sergeant major, First Confederate Regiment, Georgia Volunteers, Confederate army.

Guyton, Cincinnatus Saxon, colonel, Fifty-seventh Regiment, Georgia Infantry, Confederate army.

Harris, Henry, second lieutenant, Fifty-seventh Regiment, Georgia Infantry, Confederate army.

Holly, William B., private, Fifty-seventh Regiment, Georgia Infantry, Confederate army.

Mathews, James N., private, Phillips's Legion Cavalry (Georgia), Confederate army.

Mims, Seaborn, first sergeant, Fifty-seventh Regiment, Georgia Infantry, Confederate army.

SECONDARY SOURCES

Books

Anderson, John Q. *Campaigning with Parsons' Texas Cavalry Brigade, C.S.A.: The War Journal and Letters of the Four Orr Brothers, 12th Texas Cavalry Regiment.* Hillsboro, Tex.: Hill Junior College Press, 1967.

Arnold, James R. *Grant Wins the War: Decision at Vicksburg.* New York: John Wiley and Sons, 1997.

————. *Jefferson Davis's Own: Cavalry, Comanches, and the Battle for the Texas Frontier.* New York: John Wiley and Sons, 2000.

Bailey, Anne J. *The Chessboard of War: Sherman and Hood in the Autumn Campaigns of 1864.* Lincoln: University of Nebraska Press, 2000.

Bailey, Anne J., and Walter J. Fraser Jr. *Portraits of Conflict: A Photographic History of Georgia in the Civil War.* Fayetteville: University of Arkansas Press, 1996.

Bailey, Ronald H. *Battles for Atlanta: Sherman Moves East.* The Civil War. Alexandria, Va.: Time-Life Books, 1985, 1989.

Ballard, Michael B. *Pemberton: A Biography.* Jackson: University Press of Mississippi, 1991.

Bankston, Emmie Carnes. *History of Roberta and Crawford County, Georgia.* Macon, Ga.: Omni Press, 1976.

Barnes, Zed H. *Confederate Forts.* Natchez, Miss.: Southern Historical Publications, 1977.

Barrett, John G. *Sherman's March through the Carolinas.* Chapel Hill: University of North Carolina Press, 1956.

Barrow, Charles K., J. H. Segars, and R. B. Rosenburg, eds. *Forgotten Confederates: An Anthology about Black Southerners.* Vol. 14 of *Journal of Confederate History Series.* Atlanta: Southern Heritage Press, 1995.

Bearss, Edwin C. *The Campaign for Vicksburg.* 3 vols. Dayton, Ohio: Morningside House, 1985–86.

————. *Decision in Mississippi.* Jackson: Mississippi Commission on the War between the States, 1962.

Bell, Malcolm, Jr. *Major Butler's Legacy: Five Generations of a Slaveholding Family.* Athens: University of Georgia Press, 1987.

Bergeron, Arthur W., Jr. *Confederate Mobile.* Jackson: University Press of Mississippi, 1991.

Boatner, Mark M., III. *The Civil War Dictionary.* New York: Vintage, 1991.

Bonner, James C. *Milledgeville: Georgia's Antebellum Capital.* Athens: University of Georgia Press, 1978.

Boritt, Gabor S., ed. *Why the Confederacy Lost.* New York: Oxford University Press, 1992.

Bradley, Mark L. *Last Stand in the Carolinas: The Battle of Bentonville.* Campbell, Calif.: Savas Woodbury, 1996.

Brown, Russell K. *To the Manner Born: The Life of General William H. T. Walker.* Athens: University of Georgia Press, 1994.

Buell, Thomas B. *The Warrior Generals: Combat Leadership in the Civil War.* New York: Crown, 1997.

Cannan, John. *The Atlanta Campaign: May–November, 1864.* Conshohocken, Pa.: Combined Books, 1991.

Carse, Robert. *Department of the South: Hilton Head Island in the Civil War.* Columbia, S.C.: State Printing Co., 1976.

Carter, Samuel. *The Final Fortress: The Campaign for Vicksburg, 1862–1863.* New York: St. Martin's Press, 1980.

———. *The Siege of Atlanta, 1864.* New York: Bonanza Books, 1973.

Cash, W. J. *The Mind of the South.* 1941. Reprint, New York: Vintage, 1991.

Castel, Albert. *Decision in the West: The Atlanta Campaign of 1864.* Lawrence: University Press of Kansas, 1992.

Catton, Bruce. *The Civil War.* 1960. Reprint, Boston: Houghton Mifflin, 1987.

———. *Grant Moves South: 1861–1863.* Boston: Little, Brown, 1960.

———. *Grant Takes Command: 1863–1865.* Boston: Little, Brown, 1968.

Central Georgia Genealogical Society. *First Hundred and Ten Years of Houston County, Georgia (1822–1932).* Chelsea, Mich.: Bookcrafters, 1983.

Channing, Steven A. *Confederate Ordeal: The Southern Home Front.* The Civil War. Alexandria, Va.: Time-Life Books, 1984.

Cisco, Walter B. *States Rights Gist: A South Carolina General of the Civil War.* Shippensburg, Pa.: White Mane, 1991.

Clark, Walter, ed. *Histories of the Several Regiments and Battalions from North Carolina in the Great War 1861–1865.* Raleigh, N.C.: E. M. Uzzell, 1901.

Coffey, David. *John Bell Hood and the Struggle for Atlanta.* Abilene, Tex.: McWhiney Foundation Press, McMurry University, 1998.

Coleman, Kenneth, ed. *A History of Georgia.* Athens: University of Georgia Press, 1977.

Connelly, Thomas L. *Army of the Heartland: The Army of Tennessee, 1861–1862.* Baton Rouge: Louisiana State University Press, 1967.

———. *Autumn of Glory: Army of Tennessee, 1862–1865.* Baton Rouge: Louisiana State University Press, 1971.

———. *Civil War Tennessee: Battles and Leaders.* Knoxville: University of Tennessee Press, 1979.

———. *The Marble Man: Robert E. Lee and His Image in American Society.* Baton Rouge: Louisiana State University Press, 1977.

Conrad, James Lee. *The Young Lions: Confederate Cadets at War.* Mechanicsburg, Pa.: Stackpole Books, 1997.

Cozzens, Peter. *No Better Place to Die: The Battle of Stones River.* Urbana: University of Illinois Press, 1990.

———. *This Terrible Sound: The Battle of Chickamauga.* Urbana: University of Illinois Press, 1992.

Crabb, Martha L. *All Afire to Fight: The Untold Tale of the Civil War's Ninth Texas Cavalry.* New York: Avon, 2000.

Craven, John Joseph. *"Fiction Distorting Fact": Prison Life, Annotated by Jefferson*

Davis. Edited by Edward K. Eckert. Macon, Ga.: Mercer University Press, 1987.

Crute, Joseph H. *Units of the Confederate States Army.* Midlothian, Va.: Derwent Books, 1987.

Current, Richard N., ed. *Encyclopedia of the Confederacy.* 4 vols. New York: Simon and Schuster, 1993.

Daniel, Larry J. *Shiloh: The Battle That Changed the Civil War.* New York: Simon and Schuster, 1997.

———. *Soldiering in the Army of Tennessee.* Chapel Hill: University of North Carolina Press, 1991.

Davis, Burke. *The Long Surrender.* New York: Random House, 1985.

———. *Sherman's March.* New York: Random House, 1980.

Davis, William C. *Brother against Brother: The War Begins.* The Civil War. Alexandria, Va.: Time-Life Books, 1983.

———. *Jefferson Davis: The Man and His Hour.* New York: Harper Collins, 1991.

———. *Look Away! History of the Confederate States of America.* New York: Free Press, 2002.

———. *The Orphan Brigade.* Baton Rouge: Louisiana State University Press, 1980.

Derry, Joseph T. *Georgia.* Vol. 7 of *Confederate Military History.* Edited by Clement A. Evans. Atlanta: Confederate Publishing, 1895. Reprint, Wilmington, N.C.: Broadfoot, 1987.

Donald, David Herbert. *Lincoln.* New York: Simon and Schuster, 1995.

Dougan, Michael B. *Confederate Arkansas: The People and Policies of a Frontier State in Wartime.* Tuscaloosa: University of Alabama Press, 1976, 1991.

Dowell, Spright. *A History of Mercer University.* Macon, Ga.: Mercer University Press, 1958.

Dyer, John P. *The Gallant Hood.* Boston: Bobbs-Merrill, 1950.

Elliott, Sam Davis. *Soldier of Tennessee: General Alexander P. Stewart and the Civil War in the West.* Baton Rouge: Louisiana State University Press, 1999.

Evans, Clement A., ed. *Confederate Military History.* 17 vols. 1899. Reprint, Wilmington, N.C.: Broadfoot, 1987.

Evans, David. *Sherman's Horsemen: Union Cavalry Operations in the Atlanta Campaign.* Bloomington: Indiana University Press, 1996.

Fellman, Michael. *Citizen Sherman: A Life of William Tecumseh Sherman.* New York: Random House, 1995.

Fleming, Thomas. *Band of Brothers: West Point in the Civil War.* New York: Walker, 1988.

Foote, Shelby. *The Civil War: A Narrative, Fort Sumter to Perryville.* New York: Random House, 1958.

———. *The Civil War: A Narrative, Fredericksburg to Meridian.* New York: Random House, 1963.

———. *Shiloh: A Novel.* New York: Vintage, 1952.

Fowler, Robert H., ed. *Struggle for Vicksburg.* Harrisburg, Pa.: Stackpole Books, 1967.

Futch, Ovid L. *History of Andersonville Prison.* Gainesville: University of Florida Press, 1968.

Gallagher, Gary W. *The Confederate War.* Boston: Harvard University Press, 1997.

Glatthaar, Joseph T. *The March to the Sea and Beyond: Sherman's Troops in the Savannah and Carolinas Campaigns.* Baton Rouge: Louisiana State University Press, 1985.

Golay, Michael. *A Ruined Land: The End of the Civil War.* New York: John Wiley, 1999.

Goolrick, James T. *The Life of General Hugh Mercer.* New York: Neale, 1906.

Gottschalk, Phil. *In Deadly Earnest: The Missouri Brigade.* Columbia: Missouri River Press, 1991.

Govan, Gilbert, and James Livingwood. *A Different Valor: Joseph E. Johnston.* New York: Bobbs-Merrill, 1956.

Governor Treutlin Chapter of the Daughters of the American Revolution, Fort Valley, Georgia. *History of Peach County, Georgia.* Atlanta: Cherokee, 1972.

Greene, Francis V. *The Mississippi.* New York: Charles Scribner's Sons, 1882.

Griffith, Paddy. *Battle Tactics of the Civil War.* New Haven, Conn.: Yale University Press, 1989.

Grimsley, Mark. *The Hard Hand of War: Union Military Policy toward Southern Civilians 1861–1865.* New York: Cambridge University Press, 1995.

Groom, Winston. *Shrouds of Glory: From Atlanta to Nashville.* New York: Atlantic Monthly Press, 1995.

Hafendorfer, Kenneth A. *Perryville: Battle of Kentucky.* Louisville, Ky.: KH Press, 1991.

Hale, Douglas. *The Third Texas Cavalry in the Civil War.* Norman: University of Oklahoma Press, 1993.

Hankinson, Alan. *Vicksburg 1863: Grant Clears the Mississippi.* Oxford, U.K.: Osprey, 1993.

Harrison, Lowell H. *The Civil War in Kentucky.* Lexington: University Press of Kentucky, 1975.

Hay, Thomas R. *Hood's Tennessee Campaign.* New York: Walter Neale, 1929.

Henderson, Lillian, ed. *Roster of the Confederate Soldiers of Georgia, 1861–1865.* 7 vols. Hapeville, Ga.: Longino and Porter, 1960.

Hendrick, Burton J. *Statesmen of the Lost Cause: Jefferson Davis and His Cabinet.* New York: Literary Guild of America, 1939.

Henry, Robert S. *The Story of the Confederacy.* New York: Grosset and Dunlap, 1931.

Herring, Dorothy Holland. *Company A of the Fortieth Georgia Infantry Regiment in the Confederate Service.* Westminster, Md.: Willow Bend Books, 2000.

Hoehling, A. A. *Last Train from Atlanta.* New York: Bonanza Books, 1958.

———. *Vicksburg: 47 Days of Siege.* 1969. Reprint, New York: Fairfax, 1991.

Horn, Stanley F. *The Army of Tennessee.* New York: Bobbs-Merrill, 1941. Reprint, Norman: University of Oklahoma Press, 1953.

———. *The Decisive Battle of Nashville.* Baton Rouge: Louisiana State University Press, 1956, 1984.

Howell, Grady L., Jr. *Hill of Death: The Battle of Champion Hill.* Madison, Miss.: Chickasaw Bayou, 1993.

Hughes, Nathaniel Cheairs, Jr. *Bentonville: The Final Battle of Sherman and Johnston.* Chapel Hill: University of North Carolina Press, 1996.

————. *General William J. Hardee: Old Reliable.* 1965. Reprint, Wilmington, N.C.: Broadfoot, 1987.

————. *The Pride of the Confederate Artillery: The Washington Artillery in the Army of Tennessee.* Baton Rouge: Louisiana State University Press, 1997.

Hurst, Jack. *Nathan Bedford Forrest: A Biography.* New York: Alfred A. Knopf, 1993.

Johnson, Robert Underwood, and Clarence Clough Buel, eds. *Battles and Leaders of the Civil War.* 7 vols. 1887. N.d., Reprint, Secaucus, N.J.: Castle.

Jones, Archer. *Confederate Strategy from Shiloh to Vicksburg.* Baton Rouge: Louisiana State University Press, 1961.

Jones, Wilmer L. *After the Thunder: Fourteen Men Who Shaped Post–Civil War America.* Dallas: Taylor, 2000.

Jordan, Mary Alice, ed. *Cotton to Kaolin: A History of Washington County Georgia, 1784–1989.* Roswell, Ga.: W. H. Wolfe, 1989.

Kelly, Dennis. *Kennesaw Mountain and the Atlanta Campaign.* Atlanta: Susan Hunter, 1990.

Kennedy, Francis H. *The Civil War Battlefield Guide.* Boston: Houghton Mifflin, 1990.

Kennett, Lee. *Marching through Georgia: The Story of Soldiers and Civilians during Sherman's Campaign.* New York: Harper Collins, 1995.

Kerksis, Sydney C., Lee A. Wallace Jr., Margie Riddle Bearss, eds. *The Atlanta Papers.* Dayton, Ohio: Morningside Bookshop, 1980.

Key, William. *The Battle of Atlanta and the Georgia Campaign.* New York: Twayne, 1958.

King, Spencer. *Sound of Drums.* Macon, Ga.: Mercer University Press, 1984.

Korn, Jerry. *Pursuit to Appomattox: The Last Battles.* The Civil War. Alexandria, Va.: Time-Life Books, 1987.

————. *War on the Mississippi: Grant's Vicksburg Campaign.* The Civil War. Alexandria, Va.: Time-Life Books, 1987.

Krick, Robert K. *Lee's Colonels: A Biographical Register of the Field Officers of the Army of Northern Virginia.* Dayton, Ohio: Morningside House, 1992.

Kurtz, Wilbur G. *The Atlanta Cyclorama: The Story of the Famed Battle of Atlanta.* Atlanta: City of Atlanta, 1954.

Laine, Gary J., and Morris M. Penny. *Law's Alabama Brigade in the War between the Union and the Confederacy.* Shippensburg, Pa.: White Mane, 1996.

Lawliss, Chuck. *The Civil War Source Book.* New York: Harmony Books, 1991.

Lawrence, Alexander A. *A Present for Mr. Lincoln: The Story of Savannah from Secession to Sherman.* Macon, Ga.: Ardivan Press, 1961.

Leech, Margaret. *Reveille in Washington, 1860–1865.* New York: Harper and Brothers, 1941.

Lewis, Lloyd. *Sherman: Fighting Prophet.* New York: Harcourt, Brace, 1932.

Linderman, Gerald F. *Embattled Courage: The Experience of Combat in the American Civil War.* New York: Free Press, 1987.

Logsdon, David R., ed. *Eyewitnesses at the Battle of Franklin.* Nashville, Tenn.: Kettle Mills, 1991.

Longacre, Edward G. *Gentleman and Soldier: The Extraordinary Life of General Wade Hampton.* Nashville, Tenn.: Rutledge Hill, 2003.

Losson, Christopher. *Tennessee's Forgotten Warrior: Frank Cheatham and His Confederate Division.* Knoxville: University of Tennessee Press, 1989.

McCaffrey, James M. *This Band of Heroes: Granbury's Texas Brigade, C.S.A.* College Station: Texas A&M Press, 1996.

McCarley, J. Britt. *The Atlanta Campaign.* Atlanta: Cherokee, 1989.

McDonough, James Lee, and Thomas L. Connelly. *Five Tragic Hours: The Battle of Franklin.* Knoxville: University of Tennessee Press, 1983.

McElroy, John. *This Was Andersonville.* Edited by Roy Meredith. New York: McDowell, Obolensky, 1957.

McMurry, Richard M. *Atlanta 1864: Last Chance for the Confederacy.* Lincoln: University of Nebraska Press, 2000.

———. *John Bell Hood and the War for Southern Independence.* Lincoln: University of Nebraska Press, 1982.

McPherson, James M. *Abraham Lincoln and the Second American Revolution.* New York: Oxford University Press, 1991.

———. *Battle Cry of Freedom: The Civil War Era.* Oxford: Oxford University Press, 1988.

———. *Drawn with the Sword: Reflections on the American Civil War.* New York: Oxford University Press, 1996.

———. *What They Fought For: 1861–1865.* Baton Rouge: Louisiana University Press, 1994.

McWhiney, Grady. *Braxton Bragg and Confederate Defeat.* New York: Columbia University Press, 1969.

McWhiney, Grady, and Perry D. Jamieson. *Attack and Die: Civil War Military Tactics and the Southern Heritage.* Tuscaloosa: University of Alabama Press, 1990.

Maley, Dan, ed. *Sherman's March to the Sea.* Macon, Ga.: Macon Telegraph, 1989.

Marszalek, John F. *Sherman: A Soldier's Passion for Order.* New York: Free Press, 1993.

Martin, David. *Vicksburg Campaign.* New York: Gallery Books, 1990.

Marvel, William. *Andersonville: The Last Depot.* Chapel Hill: University of North Carolina Press, 1994.

Meade, Robert D. *Judah P. Benjamin: Confederate Statesman.* New York: Oxford University Press, 1943.

Miers, Earl S. *The General Who Marched to Hell: Sherman and the Southern Campaign.* New York: Curtis Brown, 1951.

———. *The Great Rebellion.* New York: World, 1958.

———. *The Web of Victory: Grant at Vicksburg.* Baton Rouge: Louisiana State University Press, 1955.

Miles, Jim. *Fields of Glory: A History and Tour Guide of the Atlanta Campaign.* Nashville, Tenn.: Rutledge Hill, 1989.

———. *Piercing the Heartland: A History and Tour Guide of the Fort Donelson, Shiloh, and Perryville Campaigns.* Nashville, Tenn.: Rutledge Hill, 1991.

———. *To the Sea: A History and Tour Guide of Sherman's March.* Nashville, Tenn.: Rutledge Hill, 1989.

Miller, Francis T. *The Photographic History of the Civil War: The Cavalry.* 10 vols. New York: Castle, 1957.

Mitchell, Ella. *History of Washington County, Georgia.* Atlanta: Cherokee, 1973.

Mitchell, Reid. *Civil War Soldiers: Their Expectations and Their Experiences.* New York: Viking Penguin, 1988.

Moore, Mark A. *Moore's Historical Guide to the Battle of Bentonville.* Campbell, Calif.: Savas, 1996.

Neely, Mark E., Jr. *The Last Best Hope of Earth: Abraham Lincoln and the Promise of America.* Cambridge, Mass.: Harvard University Press, 1993.

Nevin, David. *Sherman's March: Atlanta to the Sea.* The Civil War. Alexandria, Va.: Time-Life Books, 1986.

Nolan, Alan T. *Lee Considered: General Robert E. Lee and Civil War History.* Chapel Hill: University of North Carolina Press, 1991.

Northern, William J., ed. *Men of Mark in Georgia: A Complete and Elaborate History of the State from Its Settlement to the Present Time, Chiefly Told in Biographies and Autobiographies of the Most Eminent Men of Each Period of Georgia's Progress and Development.* 7 vols. Spartanburg, S.C.: Reprint Company, 1974.

Oates, Stephen B. *With Malice toward None: The Life of Abraham Lincoln.* New York: Harper and Row, 1977.

Owen, Richard, and James Owen. *Generals at Rest.* Shippensburg, Pa.: White Mane, 1997.

Owsley, Frank Lawrence. *States Rights in the Confederacy.* 1925. Reprint, Gloucester, Mass.: Peter Smith, 1961.

Paludan, Phillip Shaw. *The Presidency of Abraham Lincoln.* Lawrence: University Press of Kansas, 1994.

Parks, Joseph H. *General Edmund Kirby Smith, C.S.A.* Baton Rouge: Louisiana State University Press, 1954.

————. *General Leonidas Polk, C.S.A.: The Fighting Bishop.* Baton Rouge: Louisiana State University Press, 1962, 1990.

Parrish, Michael T. *Richard Taylor: Soldier Prince of Dixie.* Chapel Hill: University of North Carolina Press, 1992.

Parrish, Michael T., and Robert M. Willingham Jr. *Confederate Imprints: A Bibliography of Southern Publications from Secession to Surrender.* Austin, Tex.: Jenkins, and Katonah, N.Y.: Gary A. Foster, [ca. 1984].

Pemberton, John C. *Pemberton: Defender of Vicksburg.* Chapel Hill: University of North Carolina Press, 1942.

Perret, Geoffrey. *Ulysses S. Grant: Soldier and President.* New York: Random House, 1997.

Philips, Herb, *The Battle of Champion Hill, May 16, 1863.* Edwards, Miss.: privately printed, n.d.

Phillips, Charles, and Alan Axelrod, eds. *My Brother's Face.* San Francisco: Chronicle Books, 1993.

Piston, William Garrett. *Lee's Tarnished Lieutenant: James Longstreet and His Place in Southern History.* Athens: University of Georgia Press, 1987.

Purdue, Howard, and Elizabeth Purdue. *Pat Cleburne: Confederate General.* Hillsboro, Tex.: Hill Junior College Press, 1973.

Ramage, James A. *Rebel Raider: The Life of General John Hunt Morgan.* Lexington: University Press of Kentucky, 1986.

Rand, Clayton. *Sons of the South.* New York: Holt, Rinehart and Winston, 1961.

Rawley, James A. *Turning Points of the Civil War.* Lincoln: University of Nebraska Press, 1966.

Reed, John Shelton, and Dale Volberg Reed. *1001 Things Everyone Should Know about the South.* New York: Doubleday, 1996.

Robertson, James I., Jr., ed. *An Index-Guide to the Southern Historical Society Papers, 1876–1959.* Millwood, N.Y.: Kraus International, ca. 1980.

———. *Tenting Tonight: The Soldier's Life.* The Civil War. Alexandria, Va.: Time-Life Books, 1984.

Rogers, James A. *Richard Furman: Life and Legacy.* Macon, Ga.: Mercer University Press, 1985.

Rogers, William Warren. *Thomas County during the Civil War.* Tallahassee: Florida State University Press, 1964.

Sandburg, Carl. *Abraham Lincoln.* 6 vols. New York: Charles Scribner's Sons, 1926.

Savas, Theodore P., and David A. Woodbury. *The Campaign for Atlanta and Sherman's March to the Sea.* Campaign Chronicles, vol. 1. Campbell, Calif.: Savas Woodbury, 1992.

Scaife, William R. *The Campaign for Atlanta.* Atlanta: Privately printed, 1990.

———. *Order of Battle: Federal and Confederate Forces Engaged in the Campaign for Atlanta.* Saline, Mich.: McNaughton and Gunn, 1992.

Schultz, Duane. *The Most Glorious Fourth: Vicksburg and Gettysburg, July 4th, 1863.* New York: W. W. Norton, 2002.

Shea, William L., and Earl J. Hess. *Pea Ridge: Civil War Campaign in the West.* Chapel Hill: University of North Carolina Press, 1992.

Shea, William L., and Terrence J. Winschel. *Vicksburg Is the Key: The Struggle for the Mississippi River.* Lincoln: University of Nebraska Press, 2003.

Shryock, Richard H. *Georgia and the Union in 1850.* Durham, N.C.: Duke University Press, 1926.

Sifakis, Stewart. *Compendium of the Confederate Armies: Florida and Arkansas.* New York: Facts on File, 1992.

———. *Compendium of the Confederate Armies: South Carolina and Georgia.* New York: Facts on File, 1995.

———. *Who Was Who in the Civil War.* New York: Fact on File, 1988.

Simms, Kristina. *Macon: Georgia's Central City.* Chatsworth, Calif.: Windsor, 1989.

Simpson, Brooks D. *Ulysses S. Grant: Triumph over Adversity, 1822–1865.* New York: Houghton Mifflin, 2000.

Simpson, Brooks D., and Jean V. Berlin. *Sherman's Civil War: Selected Correspondence of William T. Sherman, 1860–1865.* Chapel Hill: University of North Carolina Press, 1999.

Smith, Timothy B. *Champion Hill: Decisive Battle for Vicksburg.* New York: Savas Beatie LLC, 2004.

Stephens, Robert Grier, Jr., ed. *Intrepid Warrior: Clement Anselm Evans*. Dayton, Ohio: Morningside House, 1992.

Stevens, Joseph E. *1863: The Rebirth of a Nation*. New York: Bantam, 1999.

Stockdale, Paul H. *The Death of an Army: The Battle of Nashville and Hood's Retreat*. Murfreesboro, Tenn.: Southern Heritage Press, 1992.

Strayer, Larry R., and Richard A. Baumgartner. *Echoes of Battle: The Atlanta Campaign*. Huntington, W.Va.: Blue Acorn, 1991.

————. *Kennesaw Mountain: June 1864*. Huntington, W.Va.: Blue Acorn, 1998.

Street, James, Jr. *The Struggle for Tennessee: Tupelo to Stones River*. The Civil War. Alexandria, Va.: Time-Life Books, 1985.

Swanberg, W. A. *First Blood: The Story of Fort Sumter*. New York: Charles Scribner's Sons, 1957.

Sword, Wiley. *Embrace an Angry Wind*. New York: Harper Collins, 1992.

Symonds, Craig L. *Joseph E. Johnston: A Civil War Biography*. New York: W. W. Norton, 1992.

————. *Stonewall of the West: Patrick Cleburne and the Civil War*. Lawrence: University Press of Kansas, 1997.

Thomas, Dean S. *Cannons: An Introduction to Civil War Artillery*. Gettysburg, Pa.: Thomas, 1985.

Thomas, Emory M. *Robert E. Lee: A Biography*. New York: W. W. Norton, 1995.

Thomas, Hugh. *The Slave Trade*. New York: Simon and Schuster, 1997.

Trotter, William R. *Silk Flags and Cold Steel: The Civil War in North Carolina: The Piedmont*. Winston-Salem, N.C.: John F. Blair, 1988.

Trudeau, Noah A. *Out of the Storm: The End of the Civil War, April–June 1865*. New York: Little, Brown, 1994.

Tucker, Phillip T. *The South's Finest: The First Missouri Confederate Brigade from Pea Ridge to Vicksburg*. Shippensburg, Pa.: White Mane, 1993.

Turner, George E. *Victory Rode the Rails: The Strategic Place of the Railroads in the Civil War*. 1953. Reprint, Lincoln: University of Nebraska Press, 1992.

Vandiver, Frank E. *Their Tattered Flags: The Epic of the Confederacy*. College Station: Texas A&M University Press, 1970.

Warner, Ezra J. *Generals in Blue: Lives of the Union Commanders*. Baton Rouge: Louisiana State University Press, 1964.

————. *Generals in Gray: Lives of the Confederate Commanders*. Baton Rouge: Louisiana State University Press, 1959.

Waugh, John C. *The Class of 1846*. New York: Warner, 1994.

Weitz, Mark A. *A Higher Duty: Desertion among Georgia Troops during the Civil War*. Lincoln: University of Nebraska Press, 2000.

Wellman, Manly W. *Giant in Gray: A Biography of Wade Hampton of South Carolina*. 1949. Reprint, Dayton, Ohio: Morningside Bookshop, 1988.

Wensyel, James W. *Appomattox: The Passing of the Armies*. Shippensburg, Pa.: White Mane, 2000.

Wert, Jeffry D. *General James Longstreet: The Confederacy's Most Controversial Soldier*. New York: Simon and Schuster, 1993.

Wheeler, Richard. *The Siege of Vicksburg*. New York: Thomas Y. Crowell, 1978.

Wiley, Bell I. *The Life of Billy Yank: The Common Soldier of the Union.* Baton Rouge: Louisiana State University Press, 1951.

———. *The Life of Johnny Reb: The Common Soldier of the Confederacy.* Baton Rouge: Louisiana State University Press, 1943.

Williams, T. Harry. *Lincoln and His Generals.* 1952. Reprint, New York: Dorset, 1989.

Wills, Brian S. *A Battle from the Start: The Life of Nathan Bedford Forrest.* New York: Harper Collins, 1992.

Wilson, Charles R., and William Ferris. *Encyclopedia of Southern Culture.* Chapel Hill: University of North Carolina Press, 1989.

Wilson, Douglas L. *Honors Voice: The Transformation of Abraham Lincoln.* New York: Alfred A. Knopf, 1998.

Wink, Jay. *April 1865: The Month That Saved America.* New York: Harper Collins, 2001.

Woodhead, Henry, ed. *Echoes of Glory: Arms and Equipment of the Confederacy.* Alexandria, Va.: Time-Life Books, 1991.

———, ed. *Echoes of Glory: Arms and Equipment of the Union.* Alexandria, Va.: Time-Life Books, 1991.

Woodworth, Steven E. *Jefferson Davis and His Generals: The Failure of Confederate Command in the West.* Lawrence: University Press of Kansas, 1990.

Wyeth, John Allan. *That Devil Forrest: Life of General Nathan Bedford Forrest.* Baton Rouge: Louisiana State University Press, 1989.

Young, Ida, Julius Gholson, and Clara Nell Hargrove. *History of Macon, Georgia, 1823–1949.* Macon, Ga.: Lyon, Marshall and Brooks, 1950.

Articles and Parts of Books

Barton, Dick. "Charge at Big Black River." *America's Civil War,* September 1999, 54–61.

Bearss, E. C. "Disaster in Mississippi: The Vicksburg Campaign." *Civil War* 64 (October 1997): 12–52.

Beronius, George. "Joe Johnston's Last Charge." *Civil War Times* 35, no. 2 (1996): 44–53.

Bonner, James C. "David R. Snelling: A Story of Desertion and Defection in the Civil War." *Georgia Review* 10, no. 3 (Fall 1956): 275–82.

Boswell, E. M. "Rebel Religion." *Civil War Illustrated Times* 11, no. 6 (1972): 26–34.

Bradley, Mark L. "Last Stand in the Carolinas: The Battle of Bentonville." *Blue and Gray Magazine* 13, no. 2 (1995): 8–23.

———. "Old Reliable's Finest Hour: The Battle of Averysboro, North Carolina." *Blue and Gray Magazine* 16, no. 2 (1998): 6–20, 52–57.

Brawner, Robert L. "Bloody Footprints in the Snow: Mercer's Brigade, April 28, 1864–April 25, 1865." *Confederate Veteran* (March–April 1989): 6–11.

Brennan, Patrick. "The Battle of Franklin." *North and South* 8, no. 1 (2005): 26–46.

Bruyn, DeWitt. "Major L. C. Bryan." *Confederate Veteran* 19 (1911): 130–31.

Carmichael, Peter. "Lee's Quest for the Battle of Annihilation." *North and South* 3 (June 2000): 53–59.

Cates, C. Pat. "From Santa Rosa Island to Bentonville: The First Confederate Regiment Georgia Volunteers." *Civil War Regiments* 1, no. 4 (1991): 42–73.

Catton, Bruce. "Prison Camps of the Civil War." *Civil War Chronicles* 2, no. 2 (1992): 46–59.

Cozzens, Peter. "The Last Hurrah: Bragg and Chattanooga." *Civil War Magazine* 50 (April 1995): 16–24.

Davis, Stephen. "Atlanta Campaign: Hood Fights Desperately." *Blue and Gray* 6, no. 6 (1989): 8–62.

Evans, David. "The Atlanta Campaign: A Special Issue." *Civil War Times* 28, no. 4 (1989): 12–61.

Fitzgerald, William S. "Clash of Genius: Forrest vs. Wilson in the Nashville Campaign." *Confederate Veteran* (January–February 1992): 23–32.

Frazier, Donald S. "Texas General Hiram Granbury." *America's Civil War,* January 1997, 12–20.

Gallagher, Gary W. "The Generalship of Robert E. Lee." *North and South* 3, no. 5 (2000): 10–24.

Hart, B. H. Liddell. "Sherman: Modern Warrior." *Civil War Chronicles* 2, no. 2 (1992): 114–22.

Hassler, William W. "Patrick Cleburne: 'Stonewall of the West.'" *Civil War Illustrated Times* 10, no. 10 (1972): 4–9.

Henderson, Rosemary L. "Greenwood Plantation Families of Thomas County, Georgia." *Origins* 1, no. 1 (1990):8–9.

Hopkins, Charles Ferren. "Hell and the Survivor." *Civil War Chronicles* 1, no. 2 (1992): 36–51.

Julian, Allen P. "The Siege of Fort Pulaski." In *Fort Pulaski and the Defense of Savannah,* 1–14. Yorktown, Va.: Eastern Acorn Press, 1985.

Keenan, Jerry. "Fighting with Forrest in the Tennessee Winter." *America's Civil War,* November 1995, 48–53.

Kelly, Dennis. "Atlanta Campaign: Mountains to Pass, a River to Cross, and the Battle of Kennesaw Mountain." *Blue and Gray Magazine* 6, no. 5 (1989): 8–60.

Ladd, James R. "From Atlanta to the Sea." *Civil War Chronicles* 2, no. 2 (1993): 4–11.

McDonough, James Lee. "The Battle of Franklin." *Blue and Gray Magazine* 2, no. 1 (1984): 18–39.

McMurry, Richard M. "Atlanta Campaign: Rocky Face to the Dallas Line, the Battles of May 1864." *Blue and Gray Magazine* 7, no. 4 (1989): 10–62.

McPherson, James M. "A War That Never Goes Away." *Civil War Chronicles* 1, no. 2 (1992): 5–10.

Mosser, Jeffrey M. "I Shall Make Him Remember This Insult." *Civil War Times* 32, no. 1 (1993): 24.

Neul, Robert C. "Battle Most Desperate and Bloody." *America's Civil War,* January 1995, 30–36.

Newton, Steven H. "Joe Johnston: Formidable Only in Flight?" *North and South* 33, no. 4 (2000): 43–56.

Noblitt, Phil. "Pickett's Mill." *America's Civil War,* January 1996, 39–44, 95.

Northern, William J. "George Anderson Mercer." In Northern, ed., *Men of Mark in Georgia,* 4:108–12.

———. "Hugh Weedon Mercer." In Northern, ed., *Men of Mark in Georgia* 3:379–81.

Roth, David E., ed. "The Battle of Perryville." *Blue and Gray Magazine* 1, no. 2 (1983): 21–44.

Smith, David M. "Too Little Too Late at Vicksburg." *America's Civil War,* May 2000, 38–45.

Stanberry, Jim. "A Failure of Command: The Confederate Loss of Vicksburg." *Civil War Regiments* 2, no. 1 (1992): 36–68.

Stephenson, Jon. "Literal Hill Of Death." *America's Civil War,* November 1991, 23–29.

Thomas, Gary, and Richard Andrew. "Houses of Misery and Hope." *Civil War Magazine* 59 (December 1996): 10–59.

Wilson, Thelma. "Fort Valley: Its Century of Progress." *Georgia Review* 12 (Fall 1958): 337–38.

Winschel, Terrence J. "The Guns at Champion Hill (Part II)." *Journal of Confederate History* 6 (1990): 94–105.

Theses, Dissertations, and Unpublished Sources

Braswell Family History, n.d., in author's possession.

Clauss, Errol MacGregor. "The Atlanta Campaign: 18 July–September 1864." Ph.D. diss., Emory University, 1965.

Farrant, Don. "Colonel William Barkuloo: His Story." Unpublished document. December 11, 1992. In the author's files.

Garman, James E. "Materials for the Writing of Histories of Georgia Confederate Regiments: A Bibliographical Study." Master's thesis, Emory University, 1961.

House, Myron Wade. "History of the First Volunteer Regiment of Georgia, 1864–1865." Master's thesis, Emory University, 1973.

Jackson, Diane, to author, May 29, 1992; June 17, 1992. Personal communications regarding the history of William Barkuloo after the Civil War. Jackson is a reference assistant at the Brunswick–Glynn County (Ga.) Regional Library.

Joiner, Herbert. "History of Oak Grove Cemetery." 1977. Brunswick–Glynn County (Ga.) Regional Library.

Methvin, John J. "The Autobiography of John Jasper Methvin." 1930. Private collection.

Methvin, John J. "Hotch-Potch." The handwritten notes of John Methvin, September 1, 1933. Private collection.

Smith, Gordon B. "The Fifty-seventh Regiment, Georgia Volunteer Infantry, Confederate States Army." Working paper in the author's files, April 26, 1976, Savannah, Ga.

Interviews

Braswell, Mattie Rowland. By author. Fort Valley, Ga., 1969.

Braswell, Robert S., III. By author. Waco, Tex., 1992, 1998.

Braswell-Holman, Carolyn. By author. Albany, Ga., 1998.

Mathews, Robert Braswell. By author. Los Angeles, 1998.
Platt, Shirley. By author. North Andover, Mass., 1992.
Smith, Gordon. By author. Savannah, Ga., 1992.
Stoll, Emily Ship. By author. Louisville, Ky., 1995.
Vinson, Charles. By author. Fort Valley, Ga., 1998.
Vinson, Frank. By author. Milledgeville, Ga., 1998.
Vinson-Oldham, Nell. By author. Lubbock, Tex., 1998.
Walker, Dorothy Mathews. By author. Monroe, Ga., 1998.
Williams, Reggie Mullis. By author. Waco, Tex., 1995.

Index

African Americans: roles of, in Union and Confederation armies, 31–32; and skirmish between Mercer's brigade and Union, 204

Allen, Joseph H. V., 127, 132, 240

Anderson, R. C., 104

Andersonville prison camp: "the Dead Line" of, 110–11; description of, 109–10; Fifty-seventh Georgia ordered to, 108, 109; Sherman's attempt to rescue Union prisoners at, 172

Army of East Tennessee (Confederacy): Fifty-seventh Georgia joins, 24; geographic area of defense of, 27; and invasion of Kentucky, 31–51; moved to defend Louisville, 45; organization of, 32–34; renamed Army of Tennessee, 57; and strategy at end of Kentucky campaign, 46–51. *See also* Army of Tennessee (Confederacy); Smith, Edmund Kirby

Army of Mississippi (Confederacy): and Battle of Perryville, 46–47; during early Kentucky campaign, 33, 39; moved to defend Louisville, 45; moved to Glasgow, 44; and strategy at end of Kentucky campaign, 46–49. *See also* Bragg, Braxton; Polk, Leonidas

Army of Northern Virginia (Confederacy): Heth on transfer back to, 55–56; surrender of, 241; under siege along Richmond-Petersburg line, 223–24, 229, 240; Union Army of the Potomac to attack, 115. *See also* Lee, Robert E.

Army of Tennessee (Confederacy): Army of East Tennessee renamed, 57; Atlanta campaign preparations by, 121–22; and Battle of Atlanta, 158–68; during Battle of Bentonville, 234–39; during Battle of Franklin, 193–201;

casualties of, suffered during retreat, 217, 221; during Chattahoochee engagement, 140–46; Chickamauga Creek victory of, 115; Hood replaces Johnston as head of, 147–55; Johnston's efforts to build up, 116; Johnston's surrender of, 242; Johnston takes command of, in North Carolina, 228; Johnston takes command of, in north Georgia, 115; during Kennesaw Mountain engagement, 128–29, 136; loss of faith by, in Hood, 200–201, 211, 221–22; needed in North Carolina to help R. E. Lee, 224; retreat of, from Tennessee, 209–17; retreat of, into Atlanta, 156–58; shattered by Thomas's forces, 207–8; Sherman captures Atlanta and withdraws from, 180–81. *See also* Army of East Tennessee (Confederacy)

Army of Tennessee (Union), 119, 131, 151, 158, 161–68, 173–75, 178. *See also* Howard, O. O.; McPherson, James Birdseye

Army of the Cumberland (Union), 63, 134–36, 151–54, 175, 178. *See also* Thomas, George

Army of the Potomac (Union), 115, 229, 240–41

Aspinwall, William, 83–84

Atlanta, Battle of, 156–68, 271n14

Atlanta campaign: Atlanta captured by Sherman at end of, 180–81; and Battle of Atlanta, 156–68, 271n14; and Battle of Ezra Church, 172; and Battle of Jonesboro, 174–81; and Battle of Peachtree Creek, 152–55; and fighting along banks of Chattahoochee River, 137–46; Hell Hole of, 123–27; and Kennesaw Mountain, 128–36;

Atlanta campaign (*continued*)
  preparations by Union and
  Confederate armies for, 115–22;
  replacement of Johnston by Hood
  during, 147–55; Union and
  Confederate armies meet in, 124–27

Braswell, William ("Billy"): death of, in battle, 154, 155, 156; early life of, 3; enlists in Governor Brown's Riflemen, 6; incorporated into First Confederate Regiment Georgia Volunteers, 15; motivations of, for enlisting, 4–6; reunited with brothers, 123, 151; shipped to Florida (1861), 15

Breckinridge, John C., 241, 242

Broadfoot, Charles, 235

Brown, Joseph Emerson, 5

Brunswick Riflemen, 16

Buell, Don Carlos: during Kentucky campaign, 28, 45, 46, 47, 49–50; relieved of duty by Union army, 63

Camp Davis (Ala.), 25

Camp Dick Robinson, 48

Camp Randolph, 19, 23

cannon fodder, 74

Cantrell, Oscar Alexander, 50

Carswell, Nathan, 67

Castel, Albert, 165

Chamberlin, William H., 164

Champion Hill, Battle of, 70–84

Chattahoochee River engagement, 137–46

Chattanooga (Tenn.), 23–25, 28–29

Cheatham, Benjamin Franklin: during Battle of Bentonville, 230; during battles of Spring Hill and Franklin, 194, 195, 197, 200; on need to end "French leave" of men, 226–27

Civil War: Atlanta campaign of, 115–81, 271n14; early days of, 7–8; factors leading to, 3–5; Kentucky campaign of, 28–51; military casualties during, 242; North Carolina campaign of, 221–41; and surrender of Johnston, 242; and surrender of R. E. Lee, 241; Tennessee campaign of, 185–217; Vicksburg campaign of, 55–94

Clark, Walter, A.: on Battle of Bentonville, 236, 237–38; on deterioration of

Confederate army's conditions, 223; on Forrest and rear guard, 214–15; on good fortune of Mercer's brigade, 192; on hardship of cold weather, 206; on Hood's poor strategy, 221; post–Civil War life of, 248–49; sad homecoming of, 226; on troop panic during Kennesaw Mountain engagement, 133

Cleburne, Patrick: battle flag of, 233; during Battle of Atlanta, 124–25, 157–58, 159, 165–68; during Battle of Franklin, 195, 197, 199; during Battle of Jonesboro, 174–76, 178–79; death and burial of, 200, 202; during Kentucky campaign, 34, 40, 45; Mercer's brigade assigned to, 171–72; permits Olmstead to visit wife, 186

Colston, Raleigh E., 103, 104, 105, 106

Company F, Second Regiment, First Brigade (Georgia State Troops), 9–10

Confederacy: Conscription Act (1862) of, 13, 260n14, 261n4; Kentucky in hands of, 40, 43–44; poor conditions of, in 1862, 23; secession of, from United States, 5–6; surrender of, by R. E. Lee and Johnston, 241, 242

Confederate armies: in Atlanta campaign, 124–27; Battle of Atlanta losses of, 168; delusion and denial of, 170–72; Lee, R. E., accepts command over, 228; organization of, 8; preparation of, for Atlanta campaign, 115–22; straggling and desertions from, 55, 61–62, 64. *See also specific armies and regiments*

Confederate Ordnance Department, 32

Conscription Act (1862; Confederacy), 13, 260n14, 261n4

Cooper, Samuel, 112

Cox, Jacob D., 194

Cumberland Gap (Ky.), 28, 30, 31, 35–36

Cumming, Alfred, 73–74, 75, 82, 87

Davis, Edwin Tralona: on Battle of Atlanta, 170; in command of pioneer

Davis, Edwin Tralona (*continued*)
corps, 35; decision of, to enlist, 9; on
furlough, 16; on Mercer's brigade
assignment to Cleburne's division,
171–72; promotion of, to Company B
captain, 203; on shame of surrendering
colors, 93; wounding of, at Battle of
Champion Hill, 81
Davis, Jefferson (Confederate president):
appoints Johnston head of
Confederate army, 115; consults with
Hood regarding Sherman's
movements, 187–88; impatience of,
with Johnston, 130–31; on importance
of holding Kentucky, 28; Johnston
convinces, to negotiate for peace, 241;
orders of, to hold Vicksburg, 71;
relationship between, Hood, and
Johnston, 149–50; replaces Johnston
with Hood, 147–48; support of, for
Bragg, 56; transfers Hardee to
Charleston, 186; on Union's strategy in
Tennessee, 63
Davis, Jefferson C. (Union general), 233
Davis, John M., 169–70
"Dead Line" (Andersonville), 110–11
desertions, 55, 61–62, 64; as "French
leave," 226–27
disease: and Andersonville overcrowding,
110, 111; casualties due to, 11; during
early Kentucky campaign, 34–35;
during late Kentucky campaign, 49;
during Vicksburg campaign, 66–67,
90–91
dysentery, 11
Dyson, Thomas Jefferson, 18, 19, 76, 83

Eighth Battalion, Georgia Militia, 16
Evans, Clement, 11
Everett, J. Abb, 8
Everett, James, 128
Everett Guards (Confederacy): as Fort
Valley Infantry (Confederacy), 98–101;
joins First Independent Battalion, 8;

Long elected captain of, 8;
reorganized as Fort Valley Infantry, 16
Ezra Church, Battle of, 172

Fifty-fourth Regiment Georgia Volunteer
Infantry: attempted mutiny of, 105;
incorporated into Mercer's brigade,
117; separated from Mercer's brigade,
240. *See also* Fifty-seventh Regiment
Georgia Volunteer Infantry
Fifty-seventh Regiment Georgia
Volunteer Infantry: Battle of Atlanta
losses of, 168; Battle of Champion
Hill movements of, 74–84; Battle of
Vicksburg movements of, 88–94;
crossing of, into Tennessee (1864),
185–86; delusion and denial of
soldiers in, 169–72; during early
Kentucky campaign, 32–36; Fort
Valley Infantry ordered to rejoin,
100–101; impact of combat conditions
on, 94; incorporated into Mercer's
brigade, 117; increasing desertion
from, 55, 61–62; ordered back to
Savannah, 104; ordered to advance to
Chattanooga, 24–25; ordered to
Andersonville prison camp, 108, 109;
ordered to Camp Randolph, 19, 23;
ordered to Vicksburg, 63–64;
organization of, 18; quelled mutiny of,
105–6; reassigned to Army of
Tennessee, 57; reorganized into First
Volunteer Regiment of Georgia, 240;
Savannah Republican statement of
loyalty by members of, 107–8;
Sherman's march to the sea affects
homes of, 189–91, 273n17; sullied
reputation of, 105–6, 107–8; weakened
by missing officers and companies,
103–4. *See also* Mercer's brigade
(Confederacy)
Fifty-sixth Regiment Georgia Volunteer
Infantry, 74–84
Fingal, 11

First Confederate Regiment Georgia
Volunteer Infantry, 15–16, 123,
152–54, 156, 268n1 (ch. 18)
First Independent Battalion, First
Brigade (Georgia State Troops), 8
First Regiment Georgia Volunteer
Infantry (Olmstead's): in Colston's
brigade, 103; and defense of Fort
Pulaski, 5, 12–13; incorporated into
Mercer's brigade, 117; and prisoner
exchange at Johnson's Island Prison,
268n7 (ch. 18). *See also* Mercer's
brigade (Confederacy); Olmstead,
Charles H.
Fitzpatrick, Francis, 98
Five Forks, Battle of, 240
Fontaine, Felix Gregory de, 10
Forrest, Nathan Bedford: during Battle of
Franklin, 197, 200; command of rear
guard by, during Hood's retreat,
211–17; Olmstead on interview with,
205–6; ordered to march to join
Hood's troops, 207–8, 209; rear guard
organized by, 210–12; Thomas on
capabilities of troops under, 222
Fort Bartow, 103, 106–7
Fort Donelson, 23, 27
Fort Hatteras, 7
Fort Pulaski, 5, 12, 13
Fort Valley, city of, 259nn2–3 (ch. 1),
259n8
Fort Valley Companies, 7
Fort Valley Infantry (Confederacy), 16,
18, 77, 89, 98–101, 245–46; as Everett
Guards, 8, 16
Fowler, John B., 67–68
Franklin, Battle of, 193–201
"French leave," 226–27. *See also*
desertions
Fuller, David, 37, 38, 48–49

Georgia Military Institute, 141–42
Georgia State Troops. *See specific*
regiments and brigades

Gettysburg, Battle of, 62, 198–99
Gordon, John, 243
Governor Brown's Riflemen, 6, 7, 15
Grant, Ulysses S.: appointment of, as
head of Union army, 115; arrival and
march of, through Mississippi, 70–71;
Battle of Champion Hill strategies of,
75; early strategies of, 12; Fort
Donelson captured by, 23; respect of,
for Johnston, 87–88; Sherman's letter
to, about Georgia, 187; surrender of
R. E. Lee to, 240–41; Vicksburg siege
by and surrender to, 86–94
Guyton, Cincinnatus: background and
character of, 18; Battle of Atlanta
report of, 167–68; during Battle of
Vicksburg, 89–90; duty of, as Georgia
state senator, 103; post–Civil War life
of, 249; regiment's colors hidden in
blanket of, 93

Hallek, Henry W., 25
Hammond, Paul, 37–38, 49
Hampton, Wade, 230, 231–32
Hardee, William J.: baptized by Polk, 128;
during Battle of Atlanta, 158–60, 161,
165–66, 271n14; during Battle of
Bentonville, 231–32, 234–36; during
Battle of Jonesboro, 173–76, 178–81;
during Battle of Peachtree Creek,
151–55; character of, 116; Hood
chosen over, 148, 151, 152; Olmstead's
objection to order of, 142–43;
Savannah evacuated by, 211;
transferred to Charleston (1864), 186
Harris, Philo, 77
Harris, Robert H., 93, 106–7
Harrison, Thomas J., 214
Harvey, Stan C., 179
Hatch, Edward, 212
Hawes, Richard C., 46
Hell Hole (Atlanta campaign), 123–27
Henry, Gustavus Adolphus, 56
Henry, Robert Selph, 51

Heth, Henry: during early Kentucky campaign, 32; moves troops to defend Kentucky, 45; ordered to join E. K. Smith in Lexington, 41; transferred to Army of Northern Virginia, 55–56

Hilzheim, A. M., 133

Holly, William, Sr. ("Will"), 8

Hood, John Bell: army's loss of faith in, 200–201, 211, 221–22; baptized by Polk, 128; Battle of Atlanta strategies of, 157–68; during Battle of Franklin, 193–201; during Battle of Peachtree Creek, 152–55; character of, 116, 150; confronts Sherman's troops around Atlanta, 173, 175–76; consults J. Davis on Sherman's progress, 187–88; criticizes Johnston, 147; Davis, Jefferson, declines to remove, from command, 185–86; failure of, to contain Sherman, 188–92; Forrest's forced march to join, 207–8, 209; Johnston replaced by, 147–48; paralyzed actions of, following Battle of Franklin, 203–4; relationship between, Johnston, and J. Davis, 149–50; requests relief from command, 222; retreat of, during Tennessee campaign, 209–17; Sherman captures Atlanta and withdraws from troops of, 180–81; Thomas attacks and shatters forces under, 207–8; tragic frontal attack (Battle of Franklin) ordered by, 198–99

Howard, O. O.: and Battle of Bentonville, 229; and Battle of Jonesboro, 173–75, 178; at "Hell Hole," 124–25; with Hood at West Point, 150

Johnson, Andrew, 242

Johnson, James A. W., 32

Johnston, Joseph E.: appointment of, as head of Army of Tennessee, 115–16; on Army of Tennessee reaching North Carolina, 224; Atlanta campaign preparations of, 119–22; Battle of Bentonville strategies of, 229–39; cease-fire request of, to Sherman, 241; character of, 147; during Chattahoochee engagement, 140–46; Davis's impatience with, 130–31; Davis's ultimatum to and replacement of, 147–48; Grant's respect for, 87–88; informed of R. E. Lee's surrender, 241; during Kennesaw Mountain engagement, 128–29, 136; loss of friend (Polk), 128; ordered to take command in Mississippi, 71; orders of, to Pemberton on Vicksburg, 71, 72, 85; reappointed to Army of Tennessee command, 228; relationship between, J. Davis, and Hood, 147–50; retreat of, from Mississippi, 94; surrender of, 242

Jonesboro, Battle of, 174–81

Keen, John, 80–81, 86

Kennesaw Mountain, 128–36

Kentucky: Confederate lines of occupation in, 43–44; Hawes as governor of, 45–46; neutrality of people in, 43

Kentucky campaign: Fifty-seventh Georgia in, 32–36; four regiments together in, 32; inexperience of volunteers in, 37–38; and passage through Cumberland Gap, 28, 30, 31, 35–36; and retreat from Kentucky, 47–51; strategic importance of Chattanooga in, 23–25, 28–29; strategies leading to collapse of, 46–51

Kersh, Mariah Austin, 5–6, 7, 98, 99–100

Kirkpatrick, James, 255–57

Kuglar, Jim: on being fed by local citizens, 66; on collapse of Kentucky campaign, 50–51; on Cumberland Gap passage, 36, 40; on disease afflicting soldiers, 66–67; on early Kentucky campaign, 33; on Kentucky campaign orders, 47,

48; post–Civil War life of, 249–50; on Richmond battlefield scenes, 41, 42; on soldiers preying on citizens and blacks, 64–66; on suffering during late Kentucky campaign, 49, 50

Lauman, Jacob, 88–89
Leadbetter, Daniel, 32, 35, 37–38, 39, 41, 44, 47, 57
Lee, Robert E.: appointment of, as head of Confederate armies, 228; defense of Fort Pulaski by, 12; Mathew's honorable discharge signed by, 62; opinion of, on Hood's military abilities, 148; Pickett's Charge at Gettysburg ordered by, 198; surrender of, 241; under siege along Richmond-Petersburg line, 223–24, 229, 240. *See also* Army of Northern Virginia (Confederacy)
Lee, Stephen D.: and Atlanta campaign, 131, 173–76, 179, 180; and Battle of Champion Hill, 72, 73, 81; and siege of Vicksburg, 88; and Tennessee campaign, 194, 200, 209
Lewis, Thomas, 90
Lightburn, Andrew A. J., 132, 134
Lincoln, Abraham: appoints Grant as head of Union army, 115; assassination of, 241–42; Georgia response to election of, 5; inaugurated for second term, 229
Long, A. H., 8
Longley, Charles L., 77–78, 80
Loring, William, 71, 72, 78, 82, 128, 130
Love, Laura, 100, 101, 111, 112, 246, 248
Lovejoy's Station (Ga.), 179, 180, 187

Macon and Western Railroad, 172, 173, 178
malaria, 11
Massee, Tom, 6
Mathews, James N. (Fifty-seventh Georgia), 82

Mathews, James N. (Jeb Stuart's cavalry), 62
McClernand, John A., 74, 81, 86–87
McElroy, John, 110–11
McKinley, Archibald C.: description of, 32; post–Civil War life of, 250; relationship of, with Scott, 32, 82–83, 93–94, 225–26, 245
McPherson, James Birdseye, 75, 93, 119–20, 131, 152, 157–58, 161, 167, 271n27
measles, 11
Memoirs of General W. T. Sherman (Sherman), 125, 129, 168, 190–91
Mercer, George A.: on Battle of Jonesboro losses, 179; on defense of Savannah, 11; on exhausted state of Mercer's brigade, 121; on finding Union lines empty, 173; on heavy rain conditions, 128; on losses suffered by Mercer's brigade, 172; post–Civil War life of, 250; on problems facing Hardee's troops, 180; on quelled mutiny of Fifty-seventh Georgia, 105–6; relieved of command, 171
Mercer, Hugh Weedon: during Battle of Atlanta, 161–66, 168; and challenges of serving under Walker, 118–19; early life of, 116; ordered to join Johnston's army, 116–18; post–Civil War life of, 250; regional command of Savannah by, 103, 105; relieved of command, 171
Mercer's brigade (Confederacy): assigned to Cleburne's command, 171–72; attached to Walker's division, 120–21; during Battle of Atlanta, 156–68; during Battle of Bentonville, 233, 235–36, 238, 276n17; and Battle of Franklin aftermath, 202–3; during Battle of Jonesboro, 174–81; during Battle of Peachtree Creek, 154–55; in Chattahoochee River engagement, 137–46; consolidated with Palmer's Tennessee brigade, 211; delay of, getting to Battle of Franklin, 191–92,

Mercer's brigade (Confederacy) (*continued*)

202; difficult journey of, to Forrest's headquarters, 204–5; "French leave" taken by members of, 226–27; in Hell Hole engagement, 123–27; in Kennesaw Mountain engagement, 128–36; losses of, during forced march to join Hood's troops, 207–8; losses suffered by, 172, 179; official record (December 1864) of men present in, 221; as part of Forrest's rear guard, 212–17; railroad track ripped up by, 206; regiments composing, 117–18; return home of, following surrender, 243–46; skirmish of, with black Union soldiers, 204; Smith, James, given command of, 171, 203; travel of, to North Carolina, 224–27. *See also* Fifty-seventh Regiment Georgia Volunteer Infantry

Mercer University Cadets (Ga.), 9

Methvin, John J.: on death of brother, 177–78; enlistment of, to take place of captured brother, 104; furlough of, due to poor health, 221; on homecoming, 224; post–Civil War life of, 250–51; on Union troops retreating across Flint River, 175

Methvin, Thomas J., 104, 176–78

Methvin, William K., 104, 276n11

Military Division of the Mississippi (Union), 115

Military Division of the West (Confederacy), 186

Mims, Seaborn: during Battle of Champion Hill, 77; capture of, 143; furlough of, from Virginia, 16; inheritance of, from father, 100; during late Kentucky campaign, 48; post–Civil War life of, 251; recovery of, from wound, 97; reunited with nephews, 123

Mims, Williamson, 4, 97, 98–99, 100, 254

Montgomery, L. M., 92

Morgan, George W., 28, 45

Napier, Briggs, 156, 157

Nelson, William "Bull," 40

Nisbet, James Cooper, 150–51, 154, 159

North Carolina campaign: and Battle of Bentonville, 228–39, 276n17; and Battle of Five Forks, 240; Confederate troops called up for, 221–27; and surrender of Johnston, 242; and surrender of R. E. Lee, 240–41

Oatland Bridge, 106–7

Olmstead, Charles H.: on "barefoot brigade," 213; on Battle of Franklin aftermath, 202–3; on Battle of Jonesboro, 180; on Battle of Peachtree Creek, 153; on being part of Forrest's rear guard, 213–14, 216; on burning of supplies left by Hood, 214; on Chattahoochee River engagement, 142–43, 145, 146; on Confederate rations, 139–40; on crossing Tennessee River, 189; defense of Savannah by, 12; on delay of James Smith's brigade into Tennessee, 191–92; early life of, 141; on forced march by Forrest's troops, 207–8; on "French leave" problem, 226–27; on Guyton, 18; on Hell Hole engagement, 127; on interview with Forrest, 205–6; on loss of classmates and friends, 141–42; on miserable conditions of war, 212; objection of, to Hardee's order, 142–43; permitted to visit with wife, 186; post–Civil War life of, 251; recovery of, after Hood's retreat, 221; reflections of, on war, 224–25, 243, 257–58; on relationship between Johnston, J. Davis, and Hood, 149–50; on replacement of Johnston by Hood, 149; return home of, following surrender, 244; return of, to command of First Georgia Volunteers, 187; temporary command by, of Mercer's brigade, 172; on traveling through bad weather, 204–5; visit of, to mother-in-law, 224–25

Ordinance of Secession (Ga.), 5

Palmer, J. B., 211

Peachtree Creek, Battle of, 150–55

Peddy, George W.: on army's entrance into Lexington, 43; on Cumberland Gap passage, 39; on disease suffered by men, 34, 55

Peddy, Kittie, 34, 39

Pemberton, John: during Battle of Champion Hill, 63, 70, 71, 72–73, 75, 79, 82; during siege and surrender of Vicksburg, 85, 86, 91–92

Pickett's Charge (Battle of Gettysburg), 198

Pickett's Mill, 124–25

Polk, Leonidas, 45, 46, 121, 128, 202

Porter, David, 88

Port Royal (S.C.), 8, 11

"Preacher's Regiment" (Union), 76

Randolph, George W., 18

Ransom, John, 112

rations, Confederate, 139–40

Reed, Bessie, 156

Reed, William, 156–57

Richmond, Ky., battle scenes, 41–42

Rose Dew Island, 105–6

Sanford, S. P., 9

Savannah: during early days of Civil War, 10–11; Fifty-seventh Georgia ordered back to, 103; *Fingal* slips into, 11; Georgia State Troops defense of, 12–13; Hardee's evacuation of, 211;

and mutiny scheme of Confederate troops, 105–6; and Whitemarsh Island skirmish, 106

Savannah Republican statement of loyalty (Fifty-seventh Georgia soldiers), 107–8

Schofield, John: and Battle of Atlanta, 144, 151, 157; and Battle of Franklin, 193–94, 196, 200; and Battle of Jonesboro, 175; and Battle of Kennesaw, 136; on character of Hood, 150; and command of Army of Ohio, 119; critical crossing of, at Soap's Creek, 144; Sherman's dispatch to, on Battle of Bentonville, 239

Scott ("camp servant"): description of, 32; follows McKinley through Hood's advance and retreat, 225–26; friendship of, with McKinley, 245; nurses McKinley back to health, 82–83; post–Civil War life of, 251; taunted by Union troops, 93–94

secession, of Confederacy, 5–6

Second Regiment, First Brigade, Georgia State Troops, 17, 18. *See also* Fifty-seventh Regiment Georgia Volunteer Infantry

"see the elephant," 265n43

Sexton, James A., 196

Shellman, Allie, 213

Sherman, William T.: acceptance of Confederate surrender by, 242–43; assumption of command by, of Union forces in the West, 115; Atlanta captured by, 180–81; attempt of, to destroy Macon and Western Railroad, 172, 173, 178; Battle of Bentonville strategies of, 229–39; during Chattahoochee engagement, 140–46; Hood and J. Davis's strategies for containing, 187–88; and Johnston's cease-fire request, 241; Johnston's lost opportunity to defeat, 121–22; during Kennesaw Mountain engagement, 129–31, 136; letter of, to Grant on

Sherman, William T. (*continued*)
Georgia, 187; memoirs of, 125, 129,
168, 190–91; response of, to
Johnston's replacement by Hood, 150;
and Vicksburg campaign, 87, 91
Sherman's march, 23, 123–24, 188–91,
273n17
Shinholster, Captain, 139
Sixth Regiment Georgia Volunteers, 7, 16
slaves: "contraband of war" term applied
to escaped, 267n16; owned by
W. Mims, 254; picked on by
Confederate soldiers, 65–66; and
Thirteenth Amendment, 228–29. *See
also* Scott ("camp servant")
Slocum, Henry W., 229, 231
Smith, Edmund Kirby: and command of
the Trans-Mississippi, 56; during early
Kentucky campaign, 27–28, 29, 30,
33–34, 38, 39, 40; early life and
character of, 27; occupation line
orders of, 43–44; strategies of, during
end of Kentucky campaign, 46–51. *See
also* Army of East Tennessee
(Confederacy); Kentucky campaign
Smith, Giles A., 131–32
Smith, James Argyle, 171, 203, 232
Smith, John, 132
Smith, Morgan L., 131
Smith's brigade. *See* Mercer's brigade
(Confederacy)
Snelling, David, 190, 191, 252
South Carolina, 8, 11; secession of, 5
Stanley, David, 194–95
Steedman, James, 204
Stephenson, Phil, 161
Stevenson, Carter, 57, 63–64, 98; at Battle
of Champion Hill, 70–76 passim, 86;
during Kentucky campaign, 33, 39,
40, 45; organization of division of,
265n5
Stewart, Alexander P., 151–52, 173, 179,
180, 193; at Battle of Bentonville, 229,
231, 235, 236; at battles of Spring Hill

and Franklin, 194, 200; retreat of,
from Tennessee, 216
Stones River, Battle of, 70

Taylor, T. T., 133–34
Tennessee campaign: and Battle of
Franklin, 193–201; Hood's forces
shattered by Thomas during, 202–8;
Hood's retreat during, 209–17. *See
also* Hood, John Bell; Thomas, George
Thiot, Anna, 170
Thiot, Charles Henry: on concerns for
family during Sherman's march,
222–23; death of, 243–44; on hopes for
war to be over quickly, 144; on poor
health conditions, 137–38; on rumors
in camp, 170
Third Regiment Georgia Volunteers, 7
Thirteenth Amendment, 228–29
Thomas, George: and Battle of Atlanta,
158; and Battle of Franklin, 193; and
Battle of Jonesboro, 172–73, 176–81;
and Battle of Nashville, 204, 206–7;
and Battle of Peachtree Creek,
151–55; compliments of, regarding
Forrest's rear guard, 222; and Hood's
retreat from Tennessee, 209–17; and
north Georgia campaign, 119; transfer
of, to defend Tennessee, 188, 193
Tybee Island (Ga.), 12

Union army: Atlanta campaign fighting of,
124–27; Battle of Atlanta losses of,
168; Battle of Champion Hill
movements of, 74–83; during Battle
of Vicksburg, 87–94; during Kentucky
campaign, 28, 45, 46, 47, 49–50;
preparation of, for Atlanta campaign,
115; during Stones River campaign,
63
United States: Confederate surrender to,
241, 242; Georgia's secession from,

5–6; South Carolina's Ordinance of Secession from, 5; Thirteenth Amendment of, 228–29

Vaughn, John, 91
Vicksburg campaign: and Battle of Champion Hill, 70–84; and Battle of Stones River, 70; Fifty-seventh Georgia ordered to, 63–64; siege and surrender at end of, 85–94
Vinson, Charley E., 15, 252
Vinson, Christiana, 9, 67–68, 252
Vinson, Lamar, 252
Vinson, William: decision of, to enlist, 9–10; letter of, on death of brother Wright, 68; urges brother Wright to desert, 64
Vinson, Wright: activities of, during furlough, 15; on arrival to Camp Davis, 25; and daguerreotype of wife, 31, 60; decision of, to enlist, 9–10; on early days of Kentucky campaign, 33, 34–35; first letter of, to wife, 17; illness and death of, 67–69, 252; lack of information/uneasiness of, 57–59; on mail/supplies received from home, 60–61; naive attitudes of, 23–24; on Richmond battlefield scenes, 41–42; on soldier's life in combat zone, 25–26; on temptation to desert, 64; uncertainty and loneliness of, 24–25; on visit of his father, 59–60

Waddell, J. F., 32
Waddell's Alabama Artillery, 32, 74–78
Walden, John, Jr., 89
Walker, William H. T., 118–19, 134, 142, 149, 159–61
Walthall, Edward, 210, 211, 214
Watkins, E. P., 32, 76–77
Watkins, Samuel, 134–36
Wheeler, Joe, 48, 172
Whitemarsh Island, 104, 106–7
Wigfall, Louis T., 130–31
Williams, Sidney, 141
Williams, T. J., 77, 78, 79–80
Wilson, James, 209, 213
Winship, Charles T., 244